AP HUMAN GEOGRAPHY

TestWare® Edition

Christian L. Sawyer
AP Human Geography Instructor
Hillsboro High School
Nashville, Tennessee

Research & Education Association
Visit our website at: www.rea.com

Research & Education Association
61 Ethel Road West
Piscataway, New Jersey 08854
E-mail: info@rea.com

AP HUMAN GEOGRAPHY
With TestWare®

Library of Congress Control Number 2009934469

ISBN 13: 978-0-7386-0631-6
ISBN 10: 0-7386-0631-6

Windows® is a registered trademark of Microsoft Corporation.

REA® and TestWare® are registered trademarks of Research & Education Association, Inc.

CONTENTS

About Our Author

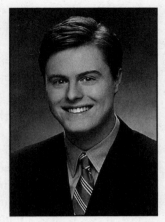

Christian Sawyer has implemented and taught AP Human Geography and other AP and standard-level social studies courses at Hillsboro High School, Hillsboro, Tennessee, and Assumption High School, Louisville, Kentucky. In addition to his high school teaching, Mr. Sawyer currently serves as the "Teacher in Residence" at Vanderbilt University's Peabody College of Education, where he teaches courses in Human Geography and Social Studies Education. Additionally, he has been a guest instructor in Taiwan, an instructor of geopolitics at the Johns Hopkins Center for Talented Youth, and an Atlantik-Brueke Fellow studying German-American relations with the Department of Education. Mr. Sawyer's work in advocating for broader geographic studies led to his being named 2006 National Outstanding Social Studies Teacher of the Year by the National Council for the Social Studies; the 2006 Tennessee Outstanding Social Studies Teacher of the Year by the Tennessee Council for the Social Studies; a White House Fellows Regional Finalist; a 2008 Tennessee Distinguished Educator; the recipient of the "2008 Educator Award" from the Nashville Mayor's Commission on People with Disabilities; and a "Local Hero" by Vanderbilt University. Mr. Sawyer has written and edited curriculum for the Modern Red Schoolhouse Institute and other publishers. He also serves on statewide committees and is a community volunteer. A native of Louisville, Kentucky, Mr. Sawyer graduated with highest distinction, Phi Beta Kappa, from the Honors Program at the University of North Carolina at Chapel Hill. After earning his master's degree and being inducted into the nation's oldest education honor society, Kappa Delta Pi, Mr. Sawyer is completing his doctorate at Vanderbilt.

About Our Expert Reviewer

Daryl Wenner earned his Ph.D. in geography at the University of Tennessee, where he specialized in cultural and urban geography. He earned his master's degree in geography at South Dakota State University and his bachelor's degree at Pennsylvania State University. He is currently an instructor at South College in Knoxville, Tennessee. Mr. Wenner is a volunteer with the Tennessee Geographic Bee and the Tennessee Geographic Alliance and has taught more than a thousand elementary and middle school students about geography.

A Note from the Author

Dear AP Human Geography Student,

Have you ever wondered how many McDonald's restaurants there are in the world? Why have the Israelis and Palestinians been in conflict for so long? What is Hinduism, and where did it start? Is English the most widely spoken language on the earth? How has the spread of Wal-Mart stores changed rural landscapes?

You have? Then you are in the right place, in perhaps one of the most powerful and useful courses you will ever take. Human geography will help you answer these types of questions and give you a new understanding of your world. Studying human geography will push you to develop a new set of tools to use in analyzing the patterns and processes that define the earth's geographic realities—its people and places. It is a course about the map and the fascinating patterns of people behind the map.

In your human geography studies, you will probably investigate interesting questions and issues related to this advanced cultural analysis. Why has India faced a population expansion crisis, while some European countries have declining birth rates? How did current economic patterns develop? For example, why is eastern Europe less well developed than western Europe? And how has colonialism continued to have an impact on newly independent states? How does the South American city structure and layout compare with the North American pattern? How does gentrification of urban areas affect the low-income residents of those areas?

In searching for solutions to these fascinating questions, you should take pride in your studies but also realize that you have a duty to learn about the world and its people with the aim of sharing that information with others. You will probably come to see the world as beautifully diverse, but often quite cruelly unequal. Take what you learn and try to improve the world in your own way. Join the efforts of an organization that you think is bettering the world—Invisible Children, Doctors Without Borders, Save Darfur, or any other program you feel is trying to improve the human condition.

You will likely feel empowered after having completed this introductory course in human geography. But remember, this is only the beginning of your geographic journey. Many students have commented that once they completed their AP Human Geography course, they were unable to look at the world in quite the same way as before. This course will change your paradigm of thought. You will develop "geographic eyes," opening your mind to finding reasons for patterns that you see in the landscapes all around.

With your new set of skills and knowledge, travel to new places, search for innovative solutions, build new bridges. After all, learning about the world is ultimately learning more about yourself. I remember a student in one of my AP human geography classes telling me, after touring a glorious Hindu temple in our region, "Mr. Sawyer, before your class, I had no idea this temple or Hindus even existed in Nashville." I smiled and thought of the words of T.S. Eliot:, "At the end of all exploring will be to arrive where we started and know the place for the first time."

May the "Geo Force" be with you,

Christian L. Sawyer

Author Acknowledgments

I am sincerely thankful for my supportive colleagues, friends, and family (especially my dear mother, father, and brothers) for their belief in me. I am especially appreciative of the insightful additions made by Daryl Wenner, who generously opened his test files to contribute several multiple-choice questions to this project. I also want to thank Anna Claire Brakefield for her impassioned dedication to Human Geography and Diane Goldschmidt for her motivational leadership as my editor. I would like to dedicate this project both to my brilliant "Geo Scholars" and to my beloved grandmother, MJ.

MJ, my book is on your nightstand.

—Christian Sawyer

About Research & Education Association

Founded in 1959, Research & Education Association is dedicated to publishing the finest and most effective educational materials—including software, study guides, and test preps—for students in middle school, high school, college, graduate school, and beyond. Today, REA's wide-ranging catalog is a leading resource for teachers, students, and professionals. We invite you to visit us at *www.rea.com* to find out how "REA is making the world smarter."

Acknowledgments

In addition to our author, we would like to thank Larry B. Kling, Vice President, Editorial, for supervising development; Pam Weston, Vice President, Publishing, for setting the quality standards for production integrity and managing the publication to completion; John Cording, Vice President, Technology, for coordinating the design and development of REA's TestWare®; Diane Goldschmidt, Senior Editor, for preflight editorial review; Jeff LoBalbo, Senior Graphic Artist, for his graphic arts contributions and post-production file mapping; Heena Patel, Technology Project Manager, for design contributions and software testing efforts; Weymouth Design for designing our cover; and Kathy Caratozzolo of Caragraphics for typesetting the manuscript. We also extend special thanks to Mapping Specialists, Inc., for rendering many of the maps contained in the book.

AP Human Geography Study Schedule

This study schedule allows for thorough preparation for the AP Human Geography exam. Although it is designed for eight weeks, it can be condensed into a four-week course by collapsing each two-week period into a single week. Be sure to set aside at least two hours each day to study. Bear in mind that the more time you spend studying, the more prepared and relaxed you will feel on the day of the exam.

Week	Activity
1	Acquaint yourself with the AP Human Geography exam by reading Chapter 1, "Excelling on the AP Human Geography Exam." You will be introduced to key aspects of the exam and be given tips for success on the exam. Take Practice Exam 1 on CD-ROM and score the exam.
2	Carefully read and study Chapter 2, "Geography: Its Nature and Perspectives." Use the Chapter Review and Pre-Exam Practice sections to be certain that you understand the content of the chapter.
3	Read and study Chapter 3, "Population." Assess your knowledge by using the Chapter Review and Pre-Exam Practice sections included at the end of the chapter.
4	Carefully read and study Chapter 4, "Cultural Patterns and Processes." Use the Chapter Review and Pre-Exam Practice sections to be certain that you understand the content of the chapter.
5	Read and study Chapter 5, "Political Organization of Space." Use the Chapter Review and Pre-Exam Practice sections to assess your knowledge of the chapter's content.
6	Carefully read and study Chapter 6, "Agricultural and Rural Land Use." Assess your knowledge by using the Chapter Review and Pre-Exam Practice sections included at the end of the chapter.
7	Read and study Chapter 7, "Industrialization and Economic Development." Use the Chapter Review and Pre-Exam Practice sections to be certain that you understand the content of the chapter.
8	Read and study Chapter 8, "Cities and Urban Land Use." Take Practice Exam 2 on CD-ROM. Use the diagnostic table included with the exam to identify areas where you may need more review. Study any areas in which you consider yourself to be weak by using the Human Geography Review in this book and any other reliable sources you have on hand. If time allows, and you would like to enhance your feel for the rhythm and flow of the exam, take the printed version of our practice exams found in this book.

CHAPTER 1

Excelling on the AP Human Geography Exam

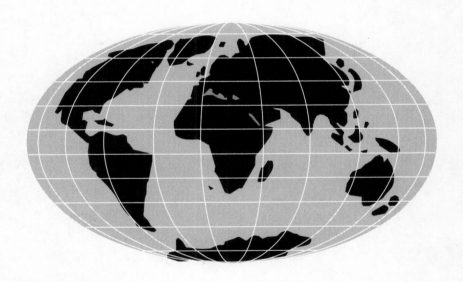

Excelling on the
AP Human Geography Exam

About This Book and TestWare®

This book, along with our companion TestWare® software, provides an accurate and complete representation of the Advanced Placement Examination in Human Geography. REA's practice exams are based on the format of the most recently administered AP Human Geography exam and each includes every type of question that you can expect to encounter on the real test. Following each of our practice tests is an answer key, complete with detailed explanations designed to clarify the material for you. By using the subject reviews, completing both practice tests, and studying the explanations that follow, you will put yourself in the best possible position to do well on the actual test.

The two practice exams are also included on the enclosed TestWare® CD-ROM. The software provides timed conditions and instant, accurate scoring, which makes it all the easier to pinpoint your strengths and weaknesses.

About the Exam

The Advanced Placement Human Geography examination is offered each May at participating schools and multi-school centers throughout the world.

The Advanced Placement Program is designed to allow high school students to pursue college-level studies while attending high school. The participating colleges, in turn, grant credit and/or advanced placement to students who do well on the examinations.

The Advanced Placement Human Geography course is designed to be the equivalent of a college introductory Human Geography course.

AP Human Geography Exam Format and Content

The AP Human Geography exam is approximately two hours and fifteen minutes long. Each section of the exam is completed separately and each counts for half of the student's score.

The exam is divided into two sections:

Section I: The multiple-choice section of the exam is 60 minutes long and contains 75 questions. The approximate breakdown of topics covered includes the following:

Topic	Approximate Percentage
Geography: Its Nature and Perspectives	5–10%
Population	13–17%
Cultural Patterns and Processes	13–17%
Political Organization of Space	13–17%
Agriculture and Rural Land Use	13–17%
Industrialization and Economic Development	13–17%
Cities and Urban Land Use	13–17%

Each question in the multiple-choice section has five possible answer choices. Each correct answer is worth one point, and 1/4 point is deducted for each incorrect answer.

Section II: This is the free-response section of the exam. Students are asked to answer three constructed-response questions in the allotted 75 minutes. Questions may be based on stimulus material such as maps, graphs, photographs, diagrams and verbal descriptions. Students are expected to use their analytical and organizational skills in writing their responses. While a formal essay is not required, a simple listing of facts will not receive a high score. All three questions are required to be answered and are weighted equally.

For more information about what to include in the essays, how to manage the time allotted, and how they are scored, please visit the AP Human Geography outline provided by the College Board at *www.collegeboard.com.*

You may find the AP Human Geography exam considerably more difficult than many classroom exams. In order to measure the full range of your ability in Human Geography, the AP exams are designed to produce average scores of approximately 50% of the maximum possible score for the multiple-choice and essay sections. Therefore, you should not expect to attain a perfect or even near-perfect score.

How to Use This Book and TestWare°

What do I study first?

To begin your studies, read over the introduction and the suggestions for test taking. Take Practice Exam 1 on CD-ROM to determine your strengths and weaknesses, and then study the course review material, focusing on your specific problem areas. Studying the review material thoroughly will reinforce the basic skills you will need to do well on the exam. Make sure to follow up your diagnostic work by taking Practice Exam 2 on CD-ROM to become familiar with the format and feel of the AP Human Geography exam.

To best utilize your study time, follow our Study Schedule, which you will find in the front of this book. The schedule is based on an eight-week program, but if necessary can be condensed to four weeks by combining each two-week period into one week.

When should I start studying?

It is never too early to start studying for the AP Human Geography examination. The earlier you begin, the more time you will have to sharpen your skills. Do not procrastinate! Cramming is *not* an effective way to study, since it does not allow you the time needed to learn the test material. The sooner you learn the format of the exam, the more time you will have to familiarize yourself with it.

SSD accommodations for students with disabilities

Many students qualify for extra time to take the AP Human Geography exam and our TestWare® can be adapted to accommodate your time extension. This allows you to practice under the same extended-time accommodations that you will receive on the actual test day. To customize your TestWare® to suit the most common extensions, visit our website at *http://www.rea.com/ssd*.

About Our Review Section

This book contains an AP Human Geography Course Review that can be used as both a primer and as a quick reference while taking the practice exams. Our course review is meant to complement your AP Human Geography textbook and is by no means exhaustive. By studying our review along with your textbook and course materials, you will be well prepared for the exam.

Scoring the Official Exams

The College Board creates a formula (which changes slightly every year) to convert raw scores into composite scores grouped into broad AP grade categories. The weights for the multiple-choice sections are determined by the Chief Reader, who uses a process called *equating*. This process compares the current year's exam performance on selected multiple-choice questions to that of a previous year, establishing a level of achievement for the current year's group and a degree of difficulty for the current exam. This data is combined with historical trends and the reader's professional evaluation to determine the weights and tables.

The AP free-response is graded by teacher volunteers, grouped at scoring tables, and led by a chief faculty consultant. The consultant sets the grading scale that translates the raw score into the composite score. Past grading illustrations are available to teachers from the College Board, and may be ordered using the contact information given in this chapter. These actual examples of student responses and a grade analysis can be of great assistance to both the student and the teacher as a learning or review tool.

When will I know my score?

In July, a grade report will be sent to you, your high school, and the colleges you choose to notify. The report will include scores for all the AP exams you have taken up to that point and will show a grade of between 1 and 5. Normally, colleges participating in the Advanced Placement Program will recognize grades of 3 or better.

Your grade will be used by your college of choice to determine placement in its Human Geography program. This grade will vary in significance from college to college, and is used with other academic information to determine placement. Contact your college admissions office for more information regarding its use of AP grades.

Tips for Success on the AP Human Geography Exam

- Invent your own "review system." Get a new binder and label it "AP Human Geo Review Binder." Place all review sheets and other pertinent material in this binder for cumulative reviewing.

- Make flashcards for each key term in the content review and cumulatively review the terms each night. Define the term in your own words, rather than copying the definition from the glossary. Write related notes and ideas to each flashcard.

- Review cumulatively. For example, during the week you are studying Chapter 3, review the flashcards and notes for the chapters you previously studied.

- Throw your flashcards in the air and stack them into related groups. Quiz yourself and others. Make a pact with yourself that if you get one key term wrong in a stack, you have to start the stack over again. Keep going until you get the entire stack correct!

- As you study each review chapter in this book, review your textbook's corresponding chapter and your class notes.

- Save magazine and newspaper articles that relate to what you learn in your AP Human Geography course. Put them in a folder to read later.

- Keep a chart of the geographic models that you encounter throughout your review. Make a flashcard for each model. Analyze each model's strengths and weaknesses.

- As you review, keep a list of questions for which you need answers. Seek the help of your teacher in getting the answers. Your questions can lead to important new ideas and further discussions.

- Form a study group with other trustworthy students studying AP Human Geography. (Remember, friends don't always make the best study partners.) Find a quiet place where the group can meet regularly to study and keep the group focused. Put one person in charge of "re-teaching" each section in the course and designing a "crash study guide" for the rest of the group.

- As you prepare for the free-response section, try writing your own free-response questions and sharing them with other students.

- As an alternative to the suggested study schedule provided in this book, try taking one of the practice exams *before* you study the content review chapters. By doing this, you can be aware of your strengths and weaknesses before you start preparing for the exam.

- If multiple-choice questions are not your strongest skill, carefully analyze your answers in each of the review chapters in this book and on the practice tests. Be sure to read the answer explanations to see why the selected choice is correct and the others are wrong. Also, remember that you do *not* have to get 100% of the multiple-choice questions correct! A student can earn a good passing score by answering less than 50% of the multiple-choice questions correctly, if he/she does well on the free-response section.

- When you take the practice tests in this book, simulate real testing conditions. Find a quiet place and time yourself. Ask your teacher to administer a "mock" AP exam.

- Trust in your ability! If you prepare in advance, apply your intelligence, and tap into what AP Human Geography is really about, then you will succeed on the exam. However, the course should be more important to you than your test score. Recent research by test-makers shows that even students who do not earn a passing score on the AP exam are more successful in college than their peers who did not attempt an AP course. You will be a more powerful thinker, a better-prepared college student, and a more enriched person for having applied your time and talents to learning about the world and its people. You're in a win-win situation—there is no way to lose!

Tips for Success on the Free-Response Section of the Exam

After the multiple-choice section of the exam, you will have a short break. Afterwards, you will move on to Section II, the free-response section. This section requires that you answer three free-response questions (called FRQs) in 75 minutes. A pen is required for this section, so bring three of your favorite black- or blue-ink pens with you (no markers or jelly pens, please!). You must answer all three questions and each question usually has multiple parts. It is recommended that you spend about 25 minutes on each one. The best way to approach this section is to spend a few minutes previewing all of the questions. After you have read through all of them, choose one and jump right in!

Begin by taking three to five minutes to outline your response to the FRQ or "free-writing" your initial thoughts. Then spend about 20 minutes on that question, formulating your official response in the answer booklet. Your proctor will not stop you until the end of the 75 minutes, so pace yourself to answer each of the three FRQs in the allotted time. Be sure to write the number of the question you are answering at the top of each answer-booklet page. Start each of your free-response answers on a new page in your answer booklet—in other words, don't cram your response to question 2 on the same page as your response to question 1.

Historically, the free-response questions have been a mix of recall and critical thinking questions. Often, the FRQs ask you to define a key term from the course and then call upon you to apply that concept to a map, figure, or analysis. For example, a recent FRQ asked the students to define "distance decay." Then, the students applied that term to a map of migration streams provided with the exam. In the past, the three FRQs on the exam have been a well-balanced mix of concepts from across the AP Human Geography curriculum.

If you have taken AP History or English courses or exams, it's highly likely that you were instructed to write a formal essay in response to the free-response questions. AP Human Geography is different—a formal essay is NOT required! Hooray! Think of the FRQs as short-answer questions. Don't bother with a thesis statement or a conclusion. Jump right into your response. The graders do not give you points for a thesis or a conclusion statement; rather, they grade the *content* that you include in your response. Look through the review chapters and the practice exams in this book to find sample AP-like scoring rubrics that are similar to the rubrics the actual AP graders are likely to use in scoring your FRQ responses. Use these to score your own responses.

In previous years, the official AP exam instructions recommended that you label and number each part of your response in the margins of your answer booklet to keep your reader aware of where you are in your response to the FRQ. For example, if you are answering FRQ 1, part A, label your response in the margin "1A." When you move to part B, write "1B" in the margin. Continue for each subsequent part. Also, as previously mentioned, remember to put the FRQ number at the top of the each answer booklet page. If you're answering FRQ 1, write "1" in the box at the top of the answer-booklet page and label each subpart of your response in the margin.

While a formal essay is not required (and not really wanted), simply listing facts is *not* enough. Write complete sentences with coherent, supporting thoughts (like a short answer). You should also support your responses with accurate geographic examples whenever possible. If the FRQ calls for examples from a particular region, be certain you use examples from that region and link your examples to the question's prompt. AP readers have commented that students often confuse geographic regions. Therefore, while studying for the exam, take time to review geographic regions: East Asia, Southwest Asia, Western Europe, Eastern Europe, North America, etc. Familiarize yourself with examples and situations in each region that you could use in your responses.

An AP reader, who is either a college professor or an experienced AP teacher, will score your answers. Teams of graders will be formed and each team will specialize in grading one of the questions. Each grader will use a scoring rubric that spells out *exactly* how to give points while grading the FRQ. Therefore, the graders don't have much flexibility in scoring your responses. They have to follow the rubric created. Remember also that they *award* points; they don't take points off. Thus, while reading FRQ 1, part A, the grader will look for specific elements in your response to give you points. If you don't have those specific parts in your response, you will not get the points. It's that simple.

So how can you make sure you get the points in each part of the FRQ? First, **make sure you answer the question being asked**. Carefully study the language used in the questions. Circle the key words in the FRQ. If it says "define," write a definition. If it says "evaluate," analyze the different parts of the issue.

Second, **make sure you answer all parts of the question**. If the question asks you to define a term and then offer an example, be sure you address both parts of that multi-part question.

Third, **check to see if the FRQ calls for a specific type of example**. The question might ask you for an example from a particular historical era or a particular region on the map. The FRQ may ask you to give an example of a *country* or it may call for you to cite a *region*—so be careful to use the appropriate example. Don't use an example that doesn't fit. Choose your example carefully and integrate it into your response.

Fourth, **be geographically analytical in your response.** Avoid injecting personal opinions and side-comments that distract from your direct response to the question. Try to draw together appropriate relationships from different parts of the course. For example, if the question asks you to discuss how globalization is threatening linguistic diversity, you might include treatment of time-space compression and the friction of distance. You might address assimilation, cultural diffusion, or other related concepts. The more you can support your response with substantive geographic examples, the better your response will be viewed. However, you should not write in random and unrelated ideas just to impress the reader with your geographic vocabulary! Instead, only integrate concepts directly tied to the FRQ's focus. Again, the object is to get right to the point and to support your point. No need for flowery language or Shakespearean prose.

Fifth, **if there is a "stimulus" in the FRQ, such as a chart, map, or graph, be sure that you integrate this into your response.** Use specifics from the "stimulus" in formulating your response. It's there for a reason—so use it! Take time to analyze what the stimulus shows you and how it relates to the FRQ. Feel free to draw on it and mark it up!

Here are some commonly asked questions and responses:

Can I include a diagram or a sketch in my FRQ?

Yes, you can include a diagram or a sketch in your FRQ. It is highly recommended that you do not include this as the only piece in your response. If you choose to use a diagram or sketch, link it to your overall response and be sure to describe what it means and how it relates to your response.

What if I have no idea how to respond to the question?

This could happen, but do not panic if it does. More than likely, you can offer some geographic analysis of the issue, even if you are truly stumped. Start writing something related to the course and an issue you think might be tied to the FRQ. In a past administration of the exam, some students were stumped by an FRQ calling for an analysis of the distribution of chicken farming in the U.S. Several stumped students started writing about agricultural changes in the U.S., the movement towards agribusiness and the decline of the family-owned farm in the U.S. They were successful because they offered a related idea. Above all else, do *not* leave a free-response question blank. Many well-prepared students find that one of the FRQs is their "challenge FRQ," meaning the one that really gave them a run for their money.

How long should my FRQ response be?

There is no right or wrong length for your FRQ answer. If your response fully answers the FRQ, then it is the right length. There is no word count or set limit. Make sure you do not spend too long on one FRQ and lose time to address the other two FRQs adequately.

Will I have enough time to write my answers?

Students generally have just enough time to write their responses to the free-response questions. Remember, though, that it is your responsibility to keep an eye on your own time and progress.

How can I prepare for the FRQs?

One of the strongest ways to prepare for these questions is to pay close attention to key terms and models throughout the course. Define the key terms and models in your own words. Look at the maps and diagrams in your book and think about how they apply to the chapter's focus. Keep a list of current events, controversies, and issues in each region of the world. If you do all this, you will have an arsenal of geographic concepts to draw from on exam day. Lastly, practice, practice, and practice! Use the practice FRQs in this book and given by your teacher to prepare for the big day.

The Day of the Exam

Before the exam

On the day of the test, you should wake up early (preferably after a good night's rest) and have a good breakfast. Make sure to dress comfortably, so that you are not distracted by being too hot or too cold while taking the test. Also plan to arrive at the test center early. This will allow you to collect your thoughts and relax before the test, and will also spare you the anxiety that comes with being late.

Before you leave for the test center, make sure that you have your admission form, social security number, and another form of identification, which must contain a recent photograph, your name, and signature (i.e., driver's license, student identification card, or current alien registration card). You will not be allowed to take the test if you do not have proper identification. You will also need to bring your school code. Also, bring several sharpened No. 2 pencils with erasers for the multiple-choice questions and black or blue pens for the free-response questions.

You may wear a watch, but only one without a beep or alarm. No dictionaries, textbooks, notebooks, compasses, correction fluid, highlighters, rulers, computers, cell phones, beepers, PDAs, scratch paper, listening and recording devices, briefcases, or packages will be permitted and drinking, smoking, and eating are prohibited while taking the test.

During the exam

Once you enter the test center, follow all of the rules and instructions given by the test supervisor. If you do not, you risk being dismissed from the test and having your scores canceled.

After the exam

You may immediately register when taking the exam to have your score sent to the college of your choice; you may also wait and later request to have your AP score reported to the college of your choice.

Contacting the AP Program

For registration bulletins or more information about the AP Human Geography exam, contact:

AP Services
Educational Testing Service
P.O. Box 6671
Princeton, NJ 08541-6671
Phone: (609) 771-7300 or (888) 225-5427
E-mail: apexams@ets.org
Website: *www.collegeboard.com*

COURSE REVIEW

AP Human Geography

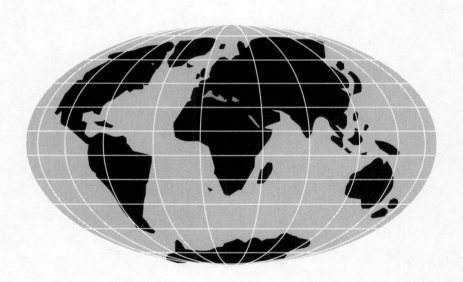

Chapter 2

Geography: Its Nature and Perspectives

Introduction

Driving through Nashville, Tennessee, the country music capital of the world, you would expect to pass numerous tourist attractions and shops devoted to that music genre, but you would likely be surprised to see a large Hindu temple built on the city's west side. The study of human geography is related to such an observation. A human geographer would be interested in studying how Hinduism spread to the United States and why this temple was built in a southern city.

Figure 2.1. Sri Ganesh Hindu Temple, Nashville, Tennessee

Or perhaps you are strolling down a crowded city street in Beijing, China, and come across a Kentucky Fried Chicken restaurant. Human geographers would be interested in analyzing the spread of KFC to China and its impact on local culture.

What is particularly interesting about human geography is its approach to studying the world by looking at the interaction between humans and the lands

Figure 2.2. Kentucky Fried Chicken restaurant in Beijing, China

they inhabit. While most *world* geography classes teach students about the earth from a regional perspective—for instance, starting with North America and moving towards Asia—*human* geography takes a *thematic* approach, looking at the earth and its many different peoples in the context of many different patterns. That is the essence of human geography: defining and explaining patterns in human interactions with the earth.

Key Questions

- *What is human geography, and how is it related to the geographic perspective?*

- *How is geography a field of inquiry?*

- *How is spatial analysis embedded in the geographic perspective?*

- *How are humans and their landscapes related?*

- *What is geographic scale, and how does it affect geographic inquiry?*

- *What is regionalization, and how is it related to human geography?*

- *What effect do globalization and spatial interconnection have on people and places?*

- *How are various map forms and spatial data used?*

- *How does technology impact our understanding of geographic patterns and processes?*

| **PART 1** | Geographical Concepts, the Geographical Perspective, and Key Skills |

Geography as a Field of Inquiry

Geography is an exciting field of investigation that focuses on understanding the world and its patterns. One geographer compared geography to a quest for the answer to a strange question: "Why of where?" Yes, geographers study the patterns that appear on a map of the earth when they chart the locations of rivers, mountains, poverty, religions, and other aspects of life. But geographers are also fundamentally concerned with trying to find the *reasons* for the patterns. For example, not only do geographers design maps that show large concentrations of Hindus in India, but they also search to understand *why* most Hindus congregate in India.

Just as an archeologist digs into the earth, geographers search through the layers of patterns in the earth's physical and human landscapes to "write about earth" (which is what *geography* means when translated literally from its Greek roots).

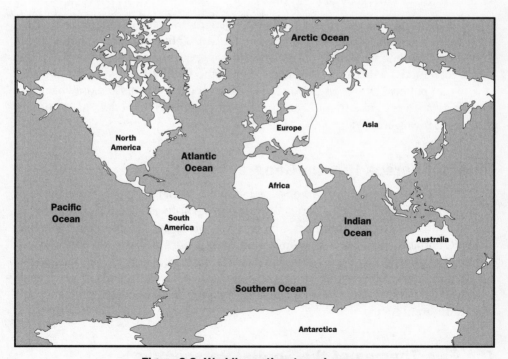

Figure 2.3. World's continents and oceans

The Spatial Perspective

At the very base of the geographer's craft is an obsession with space. No, not just outer space, where ET roams, but space in general: rooms, countries, parks, continents, cyberspace, rivers—all types of space. Geographers have a special eye for looking into space and investigating the patterns within it. For example, a geographer might look at the space of your bedroom and ask several questions: How are things distributed? What movements are occurring? What processes operate in that space? How does this space relate to other nearby spaces?

Such a way of identifying, explaining, and predicting the human and physical patterns in space and the interconnectedness of various spaces is known to geographers as the **spatial perspective**.

Often geographers create and use **geographic models** to explain and predict spatial patterns in the earth's human and physical landscapes. Geographic models are simplified versions of what exists on the earth and what might exist in the future. Models help geographers search for answers to why patterns exist the way they do—why, for example, India's population growth rate is different from South Africa's. One geographer created a model to explain rural land use patterns in his town. Then other geographers could use that model to explain and predict the patterns of farmland they saw in their towns.

You will study several models in human geography—the demographic transition model, the concentric zone model, and the von Thünen model, to name just a few—and each one will help you understand why patterns exist as they do on the earth. Each model will also give a sense of what the future might look like in terms of a spatial pattern. However, as you study each model, consider the drawbacks to applying it to every situation. Be sure to take into account the model's assumptions and where it was created.

Physical Versus Human Geography

Although all geographers are obsessed with the spatial perspective, the particular type of space they focus on varies. **Physical geography** is concerned with spatial analysis of the structures, processes, and locations of the earth's natural phenomena, like soil, climate, plants, and topography. **Human geography**, on the other hand, is primarily concerned with analyzing the structures, processes, and locations of the earth's human creations and their interactions. In essence, both fields of geography analyze the central "why of where" question, but each field approaches the question from a different focus.

The Five Themes of the Spatial Perspective

To understand the spatial perspective even more precisely, we must look into its five central themes: location, human–environment interaction, region, place, and movement. The five themes of geography are like five lenses through which

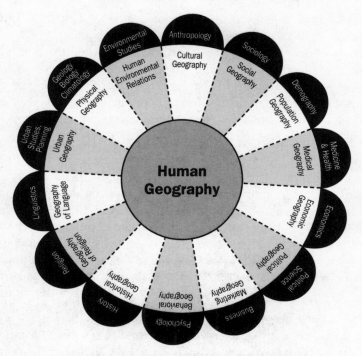

Figure 2.4. Fields of human geography

geographers look at a space, each lens giving the geographer a different sense of the patterns in that space.

Location

The theme of location is concerned with analyzing where something is on the earth and the effects that position has on human life. A location can be either absolute or relative.

Absolute Location

Absolute location refers to a position on the global grid. Technically, a location is absolute when it has only one possible reference point. That is why latitude and longitude work; only one place is 85 degrees north, 37 degrees west on the planet. Your home address is another absolute location. There is only one 28 North Main Street in Williamsport, Pennsylvania.

The U.S. Postal Service is the second-largest employer in the United States and processes more than 8,000 pieces of mail each second.

The global grid is an invisible map of latitude and longitude lines. **Lines of latitude** are measured in degrees north and south from the equator, which is 0 degrees latitude. The North Pole is 90 degrees north latitude, while the South Pole is 90 degrees south latitude. Interestingly, lines of latitude never intersect, so geographers often call lines of latitude *parallels*. Because lines of latitude encircle the earth and never intersect, the circumferences of lines of latitude decrease as they move away from the equator in both directions. Therefore, the equator has the largest circumference of all the lines of latitude.

Lines of longitude are measured in degrees east and west of one line of longitude known as the prime meridian, which runs through Greenwich, England, and is located at 0 degrees longitude. The line of longitude on the opposite side of the prime meridian is known as the international date line. The international date line is aligned with the 180-degree longitude line for some latitudes but not for others. This reflects the political influence on time zones. For example, the international date line was moved to put all of Russia ahead of Greenwich mean time (which is discussed later in this section).

Interestingly, the prime meridian was selected by a group of politicians and geographers, but any line of longitude could technically be named prime if the world wanted to change it. In fact, some geographers argue that the current prime meridian is **Anglocentric**, meaning that it orients the global grid around English (western European) culture. Critics ask why a line of longitude that runs through Asia, for example, was not selected as the prime meridian.

Thus, the absolute location of anything on the global grid—be it a city, person, boat, or Coke machine—is given as its latitude and longitude. To get more precise readings, each line of latitude and longitude can be broken down into minutes and seconds. There are 60 minutes (′) per degree (°) and 60 seconds (″) per minute.

For instance, a coordinate might be written as 75°45′32″ E, which would be a line of longitude read as "75 degrees, 45 minutes, and 32 seconds east (of the prime meridian)." Locations can be pinpointed within inches on the global grid. A degree of latitude is nearly 69 miles; a minute, nearly 1.1 miles; and a second, about 100 feet. Because lines of longitude all meet at the North and South poles, lines of longitude get closer and closer together moving toward the poles.

Geo Factoid

The earth's equatorial diameter is longer than its polar diameter, making the earth slightly "fatter" than it is tall.

Time zones revolve around the prime meridian, which establishes **Greenwich mean time (GMT)**, or **Universal time**, as the baseline for time throughout the

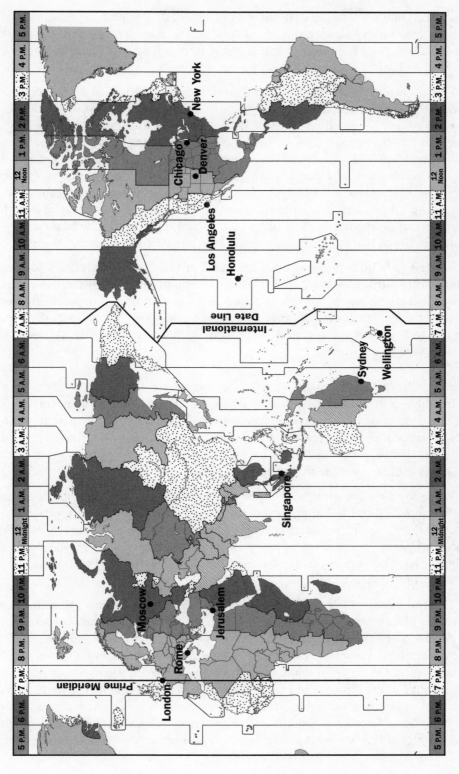

Figure 2.5. World's 24 time zones, each representing 15 degrees of longitude

world. The sun "rises in the east and sets in the west" because the earth rotates about its axis in an eastward direction. Taiwan, for example, is nearly 12 hours ahead of Louisville, Kentucky. When it is 6 p.m. on Monday in Louisville, it is 6 a.m. on Tuesday in Taiwan.

Earth's time is divided into 24 standard time zones. With each 15-degree-longitude move you make away from the prime meridian (or GMT), you go ahead or fall back by one hour and one standard time zone. For example, if you move 15 degrees east of the prime meridian, you go one hour ahead of GMT. So when it is 6 p.m. in London (GMT), it is 7 p.m. in countries 15 degrees of longitude east, and it is 8 p.m. in countries 30 degrees of longitude east. The reverse is true if you move in a westward direction from GMT. Interestingly, politics influence time zones, too. China, for example, has instituted one time zone for its entire country, even though its provinces fall into nearly three different standard time zones. The Chinese government believed that one time zone would help unify its vast country.

Related to latitude and longitude are **great circles**, which are circles formed on the earth's surface by a plane that passes through the center of the earth. The equator and every line of longitude paired with its twin on the opposite side of the earth form great circles. Any arc of a great circle shows the shortest distance between two points on the earth's surface; thus, airplanes often fly great-circle routes to save gas.

Relative Location

In addition to absolute location, anything can have a **relative location**, or its location as described in relation to places around it. The relative location of Nashville, Tennessee, could be described as being "south of Louisville, Kentucky," for example. "Hillsboro High School is located 9 miles southwest of McGavock High School" is another example of a relative location.

While the absolute location of a place remains the same (as long as the place does not move on the global grid), a description of a place's relative location can change if the place's surroundings change. For example, Kroger Grocery's relative location of being 2 miles south of Jane's Deli might change if Jane's Deli relocates to another location or goes out of business. Therefore, relative location is contextual and subject to change.

Site and *situation* are two more terms that describe a place's location. **Site** refers to a place's *internal* physical and cultural characteristics, such as its terrain and dominant religions. For example, the site of Sarasota, Florida, contains sandy beaches, Catholic churches, and humid equatorial climates, among other internal characteristics. On the other hand, **situation** refers to the location (or context) of a place relative to the physical and cultural characteristics around it. The more interconnected a place is to other powerful places, the better is its situation. A strong situation implies a place having a high degree of connectivity and accessibility, which allow for higher levels of spatial interaction. Moreover, modes of connectivity and

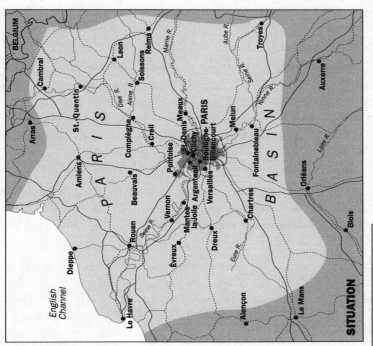

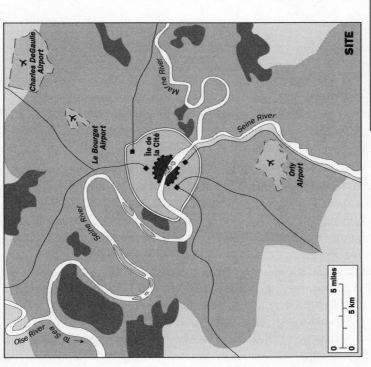

SITE AND SITUATION OF PARIS, FRANCE

Figure 2.6. Site (left) and situation (right) of Paris, France

accessibility are becoming multilayered as land, sea, and air access points increase and communication technologies like the Internet become increasingly complex.

Human–Environment Interaction

The second major theme in the geographer's toolbox is analyzing **human–environment interaction**, the study of which is referred to as **cultural ecology**. Geographers analyze both directions of this type of interaction: how human activities affect their environment and how environmental changes impact human life. Geographers also analyze the positive and negative effects of human–environment interaction.

Region

The third geographic theme is the region, a way of classifying information about places. Just as historians classify their content by epochs and centuries, geographers classify their information by **regions**, which are spatial units that share some similar characteristics.

Geographers create regions to help them classify and understand the complexity of the earth. Every region consists of an area and a location and is contained by boundaries, which are sometimes not evident. There are three types of regions: formal, functional, and perceptual. However, each region links places together that share something. The physical and cultural character of an area and people's interconnections in that area allow geographers to create and define it as a region.

Formal Regions

Formal regions (sometimes referred to as uniform regions) are areas that have common (or uniform) cultural or physical features. A country is a formal region, or an area of places linked by a shared government. A climate region is a formal region because it links places that share a climate. A map showing where Christianity is practiced is showing a formal region, or a group of places sharing that religion.

Functional Regions

A **functional region** (sometimes referred to as a nodal region) is a group of places linked together by some function's influence on them. Often the influencing function diffused, or spread, from a central **node**, or originating point. Functional regions are created through the movement of some phenomenon, like a disease, or a perceived interaction among places, like pizza delivery routes. For example, a functional region might appear on a map of Delta Airlines' flights from Atlanta, Georgia. A mapmaker would plot all the places to which Delta travels from its hub in Atlanta—the node. Then the mapmaker would draw a boundary enclosing all those places into one functional region. The area affected by the spread of a flu epidemic is a functional region. A functional region could even show the transmission of a rumor from its source to all the people who hear it. Remember, functional regions are defined by the places affected by the movement of some phenomenon from its source (or node) to other places.

Perceptual Regions

The third type of region is a **perceptual (or vernacular) region**. The boundaries of a perceptual region are determined by people's beliefs, not a scientifically measurable process. For example, the space in which the "cool kids" sit at lunch would be a perceptual region because its boundaries are totally determined by the region maker's perception of who is cool and who is not—something that could be debated by any other person in the room. Another example of a perceptual region is the South in the United States. People differ in their perceptions of which places are considered part of the South.

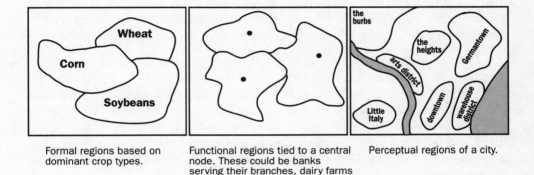

Formal regions based on dominant crop types.

Functional regions tied to a central node. These could be banks serving their branches, dairy farms providing milk to suppliers, etc.

Perceptual regions of a city.

Figure 2.7. Three types of regions: formal regions based on crop types, functional regions linked to a central node, and perceptual regions in a city

Place

The fourth geographic theme is **place**, which is a unique combination of physical and cultural attributes that give each location on the earth its individual "stamp." Human components of place include religion, language, politics, and artwork, whereas the physical attributes include climate, terrain, and natural resources. The combination of these two parts of place, the human and physical, are what differentiate each location from another, almost like fingerprints.

Humans also develop a **sense of place**, which is a person's perception of the human and physical attributes of a location that give it a unique identity in our minds. For example, you probably remember a set of smells, sounds, and images from your ninth-grade English classroom. Think of how that sense of place differs from the total set of memories you have of your childhood bedroom or a favorite vacation spot. People can even develop a sense of place for a location they have never visited—through movies, television, and interactions with others who have traveled or heard of the places. You probably have never been to Siberia, but I bet you think it is a place you never want to visit because of its harsh climate!

Movement

The fifth theme is that of **movement**. Geographers analyze the movement occurring in a space—movement of information, people, goods, and other phenomena. Geographers also evaluate how places interact through movement, a process known as **spatial interaction**. Although everything is theoretically linked to everything else, nearer things are usually related more to each other than to faraway things. Thus, the extent of spatial interaction often depends on distance.

In evaluating movement and spatial interaction, geographers often evaluate the **friction of distance**, which is the degree to which distance interferes with some interaction. For example, the friction of distance for a working-class Ohio man wanting to visit a dentist in Ethiopia is quite high, meaning that the distance gets in the way of this interaction occurring. However, the friction of distance has been reduced in many aspects of life with improved transportation and communication infrastructures.

Today, the friction of distance is not as much of a problem for a business in Kentucky to sell something to a business in Taiwan, for example. Businesses can now communicate over the Internet, buying and selling their goods in transactions that would have taken months to complete just 30 years ago. This increasing sense of accessibility and connectivity seems to bring humans in distant places closer together, a phenomenon known as **space–time compression**. Note that space–time compression is reducing perceived distance, which is the friction of distance thought by humans, not the actual distance on the land.

Related to space–time compression is the effect of **distance decay**, in which the interaction between two places declines as the distance between the two places increases. Imagine putting a magnet on your desk and putting an iron nail on it. The farther you pull the iron nail away from the magnet, the less of a pull effect the

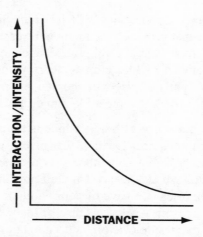

**Figure 2.8. Distance decay curve showing that
as distance increases, the level of interaction decreases**

magnet has on the nail, right? It is the same with distance decay; as the distance between two entities increases, the effect of their interaction decreases.

However, improved transportation and communication technologies have reduced the effect of distance decay on most human interactions. In 1850 on any given day, a person living in Atlanta probably never interacted with someone from 30 miles outside the city. Now a person in Atlanta can interact with people from all over the world via the Internet and improved transportation.

Mapmaking

A **map** is a two-dimensional model of the earth or a portion of its surface. The process of mapmaking is called **cartography**. All maps include a somewhat simplified view of the earth's surface. **Simplification** is when a cartographer gets rid of unnecessary details and focuses on the information needing to be displayed on the map. When designing a map of Europe for high school students to use to help them memorize the names of countries and capitals, a mapmaker would present a simplified map of Europe's political states and boundaries, eliminating details such as vegetation or climate. Another example of simplification involves a cartographer designing a map of London's underground subway for tourists. Such a cartographer might eliminate unnecessary details such as unrelated buildings and streets from their maps because tourists do not need these details to understand London's subway tracks. Tourists are simply interested in getting on and off the correct subway stops.

Distortion and Map Properties

It is impossible to take the earth's round surface and put it onto a flat surface without some form of **distortion**, or error, resulting from the "flattening" process. Think of distortion as caused by a process similar to trying to flatten an orange peel. Sorry to inform you of this, but all the maps you have memorized are wrong. As it is often said, "All maps lie flat, and all flat maps lie." Yes, that's right; every map is, in some way, wrong. The globe is the most accurate representation of the earth.

Each map has **four main map properties**: shape, size (area), distance, and direction. *Shape* refers to the geometric shapes of the objects on the map. *Size* (area) refers to the relative amount of space taken up on the map by the landforms or objects on the map. *Distance* refers to the represented distance between objects on the map. *Direction* refers to the degree of accuracy representing the **cardinal directions**—north, south, east, and west—and their **intermediate directions**—northwest, northeast, southwest, and southeast. Less accurate are the **relative directions** that people commonly use to describe a location, such as *right, left, up,* and *down,* among many others.

All four properties cannot be accurately represented, so a cartographer must choose which of the properties to distort. Cartographers make this decision by considering the map's purpose. When designing a map for navigational purposes, the cartographer would keep direction and distance accurate; size (area) and shape are not as important.

The Process of Mapmaking: Projection

In making a flat map of the round earth, geographers use geometric shapes. They can choose a cylinder, cone, or flat plane to touch to the earth and construct a map. To visualize this process, imagine that the globe has a light in it and is in a dark room. When the chosen geometric shape, such as a flat plane, is placed on the globe, the globe reflects onto this geometric shape, forming a flat image, or projection, of the round earth. The resulting projection reflects the geometric surface used in constructing it.

The projection is distorted in some way, however, depending on the geometric shape used to make the map. Geographers have different labels for maps that reflect the different properties distorted by the maps:

- **Equal-area (or equivalent) projections:** maps that maintain area but distort other properties

- **Conformal (or orthomorphic) projections:** maps that maintain shape but distort other properties (it is impossible to have a projection that is both conformal and equal area)

- **Azimuthal projections:** maps that maintain direction but distort other properties

- **Equidistant projections:** maps that maintain distance but distort other properties

The Mercator projection, described in more detail in the next section, is a conformal projection created using a cylindrical surface, and the Albers projection was created using a conic surface. Azimuthal projections are flat-plane-constructed maps of each hemisphere. Great-circle routes are apparent on azimuthal projections.

Uses of Projections

Consider the different maps you have seen in your lifetime. You probably have used a **Robinson projection** in your social studies class to memorize points on the world map because the Robinson projection shows the world according to slight distortion of all four properties, rather than getting just one correct and drastically distorting others. Before the Robinson projection was invented, social studies teachers often used the **Mercator projection**. Though the Mercator projection shows the shapes of the continents and landforms accurately, it drastically distorts the size (area) of the continents. For example, Greenland is almost as large as Africa on the Mercator. Moreover, schools in the former Soviet Union used the Mercator projection to teach its children because the map made the USSR look larger than its enemies. A geographer created the **Peter projection** to show relative sizes of

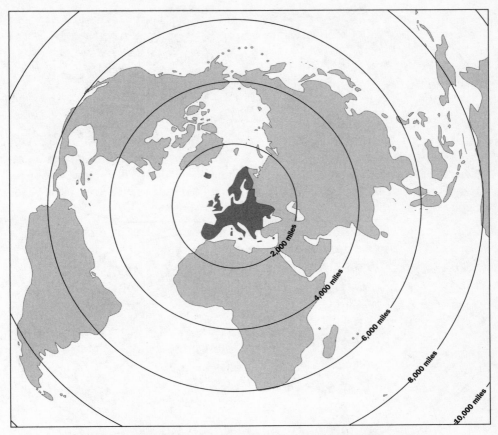

Figure 2.9. Azimuthal projection centered on Hamburg, Germany

the earth's continents accurately (equal area), but because it distorts shape, it is not conformal.

A Brief History of Mapmaking

Just as a painting is a reflection of the artist holding the brush, a map reflects the biases, experiences, and objectives of the cartographer who creates it. An evaluation of Inuit maps of Alaska shows extreme detail in the shapes of inland waterways because the Inuit people navigated those passageways every day to fish and travel to different villages. Before the Greco-Roman civilizations, maps were largely cognitive and created for spiritual and immediate travel needs.

Because the Greeks and Romans were empire builders, scholars developed an interest in mapping landholdings and charting new places. Thus, during the height

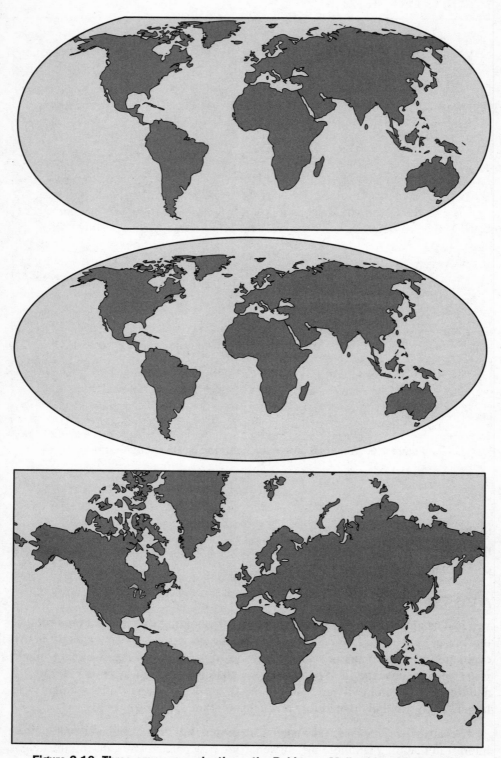

Figure 2.10. Three common projections: the Robinson, Mollweide, and Mercator

of those empires, from 1000 BCE to 500 CE, the discipline of geography was born. The Greeks and Romans had great interest in geographic inquiry. The Greek philosopher Aristotle was the first to show that the earth was spherical. Eratosthenes calculated the circumference of the earth and coined the word *geography* to mean "to write about the earth." He also created one of the earliest maps of the world and its climatic zones. Ptolemy wrote his eight-volume *Guide to Geography*, the first text to define the basic principles of geographic study and show examples of detailed maps.

After the fall of the Roman Empire in about 500 CE, maps were often oriented around religious and spiritual themes and less developed for exploration and scientific inquiry. Many medieval European maps were products of religious propaganda, chartered by the Catholic Church and oriented around Jerusalem for religious purposes. In the same way, Islamic maps often used Mecca (in Saudi Arabia, the holiest site to Muslims) as the focal point. However, cartographic progress continued outside Europe, in places like China and Southwest Asia. In the 15th century, as feudalism started to decline and western European empires were starting to search for colonies, interest in mapmaking and geographic inquiry grew. The Mercator projection, created in the 16th century, shows the influence of knowledge gained through exploration in its high degree of directional and shape accuracy. Today maps of the earth are less concerned with charting new territories and more concerned with analyzing the lands on the maps. Geographic focus has shifted away from merely asking "where" to asking the "why of where."

Cognitive Maps

Cognitive (or mental) maps are drawn from memory. A geographer can peer into the human mind by evaluating a cognitive map because it provides a glance into environmental perception. Children often draw maps with a gigantic United States surrounded by tiny neighboring countries, or all by itself. This shows children's view that their home is the center of the world.

The emphasis of a cognitive map is also useful to a geographer trying to understand a culture. While early water-based cultures produced mental maps that often emphasized fishing streams, the map your father drew on a napkin to show you how to get to the maritime museum in a nearby city probably emphasized streets and key landmarks that have been important to him (and others in the community) in navigating your region. In studying cognitive maps, it is essential to evaluate not only what you can see but also what you cannot see. The items left out of a cognitive map are a geographer's clues to both the purpose of the map and the focus (and degree of knowledge) of the individual who drew it.

Scale

Scale, another prominent feature in geographic analysis, can refer to the scope of geographic inquiry or discussion—that is, whether you are studying or discussing a topic affecting the entire world or just a village. In cartography (mapmaking), scale refers to the relationship between a distance on the map and the actual measurement in the real world. In other words, **map (or cartographic) scale** is the degree to which a map "zooms in" on the area it is representing. Scale tells you to what extent the portion of the earth represented on the map has been reduced from its original size to fit on the map.

For example, 1 inch on a map may equal 10 miles in the real world (on the portion of the earth being represented in the map). That scale might be written as "1 inch = 10 miles." Sometimes, the scale is indicated as a fraction, known as a representative fraction. For example, a scale written as "1/40 miles" (or "1:40 miles") means 1 inch on the map equals 40 miles in the real world.

One counterintuitive part of mapping is describing map scale as "large" or "small." Think of it this way: *the larger the area of space being represented on the map, the smaller its scale.* For example, a map of Africa would have a smaller scale than a map of just one country in Africa. A map of the world has a smaller scale than the map of a village. A map of a street has a larger scale than a map of its city. That is, the more "zoomed in" the map is on an area, the larger is its map scale. A large-scale map depicts a smaller area with more detail than does a small-scale map, which represents a larger area with less detail. A small-scale map is less "zoomed in."

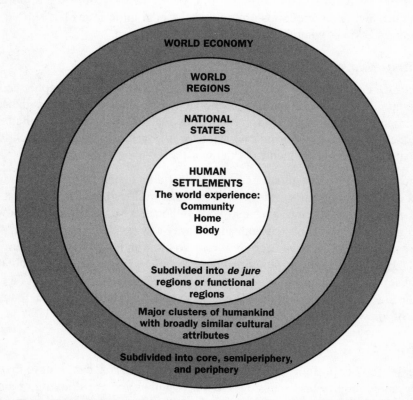

Figure 2.11. Diagram of scales commonly used in geographic research

Categories of Maps

Like a graphic designer choosing the best way to represent an image, geographers can choose from many different types of maps to use in representing different spaces. **Reference maps** show common features such as boundaries, roads, highways, mountains, and cities. A **thematic map**, however, zeroes in on one feature, such as climate, city size, or number of alligators.

Thematic maps come in various forms. **Isoline thematic maps** display the lines that connect points of equal value, as in showing elevation levels. A **choropleth thematic map** shows a pattern of some variable, such as population density or voting patterns, by using various colors or degrees of shading. A now-famous example of a choropleth thematic map is the one displaying the 2004 election results by shading conservative-voting states in red and liberal-voting states in blue. A **proportional-symbol thematic map** uses some symbol (whether it is a circle, star, triangle, or

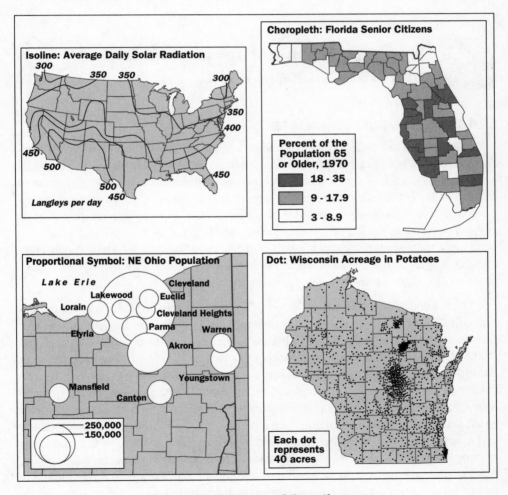

Figure 2.12. Four types of thematic maps

even Mickey Mouse ears) to display the frequency of a variable. The larger the symbol on the map, the higher is the frequency of the variable found in that region. For example, a proportional symbol of population density in the United States would have larger circles in New York City than in Bagdad, Kentucky (which really exists). **Dot density maps** are thematic maps that simply use dots to represent the frequency of a variable in a given area, such as the number of college graduates living in counties within a state. A dot density map specifies what each dot represents. In the college graduates map, for example, each dot might equal 100 graduates.

A **cartogram** is another type of map that uses proportionality to show a particular variable. In other words, cartograms use space on the map to show a particular variable. For example, a cartogram showing the frequency of factory labor throughout the world would show a large space taken up by China and a much smaller space taken up by the United States. Cartograms manage to maintain some degree of geographic accuracy in the relative positions of geographic entities.

PART 2 — New Geographical Technologies and Geographical Data

Obtaining Geographic Data

Mapmakers use data to construct thematic maps. They obtain data from various sources. **A geographic information system (GIS)** is a computer program that stores geographic data and produces maps to show those data. The city government of Nashville, Tennessee, has an entire department devoted to geographic information collection. Geographers in that department collect and manage geographic data and generate maps for the government using a GIS. For example, the city's GIS can produce a map showing property values throughout Nashville. Then it can layer another spatial characteristic such as population density on top of property values to show the relationship between the two variables.

Often geographic data are collected using **remote sensing**, which is the collection of information from satellites and distant collection systems. In other words, remote sensing is the technique of obtaining information about objects through the study of data collected by special instruments that are not in physical contact with the objects being analyzed. **A global positioning system (GPS)** uses satellites to determine exact locations on the global grid. Data directly collected by the geographer making the map or conducting the study are called **primary data**. On the other hand, **secondary data** are collected by a source that previously conducted a study and made data available for future use. For example, to make maps of the frequency of people aged 65 years and older in various cities, cartographers can use the U.S. Census Bureau's website to gather the necessary data. In doing so, the mapmakers would be using secondary data, which saves them time and eliminates the hassle of conducting their own count. However, in using secondary data, cartographers must carefully evaluate sources that gathered the data to ensure the accuracy and authenticity of the information. Be careful of what you find on the Web!

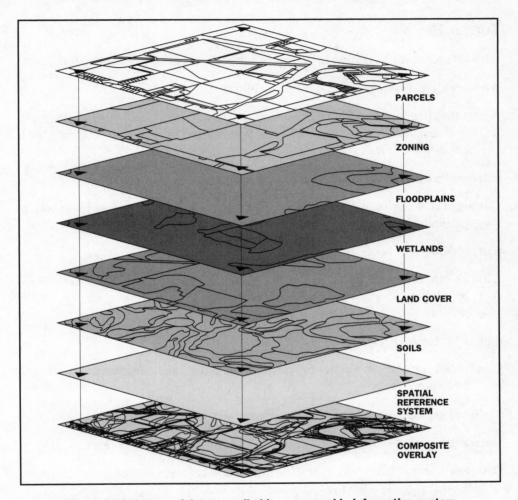

Figure 2.13. Layers of data compiled in a geographic information system

Data Aggregation

Another issue in cartography is the level of **data aggregation**, which is the size of geographic units being represented on a map. The larger the area that is being represented in a study, such as a country or continent, the "coarser" is the study's (or map's) level of data aggregation. The smaller the area that is being represented, such as a county or neighborhood, the "finer" the study's (or map's) level of data aggregation. That is, "coarser" studies show less detail than "finer" studies.

<table>
<tr><td>PART
3</td><td># Chapter Review</td></tr>
</table>

Terms Review

Absolute location—Position of an object on the global grid; latitude and longitude.

Anglocentric—Focused on the English culture.

Azimuthal projection—Map that maintains direction but distorts other properties; flat-plane-constructed map of each hemisphere; direction is accurate, and great-circle routes are apparent.

Cardinal directions—North, south, east, and west.

Cartogram—Map that uses proportionality (i.e., space on the map) to show a particular variable.

Cartography—Process of mapmaking.

Choropleth thematic map—Map that shows a pattern of a variable, such as population density or voting patterns, by using various colors or degrees of shading.

Cognitive (or mental) map—Map drawn from memory.

Conformal (or orthomorphic) projection—Map that maintains shape but distorts other properties.

Cultural ecology—Study of human–environment interaction.

Data aggregation—Size of geographic units being represented on a map.

Distance decay—Pattern in which the interaction between two places declines as the distance between the two places increases.

Distortion—Necessary error resulting from trying to represent the round, nearly spherical earth on a flat plane, or map.

Dot density map—Thematic map that uses dots to represent the frequency of a variable in a given area.

Equal-area (or equivalent) projection—Map that maintains area but distorts other properties.

Equidistant projection—Map that maintains distance but distorts other properties.

Formal region—Region composed of areas that have a common (or uniform) cultural or physical feature; sometimes referred to as uniform regions.

Four main properties of a map—Shape, size (area), distance, and direction. Shape refers to the geometric shapes of the objects on the map. Size (area) refers to the relative amount of space taken up on the map by the landforms or objects on the map. Distance refers to the represented distance between objects on the map. Direction refers to the degree of accuracy representing the cardinal and intermediate directions.

Friction of distance—Degree to which distance interferes with some interaction.

Functional region—Group of places linked together by some function's influence on them after diffusing from a central node; sometimes referred to as a nodal region.

Geographic information system (GIS)—Computer program that stores geographic data and produces maps to show the data.

Geographic model—Simplified version of what exists on the earth or what might exist in the future; helps a geographer search for answers to why patterns exist on the earth as they do.

Global positioning system (GPS)—System of satellites used to determine an exact location on the global grid.

Great circles—Circles formed on the surface of the earth by a plane that passes through the center of the earth. The equator and every line of longitude paired with its twin on the opposite side of the earth form great circles. Any arc of a great circle shows the shortest distance between two points on the earth's surface.

Greenwich mean time (GMT)—Baseline for time zones around the world, centered on the prime meridian; sometimes called Universal time.

Human–environment interaction—One theme of geography through which geographers analyze humans' impact on their environment and their environment's impact on them.

Human geography—Branch of geography primarily concerned with analyzing the structures, processes, and location of human creations and interactions with the earth.

Intermediate directions—Northwest, southwest, northeast, and southeast.

Isoline thematic map—Map displaying lines that connect points of equal value; for example, a map showing elevation levels.

Lines of latitude—Measured in degrees north and south from the equator, which is 0 degrees latitude. The North Pole is 90 degrees north latitude, and the South Pole is 90 degrees south latitude. Lines of latitude never intersect, so geographers often call lines of latitude parallels.

Lines of longitude—Measured in degrees east and west of one line of longitude known as the prime meridian, the line of longitude that runs through England's Greenwich Observatory. The prime meridian represents 0 degrees longitude.

Map—Two-dimensional model of the earth or a portion of its surface.

Map (or cartographic) scale—Relationship between distance on the map and the actual measurement in the real world.

Mercator projection—Map showing the shapes of the continents and landforms accurately but drastically distorting the size (area) of the continents. For example, Greenland appears almost as large as Africa.

Movement—Theme in geography involving the movement occurring in a space: movement of information, people, goods, and other phenomena.

Node—Place from which a diffusing phenomenon spreads to other places (its originating point).

Perceptual (or vernacular) region—Region whose boundaries are determined by people's beliefs, not a scientifically measurable process.

Gall-Peters projection—Map created by a geographer to show the relative sizes of the earth's continents accurately (equal area). However, it distorts shape, so it is not conformal.

Physical geography—Branch of geography concerned with spatial analysis of the structures, processes, and locations of the earth's natural phenomena, like soil, climate, plants, and topography.

Place—Theme in geography that involves the unique combination of physical and cultural attributes that give each location on the earth its individual "stamp."

Primary data—Data directly collected by the geographer making the map or conducting the study.

Proportional-symbol thematic map—Map that uses some symbol to display the frequency of a variable. The larger the symbol on the map, the higher the frequency of the variable found in that region.

Reference map—Map showing common features like boundaries, roads, highways, mountains, and cities.

Region—Theme in geography involving a spatial unit that has many places sharing similar characteristics.

Relative directions—Directions commonly given by people, such as *right, left, up,* and *down*, among many others.

Relative location—Location of a place or object described in relation to places or objects around it.

Remote sensing—Technique of obtaining information about objects through the study of data collected by special instruments that are not in physical contact with the objects being analyzed.

Robinson projection—Map showing the world with slight distortions to all four properties, rather than having one property correct and the other three drastically distorted.

Secondary data—Data used by a geographer but collected by another source that previously conducted a study and made the data available for future use.

Sense of place—Person's perception of the human and physical attributes of a location that give it a unique identity in that person's mind.

Simplification—Cartographer's process of eliminating unnecessary details and focusing on the information that needs to be displayed in the map.

Site—Internal physical and cultural characteristics of a place, such as its terrain and dominant religions, among others.

Situation—Location (or context) of a place relative to the physical and cultural characteristics around it. The more interconnected a place is to other powerful places, the better its situation.

Space–time compression—Increasing sense of accessibility and connectivity that seems to be bringing humans in distance places closer together.

Spatial interaction—Process in which goods, ideas, information, and people move among places.

Spatial perspective—Outlook through which geographers identify, explain, and predict the human and physical patterns in space and the interconnectedness of different spaces.

Thematic map—Map that zeroes in on one feature such as climate, population, or voting patterns.

PART 4 — Some Suggested Web Resources for Further Exploration

Association of American Geographers (AAG): http://www.aag.org/

With many of America's professional geographers among its membership, the AAG is a tremendous resource for researching a career in geography, reading about political issues in geography, and finding reviews of geography-related books and other publications.

National Council for Geographic Education (NCGE): http://www.ncge.org/

The NCGE website contains ample resources for educators looking for information on national teaching standards and lesson plans in geography.

National Geographic Society: http://www.nationalgeographic.com/

One of the most fascinating websites, National Geographic has catalogued articles and images from all over the world on virtually every interesting geographic topic.

Gallery of Map Projections: http://www.galleryofmapprojections.com/

This site displays hundreds of map projections in all forms and types and explains each kind.

Buckminster Fuller Institute: http://www.bfi.org/

Check out this site on Buckminster Fuller, one of the most intriguing minds of the 20th century, who created one of the most unique map projections known to man, based on the geodesic dome.

GIS Software: http://www.esri.com/

This is the site of a leading GIS software producer, ESRI. You can download the company's free product and explore the wonders of GIS technology.

PART 5 — Pre-Exam Practice

Terms Review Quiz

Use the Terms Review list or your own memory to determine the extent of your knowledge of key terms and concepts. Remember, the AP exam does not include this kind of exercise, but it is included here as a review tool.

1. _____ Region composed of areas that have a common (or uniform) cultural or physical feature; sometimes referred to as uniform regions.

2. _____ Outlook through which geographers identify, explain, and predict the human and physical patterns in space and the interconnectedness of various spaces.

3. _____ Location (or context) of a place relative to the physical and cultural characteristics around it.

4. _____ Region whose boundaries are determined by people's beliefs, not a scientifically measurable process.

5. _____ Southeast, southwest, northeast, and northwest.

6. _____ Branch of geography primarily concerned with analyzing the structures, processes, and location of human creations and interactions with the earth.

7. _____ System of satellites used to determine an exact location on the global grid.

8. _____ Baseline for time zones around the world, centered on the prime meridian.

9. _____ Directions commonly given by people, such as *right, left, up,* and *down,* among many others.

10. _____ Necessary error resulting from trying to represent a round, nearly spherical earth on a flat plane, or map.

11. _____ Position of an object on the global grid: latitude and longitude.

12. _____ The equator and every line of longitude paired with its twin on the opposite side of the earth form one of these.

13. _____ Process of mapmaking.

14. _____ Degree to which distance interferes with some interaction.

15. _____ Map that maintains distance but distorts other properties.

16. _____ Simplified version of what exists on the earth or what might exist in the future; helps a geographer search for answers to why patterns exist on the earth as they do.

17. _____ Two-dimensional model of the earth or a portion of its surface.

18. _____ Person's perception of the human and physical attributes of a location that give it a unique identity in that person's mind.

19. _____ Study of human–environment interaction.

20. _____ Map created by a geographer to show the relative sizes of the earth's continents accurately (equal area). However, it distorts shape, so it is not conformal.

21. _____ Map that shows a pattern of some variable, such as population density or voting patterns, by using various colors or degrees of shading.

22. _____ Internal physical and cultural characteristics of a place, such as its terrain and dominant religions, among others.

23. _____ Map showing the world with slight distortions to all four properties, rather than having one property correct and the others drastically distorted.

24. _____ Cartographer's process of eliminating unnecessary details and focusing on the information that needs to be displayed in the map.

25. _____ Map displaying lines that connect points of equal value; for example, a map showing elevation levels.

Multiple-Choice Review Questions

1. Which of the following would have the smallest map scale?

    (A) Map of Asia

    (B) Map of Kentucky

    (C) Map of the world

    (D) Map of Nashville, Tennessee

    (E) Map of Avenue of the Americas, New York City

2. Which of the following maps would be most useful for demonstrating varying levels of oceanic elevation?

    (A) Dot density   (D) Proportional symbol

    (B) Isoline topographic   (E) Azimuthal

    (C) Cartogram

3. Which of the following applies to all aspects of human geography?

    (A) Ethnicity   (D) Space

    (B) Gender   (E) Density

    (C) Climate

4. If two cities are three inches apart on a map with a scale of 1:60,200, how far apart are they on the surface of the earth?

    (A) 2.85 miles   (D) 100 miles

    (B) 4 miles   (E) 250 miles

    (C) 6 miles

5. Which of the following has the coarsest level of data aggregation?

    (A) Analysis of Asian birthrates

    (B) Analysis of lead in a classroom

    (C) Analysis of gender ratios in Kentucky

    (D) Analysis of literacy rates in Afghanistan

    (E) Analysis of copyright violations in Germany

6. If you were measuring the concentration of white Americans using a dot density map, which threshold would put the most visual emphasis on those whites living in rural areas?

    (A) One dot per 3,000 white Americans

    (B) One dot per 50,000 white Americans

    (C) One dot per 100,000 white Americans

    (D) One dot per 150,000 white Americans

    (E) The proportion is insignificant to the visual emphasis

7. Louisville, Kentucky, is located in a valley and is built on the Ohio River. Its street patterns follow the orientation of the river. These features refer most directly to Louisville's

    (A) situation   (D) site

    (B) relative distance (E) absolute location

    (C) gentrification

8. If it is 2 p.m. in your city and it is 12 p.m. in Greenwich, England, what is your city's approximate longitude?

   (A) 15 degrees west   (D) 30 degrees east

   (B) 15 degrees east   (E) 30 degrees west

   (C) 45 degrees west

9. Europe and Asia are primarily divided along the line that extends along the

   (A) Alps, Black Sea, and Indian Ocean

   (B) Himalayas and Indian Ocean

   (C) Ural Mountains, Black Sea, and Caspian Sea

   (D) Transylvanian Alps and Danube River

   (E) Volga River and Dinaric Alps

10. In approximately 365¼ days, the earth completes

    (A) one revolution   (D) one leap year

    (B) one rotation   (E) one eclipse

    (C) one solstice

11. Distortion can be defined as

    (A) the error in accuracy that occurs in all maps

    (B) a technique for giving each location on the earth a corresponding place on a flat surface

    (C) a mathematical formula for translating cultural understandings of rivers

    (D) a spherical, scaled model of the earth

    (E) the process of calculating map scale

12. Human geography is best defined as the study of

    (A) where and why human activities are located

    (B) where and why natural forces occur as they do

    (C) populations and birth rates

    (D) human conflicts

    (E) the earth's impacts on humans

13. Saying "Louisville, Kentucky, is located at 38 degrees north, 85 degrees west" is giving Louisville's

    (A) relative location   (D) functional region

    (B) region   (E) cognitive map

    (C) absolute location

14. Kentucky, Canada, the Ohio River Valley, a German-speaking region, and Northern Ireland are all classified as

    (A) functional regions   (D) heterogeneous cultures

    (B) formal regions   (E) shatter belts

    (C) perceptual regions

15. Which of the following is NOT used by geographers to determine absolute location?

    (A) Equator   (D) Prime meridian

    (B) Distance from the ocean   (E) Longitude

    (C) Latitude

16. Which of the following map projections shows the relative sizes of earth's landmasses most accurately?

    (A) Gall-Peters projection   (D) Molleweide projection

    (B) Robinson projection   (E) Buckminster Fuller projection

    (C) Mercator projection

17. Which of the following is an absolute location?

    (A) 18 degrees north

    (B) 3 miles west of Denver

    (C) the equator

    (D) 123 Main Street, Beverly Hills, CA 90210

    (E) Athens

18. Which of the following is NOT one of the five themes of geography?

    (A) Region   (D) Location

    (B) Place   (E) Movement

    (C) Maps

19. Conformal maps maintain

    (A) area   (D) distance

    (B) direction   (E) size

    (C) shape

20. Verbal, representative fraction, and graphic are all forms of

    (A) maps   (D) cardinal directions

    (B) scales   (E) intermediate directions

    (C) geographic themes

21. A map that uses a symbol to display frequency (the larger the symbol, the higher the frequency) is a(n)

    (A) isoline thematic map

    (B) choropleth thematic map

    (C) proportional-symbol thematic map

    (D) dot density map

    (E) cartogram

Free-Response Question

Of great interest to geographers are the cultural and political implications of technological innovations that affect human interaction.

(A) Define *space–time compression*, relating it to technological innovations. Give an example of its impact on human interaction.

(B) Describe the impact of space–time compression on the friction of distance.

(C) Explain one positive and one negative effect of space–time compression on one of the following regions:

- Southeast Asia
- Southwest Asia
- Eastern Europe

PART 6 Pre-Exam Practice Answers

Terms Review Answers

1. Formal regions
2. Spatial perspective
3. Situation
4. Perceptual (or vernacular) region
5. Intermediate directions
6. Human geography
7. Global positioning system
8. Greenwich mean time
9. Relative direction
10. Distortion
11. Absolute location
12. Great circles
13. Cartography
14. Friction of distance
15. Equidistant (or azimuthal) map
16. Geographic model
17. Map
18. Sense of place
19. Cultural ecology
20. Gall-Peters projection (or equal-area projection)
21. Choropleth map
22. Site
23. Robinson projection (or average projection)
24. Simplification
25. Isoline thematic map

Multiple-Choice Answers

1. **(C)**
   The smaller the map scale, the larger the area being represented on the map. The largest area from the list of choices is a map of the world.

2. **(B)**
   An isoline map uses lines (isolines) to connect areas of equal elevation. Therefore, such a map would be useful for showing varying elevations. Dot density maps are used for showing density; cartograms show some unit of analysis in a proportional, geometric pattern that is geographically accurate; proportional-symbol maps use some symbol, such as a star or circle, to represent a pattern of some measured statistic across a map; and azimuthal maps show great-circle routes.

3. **(D)**
   Just as time is essential to a historian, space is the quintessential tool to geographers. You might argue that it depends on the study, but in all geographic studies, spatial patterns are the basis of analysis.

4. **(A)**
   If 1 unit on the map represents 60,200 units in real life, then 3 inches on the map represents 180,800 inches in real life. There are 5,280 feet in a mile, which equals 63,360 inches. 180,800 / 63,360 = 2.85 miles.

5. **(A)**
   The larger the area being studied, the coarser the study's level of data aggregation. The smaller the area being studied, the finer the study's level of data aggregation. In this question, the largest spatial area listed is the level of Asian birthrates, because Asia is the largest space of the listed options.

6. **(A)**
   The threshold is the number of units represented by a dot. In this question, the threshold that would give most attention to rural white Americans would be the threshold that creates the most dots in rural areas. One dot per 3,000 whites would create the most dots on the map, rather than some of the higher thresholds.

7. **(D)**
   A city's internal characteristics make up its site, whereas its connection to other cities is its situation. Gentrification is the remodeling and revamping of urban areas by returning suburbanites who consider the areas "underdeveloped" and in need of repair and resettling.

8. **(D)**

For every hour difference from the prime meridian and Greenwich mean time (GMT), 15 degrees of longitude separate the time zones. In this question, because 2 hours separate your city from GMT, 30 degrees of longitude separate it from Greenwich. If your city's time is ahead of GMT, then it is east of Greenwich. If it is behind GMT, then it is west of GMT.

9. **(C)**

Although some geographers see Europe and Asia undivided as a continental Eurasian landmass, the two continents are typically divided along a line extending from the Ural Mountains to the Caspian and Black Seas. Places east of this boundary are considered to be part of Asia, and those west are considered to be part of Europe.

10. **(A)**

It takes one year for the earth to make a complete revolution around the sun. Interestingly, the extra one-fourth of a day is accumulated over four years for the 366th day in a leap year. The earth makes one rotation about its axis in 24 hours.

11. **(A)**

Distortion occurs on all flat maps because it is impossible to take the round earth and represent it on a flat surface. An analogy is peeling an orange peel in one piece and then trying to flatten the peel; it would crack.

12. **(A)**

Human geography is the study of people's patterns and their processes in relation to the earth's patterns and processes. (B) is too narrow in that it does not include human processes. (C), (D), and (E) are also too narrow, although all are a part of human geography.

13. **(C)**

Latitude and longitude together represent a place's absolute location on the global grid. (A) would be its relative position in relation to other places; (B) would be a group of places in which Louisville shares some commonality; (D) would be a group of places sharing some form of a movement (or function) with Louisville, perhaps an airliner's destination route; and (E) would be a map drawn from memory or recollection.

14. **(B)**

Formal regions are groups of places sharing internal uniformity, whether sharing a political affiliation, religious characteristic, topographic similarity, or language usage. All the answer choices include places linked through such a characteristic—not based on a moving function or diffusion route (functional region) and not based on people's perceptions or opinions (perceptual regions). Shatter belts are countries or areas existing in the fall-out range of larger, competing countries.

15. **(B)**

Distance from the ocean is not a part of pinpointing an absolute location on the global grid, whereas the other answer choices are all components in the determination of latitudinal–longitudinal intersection.

16. **(A)**

The Gall-Peters projection was created to more accurately portray the relative sizes of the landmasses, so that areas such as Africa are not understated on maps in relation to size, as they were on earlier maps such as the Mercator and Robinson projections.

17. **(D)**

The address in (D) is the only one of its kind; therefore, it is an absolute location. (A) and (C) are lines that run around the earth with multiple places along them. (B) changes depending on what part of Denver you leave from. (E) is the name of cities in Greece, Georgia, Tennessee and many other places.

18. **(C)**

Maps are a tool geographers use to study the earth. The other choices, along with human–environment interactions, make up the five basic themes geographers use to conduct research.

19. **(C)**

Conformal maps maintain shape. Equal-area projections (A) maintain area, azimuthal projections (B) maintain direction, and (D) equidistant projections maintain distance. Only a globe (E) can maintain all four properties.

20. **(B)**

Verbal scales state the map scale in linguistic terms (e.g., 1 inch equals 10 miles). Representative fractions give a mathematical representation of the scale (e.g., 1:24,000 or 1/24,000). A graphic scale is a pictorial representation of the scale—for example:

miles

0 ——————— 1

would mean the length of the dashes above equals 1 mile on the map.

21. **(C)**

Proportional-symbol thematic maps use a symbol (e.g., a circle) to show some feature on a map (e.g., population). The larger the circle, the larger the population. Isoline thematic maps (A) display lines that connect points of equal value. A choropleth thematic map (B) shows a pattern of some variable, such as population density or voting patterns, by using various colors or degrees of shading. A dot density map (D) uses dots to represent the frequency of a variable in a given area. A cartogram (E) uses space to show a particular variable.

Free-Response Answers

The following is a list of suggested main points for each part of the question.

Part A

- Space–time compression is the process that seems to bring places and people closer together, in terms of communicational distance, through the improvement of communication and transportation technology.

- Although the absolute distance remains the same between two places, the relative distance decreases as the places become increasingly interconnected through technological and transportation conduits.

- The distance between Taiwan and Kentucky remains the same as it was 80 years ago, but people in Kentucky and Taiwan are relatively closer because they can communicate quickly via e-mail and airline travel.

Part B

- Space–time compression is reducing the friction of distance, the degree that distance is a barrier to communication and travel.

- With improved telephone and Internet connections on top of more available and affordable air travel, the degree that distance inhibits travel and communications is diminishing. This simplifies the transmission or trade of ideas, information, and goods among individuals or groups.

Part C

- Possible topics to discuss:

  - *Southeast Asia*—movement of multinational corporations into countries and employing citizens in factories; growth of sweatshops and unchecked free trade at workers' expense

  - *Southwest Asia*—involvement of foreign powers in local political conflicts, increased media coverage of inter-religious wars, and globalization of local conflicts among Jews and Arabs; improved travel to and knowledge of Mecca and Jerusalem; improved oil-based transport and trade; perceived cultural imperialism and invasion of Arab culture by Western cultural forces (e.g., MTV)

  - *Eastern Europe*—increased advertisement and knowledge of foreign opportunities to locals, causing increased emigration from the economically depressed East; fall of communism in the East linked to knowledge of democracy; increased sex slavery/trade

Chapter 3

Population

Introduction

An essential part of human geography is the study of the earth's population, particularly the trends in population growth and change. Over the last 12,000 years, human population has been growing at rates faster than ever seen in history. The earth's population has increased 10 times in just 2,000 years. The fastest rates have been seen in the past 200 years; in fact, the global population has more than doubled in just the last 50 years.

Key Questions

- *Will the earth's population increase to a level that could lead to a global crisis?*

- *What patterns exist in the earth's population densities and distributions?*

- *Why are populations growing faster in some areas of the world than in others?*

- *How have governments and religions attempted to influence population growth trends?*

- *How do geographers measure and study human population patterns?*

- *What are the current and past patterns of population migration and movements?*

- *What political, economic, and social factors influence population migration streams?*

PART 1   Geographical Analysis of Population

Basics of Demography

Demography is the study of human populations. Currently, nearly 6.5 billion people live on the earth. Geographers use demographic analysis to study the spatial distributions of humans and their movements. Demographers are experts in demography.

The size, composition, and growth of a country's population affect its well-being. Rapid increases in population in areas like the Middle East (Southwest Asia) and sub-Saharan Africa strain their **infrastructures**, or support systems, including housing, food supplies, education, and health care.

Population Equation

Scale of inquiry, or the size of a geographic investigation (e.g., global, regional, or local) is important to demographic analysis. At the global level, demographers are looking at where the earth's populations are growing the fastest and where they are expanding more slowly. Present trends show that populations are growing fastest in poorer areas, as seen in parts of Africa and Asia.

The critical issue is not so much that children are being born at faster rates and in higher numbers. It is more concerning that populations are growing the fastest in less-developed regions that cannot support vast numbers of people.

At the subglobal level, demographers analyze population trends within regions, like continents, countries, or states. They are interested in discovering facts that only closer analysis can provide. Where are populations growing the fastest in North America? How does Africa's growth rate compare to Asia's? Locally, demographers may look at different neighborhoods or towns to get a clearer picture of what is happening to a region's population.

Two, key **demographic accounting equations** relate to scale of inquiry. Population change at the global level is calculated using the following formula:

Global Population Accounting Equation
P_0 = Size of population at *start* of interval of measurement
P_1 = Size of population at *end* of interval of measurement
B = Number of births during interval of measurement
D = Number of deaths during interval of measurement

$$P_1 = P_0 + B - D$$

This formula simply means that the new size of the population, P_1, is the original population, P_O, plus the number of people born into the population, B, minus the number of people in the population who died during the interval of measurement, D.

The formula for population change at the regional level is very similar, but it adds two important features: immigration and emigration. **Immigration** refers to people coming into a country (or region), whereas **emigration** refers to people exiting, or leaving, a country (or region). Remember that *immigration* starts with an *i* for coming "into," whereas *emigration* starts with an *e* for "exiting."

Subglobal Population Accounting Equation
P_0 = size of population at *start* of interval of measurement
P_1 = Size of population at *end* of interval of measurement
B = Number of births during interval of measurement
D = Number of deaths during interval of measurement
I = Number of immigrants moving *into* region during interval of measurement
E = Number of emigrants *exiting* region during interval of measurement

$$P_1 = P_O + B - D + I - E$$

Geo Factoid

Why are I and E not factors in the global population accounting equation? Because humans do not immigrate and emigrate from the earth to other planets enough to be included. Technically, we could petition to add astronauts to the global equation, but it is not practical.

Here is a fictitious example to demonstrate how the subglobal population accounting equation works: Country A has 1 million people in 1990. Over the next 10 years 75,000 babies are born; 50,000 people die; 10,000 people move into the country; and 5,000 people exit. In 2000, the population would be

$$P_1 = 1,000,000 + 75,000 - 50,000 + 10,000 - 5,000 = 1,030,000 \text{ people}$$

Population Distribution

Distribution of population is the pattern of people across the earth's surface—where they live. Throughout human history, people have been *unevenly* concentrated, clustering around sustaining resources, such as bodies of water, and in regions where people can farm.

Where people live is heavily influenced by physical conditions. Fewer people live in deserts and tundra, for example. Approximately three-fourths of the people in the world live on only 5 percent of the earth's surface. The part of the earth on

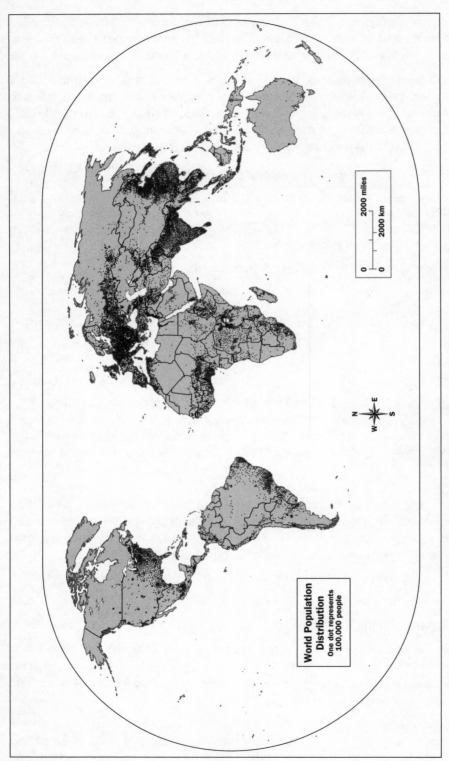

Figure 3.1. A dot density map representing world population distribution

which people *can* live is termed the **ecumene**. About 50 percent of people on the earth live in cities, while the other half lives in rural areas.

Global Population Distribution

Here are some interesting population statistics:

- Approximately 81 percent of the earth's population lives in poorer, less-developed countries in Latin America, Africa, and Asia.

- The only two countries to have more than 1 billion people are India (1.1 billion) and China (1.3 billion).

- One in three of the earth's people lives in either India or China. Combined with the rest of Asia, nearly one in two of the earth's people is Asian.

- Nearly 3 of every 5 people in the world live in Asia and Europe.

- The largest concentration of people on the earth is found in East Asia (China, Japan, Taiwan, and North and South Korea). Nearly 25 percent of all people live in this region. Most of China's population lives on the North China Plain to take advantage of the land that the Yellow River (Huang He) has made **arable**, or fit for growing crops. Most East Asians are subsistence farmers.

- The second-largest concentration of humans is in South Asia (India, Bangladesh, Sri Lanka, and Pakistan). Currently, India's rate of natural increase

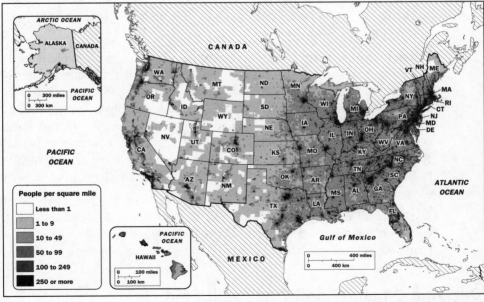

(Source: U.S. Census Bureau)

Figure 3.2. Population density map of the continental United States illustrating population per square mile in 2000

is higher than China's; thus, India is projected to overtake China by 2030 as the world's most heavily populated country. Most South Asians are subsistence farmers living on the arable land surrounding the Indus and Ganges rivers.

- The third-largest concentration of people is in Europe, from the Atlantic to the Ural Mountains (in Russia). This is highly related to Europe's climate and the coal deposits that largely facilitated a population explosion during the Industrial Revolution of the 1800s. In contrast to Asians, most Europeans are **urban** dwellers, living in cities. While Europe has the highest percentage of urban dwellers, Asia has the largest number of urban dwellers (because of its population size).

Population Density

Density is another tool geographers use to study population distributions. Density is simply the number of people in a particular land area. Demographers use several types of density to analyze population trends:

- **Arithmetic density** (also called population density) is the total number of people divided by the total land area. For example, 4.4 million people live in Minnesota, the area of which is 84,000 square miles. Therefore, Minnesota has an arithmetic density of 52 people per square mile. Arithmetic density can be deceptive because it does not show concentration patterns effectively. Egypt, for example, has an arithmetic density of 177 people per square mile. But 98 percent of Egyptians live on only 3 percent of the land nearest the Nile River.

- **Physiological density** is the number of people per unit of arable land. In other words, it is the population divided by the number of square miles of farmland in the region. This measurement can be helpful in analyzing the amount of farmland available to the population. The physiological density of the United States is 340 people per square mile, whereas that of Japan is 7,000 people per square mile. While Egypt's arithmetic density is only 177 people per square mile, its physiological density is greater than 3,000. In fact, the fertile land surrounding the Nile River in Egypt has a density of nearly 8,000 Egyptians per square mile.

- **Agricultural density** is the number of farmers per unit of arable land. A very high agricultural density means that many farmers are on each piece of farmland. A low agricultural density suggests the presence of larger farms.

Carrying Capacity and Overpopulation

Related to density is a region's or country's **carrying capacity**, the number of people the area can sustain or support. This number varies depending on a region's

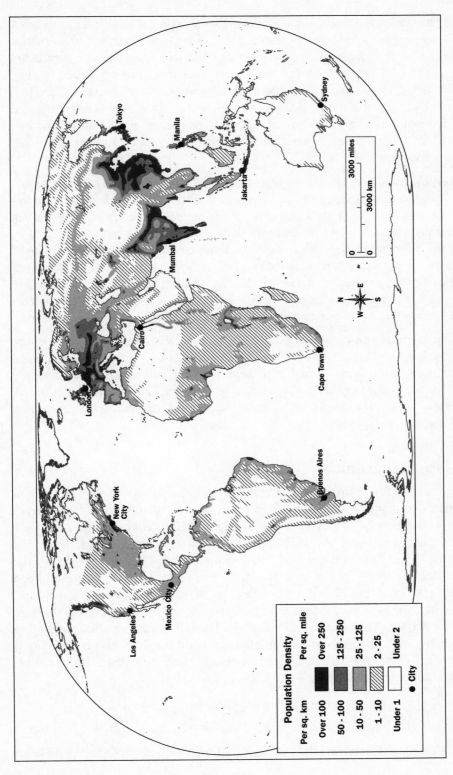

Figure 3.3. Arithmetic density throughout the world, 2007

Population Density

Per sq. km	Per sq. mile	
Over 100	Over 250	
50 - 100	125 - 250	
10 - 50	25 - 125	
1 - 10	2 - 25	
Under 1	Under 2	

● City

available technology, wealth, climate, and ability to bring in resources from other areas to support its people. For example, Japan is a classic example of a country that imports (or brings in) needed food and supplies to sustain its large population in exchange for its exportation of technologically advanced products, such as Sony products. Israel, in its largely arid (dry) environment, has developed advanced irrigation methods to create more arable lands for farming. Saudi Arabia has developed innovative **desalination** plants to remove salt from ocean water and turn it into drinking water for its people. These innovative tactics have increased these regions' carrying capacities.

Overpopulation occurs when a region's population outgrows its carrying capacity, but that carrying capacity can be increased through global trade and communication. It is not always simply a reflection of the natural resources available in that particular country or region. For example, Japan increased its carrying capacity by developing extensive trade relationships with other countries so Japan could import food for its people in exchange for trading technology. Japan is not overpopulated, although it has a high population density. Therefore, a large population can be thought of as a problem when the number of people in the area is larger than the resources available to sustain that population and keep the people living at a decent standard.

Keep in mind, though, that some places are capable of producing more resources than they are able to harvest. This is the case in some less-developed countries with infrastructures and agricultural processes that are not sufficiently productive because of the lack of advanced technology (among other factors). A region's carrying capacity can be increased through improved farming practices and economic development.

Population Pyramids

Demographers use **population pyramids**, also known as age-sex structures, to evaluate the distribution of ages and genders in a given population. A group of people of the same age is known as a **cohort**. Each cohort is split between men and women on the pyramid. The wider the base of the pyramid, the higher the percentage of young people exists in the community. The more top-heavy the pyramid, the higher the percentage of elderly people. A population pyramid can also help predict future growth of populations. Because a woman typically has a baby when she is between the ages of 15 and 45, the more women in that age range, the higher the world's birth rates will be. Let's practice with population pyramids by analyzing Algeria's population pyramid for 2000 and comparing it with Italy's pyramid for that year. Then we will look at projected 2025 pyramids for both countries.

Check to see if you can use the Algerian pyramid:

- How many males are there in the 0–4 cohort in 2000? (About 1.6 million.)

- How many females are there in the 55–59 cohort in 2000? (About 0.4 million.)

- Algeria's pyramid has a wide base and a flattened top. What does that mean? (More young people than old people live in Algeria.)

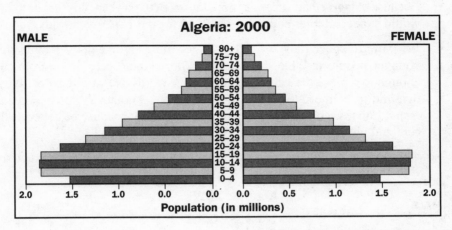

(Source: U.S. Census Bureau, International Data Base)

Figure 3.4. Algeria's 2000 population pyramid

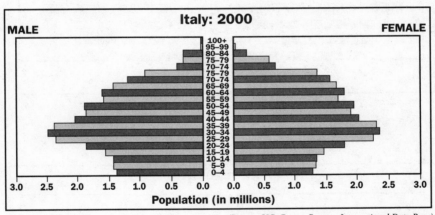

(Source: U.S. Census Bureau, International Data Base)

Figure 3.5. Italy's 2000 population pyramid

Check to see if you can use the Italian pyramid:

- How many males are there in the 0–4 cohort in 2000? (About 1.4 million.)

- How many females are there in the 55–59 cohort in 2000? (About 1.6 million.)

- Italy's pyramid is wider in the middle than at the base. What does that mean? (The population growth rate is slowing because the women in the childbearing ages of 15 to 45 are not having as many babies as their parents did.)

Before we look at each country's 2025 pyramids, let's consider what we would expect them to show:

- Because Algeria had a larger population of 0–4-year-olds in 2000, we would expect a larger population in 2025 for the 25–29-year-olds.

- We would expect Italy to have a larger number of elderly people than younger people in 2025, because in 2000 women were not reproducing enough to replace the generations. In other words, we would expect Italy's pyramid to be more top-heavy than Algeria's. Another factor to consider is that Italians typically live longer than Algerians because of better health care and higher average wealth.

Now let's look at the 2025 pyramids for both countries to check our predictions.

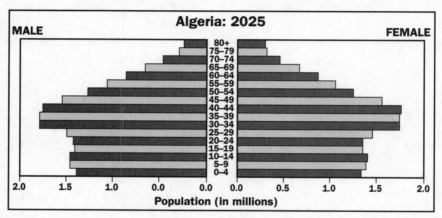

(Source: U.S. Census Bureau, International Data Base)

Figure 3.6. Algeria's 2025 population pyramid

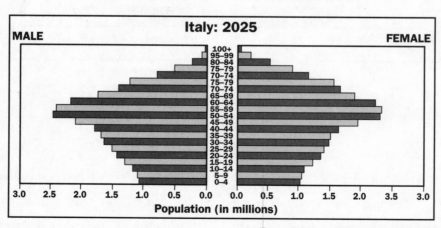

(Source: U.S. Census Bureau, International Data Base)

Figure 3.7. Italy's 2025 population pyramid

How do the pyramids compare?

- Algeria's growth rate did decrease, because the base of the pyramid is thinner than the middle section. That means the parents in the childbearing cohorts (ages 15 to 45) are not having enough babies to sustain their numbers (or the babies are not surviving).

- Italy has a more dramatic decrease in population growth rates, as indicated by the top-heavy pyramid with a thinner base. That is a sign of a **graying population,** or a population that has more middle-aged and older people than young people.

About 20 percent of western Europe's population is over the age of 60 years. By 2030 about 36 percent of its population is projected to be over 60 (Population Reference Bureau).

Let's do one more quick analysis, looking at the 2007 population pyramid for the United States.

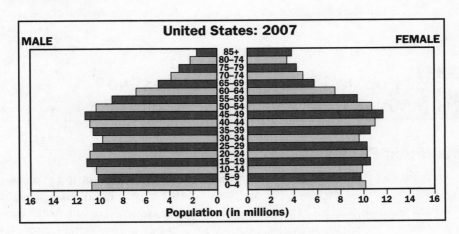

Figure 3.8. 2007 U.S. population pyramid

Notice the bulge in the U.S. population pyramid? It occurs in the 45–49 and 50–54 cohorts. People in those cohorts were born between 1953 and 1962 and are members of what has been called the baby boom generation, born in the years immediately following World War II, when the troops returned home and started families. History is important to analyzing population pyramids.

Graying Population

The **dependency ratio** is a helpful tool in analyzing the workforce and age distribution in a country. People in a country aged 15 through 64 are considered *nondependent* because they can support themselves (usually) through work. *Dependents* are usually people who are older or younger than the working group; they depend on the workers (nondependents) for their survival. Dependents are usually the elderly and children. The dependency ratio shows the relationship between the dependents and the nondependents.

A high dependency ratio means that there are more people who are dependent than are working. This can lead to problems because there are fewer workers able to pay taxes to support health care and Social Security programs for the dependents. The dependency ratio is growing in western Europe and the United States as the baby boomers age. A graying population is related to an increasing dependency ratio. Rapid growth also increases the dependency ratio and is the reason dependency ratios in Africa are fairly high.

The year 2000 marked the first time in human history that people under 14 years of age were outnumbered by people over 60 (Population Reference Bureau).

PART 2 — ## Population Growth and Decline Over Time and Space

---

Population Explosion

Over the last three centuries, the earth has experienced a **population explosion**, a dramatic population increase. Currently, the global human population of nearly 6.5 billion is growing at an **exponential growth rate**, which means that the more people that are added, the faster the population is growing. Exponential growth is different from **linear (or arithmetic) growth**, which is a fixed rate of growth. For example, if you trace the human population over time, in 1750, the population was at about 700 *million* people. However, in just over 200 years, the population has grown to 6 *billion* (one billion equals one thousand million).

Historical Trends in Population Change

Approximately 10,000 to 12,000 years ago, the **first agricultural revolution** empowered humans with the ability to domesticate crops and build stationary

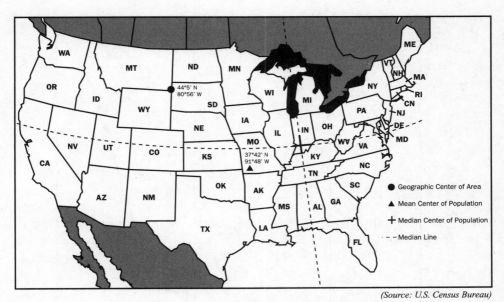

(Source: U.S. Census Bureau)

Figure 3.9. Map of the center of the U.S. population

settlements through farming, rather than always hunting and gathering on the move. Thereafter, cities began to develop and the population began to grow at faster speeds.

In the 1700s, the **Industrial Revolution,** which diffused from England, facilitated the growth of new technologies and industry. Alongside the Industrial Revolution was the **second agricultural revolution**, in which improved fertilization and food storage technology was invented. This improved and increased the food supply, fostering population growth to meet the demands of the Industrial Revolution for more workers. Cities rapidly became overcrowded as people moved from the farms to get factory jobs; urban populations boomed.

Theories of Population Growth

In response to the fast-growing urban areas and an increasing population, British theorist **Thomas Malthus** wrote in his 1798 publication *An Essay on the Principle of Population* that the world's population growth would outpace its carrying capacity. He argued that the global population was growing geometrically, while its food supply was only growing arithmetically. That is, the population was growing faster than the food supply. He advocated for birth control and celibacy, which he called positive checks. He also warned of negative checks, such as war, starvation, and disease.

Critics of Malthusian theory point to the unpredictability of the future as the theory's major flaw. Malthus could not have envisioned innovations in agriculture, such as genetic modification and improved fertilization techniques, that improved

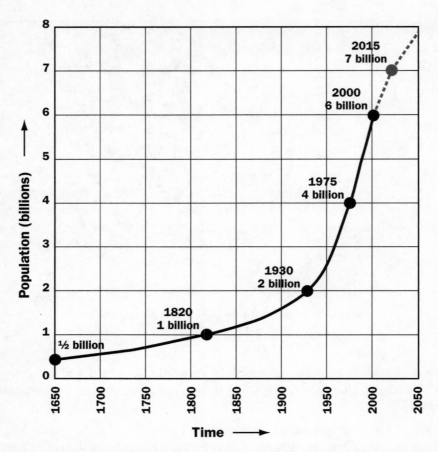

Figure 3.10. Graph demonstrating exponential global population growth over time

output. Nor could he have foreseen modern farming equipment, which enabled farmers to cover more ground than in Malthus's time, leading to greater food production. **Karl Marx** wrote that the problem was not population growth rates but the unequal distribution of resources and wages. **Ester Boserup** wrote another theory that contrasted with both Malthus and Marx. She believed that the overpopulation problem could be solved by increasing the number of subsistence farmers.

Neo-Malthusians apply some ideas in the Malthusian theory. The neo-Malthusian idea of sustainable development hinges on the Malthusian idea that human population growth must reach a "sustainable" level within carrying capacity. These arguments are more regional rather than global in that, for economic and technological reasons, different regions can support different levels of population. As mentioned earlier, many of the highest population growth rates are occurring in poorer regions with lower carrying capacities.

Population Projections for the Future

By the 1820s, the human population reached 1 billion. The **United Nations** devised **growth scenarios** to predict population growth. In its low-growth scenario, the United Nations predicts that the earth's population will begin declining, reach 7.5 billion in 2050 and 5.1 billion in 2100. In contrast, its high-growth scenario predicts a global population of 11 billion in 2050 and 16 billion in 2100. The United Nations' medium-growth scenario, the one most accepted by demographers, predicts 9.0 billion in 2050 and 9.5 billion in 2100.

Among the negative checks on population growth that have occurred throughout world history are the Black Plague of the 1300s in Europe, which decimated 40 percent of the European population and killed 13 million Chinese; the Irish potato famine, which killed nearly one in two Irish people and caused massive emigration from Ireland; and HIV/AIDS, which since the 1980s has risen to be a **pandemic,** a disease affecting very large amounts of area and people, often at a global scale (in contrast with an **epidemic**, which affects a more local group).

HIV/AIDS

Geo Factoid

The number of people living with HIV/AIDS in the Middle East and North Africa rose 75 percent between 2003 and 2005 (Population Reference Bureau).

In 2005, nearly 39 million people were living with HIV and nearly 3 million people died from AIDS. Overall the global infection rate is believed to have peaked in the 1990s, but the number of people with HIV is growing because of population growth and increased life expectancy resulting from better medicine for AIDS patients. In sub-Saharan Africa, the area most acutely affected by AIDS, some epidemics are still expanding; nearly 19 percent of all adults there are infected. Africa is the global **epicenter**, or region at the center of impact, of the AIDS pandemic. China, also facing an AIDS epidemic, is projected to see nearly 11 million infections by 2010. Death rates in sub-Saharan African countries are higher because of AIDS-related deaths.

A Demographer's Toolbox: Key Measurements

Demographers use key terms to analyze population patterns. Here is a list of the primary measurement tools:

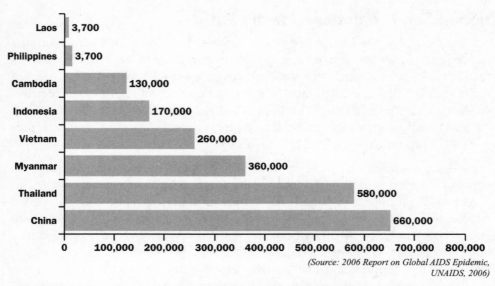

(Source: 2006 Report on Global AIDS Epidemic, UNAIDS, 2006)

Figure 3.11. Number of adults and children infected with HIV in some Asian countries

- **Crude birth rate (CBR)**: number of live births per 1,000 people in a year.

- **Crude death rate (CDR)**: number of deaths per 1,000 people in a year. One interesting aberration exists in some more-developed (richer) countries in western Europe that have higher death rates than less-developed (poorer) countries. This occurs because more-developed countries have a higher percentage of elderly people as a result of longer life expectancies and decreased birth rates.

The CBR and CDR are considered "crude" not because they are rude but because they are general statistics and do not look specifically at the age groups most likely to either give birth or die. They are calculated based on entire populations, making them general statistics.

- **Infant mortality rate (IMR)**: number of infant deaths per 1,000 live births. Infants who die before their first birthdays are counted in the IMR.

- **Life expectancy**: average number of years to be lived by a person.

- **Fecundity**: the ability of a woman to conceive. The fecund years are generally 15 to 45, but this range is believed to be expanding.

- **General fertility rate (GFR)**: number of births per 1,000 women in the fecund years. This measure of fertility is more specific than the CBR.

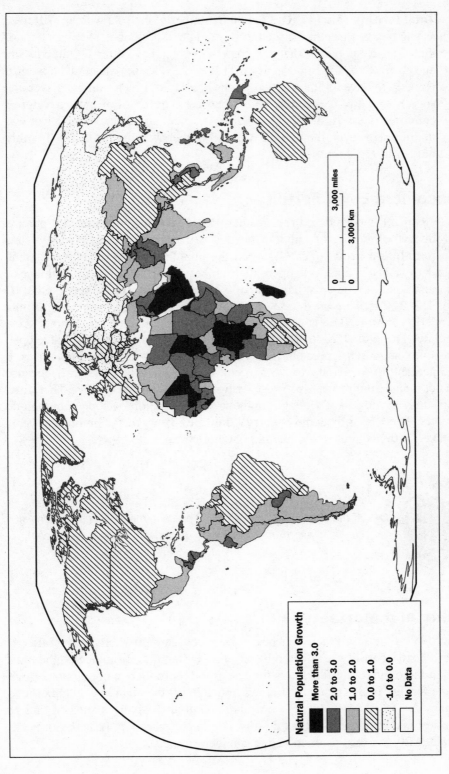

Figure 3.12. Rate of natural increase (annual percentage)

Natural Population Growth

- More than 3.0
- 2.0 to 3.0
- 1.0 to 2.0
- 0.0 to 1.0
- -1.0 to 0.0
- No Data

3,000 miles

3,000 km

- **Total fertility rate (TFR)**: predicted number of births a woman will have as she passes through the fecund years. The 2006 global TFR was greater than 3.0, which means that a woman is likely to have three children as she ages from 15 to 45. Importantly, a TFR of 3.2 does not mean that a woman is likely to have 3 kids and two-tenths of a child. It is a statistical average, so you round to the nearest whole number. The TFRs of most developed countries (western Europe and North America) and China were 2.1 or less in 2006. However, the U.S. TFR is still higher than the birth rates in other industrialized countries.

Replacement-Level Fertility

A TFR of 2.1 is considered **replacement-level fertility**, meaning that parents will produce the number of children needed to replace themselves. This leads to **zero population growth (ZPG)**, when the population size remains the same from year to year. For this to happen, the number of births minus the number of deaths must equal 0. Such a situation results in a **rate of natural increase (RNI)** of zero. The RNI is the growth rate of a population calculated using the formula CBR – CDR/10. An RNI equal to zero means that the population will neither grow nor decline. The global 2006 RNI was roughly 1.2 percent. In more-developed countries, it was only 0.1 percent, nearly ZPG. In the less-developed countries, it was 1.5 percent; in Africa, it was 2.3 percent. The RNI is called "natural" because it does not include migration—people moving in and out of the country. Therefore, a country may have a low RNI, but it might have immigration—people moving into the country. The RNI affects the country's **doubling time**, or the number of years it will take for the country to double in population size.

At the current RNI of around 1.2 percent, the global population will double in approximately 50 years (Population Reference Bureau).

Fertility and Mortality

Fertility is the reproductive behavior of a population, whereas **mortality** is related to death. Fertility is affected by several key factors. Biologically, the most important factor affecting fertility is the age of the reproductive population. Obviously, the fertility rate in a nursing home is much lower than that in a neighborhood with many 20- to 30-year-olds. For a woman, fecundity usually begins around 15 years of age and terminates in the mid-40s. For males, reproductive behavior peaks at about age 20, but the termination age is undetermined.

Geo Factoid

Studies indicate that women with lower levels of body fat tend to be less fecund than others.

A population's diet and nutritional intake also has an impact on fertility. Famine reduces fertility rates. Economic factors also play a role in shaping fertility. Industrialization tends to reduce fertility rates because families move from being rural farmers to city dwellers. Children are needed on the farms to help, but they are expensive in the cities.

Sociocultural factors, such as when men and women can marry, also affect fertility patterns. If a culture believes men and women should marry young, it is encouraging higher fertility rates. The simple fact is that the couple that is together longer has more time to have babies. Such **pronatalist population policies** encourage families to have more children.

Population Policies

Pronatalist policies promote reproduction and bigger families; they are often called expansive policies. Policies such as tax breaks for families with children and antiabortion laws are considered pronatalist. Adolf Hitler was trying to encourage the growth of his country's "Aryan" population when he established pronatalist policies to reward Aryan women with public recognition for having many babies. Hitler's racist policies were also considered **eugenic population policies** because they encouraged the reproduction of only certain groups of people and discouraged or terminated the growth of others. In the 1950s, Chairman Mao Zedong encouraged Chinese families to reproduce by rewarding families with medals and cash prizes for having many children. Currently, former East Germany is engaging in advertisements and promotions to encourage higher birth rates in an attempt to reverse the approaching **underpopulation**, when not enough people would be available to fill the jobs and fulfill the responsibilities necessary to sustain the society.

In contrast, **antinatalist population policies** encourage a reduction in fertility rates. They are often called restrictive policies because they limit population growth. India has adopted antinatalist approaches to try to reduce its fertility rates. Abortion is readily accessible, as are contraceptive measures. In fact, the government has been accused of forcing women to be sterilized, a procedure that terminates a human's ability to reproduce.

In the 1980s, China adopted the antinatalist **one-child policy**, which punished families for having more than one child in many regions of China. This policy was created under Deng Xiaoping's administration in response to the pronatalist approach of his predecessor, Mao, which created overpopulation problems in China.

Allowed to have just one child, many families preferred to have only boys to carry on the family name and be able to earn more money, since men have more earning power in Chinese society. This led to **female infanticide** problems, with some families aborting or killing their female newborns so they could try to have male children instead. It also led to gender imbalances because some regions had more men than women. This is measured by the **sex ratio**, the number of males per 100 females. Some demographers link these gender imbalances to China's HIV/AIDS rates, a result of men being unable to find wives and thus hiring prostitutes, who are more likely to be HIV positive.

For every two births in the world, at least one pregnancy is aborted. Only about half of the 60 million abortions throughout the world are legal. Abortions actually outnumber deaths on a worldwide scale (Population Reference Bureau).

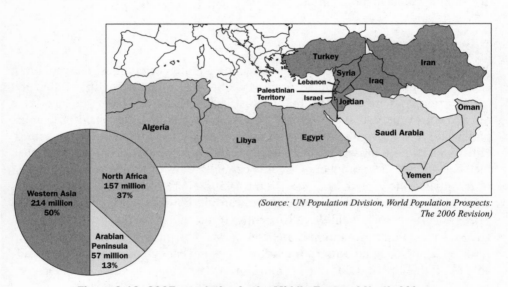

(Source: UN Population Division, World Population Prospects: The 2006 Revision)

Figure 3.13. 2007 population in the Middle East and North Africa

Global Population Conferences

The United Nations has held several conferences on controlling population growth. The **1974 UN population conference** in Romania was burdened by cold-war tensions. The Soviets (Russians) felt that population control was a conspiracy by the United States to stop the growth of communist countries, such as the Soviet Union and China. The **1984 conference** held in Mexico was colored by the advent of the Green Revolution's new technologies to increase global food production in the neediest countries. China had also enacted its one-child policy. The **1994 conference** in Egypt proposed the "Cairo Strategy" to teach contraception uses in schools in poorer countries. However, conservative elements, such as the Roman Catholic Church and Muslim countries, vehemently disagreed with the strategy and blocked its implementation. The **2004 conference** declared that the key to reducing the global RNI is to empower women throughout the world by improving women's educational and economic parity (equality) with that of men. In other words, if women have increased economic and educational opportunities, they can make career choices beyond just having children.

Worldwide, women who have completed their high school education have an average of three children; without it, the average is seven (Population Reference Bureau).

Demographic Transition Model

As described in Chapter 2, geographic models help explain and predict human patterns. The model developed to explain and predict changes in population growth is called the **demographic transition model (DTM)**, which predicts changes in

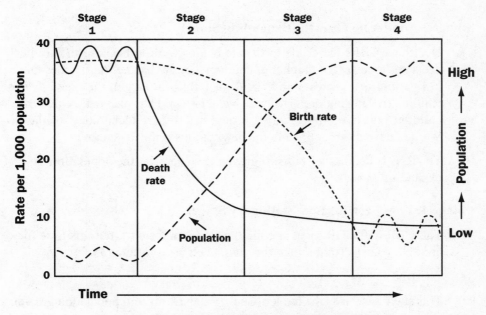

Figure 3.14. Demographic transition model

birth, death, and natural-increase rates in countries as they "transition" or mature. It is based on the assumptions that economics drive demographic change and that all countries will pass through four stages of demographic transition or change. The three measurements in the model are crude birth rate, crude death rate, and rate of natural increase. Let's look at each of the stages.

Stage 1: Low Growth (High Stationary Stage)

- High CBR and CDR, leading to low RNI.

- Fluctuation in CBR and CDR because of disease, famine, and war.

- This stage usually characterizes a subsistence farming country without an industrialized economy.

Stage 2: High Growth (Expanding Stage)

- High CBR: children are still needed on the farms to help.

- Declining CDR: the crude death rate starts to drop as new health care systems arrive, such as better medicine. Industrialization has begun, but the birth rate has not fallen because families are still living in the subsistence agriculture mode that requires lots of children, many of whom did not survive before the arrival of the new medicine and technology. It takes time for families to realize the changes in society.

- The RNI increases because the same high number of births is occurring with fewer deaths to match the high birth numbers. Therefore, population expansion is at a high rate.

Stage 3: Moderate Growth (Expanding Stage)

- Declining CBR: the crude birth rate begins to drop because of families' decisions to lower the number of children they are having. As families move to live in cities growing as a result of industrialization, they have fewer children (raising children is expensive in cities). They also realize that their children will live longer with the new health care technology available. Women have more options in the newly industrialized economy.

- The RNI is decreasing but still greater than zero, so the population is still expanding in size.

Stage 4: Low Growth (Low Stationary Stage)

- The CBR and CDR meet at equal levels (equilibrium), but this time they are at low levels (rather than the high levels seen in stage 1).

- The RNI is low.

- This stage is seen as the modern-society stage with zero population growth.

Criticisms of the DTM

Critics of the demographic transition model point to its being based on England's transition from a subsistence economy to an industrialized society. They believe not all countries will pass through the same demographic transition pattern. For example, some African countries benefited from the diffusion of medicine and food supplies from more-developed countries, a pattern not seen in England's case. Further, demographic growth in 19th-century England occurred in the millions, not the billions of people seen in today's transitions. England progressed from stage 2 to stage 3 over the course of 100 years, but today's stage-2 countries are being pushed to enter stage 3 at a much faster pace.

Some demographers propose adding a fifth stage to the DTM. This new stage would show a continuing decline in the CBR, as seen in many more-developed countries such as France and Germany. This would show the graying-population patterns noticed throughout some wealthier countries.

Demographic Momentum

Demographic momentum, sometimes called **hidden momentum**, occurs in many developing countries when the population continues to grow even after replacement-level fertility is reached. How could this happen if the TFR is 2.1 to 2.5 and parents are producing only enough children to replace themselves? Remember that the rate of natural increase is (CBR – CDR)/10. Many developing countries have population pyramids that are wide at the bottom and very thin at the top because life expectancy is not high. Therefore, when the huge number of young people start having babies, even if only two per couple, that new generation of births far surpasses the number of old people dying. Thus, you have population growth even when people are practicing replacement-level TFRs. This makes reaching zero population growth very difficult for countries with wide-based population pyramids, such as India.

Global Variations in Demographic Transition

Importantly, the DTM demonstrates that the CDR is a function of technological innovation and improvements in health care, whereas the CBR is more a function of cultural choice and individual decisions by people. The CBR often takes longer to change, unless it is forcibly changed at a governmental level, as in China's one-child policy.

Different countries are in different DTM stages. These varying stages reflect, to some degree, their economic and demographic development. All countries have progressed beyond stage 1, largely through the diffusion of medical technology from more-developed countries in the late 20th century during the **medical revolution**. With improved medicine, people in these poorer regions began having longer life expectancies, which, coupled with the already high birth rates, led to higher population growth rates.

Many of the poorest countries were pushed into stage 2. Most Latin American and Asian countries remain in stage 3 at moderate growth, while most African countries remain at high growth in stage 2. Many western European countries are at the end of stage 4's zero population growth equilibrium and pushing toward a potential stage 5, if it exists. Japan is also facing the fifth stage, or the graying-population problem. Instead of encouraging immigration to fill jobs once occupied by the growing number of elderly people, Japan is trying to increase the age of its workers.

Geo Factoid

Africa's share of the world population rose from 9 percent to 14 percent between 1950 and 2005 (Population Reference Bureau).

Epidemiologic Transition Model

One other model to mention is the **epidemiologic transition model**, which focuses on the causes of death in each of the stages of the DTM. For example, pandemics like the Black Plague affect the CDR in stage 1, while diseases (such as cholera) associated with overcrowding during massive movement into cities affect the CDR during stage 2. The CDR is most affected in stages 3 and 4 by diseases associated with the growing numbers of elderly people. Some demographers call for a fifth stage in the epidemiologic model, one showing the reemergence of infectious and parasitic diseases that were once thought to be eradicated during stage 3, such as bubonic plague and smallpox. This is speculated to occur because of improved transportation and space–time compression, allowing human contact to occur more rapidly. This was seen recently in the SARS epidemic and the swine flu outbreaks of the early 21st century.

PART 3 Population Movement

Spatial Interaction and Friction of Distance

Have you noticed that the interconnectedness of the world is increasing? It seems that we are getting closer together, even though our real distance is not decreasing. For example, communicating with someone in Taiwan today is not as big of an ordeal as it was 20 or even 10 years ago. It takes just seconds to log onto a computer and send an instant message to a person as far away as East Asia. It seems as if the difficulty of distance, known as the **friction of distance**, has been reduced. In other words, distance is not the barrier to communication and travel that it once was.

This process of coming closer together and more in contact with each other, even though the real distance remains the same, is called **space–time compression**. The friction of distance is being reduced through space–time compression, and consequently spatial interaction is increasing. **Spatial interaction** is simply the interaction between two places, whether through communication, economic transaction, or migration and travel.

Migration Defined

As we become more linked together, our ability to move across the earth's surface is increasingly more accessible. This is affecting **migration**, the process of *permanently* moving from your home region and crossing an administrative boundary, such as between counties, states, or countries. Perhaps someday it will include planets. Today more than 174 million people have moved outside the country in which they were born.

The number of migrants has more than doubled since 1975, with most living in Europe, Asia, and North America. The United States attracts the most migrants of all countries in the world.

Migration Streams

Why do people migrate? Migration patterns often give clues to what is happening in various parts of the world. A **migration stream** is a pathway from a place of origin to a destination. If hordes of people are emigrating from a place, perhaps something is pushing those masses of people out. Places attracting lots of migrants must have high **place desirability**—possession of positive features making people want to move there. If a place has more immigrants (moving into it) than emigrants (leaving it), it has a **net in-migration**. Places with more emigrants than immigrants have a **net out-migration**. A net in-migration usually indicates that an area has high place desirability; net out-migration usually indicates the opposite.

Migration streams often develop because of information exchange. People in the place of origin may hear of great opportunities in the new place, may have family members in the new community, or may be seeing advertisements for the new place. Usually, where there is a migration stream there is a **migration counterstream** of people moving back to the place of origin from the new place.

Push and Pull Factors

Migration is usually not a random act but is based on thoughtful consideration. Often migration decisions are based on a combination of push and pull factors influencing a person's movement. **Push factors** are the negative influences that make a person want to move away, such as high taxes, high crime rates, and abusive governments, among others. **Pull factors** are the positive influences that pull a person toward a particular place, such as affordable real estate, good schools, and clean parks. The assignment of what is a push and what is a pull factor is highly personal. For example, being near family members may be a positive pull factor to some people but a negative push factor to others.

Voluntary Versus Forced Migration

Voluntary migration occurs when migrants have an option of whether or not to move. However, **involuntary (or forced) migration** is when migrants are pushed from their land. The largest forced migration occurred with the North Atlantic slave trade, forcing nearly 30 million Africans from their homes to migrate to the Americas. **Refugees** are migrants fleeing some form of persecution or abuse. **International refugees** flee their country and move to another country, while *intra*national **refugees** abandon their homes but remain in their country to escape persecution. Intranational refugees are also known as **internally displaced peoples**.

In 2005, an estimated 23.7 million people were internally displaced, roughly 1.6 million fewer than in 2004 (Internal Displacement Monitoring Centre).

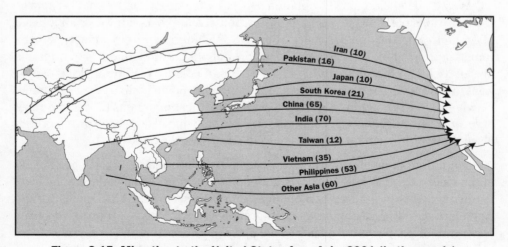

Figure 3.15. Migration to the United States from Asia, 2001 (in thousands).

Some Major Regions of Dislocation and Refugees

The following is a list of some regions of dislocation, or places where people are being forced to migrate as refugees because they are being persecuted:

- **Sub-Saharan Africa** is one area of the world with the largest refugee crisis. Millions of people fled from Rwanda and the Congo in response to tribal or ethnic conflicts. In the Darfur region of northeastern Sudan, religious and ethnic tensions between the North and the South, Muslims and animists, and the government and rebels have led to massive dislocation. Zaire, Tanzania, Uganda, Liberia, Sierra Leone, Angola, and Burundi are also seeing large numbers of war-related refugees.

- **The Middle East** (which many argue includes North Africa): A major migration stream in the Middle East includes emigration (or dislocation) of Palestinians after the formation of the Israeli state to neighboring Southwest Asian countries such as Jordan, Syria, and Egypt. Additional dislocations include the Kurdish people from the former Iraq and Afghanistan's citizens during Soviet occupation in the 1980s.

- **Europe:** The fall of Yugoslavia in the Balkans led to the largest refugee crisis in Europe since World War II. Nearly 7 million refugees fled their homes during this conflict.

- **Southeast Asia:** The Vietnam War created nearly 2 million refugees, Cambodia's violent governmental transition uprooted nearly 300,000 refugees, and the dictatorial government of Burma (now Myanmar) has dislocated thousands.

- **South Asia:** In addition to Afghani refugees fleeing to neighboring Pakistan, Sri Lanka has seen nearly 1 million of its citizens dislocated by a feud with the Sinhalese government.

More Major Migrations at Different Scales

About 3 percent of the world's people have migrated from their countries of origin. North America, Oceania, and Europe have net in-migration, while Asia, Africa, and Latin America have net out-migration. About 50 percent of Southwest Asia's population are immigrants, making it the region with the highest percentage in the world.

The United States has seen three major waves of immigration, and each wave originated from a different region. In the colonial era, from 1607 until 1776, Europe and Africa were the primary sources of migrants, both voluntary and involuntary, to the United States. Many Europeans were escaping political and religious persecution in Europe, while many Africans were forced to come to the Americas as slaves.

Country of asylum/ Leading countries of origin	Number of refugees	Country of asylum/ Leading countries of origin	Number of refugees
MENA-Western Asia		**North Africa**	
Iran	994,000	Algeria	94,500
Afghanistan	940,000	Morocco	890,000
Iraq	54,000	Former Palestine	4,000
Iraq	63,400	Egypt	86,700
Former Palestine	34,000	Former Palestine	57,000
Iran	14,300	Sudan	23,600
Turkey	13,600	Somalia	4,200
Jordan	609,500	Libya	12,000
Iraq	450,000	Former Palestine	8,700
Former Palestine	558,200	Somalia	2,900
Palestinian Territory	1,685,800	Morocco	2,300
Gaza Strip	986,000		
West Bank	699,800	**Countries outside MENA**	
Lebanon	296,800	Germany	
Former Palestine	256,800	Turkey	7,200
Iraq	9,200	Iraq	4,900
Sudan	8,300	Iran	4,400
Syria	866,300	Greece	
Former Palestine	512,100	Iraq	2,100
Iraq	351,000		
Turkey	7,300	Mauritania	
Iran	3,600	Morocco	26,700
Iraq	2,300		
Arabian Peninsula		United States	2,800
Kuwait	14,300	Iran	
Former Palestine	13,500		
Saudi Arabia	240,800		
Former Palestine	240,000		
Yemen	82,700		
Somalia	78,600		

(Source: U.S. Committee for Refugees and Immigrants, World Refugee Survey 2006)

Figure 3.16. 2005 Refugee populations in the Middle East and North Africa (MENA)

The 19th century saw continued migration from Europe. Before 1840, most immigrants in America originated in England, but in the 1840s and 1850s, massive numbers of Irish and Germans made the trip across the Atlantic in search of

Source	Destination
Europe	North America
Africa	Americas (slavery)
Southern Europe	South and Middle America
Britain and Ireland	Africa and Australia
India	Eastern Africa, Southeast Asia, and Caribbean America
China	Southeast Asia
Eastern United States	Western United States
Western Russia	Eastward

Figure 3.17. Major migration streams before 1950

opportunity. More than 4.2 million people migrated in the 1840s and 1850s, more than twice that seen since the New World had been colonized.

Many early immigrants to the New World were second sons who did not inherit land from their fathers because the land went to the first-born male. These second sons were in search of opportunity in America to build wealth.

Immigration to the United States slumped during the Civil War but surged again in the early 20th century, fueled by the Industrial Revolution. This wave, starting around 1907, came not just from northern and western Europe but also from areas like Italy, Austria-Hungary, and Russia. European migration never reached such heights after World War I.

During the Great Depression and World War II (1930s through 1940s), immigration to the United States dropped dramatically, but it picked up again thereafter and reached new heights in the 1980s and 1990s. During the 1970s and 1980s, Asia was the leading source of immigrants to the United States. By the late 1980s, Latin America was the chief source of immigrants to the United States. Many U.S. immigrants send money home to their family members in their home countries, a transaction known as a **remittance**. Many immigrants are **guest workers**, temporarily allowed in the United States on work permits.

In 1921, unrestricted immigration to the United States was halted by the **Quota Act of 1921**, which allowed the highest numbers of immigrants from European countries and discriminated against Asians and other regions.

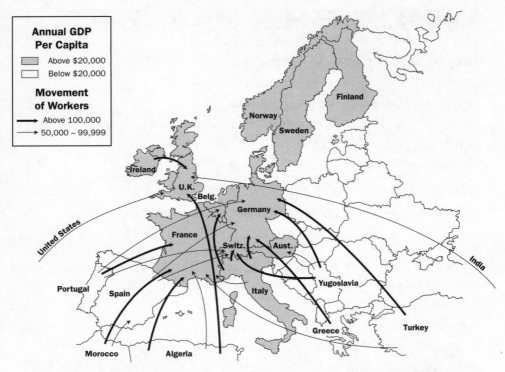

Figure 3.18. Migration streams of guest workers into Europe, circa 2001

Internal Migration

Internal migration is movement within a country, as opposed to international or external migration, which is movement outside a country. The two types of internal migration are interregional and intraregional. **Interregional migration** is moving from one region in the country to another region, whereas **intraregional migration** is moving within a region, such as from a city to a suburb. As industrialization built up cities in America, more and more Americans migrated from farms to cities in a pattern of **urban migration**. A counterstream soon developed as people left crowded cities for suburbs (intraregional migration). Recently, an increasing number of U.S. city dwellers have been moving back to the solace of rural areas in a trend known as counterurbanization.

The U.S. migration pattern has shifted its center of population consistently westward and in a southerly direction. During the Great Migration, which occurred while the nation was fighting World War I, many southern African-Americans moved north in search of industrial jobs not being filled by immigrants because of the war. By the 1970s, however, more African-Americans were returning to the South than were moving north. This pattern is part of the trend by northerners, especially baby boomers, moving south for better weather and increased job opportunities as U.S. factory jobs decrease in number. This aging of industrial-era factories in the United States is forming a **Rustbelt** in the Northeast and a **Sunbelt** in the South.

The following is a list of other prominent external (or international) migrations after World War II:

- Jewish immigrants to Israel from countries all over the world, including large sources such as Germany and Russia

- Emigration by East Germans to other countries during transition to Soviet control

- From Asia to the United States, with the largest sources being the Philippines, Vietnam, and India

- From North Africa and Turkey to Europe—namely France, Germany, and England

Migration Selectivity

The decision to migrate often fits into a predictable pattern based on age, income, and other socioeconomic factors. This is called **migration selectivity**, the evaluation of how likely someone is to migrate based on personal, social, and economic factors. Age is the most influential factor in migration selectivity. People are most likely to move between the ages of 18 and 30, the time in which they leave their parents' homes, find employment, attend college, go to war, and so on.

Most individuals move 12 times in their lives, and half of those moves occur before age 25.

Brain Drain

Education is also a factor in migration selectivity. Typically, the more educated people are, the more likely they are to make long-distance moves because of their increased knowledge of more-distant opportunities and greater job qualifications. Some places experiencing net out-migration suffer from **brain drain**, when the most educated workers leave for more-attractive destinations. The Appalachian region in Kentucky often loses its most talented cohort, causing it to suffer from brain drain. Often governments will try to create programs to try to keep the most educated in their workforce. The Kentucky Governor's Scholars Program was one such program to try to persuade the state's most talented high school students to go to college in Kentucky and stay in Kentucky's workforce.

Gravity Model

Geographers use the **gravity model** to estimate spatial interaction and movement between two places. It is known as the gravity model because it resembles Isaac Newton's theory of gravitational pull. Essentially, it says that larger places attract more migrants, just as larger planets have more gravitational pull. However, the model also asserts that closer places attract more migrants than more distant places. Therefore, migration between two places is directly proportionate to population size and inversely proportionate to the distance between the two places. In all, the gravity model proposes an equation that balances distance and size in trying to predict spatial interactions. For example, the model could be used to predict higher numbers of Mexicans choosing to migrate to the United States than to England because of distance decay factors; the United States is simply closer to Mexico. Thus, the model can be a helpful tool in predicting migration patterns, but it has some limitations: It does not factor in migration selectivity factors, such as age and educational level, and human behavior does not always fit into predicted patterns.

Ravenstein's Migration "Laws"

In the late 1800s, British geographer **Ernst Ravenstein** identified 11 generalizations about migration, some of which still apply today. Here are some of the most important generalizations:

- **The majority of migrants travel short distances.** Migration occurs step by step. A migrant moving from Massachusetts to Florida might stop in North Carolina first and then move on to his final destination of Florida. This is called **step migration**, when a person has a long-distance goal in mind and achieves it in a series of small steps. Related to this idea is the rule of short-distance migration, which states that most people never move a long distance. For example, you and your wife can't stand living with your parents so you want to move, but you still want to be close enough so your parents can watch the kids. Therefore, you only move 5 miles away.

  Often, in the process of making a long journey to a final destination, migrants will find an opportunity they like so much that they just stop their journey and stay in the new place they found along the way. This is called an **intervening opportunity**. Suppose, for instance, that on a migration to Florida you stop in Chapel Hill, North Carolina, and decide to stay there instead of proceeding on to Florida; you will have experienced the intervening opportunity of Chapel Hill. **Intervening obstacles** are barriers in a migratory journey. Financial problems, roadblocks, immigration requirements, and wars are just a few of the forms of intervening obstacles that can prevent migrants from reaching their planned final destinations.

- **Migrants who are traveling a long way tend to move to larger cities than smaller cities.** Ravenstein's idea was that the large city, with all its jobs and opportunities, has an almost magnetic pull that makes the long journey worthwhile. Keep in mind that during Ravenstein's lifetime in the 1800s, the Industrial Revolution was pulling people to big cities like Manchester and London. Today this is somewhat true, but modern technology, such as the Internet, makes many "big city" amenities and jobs available in smaller towns.

- **Rural residents are more likely to migrate than are urban residents.** This was true in Ravenstein's time, again because of the Industrial Revolution and its pull of rural dwellers to the cities in search of job opportunities. It is still true in many developing countries, such as China, because many rural folks in these developing countries are moving into large cities within their countries, such as Shanghai, Beijing, Mexico City, Brasilia, and others. Yet counter-urbanization is a noted trend in the United States, where city dwellers are leaving crowded urban places for the suburbs and rural places.

- **Families are less likely to migrate across national borders than are young adults.** Ravenstein based this generalization on the observation that it is simply easier for single people to migrate than it is for whole families. For example, it is difficult for a family to move children and all their belongings over a border. In many cases, single people are less encumbered with responsibilities and are thus more mobile.

- **Every migration stream creates a counterstream.** Therefore, net migration is the number of people in the original flow minus the number of people in the opposite flow (or counterstream). A counterstream can be caused by many factors, sometimes economic, legal, or personal. Even the out-migration of Jews from Nazi Germany had a small counterstream back into Germany because of their capture and forced return by border officials in other countries refusing fleeing Jews shelter from Nazi oppression. A less tragic example might be counterstreams of young Chinese men who originally left their rural villages for new horizons in Chinese cities only to return back to their rural villages after giving city life a try.

Chain Migration

Chain migration occurs when people migrate to be with other people who migrated before them and with whom they feel some tie—be it familial, religious, ethnic, cultural, or some other type of connection. Many immigrants to the United

States move in this pattern, following their relatives or friends to destinations that have been the arrival points for generations. For example, the author's grandparents moved from Hamburg, Germany, to the small town of Lebanon, Ohio, because their German relatives had already moved to Lebanon in previous years.

Model of Migration Transition

Wilber Zelinsky constructed a model known as the **migration transition model** to explain and predict migration changes in a country, much like the demographic transition model explains population changes. In Zelinsky's model, people from stage-1 countries are searching on a local basis for necessities but only moving on a temporary basis in their search for food and shelter materials. Stage-2 countries are experiencing such high rates of natural increase that overtaxing of resources and limited opportunities push people to migrate to the more-developed countries in stages 3 and 4. Many North Africans are currently emigrating from their stage-2 countries for new horizons in more-developed western European countries, where jobs and opportunities are often thought to be available. In stage-4 countries, most migration is intraregional, with people moving from cities to suburbs and back.

Short-Term Local Movements and Activity Space

In addition to studying migration, geographers analyze people's daily movements that do not classify as migration. The area in which you travel on a daily basis is known as your **activity space**. In some more technologically advanced societies, people's activity spaces are wide and vast because they have planes, trains, and automobiles to move them around each day. For example, United States senators may have an activity space that involves several states each day, as they fly back and forth for political meetings. However, an average citizen in South Africa, for example, may have a much smaller activity space consisting of only a few miles. There are various classifications of this shorter-term, impermanent movement:

- **Cyclic movement** is movement during your daily routine from your home and back. Commuting is a form of cyclic movement.

- **Seasonal movement** is a form of cyclic movement that involves leaving your home region for a short time in response to a change in season. Leaving New England and going to Florida for the winter is a form of seasonal movement. Nomadism, following animal herds for subsistence, is another form, with people moving their herds seasonally to better pastures.

- **Periodic movement** involves longer periods of stay, as for serving in the military or attending college.

- **Transhumance**, a pastoral farming practice of moving animals from hillsides to pastures, is periodic, seasonal movement.

PART 4	Chapter Review

Models Review

Demographic Transition Model (DTM)

In four stages of transition from an agricultural subsistence economy to an industrialized country, demographic patterns move from extremely high birth and death rates to low birth and death rates. In the process, population growth rates skyrocket and then fall again. The crude death rate first falls because of the influx of better health technology, and then the birth rate gradually falls to match the new social structure.

Epidemiologic Transition Model

Disease vulnerability shifts in patterns similar to the DTM. In the early stages, plague and pestilence spread as a result of poor medical technology. As industrialization proceeds, diseases related to urban life spread. In later stages, diseases once thought eradicated reappear as more-developed societies come into easier contact with less-developed regions struggling with the more primitive diseases, such as smallpox and the bubonic plague. Leading causes of death in later stages are related to diseases associated with aging, such as heart disease.

Gravity Model of Spatial Interaction

When applied to migration, larger places attract more migrants than do smaller places. Additionally, destinations that are more distant have a weaker pull effect than do closer opportunities of the same caliber.

Zelinsky Model of Migration Transition

Migration trends follow demographic transition stages. People become increasingly mobile as industrialization develops. More international migration is seen in stage 2 as migrants search for more space and opportunities in countries in stages 3 and 4. Stage-4 countries show less emigration and more intraregional migration.

Terms Review

Activity space—the area in which you travel on a daily basis.

Agricultural density—Number of farmers per area of farmland.

Antinatalist population policy—Restrictive policy that discourages people from having babies.

Arable land—Land that can be used for agriculture.

Arithmetic density—Number of people per area.

Brain drain—Net out-migration of the most educated individuals from a region.

Carrying capacity—Maximum number of people a region can reasonably sustain.

Chain migration—When migrants move to a new place based on information they received from family or community members who made the same journey earlier.

Cohort—Group of people usually classified by age.

Crude birth rate (CBR)—Number of live births per 1,000 people over a year.

Crude death rate (CDR)—Number of deaths per 1,000 people over a year.

Cyclic movement—Movement made on a daily basis that involves a very short move to and from one's home.

Demographic accounting equation—Equation used for evaluating population change on global and subglobal levels. At the global level, the CBR and CDR are the only two factors in the equation of change. At the subglobal level, immigration and emigration are taken into account.

Demographic momentum (hidden momentum)—Phenomenon of a growing population size even after replacement-level fertility has been reached. This occurs when the base of the population pyramid is so wide that the generation of parents will take time to cycle out before zero growth occurs.

Demography—Study of population characteristics, transitions, and projections.

Dependency ratio—Measurement in which the number of people unable to work because of age is compared with the number of workers in a society.

Desalination—Removal of salt from saltwater to make potable drinking water.

Distribution—Spread of a particular phenomenon across a given space.

Doubling time—Number of years it will take for a population to double in size.

Ecumene—Portion of the earth's surface that is habitable for humans.

Emigration—Movement out of a country or region.

Epicenter—Center, or most intensely affected region, of an outbreak or disaster.

Epidemic—Disease spread acutely over a localized area.

Ernst Ravenstein—Nineteenth-century geographer who wrote essays outlining 11 generalizations of migration, some of which still apply today, whereas others have changed since he wrote them during the Industrial Revolution in England.

Ester Boserup—Principal critic of Malthusian theory who argued that overpopulation could be solved by increasing the number of subsistence farmers.

Eugenic population policy—Policy that encourages some groups of people to have babies and discriminates against other groups, discouraging their reproduction.

Exponential growth—Growth that is compounded, like interest in a bank account; contrasts with linear (arithmetic, or regular) growth, which does not increase in rate.

Fecundity—Ability to conceive a child.

Female infanticide—In response to restrictive population policies, families kill their female infants so they can try to have male babies.

Fertility—Reproductive behavior in a population leading to births.

First agricultural revolution—Occurred 10,000 to 12,000 years ago when humans first developed the ability to remain in a settlement and domesticate crops and animals. Led to the development of cities.

Friction of distance—Negative impact that distance has on spatial interaction, including communication and travel.

General fertility rate (GFR)—Number of births per 1,000 women in the fecund range over a year.

Graying population—Evidenced by a population pyramid showing a higher number of older, or elderly, people in its projection than younger, working-age people. The pyramid is top-heavy.

Guest worker—Migrant who is temporarily permitted to stay in a country only to work.

HIV/AIDS—Human immunodeficiency virus is the onset of what turns into the acquired immunodeficiency syndrome. A global pandemic, outbreaks are most acute in Africa and Asia.

Immigration—Movement into a country or region.

Industrial Revolution—Began in England around the 1700s and later diffused in an eastward direction throughout Europe and to the United States. Saw the development of factory-based economies and urban migration at a large scale. Coincided with the second agricultural revolution and high population growth rates.

Infant mortality rate (IMR)—Number of deaths of children under 1 year of age per 1,000 births over a year.

Infrastructure— "Backbone" of a society, including communication, transportation, and other such maintenance structures.

Internally displaced person—Another name for an intranational refugee, someone who is forced from home but remains within the country.

International refugees—Refugees who flee their country and move to another country.

Interregional migration—Internal migration among particular regions in a country.

Intervening obstacle—Barrier encountered on a journey that prevents or interferes with getting to the planned, final destination.

Intervening opportunity—New opportunity that arises along a journey that is more attractive to the person making the journey and diminishes the attractiveness of the final destination.

Intranational refugees—Refugees who abandon their homes but remain in their country to escape persecution.

Intraregional migration—Internal migration within a particular region, such as from a suburb to an inner city.

Involuntary (or forced) migration—Occurs when a migrant is forced to move because of abuse, war, or similar negative circumstances against their will.

Karl Marx—Principal critic of Malthusian theory who argued that overpopulation was the fault of unchecked capitalism and unequal distribution of resources, leaving some places unable to care for their populations.

Life expectancy—Average number of years a person is expected to live.

Linear (or arithmetic) growth—Growth that is regular and not compounded over time. The growth remains at a steady pace, rather than increasing in pace over time (exponential).

Medical revolution—Period in stage 2 of the demographic transition model when lifesaving medical technology drastically reduces the CDR, leading to longer life expectancies and higher rates of natural increase.

Migration—Movement of a person across an administrative border. The move is intended to be permanent.

Migration selectivity—Combination of factors that predict a person's likelihood to migrate based on factors like age, gender, and education.

Migration streams and counterstreams—In a migration stream migrants are moving from a place of origin to a destination. When the original flow of migrants produces an opposite flow of returning migrants, a counterstream results.

Mortality—Death-related activity in a population.

Neo-Malthusians—Contemporary believers in Thomas Malthus's original ideas. They call for sustainable population growth to be achieved through birth control teachings and regional attention to birth patterns.

Net in-migration—Occurs when the number of immigrants is larger than the number of emigrants.

Net out-migration—Occurs when the number of emigrants exceeds the number of immigrants.

One-child policy—Restrictive, antinatalist policy in China that aimed at immediately reducing China's birth rate to replacement level and below.

Overpopulation—Occurs when a region exceeds its carrying capacity. This is difficult to measure because of changing technology and environmental issues that continually alter the carrying capacity.

Pandemic—Disease spread acutely over a large area or worldwide.

Physiological density—Number of people per area of farmland.

Place desirability—Degree of attractiveness of a place to a migrant.

Population explosion—Exponential, unprecedented growth in human population size over the last three centuries.

Population pyramid—Often called age-sex pyramids, a population pyramid shows the distribution of ages and genders in a particular year.

Pronatalist population policy—Expansive policy that encourages more live births in a population.

Pull factor—Factor that attracts a migrant to a region, such as good schools or nice weather.

Push factor—Factor that causes a migrant to move out of a region, such as high taxes or poor schools.

Rate of natural increase (RNI)—Natural growth rate of a population, which is CBR minus CDR expressed as a percentage. A positive RNI indicates a growing population, whereas a negative RNI indicates a population reducing in size. An RNI equal to zero indicates a stabilizing population.

Refugee—Migrant forced from his or her home by threat, real persecution, or abuse.

Remittance—Sum of money sent by a migrant to his or her family back home.

Replacement-level fertility—When the number of births equals the number of deaths. Usually reached at a TFR between 2.1 and 2.5.

Rustbelt—Decay of the once bustling factory-based economy regions of the northeastern United States.

Scale of inquiry—Level of geographic area being investigated. At a very large scale, a neighborhood may be the focus. At a very small scale, the entire earth may be the focus.

Seasonal movement—Form of cyclic movement when a person moves temporarily because of a change in season.

Second agricultural revolution—Coincided with the Industrial Revolution in England and a higher population growth rate, and saw the development of improved sanitation, storage, and fertilization techniques, allowing for greater food output.

Sex ratio—Number of males compared to 100 females in a population.

Space–time compression—Reduction of the friction of distance and distance decay effects because of improved transportation and communication technology. Often space–time compression is seen as the increasing links among people of the earth so that real distance remains the same but perceived distance decreases.

Spatial interaction—Exchange of ideas, people, money, and products among various places.

Step migration—Long migration that occurs as a journey of smaller steps from one place to another until the destination is reached.

Sunbelt—Growth of the economy in the sunny regions of the southern United States that developed as the dominance of the factory-based economy in the northeastern United States decreased.

Thomas Malthus—Malthus's *An Essay on the Principles of Population* was an alarming report during the British Industrial Revolution that predicted that food production would be outpaced by population growth rates. He warned of negative checks, such as famine, and called for positive checks, such as birth control.

Total fertility rate (TFR)—Number of children predicted to be born to a woman as she passes through the fecund years.

Transhumance—Form of pastoral nomadism in which people herd their animals from higher altitudes, such as mountains, to lower places, such as pastures.

Underpopulation—Measure that is difficult to pinpoint; occurs when a population size is below its carrying capacity and cannot sustain the economic development it has reached.

United Nations growth scenarios—Predictions by the United Nations that yield high, medium, and low population growth forecasts for the earth's future.

United Nations population conferences—United Nations conferences held in 1974, 1984, 1994, and 2004 to address population. International controversies and tensions beside population drove the approaches taken at each conference, with the most recent focusing on empowering women as a primary approach to reducing global population growth.

Urban—Pertaining to the city, as opposed to *rural*, pertaining to the farmlands.

Urban migration—Migration into cities from rural areas.

U.S. Quota Act of 1921—Immigration legislation that limited the number of people from any one country and discriminated against Asians and favored European migrants.

Voluntary migration—Move made by a migrant because he or she wants to move.

Zero population growth—Occurs when births equal deaths, leading to a stationary population level.

| PART 5 | **Some Suggested Web Resources for Further Exploration** |

Population Reference Bureau (PRB): http://www.prb.org/

This is an excellent, reliable, and user-friendly resource of demographic data and analyses. The PRB compiles an annual analysis of demographic data for the world and its countries.

Population Council: http://www.popcouncil.org/

According to its website, "The Population Council, an international, non-profit, nongovernmental organization, seeks to improve the well-being and reproductive health of current and future generations around the world and to help achieve a humane, equitable, and sustainable balance between people and resources."

United States Census Bureau: http://www.census.gov/

The Census Bureau's website contains U.S. demographic data, analyses, and helpful charts and graphs. It also has a fun population clock that estimates the U.S. population by the minute.

United Nations Population Fund (UNFPA): http://www.unfpa.org/

According to its website, "UNFPA, the United Nations Population Fund, is an international development agency that promotes the right of every woman, man and child to enjoy a life of health and equal opportunity. UNFPA supports countries in using population data for policies and programs to reduce poverty and to ensure that every pregnancy is wanted, every birth is safe, every young person is free of HIV/AIDS, and every girl and woman is treated with dignity and respect."

United Nations Statistics Division: http://unstats.un.org/unsd/

This is the UN's primary engine for distribution of demographic data and analyses. A subscription is required for retrieving much of the information on the site.

U.S. Committee for Refugees and Immigrants: http://www.refugees.org/

According to its website, the mission of the program is, "to address the needs and rights of persons in forced or voluntary migration worldwide by advancing fair and humane public policy, facilitating and providing direct professional services, and promoting the full participation of migrants in community life."

The site contains useful information on refugees, their origins, migrations, and treatment.

U.S. Citizenship and Immigration Services: http://www.uscis.gov/

This site contains data on immigration to the United States, both legal and illegal, as far back as the early 1800s.

Statue of Liberty–Ellis Island Foundation: http://www.ellisisland.org/

On this website, you can look up anyone you know that may have immigrated to the United States through Ellis Island. According to the foundation, "From 1892 to 1924, more than 22 million immigrants, passengers, and crew members came through Ellis Island and the Port of New York. The ship companies that transported these passengers kept detailed passenger lists, called 'ship manifests.' Now, thanks to the generous efforts of volunteers of The Church of Jesus Christ of Latter-day Saints, these manifests have been transcribed into a vast electronic archive, which you can easily search to find an individual passenger."

Internal Displacement Monitoring Center: www.internal-displacement.org/

Affiliated with the United Nations, The Internal Displacement Monitoring Centre (IDMC), is the preeminent international body monitoring conflict-induced internal displacement worldwide. It is an advocacy and educational agency whose site contains data, solutions, and coverage of the world's displaced peoples.

PART 6 Pre-Exam Practice

Terms Review Quiz

Use the Terms Review list or your own memory to determine the extent of your knowledge of key terms and concepts. Remember, the AP exam does not include this kind of exercise, but it is included here as a review tool.

1. _____ Exchange of ideas, people, money, and products among various places.

2. _____ Sum of money sent by a migrant to his or her family back home.

3. _____ Measure that is difficult to pinpoint; occurs when a population size is below its carrying capacity and cannot sustain the economic development it has reached.

4. _____ Form of pastoral nomadism in which people herd their animals from higher altitudes, such as mountains, to lower places, such as pastures.

5. _____ He predicted that the population growth rate would outpace the food supply and called for positive checks on population growth to prevent (or reduce) negative checks.

6. _____ Long migration that occurs as a journey of smaller steps from one place to another until the destination is reached.

7. _____ Number of children predicted to be born to a woman as she passes through the fecund years.

8. _____ Coincided with the Industrial Revolution in England and a higher population growth rate, and saw the development of improved sanitation, storage, and fertilization techniques, allowing for greater food output.

9. _____ Form of cyclic movement when a person moves temporarily because of a change in season.

10. _____ Reduction of the friction of distance and distance decay effects because of improved transportation and communication technology.

11. _____ Exponential, unprecedented growth in human population size over the last three centuries.

12. _____ When the number of births equals the number of deaths. Usually reached at a TFR between 2.1 and 2.5.

13. _____ Factor that attracts a migrant to a region, such as good schools or nice weather.

14. _____ Movement of a person across an administrative border. The move is intended to be permanent.

15. _____ Natural growth rate of a population, which is CBR minus CDR expressed as a percentage.

16. _____ Degree of attractiveness of a place to a migrant.

17. _____ Evidenced by a population pyramid showing a higher number of older, or elderly, people in its projection than younger, working-age people. The pyramid is top-heavy.

18. _____ Restrictive, antinatalist policy in China that aimed at immediately reducing China's birth rate to replacement level and below.

19. _____ Number of people per area of farmland.

20. _____ Occurs when the number of immigrants is larger than the number of emigrants.

21. _____ Occurs when migrants are forced to move against their will because of abuse, war, or similar negative circumstances against their will.

22. _____ Occurred 10,000 to 12,000 years ago when humans first developed the ability to remain in a settlement and domesticate crops and animals. Led to the development of cities.

23. _____ Barrier encountered on a journey that prevents or interferes with getting to the planned, final destination.

24. _____ Disease spread acutely over a large area or worldwide.

25. _____ "Backbone" of a society, including communication, transportation, and other such maintenance structures.

Multiple-Choice Review Questions

1. Which of the following is most clearly a pronatalist policy?

    (A) Awarding tax breaks to families with three or more children

    (B) Giving families cash rewards for not having more than three children

    (C) Forced sterilization programs

    (D) A law similar to China's one-child policy

    (E) Hospitals offering parenting classes to new parents

2. In which of the following countries is life expectancy projected to drop the most by the year 2015?

    (A) Luxembourg   (D) Japan

    (B) Namibia   (E) Mongolia

    (C) Russia

3. Which of the following countries most likely has the highest agricultural density?

    (A) Germany   (D) England

    (B) United States   (E) Egypt

    (C) Brazil

4.   The number of people a region can reasonably support, given its landscape, resources, and trading ability, is known as

(A)   infrastructure   (D)   carrying capacity

(B)   overpopulation   (E)   age-sex pyramid

(C)   physiological density

5.   Why does the rate of natural increase (RNI) not accurately demonstrate population change for subglobal regions?

(A)   RNI data do not include immigration and emigration.

(B)   RNI data are not specific enough to focus on fecund women.

(C)   The RNI does not change in a region without a cultural decision to change the birth rate.

(D)   HIV/AIDS has dramatically altered RNI data.

(E)   Mortality is increasing because of decreased fertility rates in more-developed regions.

6.   Country X's demographic transition is depicted in the following table:

Year	CBR	CDR
1975	45	12
1980	46	13
1985	40	12
1990	35	11

Based on this information, which stage of the demographic transition model best fits Country X in 1990?

(A)   Stage 1   (D)   Stage 4

(B)   Stage 2   (E)   Stage 5

(C)   Stage 3

7. Karl Marx would most likely have agreed with which of the following statements?

   (A) Overpopulation results from exponential population growth and arithmetic growth of food supply.

   (B) The unequal distribution of resources creates surplus population.

   (C) Overpopulation is a direct result of not having enough subsistence farmers in an economy.

   (D) Surplus population is impossible.

   (E) Death rates must exceed birth rates.

8. Italy's demographic data differ from Algeria's in that Italy has

   (A) a much higher percentage of women

   (B) a larger percentage of people considered dependents

   (C) a lower average life expectancy

   (D) more people who are rural dwellers

   (E) a population growing at a faster rate

9. Which of the following measurements would give a demographer the closest prediction of reproductive behavior in a fecund woman in a country?

   (A) crude birth rate   (D) total fertility rate

   (B) rate of natural increase   (E) life expectancy

   (C) infant mortality rate

10. By 2050, which country is projected to have the highest population in the world?

   (A) China   (D) India

   (B) Japan   (E) United States

   (C) Russia

11. Which factor was identified at the 2004 United Nations population conference as key to controlling population growth?

    (A) health care

    (B) political ideology

    (C) farming methods

    (D) HIV/AIDS

    (E) the status of women

12. Margaret embarked on her move to California. En route to San Diego from her home of Louisville, Kentucky, she stopped in Santa Fe, New Mexico. While in Santa Fe, she fell in love with the city and decided to stay there. In Margaret's migration, Santa Fe represents a(n)

    (A) intervening opportunity

    (B) intervening obstacle

    (C) remittance

    (D) push factor

    (E) pandemic

13. Which country is in the region with the highest concentration of people?

    (A) Brazil

    (B) Nigeria

    (C) United States

    (D) Czech Republic

    (E) South Korea

14. Which of the following trends matches the urban migration pattern of the 1880s noted by Ernst Ravenstein?

    (A) The majority of migrants move long distances.

    (B) Most migrants are young children following their young parents.

    (C) Countercurrents of migration tend to be larger than their original streams.

    (D) Migrants who move long distances tend to move to large cities.

    (E) Rural dwellers tend to be less migratory than urban dwellers.

15. Which of the following regions produced the largest migration stream into Germany in the period 1999–2005?

    (A) Latin America

    (B) China

    (C) North Africa

    (D) United States

    (E) Australia

16. Which of the following is NOT a variable in the subglobal population accounting equation?

    (A) Number of births during the interval of measurement

    (B) Number of deaths during the interval of measurement

    (C) Number of people moving into the region during the interval of measurement

    (D) Number of people moving out of the region during the interval of measurement

    (E) Number of children predicted to be born to a woman

17. In which stage of the demographic transition model does the medical revolution take place?

    (A) Stage 1   (D) Stage 4

    (B) Stage 2   (E) Stage 5

    (C) Stage 3

18. Approximately 81 percent of the earth's population lives in poorer, less-developed countries in which three regions?

    (A) Africa, Australia and Asia

    (B) Latin America, Africa, and Asia

    (C) North American, Asia, South America

    (D) Europe, Africa, Pacific Rim

    (E) North America, Europe, Africa

19. Overpopulation in a country occurs when

    (A) total population reaches 10 billion

    (B) there is more of one sex than the other

    (C) the country's population outgrows its carrying capacity

    (D) the country imports food

    (E) large parts of a country are desert

20. Population pyramids are used to show

    (A) the age of a country's population

    (B) the sex ratio of a country's population

    (C) the average income of a country's population

    (D) disease rates

    (E) both A and B

Free-Response Question

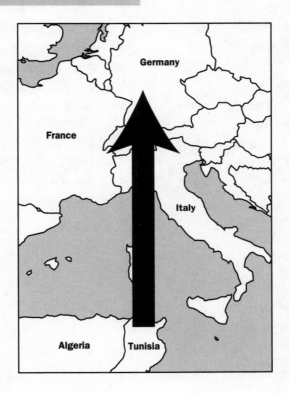

Germany is currently experiencing net in-migration.

(A) Define *net in-migration*, and describe the stream identified in the map above.

(B) Define *push factors* and *pull factors*. Give an example of and explain one push and one pull factor that a migrant in the stream shown in the map above may have experienced.

(C) Relate the immigration pattern noted on the map to Germany's negative rate of natural increase.

PART 7

Pre-Exam Practice Answers

Terms Review Answers

1. Spatial interaction
2. Remittance
3. Underpopulation
4. Transhumance
5. Thomas Malthus
6. Step migration
7. Total fertility rate
8. Second agricultural revolution
9. Seasonal movement
10. Space–time compression
11. Population explosion
12. Replacement-level fertility
13. Pull factor
14. Migration
15. Rate of natural increase
16. Place desirability
17. Graying population
18. One-child policy
19. Physiological density
20. Net in-migration
21. Involuntary (or forced) migration
22. First agricultural revolution
23. Intervening obstacle
24. Pandemic
25. Infrastructure

Multiple-Choice Answers

1. **(A)**

Pronatalist laws encourage people to have babies, whereas antinatalist policies discourage people from having babies. Cash rewards in the form of tax breaks would encourage people to have more children. (B), (C), and (D) are antinatalist policies discouraging families from having babies, whereas (E) is neither. Some might argue that (E) promotes child birth, but (A) is more clearly encouraging higher birth rates, while (E) is simply supporting new parents.

2. **(B)**

In sub-Saharan Africa, life expectancy is projected to drop nearly 10 years, on average. Namibia alone is projected to lose 26 years. These drops are primarily attributed to HIV/AIDS infections. (C) would have been the next-best choice because of Russia's struggling economy and rising HIV/AIDS rates, but sub-Saharan Africa has higher loss of life expectancy years. (A) and (D) are both in more-developed regions, and (E) is improving as a result of improved health technology.

3. **(E)**

Agricultural density is the number of farmers per unit area of farmland. (E) is the best choice because Egypt has a limited amount of farmland near the fertile Nile River; the rest of the country is desertlike. All of Egypt's many farmers crowd near the Nile, packing it densely. (A), (B), and (D) have lower agricultural densities because their farms are more technologically well developed, allowing fewer farmers to farm larger areas and thus decreasing the number of farmers in their economies. (C) has more farmland per person than does Egypt, thereby reducing its agricultural density.

4. **(D)**

Carrying capacity is like the fire capacity of a theater, which indicates the number of people who can safely sit in the theater and exit in an emergency. Carrying capacity is the number of people who can be sustained in a given region, such as a country. When a country exceeds its carrying capacity, it is considered overpopulated (B). (A) is an integral part of a region's carrying capacity, because the infrastructure is its support network of transportation, health care, communication, and so forth. (C) is the number of people divided by the amount of farmland in a region, and (E) is a demographic tool showing the size of cohorts (age groups) divided by gender in a given country or region.

5. **(A)**

RNI data only include fertility and mortality rates and therefore do not give a complete picture for a region. Although U.S. fertility rates may be moving toward replacement level, the amount of immigration to the U.S. is increasing the size of the overall U.S. population. However, immigration is not accounted for in the RNI. (B) is more applicable to the CBR rather than the RNI. (C) refers to the birth rate, not the RNI. (D) is true in regions acutely hit by HIV/AIDS, but that does not make the RNI less comprehensive in its use. (E) is also a true statement but is not a cause of the RNI's limited picture.

6. **(C)**

Stage 3 depicts a country with a birth rate that begins a substantial decline to match the already low death rate. In Country X, the crude birth rate begins to fall almost 10 points to reach the already-low (or developed-level) death rate. (B) is characterized by a plummeting death rate and a high birth rate; (D) shows a country at low birth and death rates that are at equilibrium. (E) is a suggested addition to the DTM that shows a higher death rate than birth rate, caused by graying populations.

7. **(B)**

Karl Marx argued that a "surplus population," when there are unemployed workers, is only a manifestation of the unequal distribution of resources causing some economic classes and areas to have more resources than others. (A) is the philosophy of Thomas Malthus, who believed that overpopulation results when the birth rate grows faster than the food supply, which leads to famine and chaos. (C) was a belief held by Ester Boserup in the 1960s. Marx would not have agreed with (D) because he did see surplus populations occurring in capitalistic societies. (E) would indicate population reduction, which Marx would not have advocated in by any instance.

8. **(B)**

Italy is experiencing a graying population with its lower birth rates and increasing death rates (because the older generation is larger than the younger generation). Algeria, on the other hand, has not yet moved into stage 4 of the demographic transition model and is still experiencing natural population growth. (A) is not true because the percentages of men and women are nearly equal in both countries. (C) is untrue because life expectancy is higher in Italy as a result of its more equally distributed and more well-developed health care practices. (D) is untrue and reversed, because more people are subsistence, rural farmers in Algeria than in Italy. (E) is false for the same reason (B) is true.

9. **(D)**

    The total fertility rate is the number of babies a woman is likely to have as she passes through her fecund (fertile) years, usually from 15 to 45 years of age. It is a predictive measure of the number of children a woman will have. (A) is a general statistic not specific to fecund women, (B) refers to the overall difference between fertility and mortality, (C) refers to the death rates of infants, and (E) is the average number of years a person is expected to live.

10. **(D)**

    China's growth rate was drastically controlled through its one-child policy in the 1980s, forcing its population to reach (or very nearly reach) replacement-level fertility. However, India's drastic growth was not as forcibly controlled, in part because India is a democracy and not a totalitarian state. Therefore, India's growth rate continues to increase, and through hidden momentum, its population will continue to grow for many years to come.

11. **(E)**

    The status of women was emphasized at the 2004 U.N. conference. Leaders discussed the crucial relationship between opportunities for women beyond reproductive roles and global population control. (A) is related but recognized at earlier conferences; (B) was on focus in the 1970s during the cold war; (C) was a focus in the 1980s, during the Green Revolution; and (D), though a factor discussed, this has not been considered critical to controlling growth because it reduces population growth.

12. **(A)**

    An intervening opportunity is a place a migrant comes to on her journey and, because of its high place desirability, decides to stay there rather than continue on to her planned destination. (B) is a blockage or barrier that prevents the migrant from reaching her planned destination, (C) is money an immigrant sends back home, (D) is a factor that causes a migrant to move away from a place, and (E) is a very widespread disease.

13. **(E)**

    East Asia has the highest concentration of people. South Korea is in East Asia, as is China, Taiwan, North Korea, and Japan, to name a few. The second-largest concentration on the earth is found in South Asia, composed of India, Sri Lanka, Pakistan, and Bangladesh.

14. **(D)**

In Ravenstein's time, England was industrializing, and most migrants moved only small distances. However, those who went long distances moved to cities in search of opportunities, making (D) correct and (A) incorrect. (B) is incorrect because most migrants were young adults. (C) is incorrect because most migration streams tend to produce smaller counterstreams in the opposite direction. (E) is incorrect because Ravenstein noticed the opposite trend, that rural dwellers were more migratory than urban dwellers because rural dwellers were moving into cities.

15. **(C)**

North Africans are streaming into many western European countries to fill the job vacancies created by the graying population and shrinking birth rates. Although China (B) may be a tempting choice because of its size, the country limits its emigration. A large number of immigrants into the United States come from Latin America (A), but migration to Europe is too long and difficult for many in Latin America compared with the nearer opportunity offered by the United States.

16. **(E)**

The subglobal population accounting equation only uses the actual number of births, deaths, in-migrations, and out-migrations. It does not use predicted values.

17. **(B)**

The medical revolution occurs in stage 2 and is the cause of lowering death rates. At that point, birth rates remain high, which accounts for the rapidly increasing population. (A) is a time of high birth and death rates, (C) is a time of low death rates and falling birth rates, (D) is the time of low birth and death rates, and (E) is the theoretical time when deaths overtake births because of an aging population.

18. **(B)**

Containing India and China, Asia is the world's most populated region. Africa and Latin America are also both experiencing high population growth rates.

19. **(C)**

Carrying capacity is based on the resources and technology of a people. Increasing agricultural output and international trade are two methods of increasing the sustainability levels of a country. (A) is incorrect because there is no set number for overpopulation. If you can only feed 10 people, 11 is overpopulated. Likewise if you can feed 10 billion, then a population of 9 billion is not a problem. (B) defines the sex ratio and is not related to overpopulation in this sense. (D) is a way of preventing overpopulation by increasing resources, and (E) is not a limiting factor for food production if technology can make other areas produce sufficient food.

20. **(E)**

Population pyramids show the age and sex ratios of a population. They can be useful to geographers in identifying trends in a country's population as well as pointing to potential future problems, such as a growing dependency ratio. (C) is incorrect because population pyramids do not consider income. (D) Although population pyramids can show the effects of disease on a population, they cannot specifically prove a cause. Loss of population through war, disease, migration, or famine would all appear the same on a pyramid.

Free-Response Answers

The following is a list of suggested main points for each part of the question.

Part A

- Net in-migration occurs when a region has more immigrants than emigrants. In other words, there are more people moving in than moving out of a region.

- The migration stream on the map shows a thick in-migration into Germany from North Africa.

Part B

- A push factor affects a migrant's decision by making him or her want to leave a region, with factors such as high taxes and poor schools, among others. A pull factor affects a migrant's decision by making her or him want to move to a particular location, like a magnetic force.

- Possible pull factors in Germany include better health care, better quality of life, more job opportunities, increased stability of life, and less fighting and warfare.

- Possible push factors in North Africa include civil insurrection and warfare, poor economic conditions, few job opportunities, and poor educational opportunities.

Part C

- Germany's negative rate of natural increase has created a situation in which more deaths than births occur each year. Therefore, the Germans are not able to fill the number of jobs once held by the larger, older generations that are dying out. This opens up jobs for potential migrants, who hear about the opportunities and move to find jobs once filled by German-born citizens. This relates to the net in-migration of North Africans to Germany seeking to fill the jobs as demanded by the German economy and its graying population.

Chapter 4

Cultural Patterns and Processes

Introduction

When you walk into a shop in a small German town, you are bombarded by elements of culture, just as you are when you go to the movie theater with friends. Even a study of McDonald's restaurants throughout the world leads to interesting questions about cultural differences. Visit a McDonald's in Switzerland and you might be seated at a candlelit table and served by a waiter. Across the world in Taiwan, McDonald's is considered a place for a quick snack rather than a restaurant. How about ordering a McBeer in Germany? It's on the menu.

Cultural geography is the study of people's lifestyles, their creations, and their relationships to the earth and the supernatural. It is a wide-ranging concept that involves the study of humans' tangible creations, like architecture, languages, and clothing, and their intangible creations, such as their religions and morals. For example, when you visit a Muslim mosque, you are not likely to find pictures of humans. You are much more likely to see geometric patterns on the walls because many Muslims believe that displaying the human image is a form of idolatry. The painting is a human creation, but the image depicted in the painting and where it is displayed are aspects of the Islamic belief system.

> ## Key Questions
>
> - *How do geographers define culture?*
>
> - *How do geographers look at spatial and place aspects of culture in the form of language, religion, race, ethnicity, and gender?*
>
> - *How are cultural patterns represented at different scales, from local to global?*
>
> - *How do cultural traits move through space and time?*
>
> - *What are key aspects to the geography of language and religion?*
>
> - *How does culture shape human–environment relationships?*
>
> - *How is culture expressed in landscapes, and how do different landscapes reflect different cultural identities?*

Concepts of Culture

The Basics of Culture

Culture is seen by human geographers to be a people's way of life, their behavior, and their shared understanding of life. It is a learned system of meaning that has both material and nonmaterial components. **Material components of culture** include tangible artifacts that can be physically left behind, such as clothing and architecture. **Nonmaterial components of culture** include the thoughts and ideas of a people—for example, their religions or morals—that help define a culture. **Cultural geography** is a field of study within human geography that looks at how and why culture is expressed in different ways in different places.

Cultural geography analyzes not just religion and language but all aspects of cultural expression, including governments, economies, urban structures, and much more. It is an area of geographic study largely linked to the 20th-century geographer **Carl Sauer**, who championed the study of the **cultural landscape**, sometimes referred to as the **built environment.** The cultural landscape comprises the physical implications of human culture. In other words, wherever a human culture exists, a cultural landscape exists as that culture's unique imprint on their space on the earth.

When you look at your school, for example, the buildings, lawns, flagpoles, and sports fields are all a part of the cultural landscape of that space. Interestingly, when you look at a classroom in your school, you might see remnants of earlier generations of students. For example, on the wall of a certain high school classroom in Nashville, Tennessee, is a map painted by a class of students and their teacher who occupied that space 30 years ago. This might be considered an example of **sequent occupance**, the succession of cultures leaving their mark in a shared space or territory, often over generations of time. A better example of sequent occupance might be what happened when the Romans, Saxons, Vikings, and others conquered England over a period of 3,000 years, taking over the same space, changing it to fit their needs, and in the process leaving an imprint for future occupiers. The systematic study of this human–environment interaction is called **cultural ecology**.

Environmental Determinism Versus Possibilism

In studying human–environment interactions, cultural geographers encounter the question, "Does the earth make humans take the actions they do?" They also wonder why certain regions thrive and others do not. **Environmental determinism**, a school of thought developed as early as the Greeks, argues that human behavior is controlled (or determined) by the physical environment. "Ideal" climates lead to productive civilizations, as in Egypt near the Nile River. Harsher climates, as in

Siberia, do not foster productivity. Environmental determinists would argue that people are friendlier and more outgoing in Florida but more introverted and reclusive in Minnesota because of the climate.

Possibilism developed as a counterargument to environmental determinism. Possibilists argue that the natural environment places limits on the set of choices (or possibilities) available to people. For example, people living in Florida are not likely to choose to build an igloo park. Not only are Floridians' choices limited by the state's climate, but those limitations also drive Floridians' constructions and actions. According to possibilists, therefore, it is people, not the environment, that propel human cultural development, although the environment limits the set of choices available to them.

Recently, many geographers have discounted possibilism in favor of a concept known as **cultural determinism**. These geographers argue that the environment places no restrictions on humans whatsoever. The only restrictions we face are the ones we place on ourselves. For example, golf courses require grass, water, and fertile soil. None of these is found naturally in a desert; therefore, it seems impossible for a group of people to build a golf course in the desert. But what about Arizona? If you truck in the dirt, pipe in the water, and hire a grass expert who can manage the seeds, you can have a world-class golf course in a world-class desert. So what is possible, and what is not? Cultural determinists argue that humans create everything from their cultural perspective.

Even more ideas have developed around this central question of human–environment interaction. Both environmental determinism and possibilism start with the environment. Adding to the debate is **political ecology**, a school of thought that argues the government of a region affects the environment, which in turn affects the choices (and possibilities) available to the people in the region.

The Jigsaw of Culture

Like a jigsaw puzzle, culture can be broken down into various pieces, or layers. The simplest component of culture is a **culture trait**, a single attribute of a culture, such as the trait of bowing out of respect. Although we think of this culture trait as being Japanese, bowing to show respect is also shared by other cultures outside Japan. Culture traits are not necessarily unique to one group of people. However, the combination of all culture traits creates a unique set of traits called a **culture complex**. For example, all the things Americans do makes up the American culture complex. No other culture group in the world has the exact same combination of traits in its culture complex. When many complexes share particular traits, such as bowing out of respect, those complexes can merge together to form **culture systems**. For example, people living in the northern region of Germany speak with a different accent than Germans living in the southern region. But these two complexes share many other traits and can therefore be fused into the German culture system.

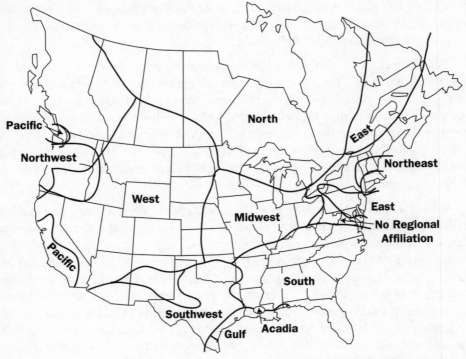

Figure 4.1. Perceptual (or vernacular) regions of North America defined by names of businesses listed in telephone books

Culture Regions and Realms

Chapter 2 introduced three types of regions: formal, functional, and perceptual. Another type of region is the culture region. **Culture regions** are drawn around places and peoples with similarities in their culture systems. Interestingly, people often share a sense of common culture and **regional identity,** or emotional attachment, to the group of people and places associated with a particular culture region. Such regional identity leads to the existence of **perceptual regions** (often called vernacular regions), regions whose boundaries are defined by people's emotions and feelings about an area, rather than objective means. It is difficult to cite examples of culture regions because they become whatever people want them to be. While some Tennesseans might argue they are "southern," some Alabamans would argue Tennesseans are not. On the other hand, a Pennsylvanian might argue that both Tennessee and Alabama are "southern" states.

Thus, the definition of culture regions often comes down to a question of perspective. The perceptual region of "the South" in the United States is a culture region defined through people's beliefs and attitudes about the Civil War, grits, and many other cultural symbols, or items through which people express their cultural

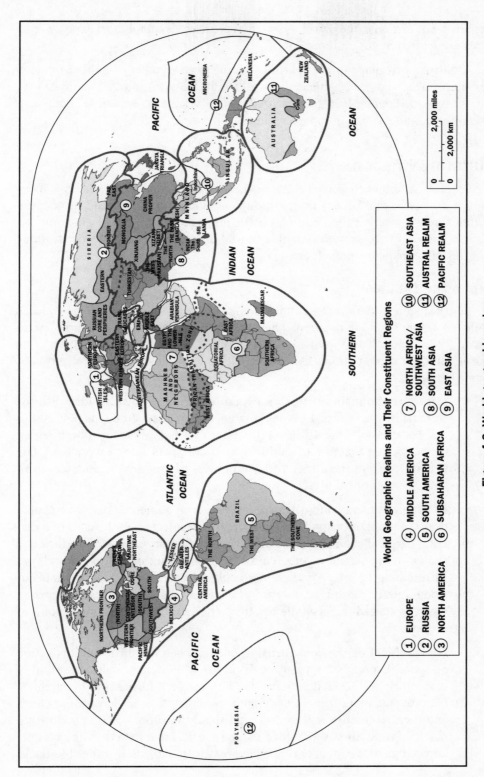

World Geographic Realms and Their Constituent Regions

① EUROPE	④ MIDDLE AMERICA
② RUSSIA	⑤ SOUTH AMERICA
③ NORTH AMERICA	⑥ SUBSAHARAN AFRICA

⑦ NORTH AFRICA/SOUTHWEST ASIA	⑩ SOUTHEAST ASIA
⑧ SOUTH ASIA	⑪ AUSTRAL REALM
⑨ EAST ASIA	⑫ PACIFIC REALM

Figure 4.2. World geographic realms

117

identities. For example, the cowboy is seen as a cultural symbol most expressive of a western United States culture region.

A **culture (or geographic) realm** is the merging together of culture regions. Commonly accepted geographic realms include the Anglo-American, Latin American, European, Islamic, sub-Saharan African, Slavic, Sino-Japanese, Southeast Asian, Indic, and Austral-European realms.

Cultural Diffusion

People's material and nonmaterial creations spread across space and time, moving to new places and being carried through generations. The spread of people's culture across space is called **cultural diffusion**. The spread of any phenomenon (such as a disease) across space is called **spatial diffusion**. There are two categories of diffusion: expansion and relocation.

Expansion Diffusion

In **expansion diffusion**, the cultural component spreads outward to new places while remaining strong in its original hearth, or place of origin. For example, Islam spread from its hearth area in Saudi Arabia to other areas around and outside of its hearth while remaining strong in Mecca and Medina. There are several forms of expansion diffusion:

- **Stimulus expansion diffusion** occurs when the innovative idea diffuses from its hearth outward, but the original idea is changed by the new adopters. For example, the diffusion of iced tea throughout the southern region of the United States was modified by southerners into "Sweet Tea." The general concept (iced tea) diffused but was altered by the adopters to fit their sweet-toothed needs.

- **Contagious expansion diffusion** occurs when numerous places or people near the point of origin become adopters (or infected, in the case of a disease). A good example of the effects of contagious expansion diffusion is shown in the spread of tuberculosis from its point of origin (or node) to surrounding people. Another, more cultural example of contagious diffusion might be the spread outward of the Green Hills Grille restaurant from where it started in Nashville to other cities and towns around its point of origin.

- **Hierarchical expansion diffusion** occurs when the diffusion innovation or concept spreads from a place or person of power or high susceptibility to another in a leveled pattern. Hip-hop music diffused in a hierarchical pattern, spreading from a few large inner cities to other large inner cities, and then to smaller inner cities, and finally to more-suburban and rural places. Information often diffuses in a hierarchical pattern. For example, knowledge of the identity of the terrorists behind the September 11 attacks in 2001 first traveled through the higher levels of the U.S. government to the media and then to the general public.

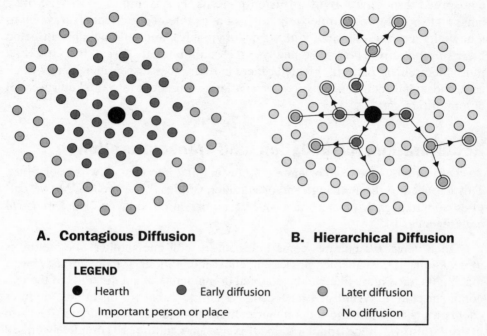

A. **Contagious Diffusion**   B. **Hierarchical Diffusion**

LEGEND

● Hearth   ● Early diffusion   ○ Later diffusion

○ Important person or place   ○ No diffusion

Figure 4.3. Contagious versus hierarchical diffusion

Relocation Diffusion

Relocation diffusion involves the actual movement of the original adopters from their point of origin, or hearth, to a new place. This movement of the adopters facilitates diffusion. Whereas in expansion diffusion it is the innovation or disease that does the moving, in relocation diffusion the people pick up and move, carrying the innovation or disease (or whatever is spreading) with them to a new place. When the capital of Russia was moved from Saint Petersburg to Moscow after the revolution, the power and prestige of the Russian government moved, through relocation diffusion, to the city of Moscow, leaving Saint Petersburg vacant of that power and prestige. The spread of HIV/AIDS in the 1980s and 1990s shows the effects of relocation diffusion, as infected individuals moved, perhaps unknowingly, with the virus to a new city and got others sick in their new cities. One form of relocation diffusion is **migrant diffusion**, in which the innovation spreads and lasts only a brief time in the newly adopting place. The flu often shows migrant patterns of diffusion, spreading to a new place and weakening in that place after already spreading to a new place of infection. Therefore, the original hearth of the innovation (or node of the disease) is sometimes difficult to find because of the fading nature of the diffusing phenomenon's presence in any one place.

Mix of Diffusion Patterns

What you have probably noticed, however, is that many diffusing phenomena spread through a mix of diffusion patterns. For example, HIV/AIDS may have first spread through relocation diffusion, as infected individuals traveled to a new city, carried the virus with them (obviously), and unknowingly infected others in that city. Then those newly infected individuals spread the virus in a more hierarchical pattern, infected others in their most susceptible groups, such as homosexual men, before spreading in larger numbers into the heterosexual communities.

Acculturation, Assimilation, and Transculturation

Diffusion involves two or more cultures coming into contact with each other. This can lead to the exchange and/or adoption of ideas. The process of two cultures adopting each other's traits and becoming more alike is called **cultural convergence**.

Often when two cultures come into contact with one another, one culture is more dominant than another, possessing either more power or more attractiveness, making its traits more likely to be adopted or maintained than the traits of the less dominant culture. **Acculturation** occurs when the "weaker" of the two cultures adopts traits from the more dominant culture. Sometimes acculturation leads to **assimilation**, when the original traits of the weaker culture are completely erased and replaced by the traits of the more dominant culture. For example, immigrants to the United States might adopt elements of U.S. culture through acculturation while maintaining some traits from their original culture. However, if assimilated, the immigrants lose most (if not all) of the original traits they brought with them from their homeland.

A heated debate surrounds the "English as the official language" controversy in America, with many people arguing that forcing immigrants to adopt the English language is a necessary step in creating a unified country and many others arguing that forced acculturation is culturally biased and erosive to the "melting pot" concept of the United States as a "nation of immigrants." **Transculturation** occurs when two cultures of just about equal power or influence meet and exchange ideas or traits without the domination seen in acculturation and assimilation.

Diffusion often follows an **S curve** adoption pattern. For example, cell phones were originally purchased by only a small number of people who knew about them and could afford their initially expensive prices. Those people were known as the "early adopters," or innovators. Once more people learned about them and the price met the demand, a much faster rate of adoption developed (the "majority adopter"

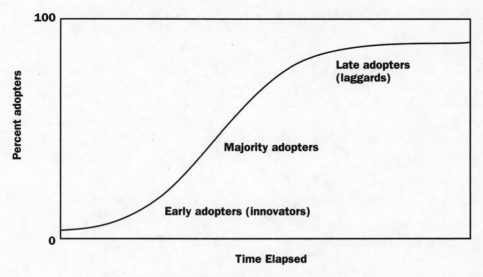

Figure 4.4. Diffusion S curve

stage). During this phase, most of the people who were susceptible (or likely) to be affected by the diffusing phenomenon became adopters.

In the last stage, most people who were likely to buy cell phones bought them (and thus became adopters). The rate of adoption therefore slowed down (note the flattening curve) in the "late adopters" stage. Only the stragglers, the "laggards," who had not yet bought cell phones purchased them in this final stage. Notice that the adoption rate does not reach 100 percent in the S curve graph. A 100 percent adoption rate would mean, for example, that everyone who could, adopted a cell phone; but surely some people have chosen not to adopt a cell phone, even though they might be able to afford one. A diffusing phenomenon (or disease) rarely reaches 100 percent adoption.

Culture Hearth

Culture hearths are areas where innovations in culture began, such as where agriculture, government, and urbanization originated. Culture hearths were the sources of human civilization. Many hearths invent similar innovations without knowing about each other, a process called **independent innovation (or invention)**. When agricultural innovation occurred in both East Asia and Mesopotamia, it did so without interaction through independent innovation. Ancient culture hearths are believed to have developed in places with the capability of innovation, all near water sources and arable land.

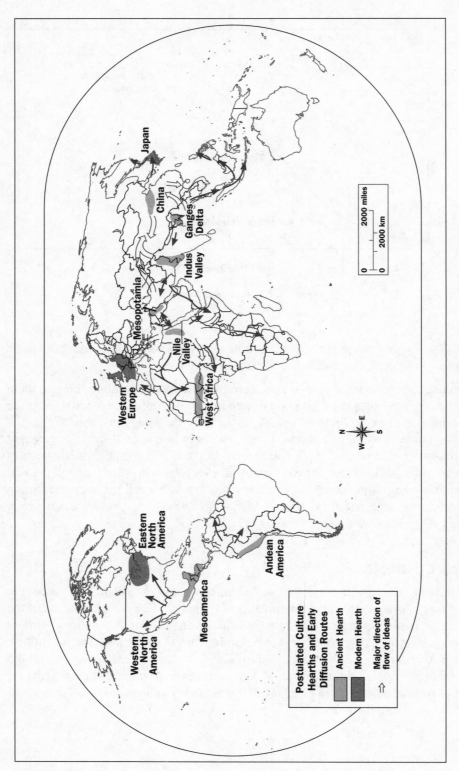

Figure 4.5. Hypothesized culture hearths and early diffusion routes

Hypothesized Ancient Hearth	Direction of Diffusion of Civilization from Ancient Hearth
Andean America (near Andes Mountains in South America)	Eastward direction throughout South America
Mesoamerica	Eastern and western North America
West Africa	Throughout Africa
Nile River valley	Throughout Africa and Southwest Asia
Mesopotamia	Throughout Southwest Asia, Europe, Central and East Asia, West Africa
Indus River valley	Throughout Southwest, Central, and East Asia
Ganges River delta	Throughout South, Southeast, and Southwest Asia
Wei and Huang rivers (China)	Throughout East and Southeast Asia

Figure 4.6. Hypothesized locations of ancient hearths and the diffusion paths of culture from those hearths

PART 2   Cultural Identities and Landscapes

Why do many people in Croatia practice Roman Catholicism, whereas most of their neighbors in Serbia practice Eastern Orthodox Christianity? Why do people in South Africa speak Afrikaans? Why are there differences in the way Christians worship? Between Muslims and Jews? Hindus and Sikhs? Why are there so many dialects of Chinese? These questions relate to the origin, diffusion, and blending of cultures. In seeking answers, cultural geographers analyze where cultures began and why they changed to understand the tapestry of human culture in the world today.

Religion

A fundamental part of human culture is **religion**, a set of beliefs and activities that are created to help humans celebrate and understand their place in the world. Religions help humans define right and wrong, good and bad. Religion can have a profound effect on human interaction with their environment and other cultures, thereby shaping the development of a people's cultural landscape.

Universalizing religions try to have a universal appeal and attract all people to their beliefs, whereas **ethnic religions** attempt to appeal not to all people but to only one group, perhaps in one place or of one ethnicity. Additionally, religions can be **monotheistic**, believing in one supreme being, or **polytheistic**, believing in more than one supreme being.

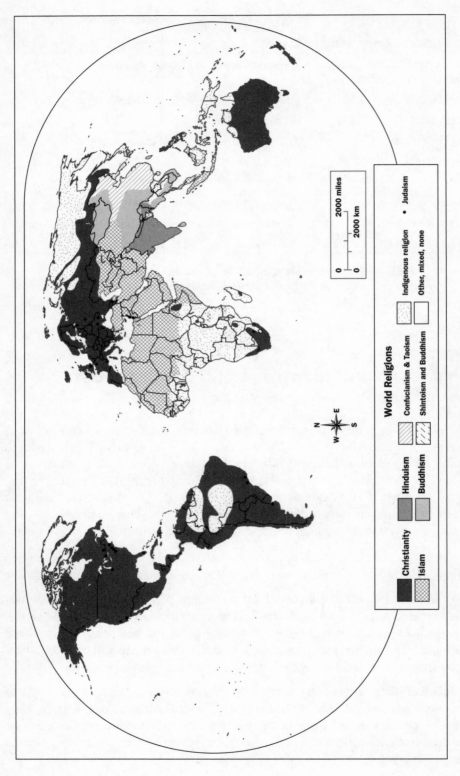

Figure 4.7. Map of world religions

Figure 4.8. Countries with the highest numbers of atheists and agnostics*

Country	Atheists, Agnostics, or Nonbelievers (%)
Sweden	85
Vietnam	81
Denmark	80
Norway	72
Japan	64–65
Czech Republic	54–61
Finland	60
France	54
South Korea	52
Estonia	49
Germany	41–49
Russia	24–48

(Source: Adherents.com)

* Many people surveyed indicated that they were nonbelievers but did not identify as atheists.

Universalizing Religions

About 60 percent of the world's people follow the universalizing religions. Universalizing religions can be broken down into branches, denominations, and sects. **Branches** are large, fundamental divisions within a religion. **Denominations** are groups of common congregations within a branch. **Sects** are smaller groups that have broken away from a recognized denomination within a branch.

Buddhism

Origins: Buddhism was the world's first universalizing religion. An outgrowth of Hinduism, Buddhism was founded in India near the **Indo-Gangetic Hearth**, the area between the Indus and Ganges rivers, by Prince Siddhartha Gautama (Buddha), born in 644 BCE (before the Common Era).

Diffusion Route: After spreading throughout India, Buddhism spread to China, Korea, Japan, Tibet, Mongolia, and Southeast Asia along the Silk Road. Buddhism is now practically extinct in India where it was founded. Nearly 350 million people world-wide are Buddhist.

Primary Branches: Theravada and Mahayana Buddhism are the primary branches in the following list:

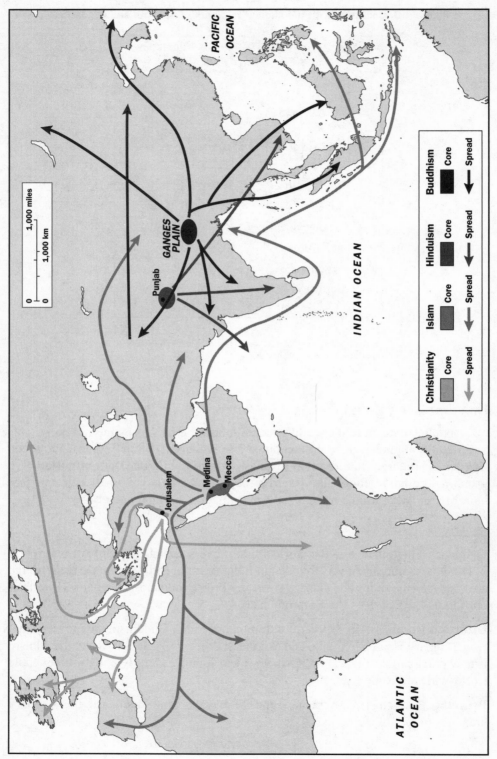

Figure 4.9. Map of origins and diffusion routes for selected religions

- *Theravada Buddhism* is monastic, meaning its followers are monks and nuns. It is practiced by nearly 55 percent of all Buddhists, mainly in Southeast Asian countries such as Sri Lanka, Myanmar (Burma), Thailand, Laos, and Cambodia.

- *Mahayana Buddhists* do not spend time as monks but find salvation through meditation and prayer. It is practiced by nearly 40 percent of all Buddhists and is found primarily in Korea, Vietnam, Japan, and China.

- *Lamaism in Tibet* (now part of China) combines the monasticism of Theravada with local images of deities and demons. It is practiced by only about 5 percent of all Buddhists. The Chinese government is seen by many to be trying to suppress this branch of Buddhism because the government sees it as a threat to its total control over the region. The Dalai Lama is a prominent adherent of this sect of Buddhism but has been exiled from Tibet by the Chinese government.

- *Zen Buddhism* exists primarily in Japan.

Cultural Landscape Features: Buddhism's most famous structure is the pagoda, which is derived from ancient burial mound shapes. According to Buddhism, Gautama (Buddha) reached enlightenment under the Bodhi tree in India, which is the site of many pilgrimages.

(Photo by: Ryuch)

Figure 4.10. A pagoda structure, typical of Buddhist architecture

Christianity

Origins: Christianity, the second universalizing religion to develop, began about 600 years after Buddhism and is an offshoot of Judaism. It originated in the **Semitic Hearth**, which is near modern-day Israel. It originated when its prophet, Jesus Christ, was seen as the expected messiah by disciples. A monotheistic religion, Christianity's main holy book is the Bible.

Diffusion Route: Christianity diffused through expansion and relocation diffusion from its hearth in Palestine. It currently contains the largest number of adherents, nearly 2 billion. The expanse of its spread was widened and accelerated in 312 CE when the Roman Empire adopted Christianity as its official religion. The European colonial efforts starting in the 15th century also carried Christianity throughout the world to new places. Nearly 90 percent of people in the Western Hemisphere are Christians.

Primary Branches: Christianity has three major branches:

- *Roman Catholics* make up the largest and original piece of Christianity, with nearly 830 million adherents (believers). It is considered a hierarchical religion because of its well-defined, organized, territorial governance structure, with the pope at its helm and cardinals, archbishops, and priests at its lower organizational levels. Unlike Protestantism, there are no prominent divisions, or denominations, within the Roman Catholic branch of Christianity. The Roman Catholic Church's headquarters is in Vatican City, an autonomous region in Italy.

- *Protestant Christians* total nearly 503 million adherents throughout the world, about 25 percent of all Christians. The Protestant branch is broken into denominations, of which the Baptist, Methodist, Pentecostal, and Lutheran are the largest. Protestantism has its origins in the Reformation, which occurred around the 15th century.

- *Eastern Orthodox Christianity* developed in 1054, when the Roman Catholic Church split (notice this was long before Protestantism began). It is a collection of 14 self-governing churches, the largest of which is the Russian Orthodox Church. The Eastern Orthodox branch, with nearly 192 million adherents, is dominant in eastern Europe and Russia (which is considered a part of eastern Europe). It has its roots in Constantinople, modern-day Istanbul.

Cultural Landscape Features: The varied nature of Christian-influenced cultural landscapes reflects the changes that have occurred in the religion throughout its history. Prominent cathedrals in the cityscape tower above feudal villages as symbols of the leading influence in medieval life, the Roman Catholic Church. Defiantly simple, wooden, plain churches define Protestant communities and outposts in what was the "New World," a haven for Protestants from England before the Revolutionary War in "America." Baroque cathedrals with ornate sculptures and domes were

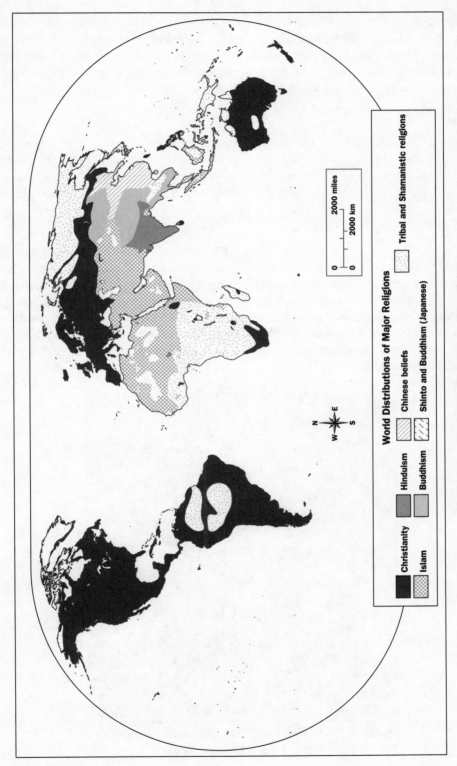

Figure 4.11. Global distribution of major religions

constructed by Catholics trying to combat the growing Reformation movement in 17th century Europe. Christians also use up the most land of all religions for burial, whereas Hindus, Buddhists, and Shintoists cremate their dead. Class differences are evident in burial yards where the gravestones of wealthier Christians often were more prominent than those of poorer adherents.

Islam

Origins: Islam, the third major universalizing religion to develop, originated in Mecca, Saudi Arabia, around 600 CE through its prophet, Muhammad (sometimes spelled Mohammed), who carried Islam to Medina, Saudi Arabia, from where it diffused globally. With nearly 1.2 billion adherents, it is the second-largest religion on the earth, but it is the fastest growing. A monotheistic religion, Islam's holy book is the Koran.

Diffusion Route: Islam diffused through Muhammad's followers, who organized armies to spread the religion throughout extensive areas of Africa, Europe, and Asia. Its successful diffusion led to the Crusades, which were efforts by Christians in the 11th and 12th centuries to "take back" and "save" lands from the diffusing Muslims. Today there is ongoing tension in parts of Africa between the missionary forces of Islam and Christianity, both competing to convert Africans to their faiths. Most Muslims are concentrated in Asia (note that much of the Middle East is part of Southwest Asia).

Figure 4.12. A Muslim mosque

Primary Branches: There are two principal branches of Islam:

- **Sunni Muslims** (*Sunni* means "orthodox") account for about 85 percent of Muslims. Sunnis dominate in the Arabic-speaking areas of Bangladesh and Pakistan. Whereas Shiites (or Shia) believe that only decendents of Ali, and therefore Muhammad, should be the head of Islam, Sunni caliphs, or religious emperors, in the Umayyad Dynasty were not descendants of Muhammad, nor were Ottoman emperors.

- **Shiite Muslims** are the majority in Iran and Iraq, though the Sunnis controlled the government of Iraq's former president, Saddam Hussein. They account for nearly 15 percent of all Muslims. As stated previously, in contrast to Sunnis, Shiites believe that descendants of Ali were acceptable authorities in Islam.

Cultural Landscape Features: Most prominent in the Islamic religion is the mosque, the center of Muslim worship. The mosque is often the center of a Muslim town's focus; it often has four minarets, or towers used to call worshippers, surrounding it. Islam's prohibition of depicting human form in architecture is the primary reason so many mosques are ornately designed with geometric patterns. One of the Five Pillars of Islam, which are analogous to the Ten Commandments to Christians and Jews, requires most Muslims to make a pilgrimage to Mecca, the holiest site to Muslims where Muhammad was born. The second-holiest site is Medina, where Muhammad moved with his knowledge of the religion. Third holiest is the Dome of the Rock in Jerusalem, where Muslims believe Muhammad ascended into heaven and returned to the earth with divine inspiration.

Sikhism

With nearly 22 million adherents, Sikhism is one of the smaller universalizing religions but is larger than the ethnic religion of Judaism. Founded in the late 15th century in present-day Pakistan, Sikhism is seen by many to be a **syncretic religion**, or a blend of the beliefs and practices of Hinduism and Islam. It follows the teachings of Guru Nanak and has its holiest site at the Golden Temple in Amritsar, India. In India, there are continuing tensions between the Sikhs and Hindus, and a high concentration of Sikhs live in the Punjab region, which straddles northwestern India and northern Pakistan. Sikhism is a monotheistic religion, and its holy book, known as the Guru Granth Sahib, contains the teachings of its prophets, called gurus.

Ethnic Religions

The major ethnic religions developed before the major universalizing religions. The largest ethnic religions are Hinduism and Judaism.

Hinduism

Origins: Hinduism claims more than 900 million adherents, most living in India. It evolved in the Indo-Gangetic Hearth in about 2000 BCE. Hinduism was the first

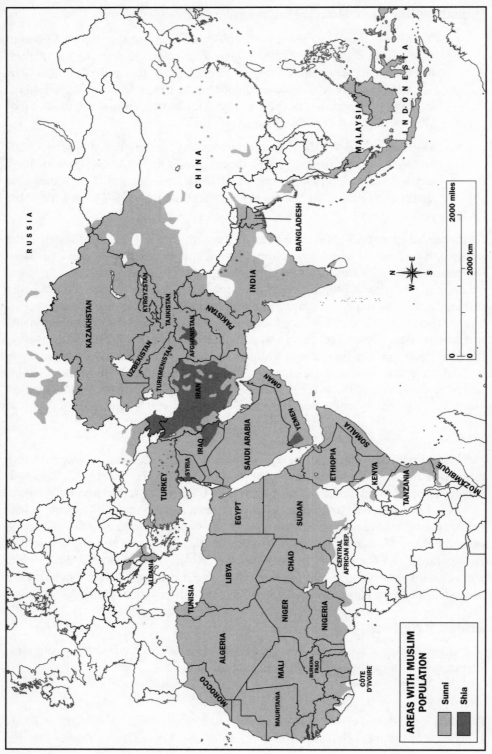

Figure 4.13. Distribution of Sunni and Shiite Muslims

major religion to originate in this area, before Buddhism. Instead of one holy book, Hinduism has a collection of ancient scriptures called the Vedas.

Diffusion Route: Hinduism spread from its Indo-Gangetic Hearth eastward via the Ganges and south through India. As it spread, Hinduism blended with other faiths. Though it diffused to places beyond India, it never developed a dominant presence elsewhere. It is considered an ethnic religion because of its close identity with its Indian origins.

Primary Branches: There are no formal branches in Hinduism, although among its believers there are definite variations in practices. Hinduism is believed to be a polytheistic religion by some but a monotheistic religion by others. Some Hindus say there is only one supernatural being reflected in Hinduism's hundreds of deities.

Cultural Landscape Features: One of Hinduism's principal beliefs is reincarnation, or the rebirth of souls from one generation of life to another. Alongside reincarnation is Hinduism's link to India's tradition of a **caste system**, or a social hierarchy into which people are born. According to the caste system, some people are born into power, others into destitution. In recent years, India's caste system has been lessening in influence because of political pressure. Perhaps the most famous Hindu was Mahatma Gandhi, who worked to free India from England's colonial rule in the 20th century. Because Hindus believe temple builders receive divine reward, the Hindu landscape is dotted with countless shrines and temples to Hindu gods, often adorned by food offerings from local believers. Further, because Hindus believe in cremating their dead, corpses are often burning along the streets and beside rivers in Hindu areas. It is considered a very holy act to bathe in the Ganges River in India, so many Hindus make a pilgrimage to the river's banks to bathe.

Judaism

Origins: The oldest monotheistic religion on the earth, Judaism originated around 2000 BCE in its Semitic Hearth. Judaism grew out of the belief system of a tribe in Southwest Asia known as the Jews, whose headquarters became Jerusalem. The roots of the faith exist in the teachings of Abraham, who is believed to have united his people. Interestingly, Christianity's Jesus Christ and Islam's Muhammad both trace their ancestry through Abraham. Jesus Christ even considered himself a Jew. A monotheistic religion, Judaism's holiest books are the Torah, which consists of Old Testament teachings, and the Talmud, the collection of rabbinical and historical teachings passed down from one generation to the next.

Diffusion Route: After the Roman Empire destroyed their holy city of Jerusalem, the Jews were scattered throughout the world. A scattering of any ethnic group is known as a **diaspora**. The Jewish people scattered north into central Europe and toward the Iberian Peninsula. Currently, there are about 18 million Jews worldwide, with about 7 million in North America and 5 million in Europe and Russia. A heavy concentration of Jews is in Israel, the only country in which Judaism is not a minority religion, one practiced by less than half of the people. Sixty-six percent of all Jews live in the United States and Israel. In 1948, Israel was declared the official Jewish homeland, much to the disagreement of some of its Arab neighbors.

Primary Branches: Judaism has three primary branches: Orthodox Judaism, which seeks to retain the original traditions of the faith; Reform Judaism, which developed in the 1800s as a branch attempting to adjust the religion to fit more modern times; and Conservative Judaism, which is the most recent of the branches and is a more moderate approach to the religion than either the Reform or Orthodox branches.

Cultural Landscape Features: Perhaps the most prominent feature in the Jewish-influenced cultural landscape is the synagogue, or Jewish house of worship and community gathering. Though architecturally varied, all synagogues have an ark housing their sacred book, the Torah, written in Hebrew. An important symbol in Judaism is the six-pointed star. Perhaps the holiest site to Jews is Jerusalem's Western Wall, which is believed by Jews to be the western side of the holy Temple Mount complex that once housed two holy temples destroyed by invaders. Many Jews try to make pilgrimages to the Temple Mount to see the Western Wall and offer prayers and mourn the destruction of their holy temples. Importantly, the Muslims' holy Dome of the Rock is only feet from the Jews' holy Western Wall. This intersection of religions in Jerusalem's cultural landscape has led to a centuries-long conflict over control of this sacred space.

East Asian Ethnic Religions

Shintoism is a syncretic, ethnic religion blending principles of Buddhism with a local religion of Japan. From the 1800s until after World War II, Shintoism was the state religion of Japan. There are about 118 million worshippers, by some estimates.

Taoism (or Daoism) and **Confucianism** both have had a profound impact on Chinese life. Taoism is linked to the philosopher Laozi, who lived around the 6th century BCE, the same time as another philosopher, Confucius. In his writings, Laozi taught that people should live in harmony with nature in all aspects of their lives. This created feng shui, the practice of organizing living spaces in harmonious ways. Geomancers are considered truth-knowing, wise advisers in the Taoist faith.

Confucius built a system of morals and a way of life for Chinese in areas such as government, education, religion, and philosophy. Confucianism focuses more on the worldly life rather than the ideas of a heaven and a hell. Confucius rejected the Chinese aristocrats' claim that they were divine and the poor were not.

Both Taoism and Confucianism have spread beyond China to the Korean Peninsula, Japan, Southeast Asia, North America, and Europe. There has been some conflict between China's communist government and these faiths. Collectively, there are an estimated 263 million followers of these faiths. Many adherents of East Asian ethnic religions are also Buddhists.

Shamanism and Animism

Shamanism is a term given to any ethnic religion in which a community follows its shaman, or religious leader, healer, and truth knower. It has strongest presence in Africa, but shamanism has historically existed in North America, Southeast Asia, and East Asia. Some shamans teach **animism**, a belief that objects such as trees, mountains, and rivers have divine spirits in them.

Figure 4.14. Top-10 largest international religious bodies*

Religious Body	Number of Adherents
Catholic Church	1,100,000,000
Sunni Islam	875,000,000
Eastern Orthodox Church	225,000,000
Anglican Communion**	77,000,000
Assemblies of God	50,000,000
Seventh-day Adventists	16,811,519
Jehovah's Witnesses	16,500,000
Church of Jesus Christ of Latter-day Saints	12,275,822
New Apostolic Church	10,260,000
Ahmadiyya	10,000,000
Bahá'í World Faith	6,000,000

(Source: Adherents.com)

* These are religious bodies in which at least 30% of their world membership lives outside the core country (the country with the largest number of members).

** This figure represents the Anglican Church, Episcopal Church, and other derivatives throughout the world.

Secularism and Theocracy

Worldwide, there are more than 4 billion believers in some religion or faith. However, millions of people, called secularists, have rejected or are indifferent to religion. **Secularism** is the movement away from control of life by a religion. On the other hand, a **theocracy** is a government run by a religion. For example, a theocracy existed in the former government of Afghanistan, in which the Taliban, a group of fundamentalist Muslims, controlled all aspects of life for the Afghani people. Currently, Iran is another example of a theocracy.

Religion and Conflict

Humans have consistently warred over land, particularly when it involves sacred space. They have also warred for their right to practice their religions or to terminate others' rights to do so. If history is our teacher, then humans will forever war over similar issues. **Interfaith boundaries** divide space between two or more religions. **Intrafaith boundaries** divide space within one religion, often among denominations.

Such boundaries can lead to conflicts, often very passionate in nature. Figures 4.15 and 4.16 list some recent conflicts that have occurred in each category.

Figure 4.15. Examples of interfaith boundary conflicts

Place	Interfaith Boundary	Conflict
China (Tibet)	Tibetan Buddhism and Atheism	The atheist Chinese government is allegedly destroying Tibetan Buddhist monasteries and arresting and exiling its adherents to suppress religion in the area and assimilate the region to Chinese control.
Nigeria	Islam and Christianity	Islam prevails in the northern region, while Christianity and local religions prevail in the south. Such division causes power-based tensions for control of the one government.
India	Hinduism and Sikhism	Sikhs in the northwestern state of Punjab demand autonomy from the Hindu-controlled government of India.
India and Pakistan	Hinduism and Islam	Pakistan, once a part of India, was established in 1947 as a Muslim state. Pakistan and India are raging over control of the northern territory known as Jammu and Kashmir.
Former Yugoslavia	Christianity and Islam	In the Yugoslavian civil wars of the 1990s, Serb leader Slobodan Milosevic (an Eastern Orthodox Christian) tried to kill or evict the Muslim population in Bosnia and other Serb-controlled lands in the region.
Palestine (modern-day Israel)	Judaism and Islam	For centuries, Jews and Muslims have warred for control of Palestine. This fight intensified after the creation of Israel following World War II.

Language

Language and religion are fundamental components in cultural identity; they define human culture. Language is a cultural trait, learned from one generation to another. It is speculated that nearly 2.5 million years ago language first developed to organize human activity. All original speakers communicated in the prototongue, or original language. Once those speakers diffused to various places on the earth, language divergence occurred, and new languages and dialects were spawned from

Figure 4.16. Examples of intrafaith boundary conflicts

Place	Intrafaith Boundary	Conflict
Iraq	Sunni Islam and Shiite Islam	After the fall of the largely Sunni government controlled by Saddam Hussein, both Sunnis and Shiites are warring for control of the newly forming political landscape.
United States	Christian fundamentalism and moderate, liberal Christianity	Christians have conflicted not just in the U.S. but worldwide over political-cultural issues such as homosexuality, evolution, and abortion. In some cases, violent tactics have been used.
Northern Ireland	Protestant Christians and Roman Catholics	British colonialism deposited large numbers of Protestants in traditionally Catholic Northern Ireland. This intrafaith boundary has caused violent conflicts between the two groups in the region.

the original source. **Language divergence** occurs when speakers of the same language scatter and develop variations of that original form of the language to meet their needs in the new surroundings. For example, the original language may not have had words for concepts such as a *snake* or *iceberg*. Once the human group came into contact with these new concepts, they created new words for them.

Nearly 50 million Americans speak a language at home other than English.

A blending of two or more languages can take place when speakers come into contact with other languages. **Language replacement** occurs when invaders replace the language of those places they conquer. This can lead to **language extinction**, when a language is no longer used by people in the world.

Geographers can trace diffusion paths of language through **reverse reconstruction**. For example:

✓ If two languages share a common word for an extinct animal that no longer exists

✓ And that animal only existed in one of the many places where the two languages are now spoken,

✓ Then one possible conclusion is that the language diffused from the place where the extinct animal once existed, and the speakers carried with them the word for the hearth's extinct animal.

Geographers have organized languages into a language tree. The tree is subdivided into the following hierarchy:

19 language families

Each family has its own branches

Each branch has its own groups

Each group has its own language

Each language has its own dialects

Figure 4.17. Some major language families

Language Family	Approximate Number of Languages	Percentage of World's Speakers	Approximate Number of Speakers (in millions)
Indo-European	430	44.78%	5,960 (5.9 billion)
Sino-Tibetan	399	22.28%	1,275 (1.2 billion)
Niger-Congo	1,495	6.26%	358
Afro-Asiatic	353	5.93%	339
Austronesian	1,246	5.45%	311
Dravidian	73	3.87%	221

(Source: ethnologue.com)

Indo-European Hearth

About 50 percent of all people speak an Indo-European language, most prominently, English. English is part of the Germanic branch of the Indo-European language family. Other major branches include the Balto-Slavic, Romance, and Indo-Iranian branches. The original Indo-European language is referred to as **Proto-Indo-European**. New languages developed through language diversification as a result of migration of Proto-Indo-European speakers from the hearth of this language family.

The location of the hearth of the Proto-Indo-European language is the subject of speculation. The **conquest theory** argues that it began in the empire-building Kurgan culture located in the steppe region of Russia, north of the Caspian Sea. The **agriculture theory** argues that Proto-Indo-European started in a farming community in the Europe's Danube River region. Because modern Indo-European languages share words for *snow* but not *sea*, the hearth is believed to have been somewhere with snow but distant from the sea. Geographers estimate its origin to have been between 6000 and 4500 BCE. As the Proto-Indo-European speakers diffused using the horse and wheel, the language evolved into various forms.

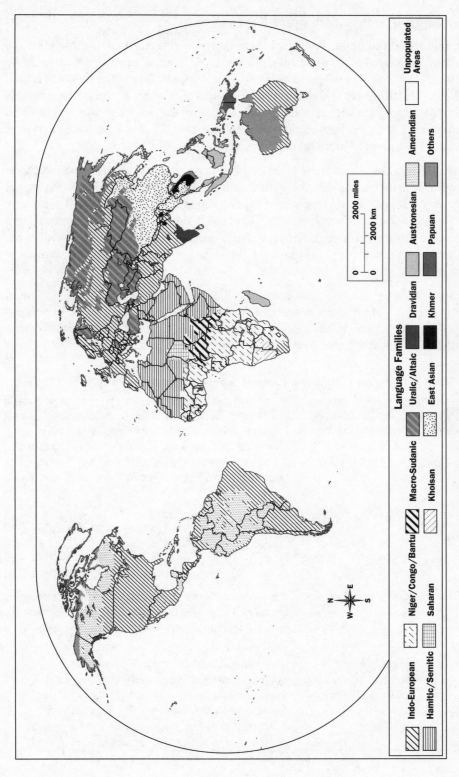

Figure 4.18. Distribution of language families

Monolingual and Multilingual States

Language often defines national identity and is linked to territorial claims. A common language makes communication possible among a people. It can also be used to declare "sameness" or unity. However, linguistic boundaries are often hard to define. **Multilingual states** are countries in which more than one language is spoken. Multilingual states contain linguistic minorities, or groups of speakers who are outnumbered by another language in the country. This can lead to conflict over language and its ties to national identity and power.

Monolingual states, on the other hand, contain speakers of only one language. Because of the increasing pace of spatial–cultural interaction globally, monolingual countries no longer exist. One might argue that Japan, for example, is relatively monolingual with its stringent immigration laws. Countries like France have fought to preserve their monolingual heritage. For example, French politicians called for laws to keep French pure and prohibit the infusion of English words into their vocabulary.

Figure 4.19 lists some recent conflicts related to multilingualism. Keep in mind that the conflicts highlighted in the table reflect multi-faceted conflicts, not singularly related to language. Instead, language is an important symbol of the ethno-cultural divisions at the root of the conflicts in these regions.

Figure 4.19. Some conflicts related to multilingualism

Place	Languages	Conflict
Canada	English and French	French speakers, concentrated in Quebec, have fought for increased recognition and power against the English-speaking Canadian majority. Some Quebec citizens have even called for secession from Canada.
Belgium	Dutch and French	The Dutch-speaking north and French-speaking south compete for power and control. The nation's capital city, Brussels, is located in the Dutch-speaking south, but most inhabitants are French speakers.
Cyprus	Greek and Turkish	The Greek majority and Turkish minority compete for control of this island-country. Cyprus is divided by a "Green-Line" partition separating the two cultures.
Nigeria	Hausa, Yoruba, Ibo and nearly 230 other languages	Hausa speakers in the north, Yoruba in the southwest, and Ibo in the southeast paint a divided Nigeria in which some 230 other languages complicate Nigeria's unification. English was declared the official language as an attempt to create a tool of common communication.

Official and Standard Languages

Often countries declare official languages to define and declare national identity. An **official language** is declared by the leaders of a country to be the language used in legal and governmental proceedings. It often is the language of the powerful, linguistic majority. In 2006, the United States engaged in a national debate surrounding the longstanding call for a declaration of English as its official language. Declaration of an official language in multilingual states is often very controversial. In Nigeria, for example, English was chosen as a neutral choice, rather than one of the three largest languages in the country, to prevent calls of dominance by one group over another. Canada declared both French and English to please both culture groups within the state.

Figure 4.20. Top 10 *native* languages

Language	Speakers
Mandarin Chinese	885,000,000
Spanish	332,000,000
English	322,000,000
Bengali	189,000,000
Hindi	182,000,000
Portuguese	170,000,000
Russian	170,000,000
Japanese	125,000,000
German (Standard)	98,000,000
Wu Chinese	77,175,000

(Source: ethnologue.com)

Related to the concept of *official language* is the concept of *standard language*. **Standard language** is the acceptable form of a given language as declared by political or societal leaders. For example, the British government declared British Received Pronunciation (BRP) English as the standard form of the language to be taught in all schools, rather than American English. German schools teach High German (Hoch Deutsch), the form of German originally spoken by the powerful in the upper Rhine region of Germany.

Lingua Franca, Pidgin, and Creole Languages

When many languages are spoken in one region, people living in the region will often use one language when speaking with one another and conducting trade, almost like a bridge between two cultures. A **lingua franca** is a language used to facilitate trade among groups speaking different languages. For example, in the very multilingual East Africa, where hundreds of native languages are spoken in villages and cities, people turn to Swahili as their lingua franca to communicate with speakers of other languages.

When regions are invaded or economically dominated by a particular foreign-language-speaking group, the people being dominated are forced to pick up on the language of the dominators in order to trade with them and conduct business. When the dominated culture picks up on the new language, they usually speak a simplified version of it known as a **pidgin** of the dominators' language. For example, when the French dominated the Caribbean region, the native people began speaking a simplified version of French, known as pidgin French. Eventually, the speakers of this simplified pidgin language taught their children to speak the pidgin. Once a pidgin becomes part of a culture and is even written, it is known as a **creole** (or creolized) language, a pidgin language that becomes the main language of a group of people. In the Caribbean, pidgin French became such a part of life that it became the mother language of the dominated people, thus becoming a creole.

Toponyms

Toponyms are place names that reflect cultural identity and impact the cultural landscape. Just as parents take pride in naming their child, a people take pride in naming their place, often a controversial task. Determining a toponym indicates ownership and control over space. For example, controversy erupted in India when the government announced it would rename the city of Bombay. The Indian government wanted to rid the city of the name its English colonizers had given the city and replace it with a name that reflected Indian culture and ownership. However, the new toponym of Mumbai reflects Hindu dominance because it relates to a Hindu god. Non-Hindus were angered that their cultures were not being reflected in the new toponym for the city.

Toponyms can also give geographers clues into the origins and aspirations of the related cultures. Saint Petersburg, Russia, was named by Czar Peter the Great, perhaps conveniently, after his patron saint, Peter. Toponyms can also indicate the dreams of a people for their place, such as Paradise, California; Hope, Arkansas; and even Hell, Michigan. The toponym Santa Barbara in California reflects the Spanish-Portuguese language and Catholic religious influences on the region. Santa (Spanish for *Saint*) Barbara was a Catholic martyr.

Ethnicity

Cultural identity also includes ethnicity. **Ethnicity** relates to sets of norms that people create to define their group through actual or perceived shared culture traits, such as language, religion, and nationality. It is a much-debated term because different groups express ethnicity in different ways. Territory is often a unifying trait for ethnicities, such as Albanians' attachment to Albania. Ethnic groups may be spatially divided, as were the Jews who were forcibly segregated from non-Jews in Nazi Germany into a Jewish ghetto. A **ghetto** is a region in which an ethnic minority is forced to live by economic, legal, or governmental pressures. An **ethnic enclave** is a place in which an ethnic minority is concentrated, sometimes in the form of a ghetto. The term **enclave** can indicate a place in which a minority group is concentrated and surrounded by a hostile or unwelcoming majority. An ethnic *neighborhood* tends to be a place in which an ethnic minority is concentrated but is not surrounded by a majority as unwelcoming as that in an enclave. However, an enclave is just a group that is surrounded by another group; it does not have to be hostile. The only real difference is that neighborhoods do not have to be surrounded, whereas enclaves do. A **barrio** is a Spanish-speaking ethnic neighborhood (or enclave) in a city, although the term is often used with negative racial connotations.

Within ethnic landscapes, ethnicities often use space to celebrate their group, such as through parades and festivals. Ethnic enclaves indicate social segregation in space. In addition to the often-present discriminatory pressures, chain migration processes can foster the development of an ethnic enclave. As discussed in Chapter 3, chain migration occurs when family members and associates migrate to the same places because they have heard from others who have made the journey that the region is "safe" or "welcoming" to them. Often migrants move into these ethnic enclaves because they have relatives or friends there.

Race

Race is another factor that can influence ethnic definition. **Race** refers to a classification system of humans based on skin color and other physical characteristics. Race has been used to separate people within a territory, such as its use by South Africa's **apartheid** government, which separated whites and blacks by racial categories. In that example and others, race affects humans' use and division of space. What differentiates race and ethnicity is unclear, but ethnicity is usually seen to incorporate more than just race. For example, Puerto Rican ethnicity includes more than a "Hispanic race," because it includes a national, territorially based cultural identity. Your ethnicity is made up of the cultural traits you acquire while attached to some national group. So people from Armenia living in Germany may consider themselves ethnically Armenian. After living in Germany for five generations, their children would probably have picked up enough German cultural traits that they might consider themselves ethnic Germans, even if they still looked like their great-great-grandparents.

Social Distance

Tensions often arise when ethnicities and races compete for political and territorial control. **Social distance** is a measurement of how "distant" two ethnicities or social groups are from each other, but not in a spatial sense of distance. Often groups perceived as very different from the majority or powerful group are cast into the marginalized social periphery. Such marginalized groups are often the targets of discrimination and hatred by the more powerful social group. **Ethnocentrism**, or one group's use of its cultural identity as the superior standard by which to judge others, often causes such discriminatory behavior.

Ethnic Conflict

In their divisive powers, race and ethnicity have been used by leaders to motivate warfare and forced expulsion of people perceived as being "different" from the majority's classification. **Ethnic cleansing** is a process in which a racial or ethnic group attempts to expel from a territory another racial or ethnic group. An extension of ethnic cleansing is **genocide**, when a racial or ethnic group tries to kill another racial or ethnic group. Slobodan Milosevic, the Serb leader of former Yugoslavia, led a genocide campaign against ethnic Albanians living in Kosovo, a region in Serbia. Adolf Hitler targeted the Jews and other minority ethnic groups; and Sudan's government is accused of attempting to eliminate ethnic groups in Darfur, a region in northwestern Sudan.

Gender

Gender is another category of classifying humans reflecting not just biological but also social differences between men and women. Social concepts of what is "masculine" and what is "feminine" vary across space and time. For example, having long hair is considered masculine for men in some East Asian cultures but considered feminine in others. Globally, women do not have the opportunities men do; male dominance economically, politically, and socially remains the pattern, a situation referred to as the **gender gap**. Following are some problems related to gender:

- High **maternal mortality rates**, or death rates among women giving birth, indicate that women in poorer regions are 100 to 600 times more likely to die giving birth that are women in wealthier regions.

- High **female infanticide** rates, or the murder of female infants, exist in regions where families want male children to carry on the family name or be able to earn more money for the family. Population control policies, such as the one-child policy in China, can cause higher female infanticide rates. In places like India, for example, the female bride's family must pay a sum of money, called a dowry, to the male groom's family. Therefore, some families may try to abort female children in favor of profit-creating male children.

- Dowry deaths in India were rising in the 1980s but have been statistically declining. A **dowry death** occurs when a bride is murdered by her husband's family because her father failed to pay the dowry.

- Women were not given the right to vote, called **enfranchisement**, until the 20th century in most places. Although high in northern Europe and most industrialized countries, on average the election of females to legislative bodies remains much lower than men's.

- **Gender imbalances** also exist in places like India and China, where men outnumber women. This can lead to higher rates of male depression as a result of their inability to find female mates. It can also lead to more men employing prostitutes and thus higher rates of HIV infection.

Despite these discriminations, women typically live longer than men, a fact described as the **longevity gap**.

A global average of life expectancies shows women live about four years longer than men.

Folk and Popular Culture

Culture traits may be defined as being either folk or popular culture. **Folk culture** is limited to a smaller region and a smaller number of people than popular culture. Folk cultures are usually isolated groups that have had long-lasting culture traits that have not changed substantially over long periods. **Popular culture** is mass culture that diffuses rapidly (the reason it is called popular). Folk cultures either have not been exposed to more common, or popular, culture or they have chosen not to adopt popular culture.

A well-known example of folk culture is the Amish use of horse-drawn carriages in their communities instead of the popular culture trait of using cars. Folk culture is evident in its people's cultural landscape, in housing styles that are found only in the region of their origin, and even in the artistic and musical components of the folk culture's landscape. Usually, folk culture spreads through relocation diffusion, when the original group moves to another location and takes their folk traits with them. Country music originated as a folk music in various places in the Appalachian region, each with its own sound and set of instruments. As the various strains of what became known as country music diffused, they started to popularize and become more uniform in sound to please the masses of listeners.

Maladaptive Diffusion

Popular culture diffuses rapidly, primarily through expansion diffusion, across space and varied cultures. Popular culture does not necessarily reflect its original environment. Wearing blue jeans, for example, is a popular culture trait that has diffused across space and cultures. Listening to the Beatles and Snoop Dogg are examples of pop(ular) music that diffused globally. Sometimes this can lead to **maladaptive diffusion**, the adoption of a diffusing trait that is impractical for a region or culture. The diffusion of blue jeans has popularized wearing them even in very warm months, even though jeans can be quite hot (in terms of temperature, that is).

Cultural Imperialism

The diffusion of popular culture can create cultural conflict, when a part of a culture group may protest the arrival of a type of popular culture in its region. For example, when McDonald's arrived in one African city, protesters attacked the restaurant, claiming McDonald's represented **cultural imperialism**—the invasion of a culture into another with the intent of dominating the invaded culture politically, economically, and/or socially. Many Middle Eastern cultures resent the influx of Western popular culture into their cultures. Even in the United States, some people resent the arrival of Starbucks, for example, which is argued to cause the demise of local coffee shops that represent their local people. **Cultural nationalism** is the rise of anticultural imperialism forces; it is the fight by regions and cultures to resist cultural convergence and imperialism and remain distinct.

McDonald's on average opened two new restaurants a day in 2006. Nearly 31,000 McDonald's restaurants are operating worldwide. (www.McDonalds.com)

Cultural Homogeneity

With increasing access to the Internet, efficient transportation tools, and other communication technology, the diffusion of popular culture is increasing in speed and scope. One of the concerns about the increasing dominance of popular culture is that it is threatening regional and cultural diversity because the diffusion of popular culture makes everyone look, sound, act, and believe more of the same rather than in unique, local ways. When cultures become more similar, the result is **cultural homogeneity**, or cultural sameness. However, the arrival of popular culture can also be perceived as increasing opportunities and access.

Popular Culture and Consumption

Another related concern about popular culture is its impact on the environment. Many popular culture traits lead to increased consumption of the earth's limited natural resources and increases waste production. For example, whereas people once carpooled or rode public transportation, the popularizing of every individual owning and driving a car has led to increased fuel consumption and pollution.

Americans' consumption of resources grew faster than its population, which doubled between 1950 and 2005 (Population Reference Bureau).

Landfills are stockpiled with people's plastic water bottles, a fad that has recently developed instead of drinking tap water. In fact, one city government in California recently banned selling bottled water in government offices to try to reduce this waste.

PART 3 Chapter Review

Major Religions Review Chart

The following chart includes an overview of some of the world's largest religions.

Religion	Hearth	Prophet or a Founding Thinker	Sacred Text and Worship Center	Significant and/or Holy Places (list contains only a select few, in some cases)	Classification	Major Branches or Divisions
Buddhism	Indo-Gangetic	Siddhartha Gautama	Tipitaka; temple	Bodh Gaya in India	Universalizing; neither monotheistic nor polytheistic	Theravada, Mahayana, Lamaism, Zen
Christianity	Semitic	Jesus	Holy Bible; church	Jerusalem, Vatican City, Constantinople	Universalizing, monotheistic	Roman Catholic, Protestant, Eastern Orthodox
Hinduism	Indo-Gangetic	Unknown	Veda; temple	Ganges river, many sites in India	Ethnic, debatable whether monotheistic or polytheistic	No formal major branches, though various local forms exist
Islam	Arabian peninsula	Muhammad	Koran; mosque	Mecca, Medina, Jerusalem	Universalizing, monotheistic	Sunni, Shiite
Judaism	Semitic	Abraham	Torah; synagogue	Jerusalem, Israel	Ethnic; monotheistic	Conservative, Reform, Orthodox
Sikhism	Indo-Gangetic	Guru Nanak	Guru Granth Sahib; temple	Golden Temple in Amritsar, India; Punjab, India	Universalizing, monotheistic	No major divisions

Terms Review

Acculturation—Occurs when a less-dominant culture comes into contact with and adopts traits from a more dominant culture.

Animism—Belief that objects such as trees, mountains, and rivers have divine spirits in them.

Apartheid—South Africa's English-Dutch imposed government segregating white and black inhabitants.

Assimilation—Final completion of the cultural acculturation process, when a culture group loses all its original traits and becomes fully a part of a different, dominating culture.

Barrio—Spanish-speaking ethnic neighborhood.

Branch of a religion—Large division within a religion.

Carl Sauer—Prominent geographer in the 20th century who championed the study of cultural landscapes and built environments in human geography.

Caste system—System of social levels defined by one's ancestry and job, traditionally in India.

Confucianism—East Asian belief system originally taught by Confucius, stressing morals for all aspects of life.

Creole—Pidgin language that has become the language of the people being dominated by invaders.

Cultural convergence—Occurs when one culture adopts a cultural attribute of another.

Cultural diffusion—Process by which a cultural element spreads from its hearth across space and time. There are two forms: expansion and relocation.

Cultural ecology—Study of a human group's interaction with its natural environment.

Cultural geography—Field of human geography that analyzes how and why culture is expressed in different ways in different places.

Cultural homogeneity—Occurs when cultures become the same, or uniform, and local diversity is decreased.

Cultural imperialism—Invasion of a culture into another with the intent of dominating the invaded culture politically, economically, and/or socially.

Cultural landscape (or built environment)—Tangible result of a human group's interaction with its environment.

Cultural nationalism—Movement to protect one's culture from invasion or influence from another culture's perceived invasion or influence and threat to one's own culture. Highly related to the emotional attachment an individual has for his/her culture.

Culture complex—Unique combination of culture traits for a particular culture group.

Culture hearth—Area where innovations in culture began and from which such cultural elements spread.

Culture (or geographic) realm—Cluster of culture regions in which common culture systems are found. Examples include Latin America and sub-Saharan Africa.

Culture regions—Area in which a culture system is found or is prevalent.

Culture system—Collection of culture complexes that shape a group's common identity.

Culture trait—Single piece of a culture's traditions and practices.

Denomination of a religion—Group of common congregations within a branch of a religion.

Diaspora—Scattering of any ethnic group; originally referred to the Jews.

Dowry death—Murder of a bride by her husband's family because her father failed to pay the dowry.

Enfranchisement—Right to vote.

Environmental determinism—School of thought that believes human activities are controlled by their environment.

Ethnic cleansing—Process in which a racial or ethnic group attempts to expel or exterminate from a territory another racial or ethnic group.

Ethnic enclave—Another name for an ethnic neighborhood surrounded by an unwelcoming, discriminatory, or hostile ethnic group or groups.

Ethnicity—Complex identity created by a people to define their group through actual or perceived shared culture traits, such as language, religion, and so forth.

Ethnic religion—Religion that comprises one group of people or exists in one place and does not seek converts.

Ethnocentrism—Using one's own cultural identity as the superior standard by which to judge others; often causes discriminatory behavior.

Expansion diffusion—Subtype of diffusion in which a phenomenon spreads outward from its hearth while remaining strong in the original location through hierarchical, contagious, or stimulus patterns.

Female infanticide—Murder of female infants.

Folk culture—Isolated group that has had long-lasting culture traits that have not changed substantially over time.

Gender—Category of classifying humans reflecting not just biological but also social differences between men and women.

Gender gap—Difference in social, economic, and political power and opportunity between men and women.

Gender imbalance—Unequal number of men and women in a place.

Genocide—Killing of one racial or ethnic group by another.

Ghetto—Ethnic neighborhood created by government, social, or economic pressures, causing people of one ethnicity to live together.

Independent innovation (or invention)—Invention of the same phenomenon by two culture hearths without each knowing about the other's invention or, sometimes, existence.

Indo-Gangetic Hearth—Hearth near the Indus and Ganges rivers where Hinduism, Buddhism, and Sikhism originated.

Interfaith boundary—Boundary that divides space between two or more religions.

Intrafaith boundary—Boundary that divides space among different groups within a particular religion, such as among branches, denominations, or sects.

Language divergence—Occurs when new languages or dialects grow from one original source because of the migration of original speakers to new lands or contact with new languages.

Language extinction—Occurs when a people's language is no longer used in the world.

Language replacement—Occurs when invaders replace with their own language the language of the people whom they conquer.

Lingua franca—Language used to facilitate trade among groups speaking different languages.

Longevity gap—Difference between life expectancies of men and women.

Maladaptive diffusion—Adoption of a diffusing trait that is impractical for a region or culture.

Material components of culture—Pieces of a cultural landscape that are tangible, such as clothing and architecture.

Maternal mortality rate—Death rate among women giving birth.

Migrant diffusion—Type of relocation diffusion in which the spreading phenomenon's epicenter (or place of most infection or adoption) moves with the relocating group of users or carriers, like the influenza's usual diffusion pattern.

Monolingual state—Country in which only one language is spoken.

Monotheistic religion—Religion based on belief in one god or deity.

Multilingual state—Country where more than one language is spoken.

Nonmaterial components of culture—Pieces of a culture that are intangible, such as beliefs and attitudes.

Official language—Language selected by a country to represent its identity in courts and government proceedings.

Perceptual regions—Area with boundaries defined by people's beliefs, emotions, and attitudes. Often called a vernacular region.

Pidgin language—Simplified version of a lingua franca adopted by a group of people to trade and communicate.

Political ecology—Study of cultural geography through the lens of the relationships government and economic systems create between human cultures and their environments.

Polytheistic religion—Religion based on belief in many gods or deities.

Popular culture—Mass culture that diffuses rapidly.

Possibilism—School of thought suggesting that humans' natural environments present a set of choices from which humans choose their actions.

Proto-Indo-European—First form of language that gave rise to the Indo-European family. Believed to have spread through either the Kurgan conquests or through farming technology.

Race—Classification system of humans based on skin color and other physical characteristics.

Regional identity—Common identification a group of people has with a particular place.

Religion—Set of beliefs and activities created to help humans celebrate and understand their place in the world.

Relocation diffusion—Subtype of diffusion in which the phenomenon spreads through the movement of its users from one place to another.

Reverse reconstruction—Process of tracing a language's diffusion. The process begins with the most recent places of the language's existence and moves backward through time, comparing words with geographic places and groups of people using the same or similar words.

S-curve diffusion pattern—Diffusion often follows this pattern of a slower pace in the innovation stage, followed by a rapid diffusion pattern in the majority-adopter stage, and finishing in a slower-paced "laggard" stage.

Sect—Small group that breaks away from a denomination within a religion's branch.

Secularism—Movement away from control of life by a religion.

Semitic Hearth—Hearth near modern-day Israel where Judaism, Christianity, and Islam originated.

Sequent occupance—Theory that a place is occupied by different groups of people, each group leaving an imprint on the place from which the next group learns.

Shamanism—Any ethnic religion in which a community follows its shaman, or religious leader, healer, and truth knower.

Shintoism—Syncretic faith blending Buddhism with local practices predominant in Japan.

Social distance—Measurement of how "distant" or different two ethnicities or social groups are from each other.

Spatial diffusion—Spread of any phenomenon (such as a disease) across space and time.

Standard language—Acceptable form of a given language as declared by political or societal leaders.

Stimulus expansion diffusion—Occurs when an innovative idea diffuses from its hearth outward, but the original idea is changed by the new adopters.

Sunni and Shiite Muslims—Two major branches of Islam; Sunnis, the largest branch, are known as the orthodox branch supporting only descendants of Muhammad, whereas Shiites support descendants of Ali as religious leaders.

Syncretic religion—Religion blending elements from various religions.

Taoism (Daoism)—East Asian belief system stressing balancing the forces of humanity and nature, taught originally by Laozi.

Theocracy—Government run by a religion.

Toponym—Name given to a place.

Transculturation—Equal exchange of cultural traits between two cultures; a form of cultural convergence.

Universalizing religion—Type of religion that believes that its truth is the one and only truth and is applicable to all humans, a belief often leading to proselytizing and missionary work.

PART 4 — Some Suggested Web Resources for Further Exploration

United Nations Educational, Scientific, and Cultural Organization: http://www. unesco.org/

This is the primary portal for cultural information collected by the United Nations. It contains valuable maps, statistics, and descriptions of cultural issues around the globe.

American Folk: http://www.americanfolk.com/

This site contains interesting information on American folk and popular culture.

Ethnologue: http://www.ethnologue.com/

This site contains a fascinating, online encyclopedia of the thousands of languages spoken in the world.

U.S. Board on Geographic Names: http://geonames.usgs.gov/

This is the official website of the U.S. government's main organ of toponyms. It has searchable databases on place names.

Voice of America (VOA) News Portal: http://www.voanews.com/english/portal.cfm

This site is a radio station run by the U.S. government and disseminated throughout the world. The interesting part of this website is that you can listen to the news (as reported by the VOA) in different languages.

Adherents.com: http://www.adherents.com/

This website contains helpful statistics and graphics related to the religions of the world, though such statistics are often debated. Information on branches, sects, and other divisions are included. It also has links to other websites that focus on religions.

**PART
5**
Pre-Exam Practice

Terms Review Quiz

Use the Terms Review list or your own memory to determine the extent of your knowledge of key terms and concepts. Remember, the AP exam does not include this kind of exercise, but it is included here as a review tool.

1. _____ Acceptable form of a given language as declared by political or societal leaders.

2. _____ System of social levels separating people on the basis of ancestry and job, traditionally in India.

3. _____ Field of human geography that analyzes how and why culture is expressed in different ways in different places.

4. _____ The tangible result of a human group's interaction with its environment.

5. _____ Unique combination of culture traits for a particular culture group.

6. _____ Groups of common congregations within a branch of a religion.

7. _____ Type of religion that exists in one group of people and/or place that does not seek converts.

8. _____ Using one's own cultural identity as the superior standard by which to judge others; often causes discriminatory behavior.

9. _____ Pieces of a culture that are intangible, such as beliefs and attitudes.

10. _____ School of thought suggesting that humans' natural environments present a set of choices from which humans choose their actions.

11. _____ Region with boundaries defined by a people's beliefs, emotions, and attitudes.

12. _____ Occurs when a less-dominant culture comes into contact with and adopts traits from a more dominant culture.

13. _____ Type of diffusion in which the phenomenon spreads through the movement of its adopters from one place to another.

14. _____ Final step of the acculturation process, when a culture group loses all its original traits and becomes fully a part of a different, dominating culture.

15. _____ Area where innovation in culture began and from which such cultural elements spread.

16. _____ Invention of the same phenomenon by two culture hearths without each knowing about the other's invention or, sometimes, existence.

17. _____ Currently, the religion based on belief in many gods or deities.

18. _____ Scattering of any ethnic group, originally referring to the Jews.

19. _____ Religion with the largest number of adherents in the world.

20. _____ Occurs when an innovative idea diffuses from its hearth outward, but the original idea is changed by the new adopters.

21. _____ Principal religious text for Muslims.

22. _____ First person to spread teachings of Buddhism; known as the Buddha.

23. _____ Three monotheistic religions originating in the Semitic Hearth.

24. _____ Government run by a religion.

25. _____ Killing of one racial or ethnic group by another.

Multiple-Choice Review Questions

1. Which of the following best represents a possibilist interpretation of human activity?

    (A) Shanghai developed into a world city because of its navigable rivers.

    (B) Lesoto's economy has not developed to be globally competitive because of its lack of water access.

    (C) Minnesota's people are usually quieter than Florida's because of the harsher weather people endure in Minnesota.

    (D) Germany's success in gaining land early in World War II was linked to its use of coal deposits in the Ruhr region, which facilitated a more powerful military.

    (E) Civilization was born in arable areas because fertile land created human innovation beyond nomadic lifestyles.

2. A formal caste system of socioeconomic segregation based on family and occupation was prominent in which country's tradition?

    (A) Vietnam   (D) Saudi Arabia

    (B) Russia   (E) China

    (C) India

3. If a Spanish speaker and a French speaker come together to conduct trade and revert to the authentic form of English they both learned in their schools, English is known to them as a(n)

    (A) creolized language   (D) pidgin language

    (B) language branch   (E) lingua franca

    (C) isogloss

4. In the 1800s, Czar Peter the Great of Russia returned to Russia from his travels in Europe and taught his people Western-style dance. This diffusion of Western-style dance to Russia is most closely an example of

    (A) cultural convergence   (D) cultural isolation

    (B) sequent occupance   (E) theocracy

    (C) folk culture

5. Which of the following lists religions that all started in Southwest Asia?

    (A) Buddhism, Hinduism, Islam

    (B) Islam, Judaism, Christianity

    (C) Shintoism, Sikhism, Judaism

    (D) Taoism, Christianity, Hinduism

    (E) Judaism, Animism, Buddhism

6. Which of the following is the dominant language family in India?

    (A) Sino-Tibetan   (D) Indo-European

    (B) Dravidian   (E) Altaic

    (C) Afro-Asiatic

7. The above image comes from Beijing, China, and is of a Kentucky Fried Chicken restaurant that bought out and replaced a local family's restaurant. Some might argue this is an example of

    (A) language replacement   (D) ethnic enclave

    (B) creolized language   (E) ghettoization

    (C) cultural imperialism

8. A geographer studying the northern Canadian Inuit culture's intricate river navigation routes is best described as analyzing

    (A) demography
    (B) cultural ecology
    (C) linguistics

    (D) territorial morphology
    (E) boundary classification

9. In which of the following countries has conflict related to its multilingualism escalated to widespread threats of secession?

    (A) United States
    (B) Germany
    (C) Japan

    (D) Canada
    (E) India

10. Which of the following is most closely an example of nonmaterial culture?

    (A) Blue jeans
    (B) Indian naan bread
    (C) Dome of the Rock

    (D) Teachings of Confucianism
    (E) New England saltbox house style

11. Which of the following has the highest concentration of Muslims?

    (A) Vatican City
    (B) Northern Ireland
    (C) Pakistan

    (D) Sri Lanka
    (E) Vietnam

12. The excitement created by attending a Bon Jovi concert diffused in a pattern with an epicenter, or (node), that followed Bon Jovi's band as it toured through Europe between large and small towns in no particular order. About two weeks after Bon Jovi's visit, the excited crowds in each city died down and returned to normal lifestyles, while sometimes listening to his CDs in their homes. The pattern of excitement surrounding the traveling Bon Jovi concert is best classified as

    (A) hierarchical diffusion
    (B) migrant diffusion
    (C) stimulus diffusion

    (D) reverse hierarchical diffusion
    (E) contagious diffusion

13. Which of the following is a universalizing religion?

    (A) Shintoism   (D) Confucianism

    (B) Judaism   (E) Taoism

    (C) Islam

14. In which region does shamanism currently have the highest presence?

    (A) Western Europe   (D) South America

    (B) North America   (E) Southwest Asia

    (C) Sub-Saharan Africa

(Photo by: Aubrey Stoll)

15. The holy site shown in the picture above exists in Amritsar, India. With which religion is this site primarily associated?

    (A) Islam

    (B) Hinduism

    (C) Eastern Orthodox Christianity

    (D) Sikhism

    (E) Buddhism

16. Which prominent geographer in the 20th century championed the study of cultural landscapes and built environments in human geography?

    (A) Ellen Churchill Semple   (D) Joel Garreau

    (B) Walter Christaller   (E) Alfred Weber

    (C) Carl Sauer

17. What are the two major branches of Islam?

    (A) Sunni and Shintoism   (D) Shiite and Shamanism

    (B) Shiite and Sunni   (E) Shiite and Shintoism

    (C) Sunni and Shamanism

18. The simplest component of a culture is a

    (A) culture trait   (D) cultural diffusion

    (B) culture complex   (E) cultural identity

    (C) culture system

19. Religions that attempt to attract all people to their beliefs are known as

    (A) ethnic religions   (D) polytheistic religions

    (B) universalizing religions   (E) syncretic religions

    (C) monotheistic religions

20. Mecca, Saudi Arabia, is the holiest site for which religion?

    (A) Buddhism   (D) Sikhism

    (B) Shintoism   (E) Islam

    (C) Hinduism

Free-Response Review Questions

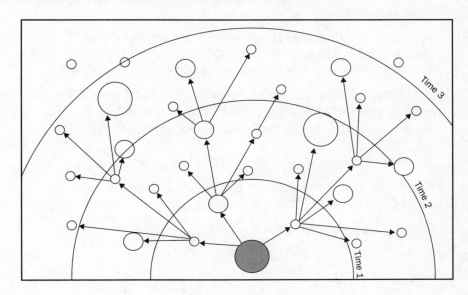

Vector 5 diffusion pattern

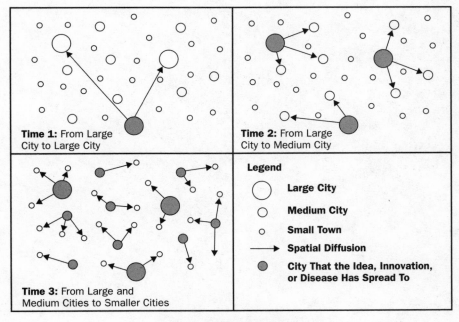

Vector 6 diffusion pattern

The maps on the previous page depict the diffusion patterns of two new diseases, vector 5 and vector 6.

(A) Define *spatial diffusion*.

(B) Look at the diffusion pattern of vector 5. Define and explain the diffusion type indicated in the map of vector 5's diffusion as relocation, hierarchical expansion, stimulus expansion, or contagious expansion diffusion.

(C) Look at the diffusion pattern of vector 6. Define and explain the diffusion type indicated in the map of vector 6's diffusion as relocation, hierarchical expansion, stimulus expansion, or contagious expansion diffusion.

PART 6 — Pre-Exam Practice Answers

Terms Review Answers

1. Standard language
2. Caste system
3. Cultural geography
4. Cultural landscape (or built environment)
5. Culture complex
6. Denomination
7. Ethnic religion
8. Ethnocentrism
9. Nonmaterial components of culture
10. Possibilism
11. Perceptual regions (vernacular regions)
12. Acculturation
13. Relocation diffusion
14. Assimilation
15. Culture hearth
16. Independent innovation (or invention)
17. Polytheistic religion
18. Diaspora
19. Christianity
20. Stimulus diffusion
21. Koran
22. Siddhartha Gautama
23. Judaism, Christianity, Islam
24. Theocracy
25. Genocide

Multiple-Choice Answers

1. **(D)**

    Possibilism teaches that humans take the natural environment's opportunities and limitations and innovate from them. It is an argument against environmental determinism, which says that human behavior is directed by the environment. (D) represents possibilism because humans took the coal deposits in the Ruhr region and used them to industrialize and create army technology. The other choices represent the principle from environmental determinism that the environment *directed* human activity and outcomes.

2. **(C)**

    India's formal caste system involved a strict segregation of society based on a person's family and occupation. The untouchables were the lowest caste and suffered almost complete social isolation. Recent political reforms have reduced the effects of the caste system in attempting to create more of a meritocracy, in which people's education and effort play more of a role in economic and social promotion.

3. **(E)**

    A lingua franca is a language used by speakers of different languages to facilitate trade-based communication or some sort of transaction. A pidgin language (D) is a simplified form of a language used by a people dominated by the speakers of that new language, usually in the case of a colonized people. It is not the correct answer to this question because the two groups are using a third language, English, to communicate. The question even stipulates that it is "authentic" English, not a simplified, pidginized form of English. (A) is a pidgin that has been adopted by a people and formalized into a language or dialect, taught even to the children. (B) is a major division in a language family, and (C) is a geographical boundary of a certain linguistic feature, such as word usage.

4. **(A)**

    Cultural convergence occurs when a culture adopts traits from another culture with which it comes into contact. Peter the Great brought the culture trait of Western dance back with him to the Russian people, many of whom adopted that European trait. (B) is the theory that a generation of inhabitants of a space leave behind imprints from which succeeding generations learn, as when occupiers of a region leave buildings behind for the next occupiers to use and adapt. (C) is usually an isolated, unique culture that is not infused with popular culture. (D) implies a culture that is not in contact with other cultures, which is not the case in this scenario of Peter the Great's contact with Western culture. (E) is when religious leaders control a government.

5.   **(B)**

The Semitic Hearth in Southwest Asia is home to the origins of the three largest monotheistic religions on the earth: Judaism, Christianity, and Islam. Hinduism and Buddhism have their hearths in the land near the Indus and Ganges rivers, and the Chinese religions (or faiths), Shintoism, Taoism, and Confucianism, started in China.

6.   **(D)**

The dominant, native language in India is Hindi, which is an Indo-European language. Dravidian languages also have a presence in India, but not dominance. (A) dominates in East Asia, (C) in Africa, and (E) in Central Asia and Turkey.

7.   **(C)**

Cultural imperialism is the diffusion of a dominating set of culture traits or systems that are seen to threaten the existence of local cultures. Moreover, it is seen as a use of cultural invasion as a way to gain dominance politically, economically, or socially over the people in that region. The diffusion of KFC into the region represents the diffusion of Western, specifically American, culture and its threat to local culture—in this scenario, the ouster of a local restaurant. Some may see this as a way for American culture's invasion to pave the way for economic dominance of the region. (A) occurs when a language in a region is replaced by another, (B) occurs when by a dominated people adopts a pidgin as a language, (D) is a region wherein a particular ethnicity is concentrated and surrounded by another ethnicity or group of ethnicities, and (E) is the process of ghetto formation in cities.

8.   **(B)**

Cultural ecology is the study of human interaction with the environments. The Inuit's interaction with their landscape is evident in their navigation routes because they are interacting with their environment, their rivers. (A) is the study of human population and its related patterns, such as birth and death rates. (C) is the study of language origins and diffusions. (D) is the shape of a country; (E) is the analysis of different types of boundaries, such as subsequent and antecedent boundaries.

9.   **(D)**

Canada's French-speaking minority (known as Francophones) has pushed for greater political and cultural recognition from the English-speaking (Anglophone) majority-run government and culture. Canadians have been considering a voting referendum on whether Quebec's French-speaking region should secede from Greater Canada. Though there have been tensions in (A), (B), and (E) surrounding multilingualism, widespread threats of secession have not arisen. (C) is nearly monolingual.

10. **(D)**

Nonmaterial culture refers to components of culture that are not physically graspable, such as religious beliefs, communication patterns, customs, and philosophies, such as (D). The other choices are examples of material culture—that which is tangible or physical—such as technology, architecture, food, and clothing.

11. **(C)**

The country of Pakistan was formed in 1947 as a Muslim state in an attempt to end infighting within India between Hindus and Muslims. It is nearly 97 percent Muslim, making it one of the most populated countries in the world with a Muslim majority. (A) is heavily Roman Catholic, (B) has tensions between Roman Catholics and Protestants, (D) is nearly 70 percent Buddhist, and (E) is nearly 81 percent nonbelievers (people who do not identify with a religion or faith).

12. **(B)**

Migrant diffusion is a form of relocation diffusion in which the core (or epicenter) of the diffusing phenomenon follows its wave of diffusion, such as the wave in a stadium, when crowds stand and then sit. The phenomenon tends to die out after a short time and after the wave of diffusion has moved on to new sites of adoption (or infection). The diffusion of excitement surrounding Bon Jovi's concerts is similar in that the crowds in cities where he played were energized by the concert, but that excitement died down shortly after the concert finished. New excitement was drummed up (pun intended) in the next city Bon Jovi went to. (A) occurs when a phenomenon diffuses from large or powerful places (or people) to smaller ones. The question states that there was no order of large or small city in Bon Jovi's pattern, which also rules out (D) because it is a pattern of diffusion from smaller to larger places or importance levels. (C) occurs when the diffusing phenomenon is adapted by the new adopters to fit their needs. (E) is a form of expansion diffusion when the phenomenon spreads according to proximity to the core, regardless of size or importance level. However, in (E), the phenomenon tends to maintain its strength in all places infected rather than weakening, as in migrant diffusion.

13. **(C)**

Islam is a universalizing religion, meaning that it believes its teachings are appropriate for all people. Therefore, like Christianity and Sikhism, it seeks converts. The other choices are ethnic religions, which are based in a particular place or cultural group. Ethnic religions do not actively seek converts.

14. **(C)**

Shamanism is a practice in many traditional societies in which there is a spiritual truth knower, a shaman, who is a guide for the local community or tribe. It has its greatest presence in sub-Saharan Africa, a region in which missionary work of universalizing religions is competing for dominance.

15. **(D)**

The image is of the Golden Temple, the holiest site to Sikhs, located in the holy city of Amritsar, in India's northwest.

16. **(C)**

Carl Sauer was one of the first to realize that humans modified the landscape in ways that told something about their culture. (A) championed the idea of environmental determinism; (B) developed the central place theory; (D) wrote the book *Edge Cities*, which discusses the development of areas outside metropolises; and (E) developed least cost theory.

17. **(B)**

The two major branches of Islam are Sunni and Shiite. Shintoism is a blending of Buddhist teachings and local beliefs in Japan. Shamanism is an ethnic religion that follows a shaman, or holy man.

18. **(A)**

Traits are the basic components of a culture group. They include everything from how a people greet each other to what foods are "good" and "bad" to eat. (B) is the combination of a group's cultural traits into a unique set of characteristics. (C) occurs when a trait is present in several culture complexes; for example, soccer is played by many culture groups. (D) is the process by which traits move between groups. (E) is the set of culture traits an individual or group uses to try to answer the question "Who am I?"

19. **(B)**

Universalizing religions, such as Christianity and Islam, believe their faith is valuable to all people and attempt to show nonbelievers the value of the religion. (A) are religions that attempt to appeal to only one group of people, perhaps in one place or of one ethnicity. (C) and (D) refer to the number of deities worshipped or believed in by a religion. (E) are blendings of elements from different religions.

20. **(E)**

Mecca, Saudi Arabia, is the holiest site for all Muslims, followed by Medina and then Jerusalem.

Free-Response Answers

The following is a list of suggested main points for each part of the question.

Part A

- Spatial diffusion is the spread of a phenomenon, such as a disease, across space and time.

Part B

- Vector 5 is spreading through contagious expansion diffusion, when a phenomenon spreads like a wave through space.

- Expansion diffusion is the spread of a phenomenon geographically from one adopter (or place) to another while remaining with the first adopter (or place).

- Contagious expansion diffusion is the spread of a phenomenon outward without regard to the size of the places surrounding it; places near the origin (or hearth) are affected first. The farther away a person or place is from the origin, the later will it be affected by the diffusing phenomenon.

- Vector 5 is spreading outward from its point of origin to the nearest cities, large and small, in each wave of spread. It is not discriminating based on size, only based on proximity to the point of origin.

Part C

- Vector 6 is spreading through hierarchical expansion diffusion.

- Hierarchical expansion diffusion is the spread of a phenomenon geographically from its place of origin in an outward pattern, like in the contagious pattern. However, unlike contagious expansion diffusion, it spreads outward with respect to size of place or level of susceptibility.

- Vector 6 is spreading outward from its place of origin but is discriminating in its spread pattern to larger cities before hitting smaller places, in a hierarchical pattern.

Chapter 5

Political Organization of Space

Introduction

The lines on the map we refer to as boundaries show which lands belong to which peoples, but long before humans imposed their jigsaw puzzle of division onto the earth, the land was unified as one piece. Throughout history, the often-imaginary lines marking territorial divisions have shifted as humans fought for control over precious land and its resources. In fact, people may have such deep attachments to a territory that they are willing to risk their lives to defend it. Perhaps that is why nearly 200 wars are fought each year, usually conflicts related to territorial claims and desires.

Political geography is the study of human political organization of the earth at various geographic levels. Political geographers study the spatial layout of political organization at, above, and below the country level. Above the country level, political geographers study organizations such as the United Nations, which includes many countries. At the country scale, political geographers look at how a country's government is organized. Below the country level, political geographers might study the boundaries of voting districts. Political geographers study the changing role of the country in the world's political dealings.

Key Questions

➤ *How do political patterns reflect ideas about how the earth should be organized?*

➤ *How do political patterns affect human activities and understandings?*

➤ *What is the evolution of the nation-state from its original form to its modern form?*

➤ *What forces have shaped the world political map into its current form? How are those forces related to the rise of the modern state in Europe and to colonialism?*

➤ *How do political boundaries relate to economic, cultural, and environmental boundaries?*

> ➤ *What is the role of the modern country in the contemporary political landscape? How do forces such as ethnic separation, economic globalization, regional supranationalism, and regional environmental problems affect the role of the country in the modern world?*
>
> ➤ *What are the forms and roles of political units above and below the country level?*
>
> ➤ *How do specific political policies, such as racial segregation, affect the organization of spatial and cultural life?*

PART 1 — Territorial Dimensions of Politics

Human Territoriality

Territoriality is creating ownership over a defined space. Territoriality can apply to your bedroom or an entire country and often evokes an emotional response. Just as when your sibling "invades" your room uninvited causes you to feel angry (and even to retaliate), a country's threatening the defined space of another country often provokes an aggressive response. Consider, for example, when Iraq invaded Kuwait's territory and triggered the first Gulf War; or when Germany invaded Poland in 1939 and England and France came to Poland's defense, fearing that Germany would be moving toward taking their lands.

Some political geographers claim that human territoriality is equal to animals' aggressive defense of their territories, such as when a dog runs into another dog's yard. However, American geographer Robert Sack argued that humans are far more complex than animals in their territorial behavior. He posited that human territoriality is contextual and depends on time and place. For example, a country may allow people to cross its administrative border if they have the correct paperwork, and countries enter into and get out of treaties to work together to protect their lands. Such allowances are rare in the animal world.

Territoriality also applies to the geography of personal space. **Personal space** is the area we claim as our own territory into which others may not enter without our permission. A student sitting in a classroom desk, for example, may claim that her personal space extends around her desk like a bubble. If someone invades that space—getting close to her face, for instance—she may feel an immediate sense of anxiety, discomfort, or even anger. How much space is considered "personal" often varies with time and place. For example, people living in small towns often have larger bubbles of personal space than do New Yorkers, who deal with crowded subways and streets. How many times have you accidentally brushed someone's leg

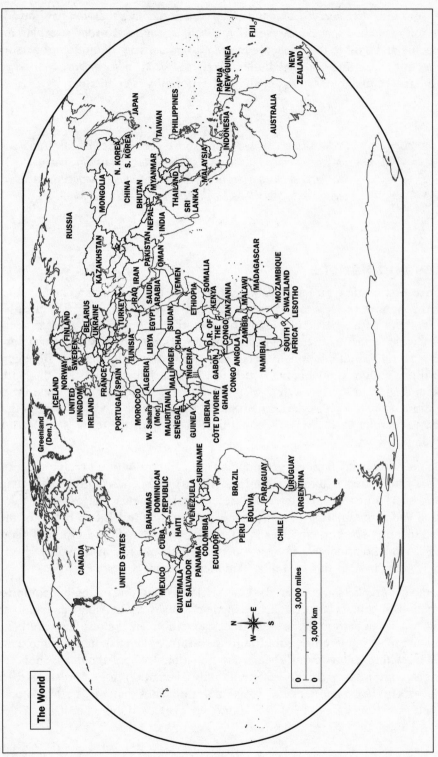

The World

Figure 5.1. A map of the world's countries

or arm and said, "I'm sorry"? This indicates your perception that you have invaded that person's personal space. However, if you walk through a crowded street jammed with people and have to touch people in order to move, your definition of personal space reconfigures, and you may be less likely to say "I'm sorry" every time you make contact with another human. Human territoriality is contextual.

Proxemics is the study of personal space. One commonly established method of claiming personal space is through use of spatial markers, such as a jacket that a man attending a concert places on a seat to mark it as his personal space in the auditorium.

States and Nations

Since first grade, you have probably been referring to England as a country. Political geographers use a more exact term: *state*. In political geography, a **state** is a political unit with a permanent population, territorial boundaries that are recognized by other states, an effective government, a working economy, and sovereignty. **Sovereignty** is the internationally recognized control a state has over the people and territory within its boundaries. Germany, Russia, Japan, Indonesia, the United States, and Mexico are just a few of the nearly 200 states (or countries) on the earth. Some states, such as the United States, have smaller divisions within them that they also refer to as "States." In political geography, the term "state" is used interchangeably with "country."

On the other hand, political geographers use the term **nation** to refer to a group of people who share a common culture and identify as a cohesive group. Language, religion, shared history, and territory are cultural elements that can create such cohesion and form a nation. Usually, people are willing to fight on behalf of their national identity. The United States is often considered a nation, a group of people unified around the principle of being American. Perhaps the constitutional sense of liberty is at the base of this idea of an American nation.

Some geographers argue that the United States is not one nation but comprises many nations within its borders, such as, perhaps, the Mexican American nation, the Islamic American nation, the Jewish American nation, and so on. They argue that the United States is, therefore, a **multinational state**, a state that includes more than one nation within its borders. Russia is a multinational state that contains hundreds of nations within its borders. A state with only one nation in its borders is called a **nation-state**. Japan and Iceland are examples of states that are as close to being classified as nation-states as possible in today's world. On the other hand, when a nation does not have a territory to call its own, it is referred to as a **stateless nation**. The Assyrian Christians of Iraq and the Ughirs of western China do not have their own countries. They are considered stateless nations.

Ethnonationalism and Conflict

Ethnonationalism is a powerful emotional attachment to one's nation that is a minority within a state and feels different from the rest of the state's people. When minority nations feel that they do not have enough **self-determination**, or the power to control their own territory and destiny, ethnonationalism can lead to conflict. For example, the Chechen people comprise a minority nation that live in Russia and have a strong sense of ethnonationalism that has even led to violent conflict with the Russian government. Chechnya is a republic within the Russian state, but the Chechens want more autonomy and feel discriminated against by the Russian government. Terrible violence has exploded over threats of secession, or breaking off into a separate state.

Irredentism

Nations do not always refer to groups of people only living in one place. For example, the Serbs are a nation, or a group of people that share a sense of brotherhood and identify as a group, but they exist in several countries, not just the land that is considered Serbia. The Chinese nation comprises the group of people identifying as part of that cultural group but not necessarily residing just in China.

Conflict can arise when a nation's homeland is spread into the territory of another state or several states. For example, Hitler believed the German homeland had spilled into Czechoslovakian territory. He wanted to take control of that land in Czechoslovakia to reunite all Germans into one state. A movement to reunite a nation's homeland when a part of it is spread into another state's borders is called **irredentism**. Albania's people live primarily in Albania, but a large pocket of Albanians live in a piece of Serbia's territory called Kosovo. Irredentism can lead to violence, as in the 1990s, when the Serb government engaged in a ruthless effort to "ethnically cleanse" Kosovo of all Albanians.

Some Recent Conflicts Related to Ethnonationalism

Place	Conflicting Parties	Reason
South Asia, Indian subcontinent	Indians versus Pakistanis	These two parties are fighting over control of Kashmir, a region overlapping each country's sovereignty and homelands.
Palestine, Southwest Asia	Jewish Israelis versus Muslim Palestinians and Arab allies	The stateless nation of Muslim Palestinians and their Arab allies are warring against the Jewish-controlled state of Israel for autonomy in a deeply layered historical conflict.
Southeast Asia	Mainland China versus Taiwan	Taiwan was founded in the 1940s after anticommunists fled the communist government established on Mainland China. China does not recognize Taiwan as a sovereign state and sees Taiwan as an island belonging to it, although Taiwan feels it is independent of China and is its own democratic state.
Former Yugoslavia	Serbs versus all the other nationalities that were once part of "Yugoslavia"	The former Yugoslavia comprised many nations, including Serbs, Croats, Kosovar Albanians, and Bosnian Muslims. In the 1990s, various nations in the multinational state of Yugoslavia warred to break away from the Serb-dominated government in Belgrade. Several newly independent states were created as a result of that war, the bloodiest since World War II.
Russia	Russia versus Chechnya	Chechnya is a territory in the Russian republic, governed by Moscow. The Chechen people want independence from Russia, which has caused massive fighting between the two groups.

Buffer States and Shatterbelts

Sometimes a buffer state or zone is used to try to calm two conflicting states or prevent them from further violence. A **buffer state** is an independent country located between two larger countries that are in conflict. Russia and China have warred over boundaries for centuries, but Mongolia has helped reduce direct confrontation between the two states. A **buffer zone** exists when two or more countries sit between two larger countries in conflict. After World War II, Eastern Europe was a buffer zone between the Soviet Union and Western Europe. However, the Soviets worked to dominate that buffer zone and install communist satellite states in Eastern Europe. **Satellite states** are countries controlled by another, more powerful state. For example, Poland became a satellite state of the Soviet Union, controlled by Moscow almost as tightly as a colonized state. The installation of communist satellite states in Eastern Europe erected what was coined by Winston Churchill as an "iron curtain" boundary between Western Europe and Soviet-controlled Eastern Europe.

A **shatterbelt** is a state or group of states that exists within a sphere of competition between larger states, as Poland was between Russia and Germany in World War II. Often states in a shatterbelt are the victims of invasion, boundary changes, and poor economic development.

Boundaries

Whether it is two states warring or two neighbors on a block arguing over a fence, the locations and definitions of boundaries are at the root of many conflicts at varying scales. Boundaries and their meanings shape our lives. Whether you are crossing into your neighbor's yard or into another country, these human-created lines represent ownership and identity, and they affect human behavior. Boundaries also exist within states at many levels: territories, municipalities, towns, villages, and so forth. *International* political boundaries separate states' territories; this type of political boundary actually extends to define what the state owns above and below the ground. There are several types of political boundaries.

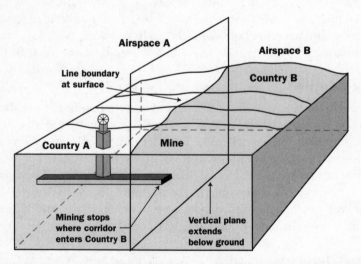

Figure 5.2. Vertical plane of a political boundary, reaching above and beneath the ground

Geometric political boundaries are straight-line boundaries that do not relate to the cultural or physical features of the territories involved. The original boundary separating North and South Korea followed a line of latitude. **Physical (or natural) political boundaries** separate territory according to natural features in the landscape, such as mountains, deserts, or rivers. France is divided from Spain by the Pyrenees Mountains. **Cultural political boundaries** mark changes in the cultural landscape, such as boundaries dividing a territory according to religion or language. Sometimes cultural political boundaries are also drawn according to geometric straight lines. The borders that carved modern-day Pakistan were created to give Muslims a territory.

Frontiers are regions where boundaries are very thinly or weakly developed, zones where territoriality is unclear and not well established. Antarctica is a frontier region at the international scale because it does not have clear boundaries of territorial control. Local communities can have frontier regions between neighborhood boundaries. Whereas boundaries are lines, frontiers are regions.

Another way to classify boundaries depends on how they have evolved over time, rather than just how they were created. **Antecedent boundaries** existed before human cultures developed into their current forms. Many physical political boundaries grew as antecedent boundaries. For example, the states of Kentucky and Indiana grew as distinct cultures around an already present divisor, the Ohio River. **Subsequent boundaries** grow to divide space as a result of human interaction and negotiation after significant settlement has occurred. The division between Canada and the United States is an example of a subsequent boundary. **Superimposed boundaries** are forcibly put on a landscape by outsiders, such as invaders or an organization like the United Nations. The boundary creating the modern state of Israel was superimposed by the United Nations. A **relict boundary** no longer functions as a boundary but only as reminders of a line that once divided space. Perhaps one of the most famous relict boundaries is the Berlin Wall, which no longer serves as an administrative border as it once did in dividing East and West Berlin.

Boundary Creation

There are several steps in the growth of boundaries into final form. **Definition** is the phase in which the exact location of a boundary is legally described and negotiated. **Delimitation** is the step when the boundary's definition is drawn onto a map. **Demarcation** is the visible marking of a boundary on the landscape with a fence, line, sign, wall, or other means. Not all boundaries are demarcated, because it can be an expensive process. One of the longest, most impressively demarcated boundaries is the Great Wall of China, though now it is a relict boundary. **Administration** is the enforcement by a government or people of the boundary that has been created.

Ocean Boundaries

How much of a claim can a country make on the waters that touch its borders? The United Nations has led the world's efforts in creating boundaries of shared waters. In its **Convention on the Law of the Seas (UNCLOS)**, the United Nations has generally paved out the following guiding provisions:

- Coastal states can stake their claims to the sea up to 12 nautical miles from their shorelines. However, ships from other countries have the right to pass through these waters.

- A coastal state can claim up to 200 nautical miles of territory beyond its shoreline as an **exclusive economic zone**, over which that state has economic control, to explore and mine natural resources that may be in the waters.

- When there is not enough water for each country on opposite sides of the sea to have 200 nautical miles of exclusive economic zone, the two or more countries involved will divide up the water evenly, a rule called the **median-line principle**.

Types of Boundary Disputes

Conflicts over boundaries sometimes involve a mix of the following categories. A **definitional boundary dispute** is a fight over the language of the border agreement in a treaty or boundary contract. Japan and Russia have still not agreed on the definition of territorial boundaries surrounding islands north of Japan. A **locational boundary dispute** is a conflict over the location of a boundary, not the definition. The conflicting parties agree on the definition but not on where it exists on the earth or the map. An **operational boundary dispute** is a conflict over the way a boundary should operate or function. For example, two states might disagree about allowing migration across their respective borders. An **allocational boundary dispute** is a fight over resources that may not be divided by the border, such as natural gas reserves beneath the soil.

Territorial Morphology

Territorial morphology is the relationship between a state's geographic shape, size, relative location, and political situation. In other words, factors like shape, size, and relative location affect the political issues facing its people internally and internationally. There are five classifications of geographic shapes of states.

A **fragmented state** geographically exists in several pieces. Indonesia, for example, has more than 16,000 islands within its fragmented boundary. Malaysia is broken into two chunks. A fragmented shape can lead to problems for a state in maintaining unity among its constituent parts, as in East Timor, which broke away from Indonesia.

Elongated states are long and thin in shape. Vietnam has an elongated shape. Sometimes problems can arise with this shape when a state's power base, or capital, loses influence over one end of the elongation. It can also pose transportation problems because of the distances involved.

Figure 5.3. Shapes of various states

A **compact state** does not vary greatly in distance from its center point to any point on its boundary. Compact states can be nearly square or circular in shape. Switzerland has a relatively compact shape. A compact shape is often the political ideal because no one part feels too far away from the center of control.

A **prorupt (or protruded) state** has a piece that protrudes from its core area, like an arm of a leg jutting off from the main body. Thailand has a prorupt shape with its protrusion jutting off from its core. Prorupt states often face problems similar to those of elongated states, because that jutting piece may try to break away or may be invaded.

A **perforated state** has a hole punched in it by another state, like South Africa, which is perforated by Lesotho, a tiny country. In other words, a perforated state completely surrounds another state. Relationships between the perforated state and its perforating state can be difficult and can cause tension, particularly if the perforated state is not welcoming of the perforating state's people.

Unitary and Federal States

A state's size and cultural composition are also factors in its political situation and internal organization. States that are smaller in geographic size and population may be more politically unified, but not always. A **microstate** is a very small state, such as Singapore. Often these smaller homogeneous states will organize using a **unitary governmental structure**, in which one main decision-making body governs the entire state. Regions within the country may have their own local governments, but usually they are weak and serve only as administrative organs of the unitary government based in the country's capital. A unitary government can even take the form of a dictatorship.

A larger, more diverse state often adopts a **federal governmental structure**, with a central government and strong regional governments that share power with the central government; the United States and Germany have this form of government. The regional governments have different names; called "States" (the word "State" is capitalized when referring to provincial units, such as the State of California) in the United States, Germany, and India; provinces in Canada; and *estados* in Mexico. Federal governmental organization is ideal for countries that may be geographically large and/or have regions that want a sense of self-determination, free from domination by the central government. The United States organized into a federal structure so that each State was given a sense of power and agreed to unify into one country. However, the threat of organizing a multinational state into a federal structure is that some regions, when given autonomy, may choose to break away from the unified state and demand complete independence.

Additionally, a state's relative location, or geographic situation, also affects its ability to survive and thrive. For example, countries that are **landlocked**, or without coastal access to a body of water, must depend on their neighbors to get to water sources for trade and navigation.

One other internal governmental structure is the **confederate governmental structure,** in which a weak central government exists with regional governments holding most of the power. The Articles of Confederation was the first document binding together the 13 American colonies, primarily for the purpose of defense during the Revolutionary War.

Political Exclaves and Enclaves

As defined in Chapter 4, an ethnic enclave is an area in which an ethnicity is concentrated and surrounded by another ethnic group or groups. A political enclave exists in a similar way. Similarly, a territorial **enclave** is a state, or part of a state, surrounded completely by another state. Lesotho is an enclave territory surrounded by South Africa, and West Berlin was an enclave within the state of East Germany. The state surrounding an enclave is a perforated state.

When an enclave is land that is a political extension of another state, it is called an **exclave**. For example, the West Berlin enclave in East Germany was technically part of the West German state, making that West Berlin enclave also an *exclave* of West Germany. Lesotho, though, is not an exclave of any other state. It is, in and of itself, a country, and not an extension of another state. Alaska is an exclave of the United States because it is cut off from the rest of the country by Canada.

Enclaves and exclaves can cause conflict over boundaries. Azerbaijan has a Muslim majority, while its neighbor Armenia has a Christian majority. Within Azerbaijan, a minority nation of Christian Armenians lives in an enclave called Nagorno-Karabakh. Because this enclave has fought to be controlled by Armenia, it is also an exclave of Armenia, or an Armenian territory existing in Azerbaijan. Therefore, Azerbaijan is a perforated state, perforated by the Christian Armenian enclave, also an exclave of the Armenian state.

Figure 5.4. A map of Azerbaijan. Take note of its political exclave.

PART 2	**Evolution of the Contemporary Political Pattern**

The Rise of the Nation-State Concept

Humans have organized political space throughout their existence in different forms. Early humans organized into clans, tribes, and villages. Conquerors collected such smaller groupings into kingdoms and empires. The ancient Greeks and Romans refined a component of their empires into the **city-state**, in which political space revolved around a central city and surrounding farmland.

Prior to the consolidation of powerful nation-states in Europe, sovereignty of the rulers depended on the loyalties of the people they ruled rather than clearly defined territories. After the fall of the Romans around 500 CE, European territory was typically divided in a feudal structure according to religion. The feudal structure was based on a system of many rulers exercising control over their own groups of dependent peoples and the dominance of the Catholic Church on everyday life. Therefore, the European political organization before the 1500s was loosely organized and not centralized.

In the 1500s, many western European places began integrating these feudal structures into more-centralized kingdoms. Strong monarchies grew in France and England, where kings developed central powers over their subjects. The loosely organized feudal state began to disappear in England and France as a strong monarchy emerged. With the stronger monarchy came more internal cohesion in the political organization, which led to the rise of nation-states, states that contain one nation, a cohesive group of people linked to their territory through a shared government and common goals. The pattern of integration into nation-states diffused throughout Europe and became a common goal even through World War II. Simply, the idea of linking people who share a strong sense of unity (a nation) under one government seemed to be the best way to prevent ethnonational violence from erupting, as it did in both of the world wars. However, creating political boundaries that match national (or cultural) boundaries was not often in the best interest of the boundary makers, as we will see.

Colonialism and Imperialism

European nation-states began building world empires in the 16th century and competed for territories across the globe through World War II. **Colonialism** is the control by a state over another area or people. Often a state that is colonizing has a more industrialized economy than the region it is overtaking. The first major period of colonialism occurred after European explorers, such as Columbus, discovered land in the Western Hemisphere in the 15th century. Europeans raced to form colonies in those lands and extract resources to send back home, an economic system called **mercantilism**. Under mercantilism, a state acquires colonies that can

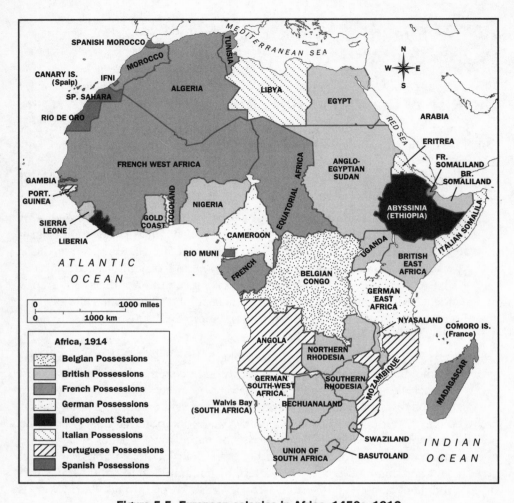

Figure 5.5. European colonies in Africa, 1450s–1912

provide it with the raw materials to ship back home and use in making products for the population in the mother country. Other motives for colonization were to spread Christianity and to bask in the glory of having more land than other states.

The second major wave occurred in the late 1800s, as western European powers were competing to "carve up" Africa, gaining more land to make them appear more powerful and to feed their industrializing economies. England and France occupied nearly 70 percent of the colonial territory in Africa. Portugal, Germany, Spain, Italy, and Belgium also colonized Africa.

Colonization fueled **imperialism**, the process of establishing political, social, and economic dominance over a colonized area. Europeans acculturated indigenous peoples to European Christianity and culture, even destroying indigenous landscapes and imposing European architecture that signified dominance.

Dependency Theory and Neocolonialism

According to the **dependency theory**, many countries are poor today because of their colonization by European powers. Proponents of this theory assert that former colonies in South America, Africa, and Asia have not been able to heal from the imperial domination established by the European colonizers and are still dependent on them. In most cases, the Europeans drew political boundaries according to the resources available to the colonizers, not according to the cultural (national) groupings of the native peoples. Therefore, when the Europeans left and the lands became independent states, the populations in those states were not unified, which often fueled violent ethnonational conflicts, as seen in Nigeria and Sudan, for example.

The number of states in the world has increased from 70 in 1938 to more than 200 in 2007. Most of the new states have recently achieved independence from a European colonizer.

Additionally, the political and economic structures established by the Europeans benefited the colonizers, not the local people, in most cases. Educational systems, health care networks, roads, communication lines, and other basic elements of infrastructure were not built in most colonized lands. As a result, many countries that were once European colonies are now in deep debt to their former colonial masters, burdened by loans they arranged with their former colonizers as a means of building up their economies that were, arguably, destroyed by their colonizers. The continued economic dependence of new states on their former colonial masters is called **neocolonialism (or postcolonial dependency)**.

World-Systems Analysis

As developed by Immanuel Wallerstein, **world-systems analysis** looks at the world as a capitalistic system of interlocking states. It posits that the situation in one country is directly linked to that country's role in the greater capitalistic system. Therefore, neocolonialism and its related dependency is not necessarily just a result of internal struggles within a poor country but is a consequence of that country's relationship to a larger system. World-systems analysis argues that the world is divided into three categories and that countries shift among these categories over time:

- The global economic core consists of the industrialized, developed countries that drive the global economy.

- The global economic periphery consists of countries that are underdeveloped and were, usually, once the core's colonies.

- The global economic semiperiphery is a third region in the world system in which countries are between the economic core and the periphery.

Geopolitics

Geopolitics is a branch of political geography that analyzes how states behave as political and territorial systems. In other words, geopolitics is the study of how states interact and compete in the political landscape. Nineteenth-century geopolitical thinker Friedrich Ratzel's **organic theory** argued that states are living organisms that hunger for land and, like organisms, want to grow larger and larger by acquiring more nourishment in the form of land. Adolf Hitler and the Nazis used Ratzel's theory as justification for invading other states to feed Germany's organic hunger for land.

In 1939, Adolf Hitler had the Olympic Village in Berlin laid out in the shape of the German map. In May of that year, Hitler used the viewing room at the Olympic Stadium to make his speech on his geopolitical justifications for gaining more land, or lebensraum, for the German state. By September, he had activated his theory by invading Poland.

Another prominent geopolitical thinker was Halford J. Mackinder, author of the heartland theory. According to the **heartland theory**, the era of sea power was ending and control over land would be the key to power. He believed that Eurasia was the "world island" and the key to dominating the world. Ruling this world island necessitated controlling eastern Europe. Mackinder's theory is linked to the Communists' efforts to dominate eastern Europe and to the U.S. "containment policy"

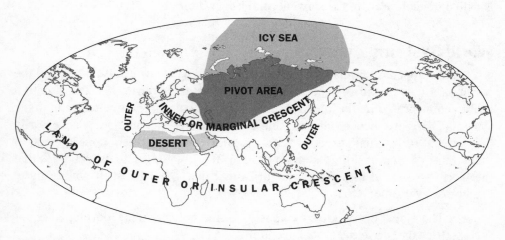

Figure 5.6. Mackinder heartland theory: The "pivot area" shown is the "heartland" in the Mackinder Theory. Mackinder argued that whoever controlled this pivot area would rule the world.

of keeping the Russians from gaining additional territories in the heartland, which the United States believed, based on the **domino theory**, would cause a fall of the world island to the Soviets.

Another geopolitical thinker, Nicolas Spykman, built off of Mackinder's theory and wrote of the "rimland." In his **rimland theory**, Spykman defined the rimland to be all of Eurasia's periphery, not its core of Russia and Central Asia. Therefore, the rimland encompasses western Europe and Southeast, South, and East Asia. He thought it was important to balance power in the rimland to prevent a global power from emerging. His theory is linked to the Vietnam and Korean wars, in which Communists and non-Communists fought for control of peripheral lands in the rimland.

PART 3 | **Challenges to Inherited Political-Territorial Arrangements**

Core Areas and Multicore States

A region's internal organization of power can affect its level of unity and cohesion. The region in a state wherein political and economic power is concentrated, like the nucleus of a cell, is called a state's **core**. A well-integrated core, one that functions as a healthy part of its state, not in isolation, helps spread development throughout the country. Countries having more than just one core region are called **multicore states**. When these core areas are competing for political and economic power and none is dominant, the result can be internal division within the state. Nigeria, for example, has several core regions competing for control and thus jeopardizing Nigeria's unification. Strong infrastructure development, in the form of roads, communication lines, and so forth, can help distribute the growth generated in a core to less developed areas in a state.

Capital Cities

The capital of most countries is its political nucleus. Some countries have a capital city, called a **primate city**, that is not only the political nucleus but also many times more economically powerful than any other city in the state. Primate cities often exist in less-developed countries, where most of the resources are attracted, like a magnet, to one city that grows and grows and is supplied by the smaller cities in the state that do not get an equal share of the development. Ulaanbaatar, Mongolia, is an example of a primate city that is many times larger and more powerful than the next-largest city in Mongolia. In many such cases, governments are trying to spread the growth and development out among different cities, rather than allowing it to focus on the primate city. Primate cities are also common in old nation-states, like France and Britain. In these places, the primate city has been the cultural center for a long time and still attracts many migrants.

States also move their capital cities for various reasons. A **forward capital** is a capital city built by a state to achieve some national goal. The Russian czar Peter the Great built the forward capital of Saint Petersburg, moving the capital of Russia from Moscow to bring Russia's capital city and its focus closer to Europe; Moscow is farther east and thus farther from Europe than is Saint Petersburg. After the fall of the Berlin Wall in 1990, Germany chose to move its capital city back to Berlin, a forward capital, to show unification.

Gerrymandering

Internal political boundaries often are the subject of debate and manipulation. Electoral boundaries affect voting patterns and outcomes. In the United States alone, considerable debate surrounds the placement of electoral district boundaries. The definition of these boundaries can give one party an advantage over another in competing for a spot in a legislature. For example, boundaries can be drawn to give the number of registered Republicans a majority in a particular district, or registered Democrats in another. Redrawing electoral boundaries to give a political party an advantage is called **gerrymandering**. In total, the spatial organization of electoral geography can have a profound effect on power structures in a state.

Figure 5.7. Political cartoon from 1812 demonstrating voting-district gerrymandering in the still-young United States.

In 2000, only 57 of the 435 seats in the U.S. House of Representatives were decided by margins of 10 percent or less.

Centrifugal and Centripetal Forces

Within every state are forces that unify its regions and people and other forces that work to divide its regions and people. **Centrifugal forces** divide a state's people and regions (think "centrifugal," *F*, for "fracture"). **Centripetal forces** unify a state's people and regions (think "centripetal," *T* for "together"). In states that are unified, centripetal forces are more dominant than centrifugal forces. The inverse holds when a state is breaking apart: centrifugal forces are dominant.

Examples of Centripetal and Centrifugal Forces Within States*

Centripetal	Centrifugal
Unifying symbols, such as flags	Separatism in a region
A national pledge of allegiance	Internal boundary conflicts
A strong identity based on language, religion, or other cultural traits	Deep religious divisions

    * These examples could be reclassified within a particular situation. A flag, for example, might be a unifying force in the United States of America but a force of division and conflict in a state that has many nations that cannot agree on what the flag should look like. A culture trait like religion can also help strengthen national ties or weaken them.

Centrifugal forces broke apart the former state of Czechoslovakia in 1993 when the Czechs and Slovaks each wanted their own regions, leading to the creation of the Czech Republic and Slovakia. Centripetal forces worked to keep the Canadian French speakers united with the English-speaking Canadian nationality, despite the centrifugal forces calling for secession and an independent French-speaking state. Centrifugal forces tore apart the former Soviet Union, leading to independent states such as Latvia, Lithuania, and Estonia, once a part of the Russian union. **Balkanization** occurs when centrifugal forces break apart a state into smaller pieces. The term is rooted in the violent breakup of the Balkan region of Yugoslavia into smaller autonomous states.

Devolution

States facing centrifugal forces, such as strong regional separatism or internal dispute, often move to transfer more power to regional governments to help

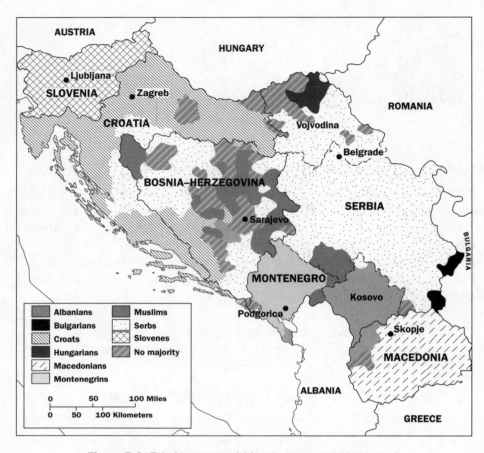

Figure 5.8. Ethnic groups within what was once Yugoslavia

reduce the divisive tensions by giving angry groups more regional power and autonomy. **Devolution** is the process of transferring some power from the central government to regional governments. For example, Scotland was pushing for more autonomy from England. In the 1990s, England devolved more power to Scotland, when Scotland was given its own representative parliament instead of being governed only by England's parliament in London. In France, the Corsicans were a threat to national unity, so France's Paris-based government devolved more power to the Corsicans to keep them from moving toward violently seceding (breaking away). Yet such devolutionary measures do not always prevent regionalism from splitting a state apart. Montenegrins were vying for increased autonomy, but despite Serbia's devolutionary efforts to give them more regional control, the Montenegrins declared independence in 2006.

Supranationalism

Although the current political landscape is characterized by a trend in ethno-nationalism leading to newly independent states, a trend toward increased integra-

(Photo by: AP Wide World Photos)

Figure 5.9. A meeting of the UN General Assembly

tion among states, or growing supranationalism, is also evident. **Supranationalism** is the growing trend of three or more countries forming an alliance for cultural, economic, or military reasons. Supranational alliances are created so that states can collectively reach a common goal that they may not be able to reach independently. If a country threatens other states, the affected supranational organizations may impose **international sanctions**, or punishments in the form of economic or diplomatic limits or even isolation. When Iraq was threatening members of the United Nations, the UN imposed economic sanctions on Iraq, including trade embargoes, or complete bans on trade with Iraq.

After the bloody conflict among states during World War I, U.S. President Woodrow Wilson, along with other world leaders, founded the League of Nations. That organization was the precursor to the current **United Nations (UN)**, which was formed in the aftermath of World War II. The countries came together as the UN for collective security, trying to ensure that a global war would not happen again. With nearly 200 members, the United Nations is the world's most extensive supranational organization ever established. During the Cold War, the **Warsaw Pact** was a supranational organization of communist allies, while the **North Atlantic Treaty Organization (NATO)** was formed to combat the expansion of communist states. The Association of Southeast Asian Nations (ASEAN), another example of political supranationalism, was formed in the 1960s to protect its member states from invasion by China.

(Photo by: Kjetil Ree)

Figure 5.10. The meeting room of the UN Security Council

The United Nations

Formed in 1945, the United Nations is the closest structure to a world government on the earth. Its headquarters and all its main organs, except the International Court of Justice, are located in New York City on a plot of land considered international territory. Bounded by the UN Charter, a constitution of sorts, the United Nations' nearly 200 member-states decide on common issues and policies. The UN Charter states that the organization's purposes are "to maintain international peace and security; to develop friendly relations among nations; to cooperate in solving international economic, social, cultural and humanitarian problems and in promoting respect for human rights and fundamental freedoms; and to be a centre for harmonizing the actions of nations in attaining these ends."

The structure of the UN includes the following main components:

- **General Assembly:** All member-states send a representative to this parliament-like deliberative body. Each member-state has an equal vote in the General Assembly, regardless of the state's size or power.

- **Security Council:** This organ of the UN has 15 member-states that make decisions related to war and peace and sending in UN "peacekeepers," which are the UN's force of troops meant only to be used to defend member-states and their people from threats to their sovereignty on peace-keeping missions. The Security Council also assigns sanctions to punish states for threatening collective security. Currently, 10 states are elected by the General Assembly to rotate onto the council, and five states of the council are permanent members. These five are the Russian Federation, China, the United States, France, and England. Each permanent country has a veto power that can cancel any resolution or action in the council. The Security Council's decisions must be carried out by the general member-ship, as stated in the UN Charter.

- **Economic and Social Council:** This is the arm of the UN that coordinates antipoverty and prohumanitarian efforts throughout the world. It is also charged with promoting cultural awareness and improving global health.

- **International Court of Justice (ICJ):** This is the UN's principal judicial organ located at the Peace Palace in the Hague, the Netherlands. The ICJ settles all legal disputes submitted to it by UN member-states in addition to giving legal advice to the UN. Composed of 15 judges who are elected for nine-year terms by the Security Council and the General Assembly, the ICJ has declared English and French as its official languages.

- **Secretariat:** This is the executive branch of the UN in charge of all administrative issues to keep the UN operating. The head of the secretariat is the UN secretary general, who is appointed by the General Assembly on recommendation of the Security Council.

The UN headquarters in New York has a Meditation Room with a guest book for signatures of people who have visited the room to meditate and pray for world peace.

Critics of the UN have called for restructuring it, including revising the UN Security Council's organization. Some analysts feel that global tensions can be linked to the lack of Arab representation among the Security Council's permanent members. Others call for reducing the UN's bureaucracy and distribution of money.

Palestine and the Vatican are not voting members of the United Nations but are considered "permanent observers."

The United Nations System

Principal Organs

Trusteeship Council	Security Council	General Assembly

Subsidiary Bodies

Military Staff Committee

Standing Committee and ad hoc bodies

International Criminal Tribunal for the former Yugoslavia (ICTY)

International Criminal Tribunal for Rwanda (ICTR)

Subsidiary Bodies

UN Monitoring, Verification and Inspection Commission (Iraq) (UNMOVIC)

United Nations Compensation Commission

Peacekeeping Operations and Missions

Subsidiary Bodies

Main committees

Human Rights Council

Other sessional committees

Standing committees and ad hoc bodies

Other subsidiary organs

Programmes and Funds

UNCTAD United Nations Conference on Trade and Development

  ITC International Trade Centre (UNCTAD/WTO)

UNDCP[1] United Nations Drug Control Programme

UNEP United Nations Environment Programme

UNICEF United Nations Children's Fund

UNDP United Nations Development Programme

  UNIFEM United Nations Development Fund for Women

  UNV United Nations Volunteers

  UNCDF United Nations Capital Development Fund

UNFPA United Nations Population Fund

UNHCR Office of the United Nations High Commissioner for Refugees

Advisory Subsidiary Body

United Nations Peacebuilding Commission

WFP World Food Programme

UNRWA[2] United Nations Relief and Works Agency for Palestine Refugees in the Near East

UN-HABITAT United Nations Human Settlements Programme

Research and Training Institutes

UNICRI United Nations Interregional Crime and Justice Research Institute

UNITAR United Nations Institute for Training and Research

UNRISD United Nations Research Institute for Social Development

UNIDIR[2] United Nations Institute for Disarmament Research

INSTRAW International Research and Training Institute for the Advancement of Women

Other UN Entities

OHCHR Office of the United Nations High Commissioner for Human Rights

UNOPS United Nations Office for Project Services

UNU United Nations University

UNSSC United Nations System Staff College

UNAIDS Joint United Nations Programme on HIV/AIDS

Other UN Trust Funds[7]

UNFIP United Nations Fund for International Partnerships

UNDEF United Nations Democracy Fund

NOTES:

1 The UN Drug Control Programme is part of the UN Office on Drugs and Crime

2 UNRWA and UNIDIR report only to the GA

3 The United Nations Ethics Office and the United Nations Ombudsman's Office report directly to the Secretary-General

4 IAEA reports to the Security Council and the General Assembly (GA)

5 The CTBTO Prep.Com and OPCW report to the GA

6 Specialized agencies are autonomous organizations working with the UN and each other through the coordinating machinery of the ECOSOC at the intergovernmental level, and through the Chief Executives Board for coordination (CEB) at the inter-secretariat level

7 UNFIP is an autonomous trust fund operating under the leadership of the United Nations Deputy Secretary-General. UNDEF's advisory board recommends funding proposals for approval by the Secretary-General.

Figure 5.11. Organizational chart of the United Nations

The United Nations System

Economic and Social Council

Functional Commissions

Commissions on:
  Narcotic Drugs
  Crime Prevention and Criminal Justice
  Science and Technology for Development
  Sustainable Development
  Status of Women
  Population and Development
Commission for Social Development
Statistical Commission

Regional Commissions

Economic Commission for Africa (ECA)
Economic Commission for Europe (ECE)
Economic Commission for Latin America and the Caribbean (ECLAC)
Economic and Social Commission for Asia and the Pacific (ESCAP)
Economic and Social Commission for Western Asia (ESCWA)

Other Bodies

Permanent Forum on Indigenous Issues (PFII)
United Nations Forum on Forests
Sessional and standing committees
Expert, ad hoc and related bodies

Related Organizations

WTO World Trade Organization

IAEA[4] International Atomic Energy Agency

CTBTO Prep.Com[5] PrepCom for the Nuclear-Test-Ban-Treaty Organization

OPCW[5] Organization for the Prohibition of Chemical Weapons

International Court of Justice

Specialized Agencies[6]

ILO International Labour Organization

FAO Food and Agriculture Organization of the United Nations

UNESCO United Nations Educational, Scientific and Cultural Organization

WHO World Health Organization

World Bank Group

IBRD International Bank for Reconstruction and Development

IDA International Development Association

IFC International Finance Corporation

MIGA Multilateral Investment Guarantee Agency

ICSID International Centre for Settlement of Investment Disputes

IMF International Monetary Fund

ICAO International Civil Aviation Organization

IMO International Maritime Organization

ITU International Telecommunication Union

UPU Universal Postal Union

WMO World Meteorological Organization

WIPO World Intellectual Property Organization

IFAD International Fund for Agricultural Development

UNIDO United Nations Industrial Development Organization

UNWTO World Tourism Organization

Secretariat

Departments and Offices

OSG[3] Office of the Secretary-General

OIOS Office of Internal Oversight Services

OLA Office of Legal Affairs

DPA Department of Political Affairs

DDA Department for Disarmament Affairs

DPKO Department of Peacekeeping Operations

OCHA Office for the Coordination of Humanitarian Affairs

DESA Department of Economic and Social Affairs

DGACM Department for General Assembly and Conference Management

DPI Department of Public Information

DM Department of Management

OHRLLS Office of the High Representative for the Least Developed Countries, Landlocked Developing Countries and Small Island Developing States

DSS Department of Safety and Security

UNODC United Nations Office on Drugs and Crime

☙❧

UNOG UN Office at Geneva
UNOV UN Office at Vienna
UNON UN Office at Nairobi

Published by the United Nations Department of Public Information

06-39572—August 2006—10,000—DPI/2431

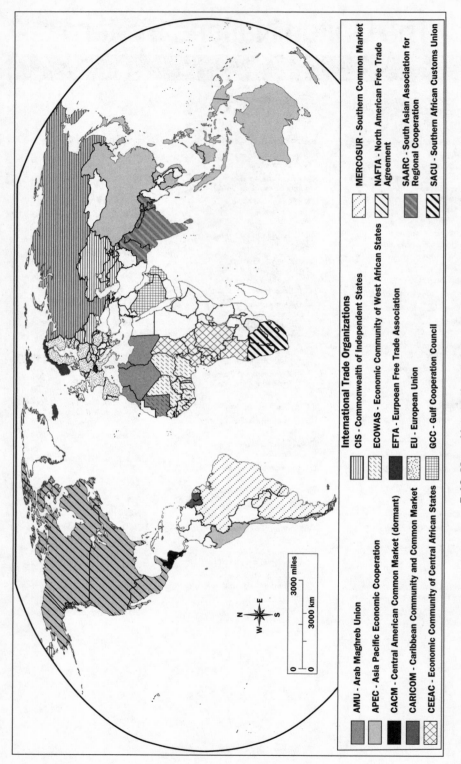

International Trade Organizations

CIS - Commonwealth of Independent States

ECOWAS - Economic Community of West African States

EFTA - Eurpopean Free Trade Association

EU - European Union

GCC - Gulf Cooperation Council

MERCOSUR - Southern Common Market

NAFTA - North American Free Trade Agreement

SAARC - South Asian Association for Regional Cooperation

SACU - Southern African Customs Union

AMU - Arab Maghreb Union

APEC - Asia Pacific Economic Cooperation

CACM - Central American Common Market (dormant)

CARICOM - Caribbean Community and Common Market

CEEAC - Economic Community of Central African States

5.12. Map of international trade organizations

The Preamble to the UN Charter, Written in 1945

Preamble

We the peoples of the United Nations determined

- to save succeeding generations from the scourge of war, which twice in our lifetime has brought untold sorrow to mankind, and

- to reaffirm faith in fundamental human rights, in the dignity and worth of the human person, in the equal rights of men and women and of nations large and small, and

- to establish conditions under which justice and respect for the obligations arising from treaties and other sources of international law can be maintained, and

- to promote social progress and better standards of life in larger freedom,

and for these ends

- to practice tolerance and live together in peace with one another as good neighbors, and

- to unite our strength to maintain international peace and security, and

- to ensure, by the acceptance of principles and the institution of methods, that armed force shall not be used, save in the common interest, and

- to employ international machinery for the promotion of the economic and social advancement of all peoples,

have resolved to combine our efforts to accomplish these aims

Accordingly, our respective Governments, through representatives assembled in the city of San Francisco, who have exhibited their full powers found to be in good and due form, have agreed to the present Charter of the United Nations and do hereby establish an international organization to be known as the United Nations.

The European Union

Economic supranationalism is the integration of three or more states for achieving collective economic goals. The **European Union (EU)** is an example of economic supranationalism and represents the growth of a European economic community that has been formally developing since the 1950s.

With more than 25 member states, the EU has a population of nearly 500 million.

Figure 5.13. A map of the European Union membership

Historically, the EU started to grow with the formation of the **Benelux**, an economic alliance among Belgium, the Netherlands, and Luxembourg, before the end of World War II. Through Benelux, these three countries benefited from reduced trade barriers, more easily crossable (or permeable) borders, and common goals. Other European countries learned from this idea, and in 1958, the **European Economic Community** (also called the **Common Market**) was formed among some states wanting economic integration and cooperation. Out of the Common Market developed an even larger grouping of states, the European Community, called "Community" with hopes of becoming more than just an economic union. By 1992, the European Union was born with economic, political, cultural, and judicial integration goals.

The EU forms the largest free-trade zone in the world; NAFTA is the second largest.

The EU is perhaps the most powerful supranational alliance in the world, because its member states have bound together their economies, currencies, and environmental policies to create a powerful internal market in Europe. Most member-countries use the Euro, a common currency. Some geographers project that the EU will soon evolve into a military alliance as well among member-states. Nonetheless, its economic integration has created a rival to the economic superpower status of the United States.

The growth of supranational alliances challenges conceptions of state sovereignty. To join such an alliance, states must often give up some powers they have to the organization. Some European countries, particularly England, were reluctant to give up their currencies and use the Euro. The United States' Congress chose not to enter the League of Nations, despite President Woodrow Wilson's advocacy for joining it. Congress also did not agree to enter the League of Nations after World War I, in part because the United States did not want to have to abide by the decisions of a supranational organization, which would have meant giving up some sovereignty.

Collapse of the USSR

Following the Russian revolution of 1917, the monarchy was overthrown by the Communists, who created the communist state called Union of Soviet Socialist Republics, or the USSR. The USSR was organized as a federation of states, called union republics, with Russia as its largest union republic; by 1960, the USSR was comprised of 16 republics. Its geographic expanse extended throughout what was the Russian empire into Eastern Europe after World War II.

The effects of the competition between the democratic U.S. allies and the USSR's communist allies, a conflict known as the cold war, led to the eventual devolution and balkanization of what was the USSR. After a period of fierce crushing of political dissent in the 1950s to 1970s in Russia, a new leader, Mikhail Gorbachev, was elected as the USSR's leader and ushered in a period of devolutionary reforms, such as allowing more freedom of speech and regional political sovereignty. The destruction of the Soviet-administered Berlin Wall that divided democratic West Berlin from communist-controlled East Berlin foreshadowed the fall of Soviet control of its satellite states and constituent regions calling for independence. By 1991, several union republics had formally voted to

Other Supranational Organizations	Purpose
Economic Community of West African States (ECOWAS)	Founded in 1975 to create a more cooperative economic union among 15 West African states.
Latin American Integration Association (LAIA)	Formed in 1980 by Argentina, Bolivia, Brazil, Chile, Colombia, Ecuador, Mexico, Paraguay, Peru, Uruguay, and Venezuela to promote free trade.
Organization of Petroleum Exporting Countries (OPEC)	Formed to coordinate petroleum policies among its members in order to secure fair and stable prices for petroleum producers; a regular supply of petroleum to consuming nations; and a fair return on capital to those investing in the industry. Its five founding members in 1960 were Iran, Iraq, Kuwait, Saudi Arabia, and Venezuela.
Organization of African Unity (African Union)	In a fashion similar to the European Union's integration efforts, the African Union was formed in 1999 with the aim of economically, socially, and politically aligning the African states toward attaining greater efficiency and reducing the strains of their colonial roots.
Arab League	Founded in 1945 in Cairo, Egypt, the Arab League combines voluntary members of primarily Arabic-speaking countries in a supranational union aimed at promoting common interests. In addition to Egypt, founding member-states are Iraq, Lebanon, Saudi Arabia, Syria, and Jordan.
North American Free Trade Agreement	Made effective in 1994, NAFTA is an economic alliance among the United States, Canada, and Mexico with the aim of fostering free trade throughout North America. The gradual removal of tariffs and trade barriers is the primary aim of NAFTA.

secede from the USSR and form their own nation-states. The USSR was declared "dissolved" that same year by its communist government, from which Mikhail Gorbachev resigned. Gorbachev's successor, Boris Yeltsin, became president of Russia, no longer called the Soviet Union.

A New World Order?

During the cold war, in the aftermath of World War II, states were divided into two camps, procommunist and prodemocratic. This "bipolar" world was relatively balanced. A geopolitical transition has occurred since the fall of the Soviet Empire in the 1990s. In this **new world order**, international relations are no longer driven by the bipolar communist/anticommunist groups. Instead, international relations are multilayered and complex. Economically, many poles of superpower exist, including the U.S. economy, the European Union, and the growing Chinese economy. Militarily, the United States maintains superpower status, but it is increasingly challenged by terrorism and other types of warfare.

PART 4

Chapter Review

Terms Review

Administration phase of boundary creation—Phase in which a government enforces the boundary it has created.

Allocational boundary dispute—Conflict over resources that may not be divided by the border, such as natural gas reserves beneath the soil.

Antecedent boundary—Boundary that existed before the human cultures grew into current form.

Balkanization—Division of a region or state into smaller units, usually along ethnic lines.

Benelux—Economic alliance (and precursor to the current European Union) among Belgium, the Netherlands, and Luxembourg established before the end of World War II.

Buffer state—Independent country that exists between two larger countries that are conflicting

Buffer zone—Area consisting of two or more countries located between two larger countries in conflict.

Centrifugal force—Force that divides a state's people and regions.

Centripetal force—Force that unifies a state's people and regions.

City-state—Political space comprising a central city and surrounding farmland.

Colonialism—Control by a developed state over an underdeveloped area.

Compact state—State with little variation in distance from its center point to any point on its boundary.

Confederate governmental structure—Organizational structure comprising a weak central government and regional governments holding the majority of power.

Core of a state—Region in a state wherein political and economic power is concentrated, like the nucleus of a cell.

Cultural political boundary—Political boundary that marks changes in the cultural landscape, such as a boundary dividing territory according to religion or language.

Definitional boundary dispute—Conflict over the language of the border agreement in a treaty or boundary contract.

Definition phase in boundary creation—Phase in which the exact location of a boundary is legally described and negotiated.

Delimitation phase in boundary creation—Phase in which a boundary's definition is drawn onto a map.

Demarcation phase of boundary creation—Phase in which the boundary is visibly marked on the landscape by a fence, line, sign, wall or other means.

Dependency theory—According to this theory, former colonies in South America, Africa, and Asia have not been able to heal from imperial domination and are still dependent on their former European colonizers.

Devolution—Process of transferring some power from the central government to regional governments.

Domino theory—Notion that democratic allies must protect lands from falling to the communists because one such communist acquisition creates others, ultimately resulting in communist domination of the world. This theory led to the containment doctrine, intended to keep the communists from acquiring new lands, such as Vietnam.

Elongated state—State with a long, thin shape.

Enclave (political)—Part of a state surrounded completely by another state. Also see ethnic enclave.

Ethnonationalism—Powerful emotional attachment people have for their nation when it is a minority within a state, making them feel they are different from the rest of the state's people.

European Economic Community (Common Market)—Supranational economic alliance of European countries wanting to form a European market. Established in1958, it was a precursor to the current European Union.

European Union (EU)—Supranational organization of nearly 25 member-states in Europe that have integrated for improved economic and political cooperation.

Exclave—Enclave that is a territorial political extension of another state.

Exclusive economic zone—According to the UNCLOS, a 200-nautical-mile area extending along a state's coast to which that state has economic rights.

Federal governmental structure—Organizational structure with a central government that shares power with strong regional governments.

Forward capital—Capital city built by a state to achieve a national goal.

Fragmented state—State geographically existing in more than one piece, or in fragments.

Frontier—Region where boundaries are very thinly or weakly developed; zone where territoriality is not well established and is unclear.

Geometric political boundary—Straight-line political boundary separating territories that do not relate to cultural or physical features.

Geopolitics—Branch of political geography that analyzes how states behave as political and territorial systems.

Gerrymandering—Redrawing electoral boundaries to give one political party an advantage over others.

Imperialism—The process of establishing political, social, and economic dominance over a colonized area.

International sanctions—Punishments in the form of economic and/or diplomatic limits or even isolation.

Irredentism—Movement to reunite a nation's homeland when part of it extends into another state's borders.

Landlocked state—State without coastal access to a body of water.

Locational boundary dispute—Conflict over the location or place of a boundary.

Mackinder's heartland theory—Geopolitical theory that Eurasia was the "world island" and the key to dominating the world. Ruling this world island required controlling eastern Europe; linked to the domino theory.

Median-line principle—Statement in UNCLOS declaring that when there is not enough water for each country on opposite sides of the sea to have 200 nautical miles of exclusive economic zone, the two or more countries involved will divide the water evenly.

Mercantilism—Economic system in which colonies are obtained to supply the colonizer with raw materials to ship back home and use in making products for the population in the mother country.

Microstate—Very small state, such as Singapore.

Multicore state—State with more than one core region.

Multinational state—State with more than one nation within its borders.

Nation—Group of people who share a common culture and identify as a cohesive group.

Nation-state—State containing one nation, a cohesive group of people linked to their territory through a shared government and common goals.

Neocolonialism (or postcolonial dependency)—Continued economic dependence of new states on their former colonial masters; the basic principle of dependency theory.

New world order—Multilayered international situation, or landscape, that has existed since the end of the cold war.

North Atlantic Treaty Organization (NATO)—Supranational organization formed during the cold war to combat the expansion of communist states.

Operational boundary dispute—Conflict over the way a boundary should operate or function, such as the conflict over allowing migration across the border.

Organic theory—Friedrich Ratzel's geopolitical theory that states are living organisms that hunger for land and, like organisms, want to grow larger by acquiring more nourishment in the form of land.

Perforated state—State with a hole punched in it by another state, like South Africa perforated by Lesotho.

Personal space—Amount of area a person claims as his or her own territory into which others may not enter without permission.

Physical (or natural) political boundary—Political boundary that separates territories according to natural features in the landscape, such as mountains, deserts, or rivers.

Political geography—Study of human political organization of the earth at various geographic levels.

Primate city—City that is not only the political nucleus but also is many times more economically powerful than any other city in the state.

Prorupt (or protruded) state—State with a piece that protrudes from its core area, as an arm juts off from the main body.

Relict boundary—Boundary that no longer functions as a boundary but only as a reminder of a line that once divided space.

Rimland theory—Nicolas Spykman's theory defining the rimland to be all of Eurasia's periphery, not its core of Russia and Central Asia. This rimland was the key to controlling the world island.

Satellite state—Country controlled by a more powerful state

Self-determination—Power of a nation to control its own territory and destiny.

Shatterbelt—State or group of states that exists within a sphere of competition between larger states

Sovereignty—Internationally recognized control of a state over the people and territory within its boundaries.

State—Political unit with a permanent population, territorial boundaries recognized by other states, an effective government, a working economy, and sovereignty.

Stateless nation—Nation without a territory to call its own.

Subsequent boundary—Boundary that grows after significant settlement has occurred, rather than existing before the growth of human cultures, as with an antecedent boundary.

Superimposed boundary—Boundary forcibly put on a landscape by outsiders.

Supranationalism—Growing trend of three or more countries forming an alliance for cultural, economic, or military reasons.

Territoriality—Control over a space and the assumption of ownership to that space.

Territorial morphology—Relationship between a state's geographic shape, size, relative location, and political situation.

Unitary governmental structure—Organizational structure in which one main governmental decision-making body exists for the entire state. Regions within the country may have their own local governments, but they are weak and usually serve only as administrative organs of the primary government based in the country's capital.

United Nations (UN)—Supranational organization of nearly 200 member-states bound together to create collective security through diplomatic cooperation.

United Nations Convention on Law and the Seas (UNCLOS)—UN document of agreement among coastal states defining how they should divide the earth's bodies of water.

Warsaw Pact—Supranational organization of communist allies formed during the cold war.

World-systems analysis—Viewpoint that the situation in one country is directly linked to that country's role in the greater capitalistic system, divided into core states, peripheral states, and semiperipheral states.

PART 5: Some Suggested Web Resources for Further Exploration

European Union (EU): http://www.europa.eu/

The portal for the EU's official website (to view the English page, select ENG). The site contains organizational charts, maps, biographies, and transcripts of resolutions.

United Nations (UN): http://www.un.org/

This is the official site for the United Nations and all its components. In addition to resources on each of the major institutions governed by the UN, you can watch live Web casts of the UN's components in their sessions, including videos of the UN Security Council. Information on peacekeeping missions and maps are also available on the site.

Central Intelligence Agency (CIA): http://www.cia.gov/

The CIA maintains on its website a database of the world's countries called the World Factbook. This is an invaluable resource detailing each of the world's recognized states and their governmental, economic, and social elements.

Organization of the Petroleum Exporting Countries (OPEC): http://www.opec.org/

The official site of OPEC, a supranational organization of 11 oil-exporting countries.

North Atlantic Treaty Organization (NATO): http://www.nato.int/

This website is dedicated to NATO, a supranational alliance formed to create collective security.

UN Convention on the Law of the Seas: www.un.org/Depts/los/

This site contains information on UNCLOS and its effects on sea boundaries for coastal states.

African Union: http://www.africa-union.org/

The official site of the African Union includes helpful maps, graphs, and information on the union and its missions.

PART 6

Pre-Exam Practice

Terms Review Quiz

Use the Terms Review list or your own memory to determine the extent of your knowledge of key terms and concepts. Remember, the AP exam does not include this kind of exercise, but it is included here as a review tool.

1. _____   Group of people who share a common culture and identify as a cohesive group.

2. _____   Control over a space and the assumption of ownership to that space.

3. _____   Phase in which a boundary's definition is drawn onto a map.

4. _____   State with more than one nation within its borders.

5. _____   Region where boundaries are very thinly or weakly developed; zone where territoriality is not well established and is unclear.

6. _____   Conflict over the way a boundary should operate or function, such as the conflict over allowing migration across the border.

7. _____   State with a hole punched in it by another state, like South Africa perforated by Lesotho.

8. _____   Economic alliance (and precursor to the current European Union) among Belgium, the Netherlands, and Luxembourg established before the end of World War II.

9. _____   Supranational organization of communist-state allies formed during the Cold War.

10. _____   Multilayered international situation, or landscape, that has existed since the end of the Cold War.

11. _____ Geopolitical theory that Eurasia was the "world island" and the key to dominating the world. Ruling this world island required controlling eastern Europe.

12. _____ Capital city built by a state to achieve a national goal.

13. _____ Force that unifies a state's people and regions.

14. _____ Branch of political geography that analyzes how states behave as political and territorial systems

15. _____ Economic system in which colonies are obtained to supply the colonizer with raw materials to ship back home and use in making products for the population in the mother country.

16. _____ Organizational structure with a central government that shares power with strong regional governments.

17. _____ Statement in UNCLOS declaring that when there is not enough water for each country on opposite sides of the sea to have 200 nautical miles of exclusive economic zone, the two or more countries involved will divide the water evenly.

18. _____ Boundary that grows after significant settlement has occurred, rather than existing before the growth of human cultures, as with an antecedent boundary.

19. _____ State with little variation in distance from its center point to any point on its boundary.

20. _____ Powerful emotional attachment people have for their nation when it is a minority within a state, making them feel they are different from the rest of the state's people.

21. _____ Internationally recognized control of a state over the people and territory within its boundaries.

22. _____ Political unit with a permanent population, territorial boundaries recognized by other states, an effective government, a working economy, and sovereignty.

23. _____ Relationship between a state's geographic shape, size, relative location, and political situation.

24. _____ Process of establishing political, social, and economic dominance over a colonized area.

25. _____ Viewpoint that the situation in one country is directly linked to that country's role in the greater capitalistic system, divided into core states, peripheral states, and semiperipheral states.

Multiple-Choice Review Questions

1. To try to reduce the calls for revolutionary secession from Canada, the Canadian parliament has given Nunavit regions more autonomy, or local control. This situation best represents the geographic concept of

    (A) exclave

    (B) buffer state

    (C) ministate

    (D) gerrymandering

    (E) devolution

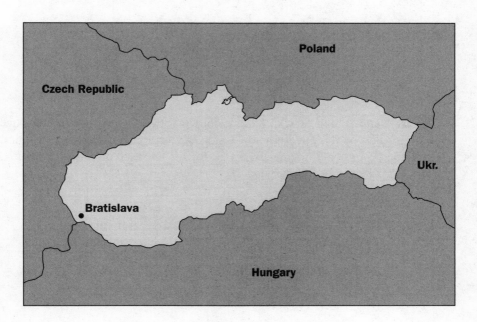

Map of Slovakia

2. Which of the following morphological classifications best describes Slovakia, shown in the map above?

    (A) Fragmented

    (B) Compact

    (C) Elongated

    (D) Prorupt, or protruded

    (E) Perforated

STATE X

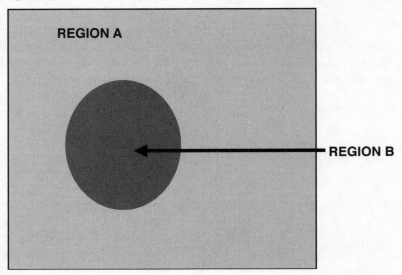

3. Regions A and B both exist in State X shown above. The shaded areas above are both ruled by the government of State X. Region B includes one nation surrounded by other ethnicities living in Region A. Based on this information, Region B is best classified as a(n)

(A) exclave

(B) enclave

(C) centripetal force

(D) core

(E) exclusive economic zone

STATE Y

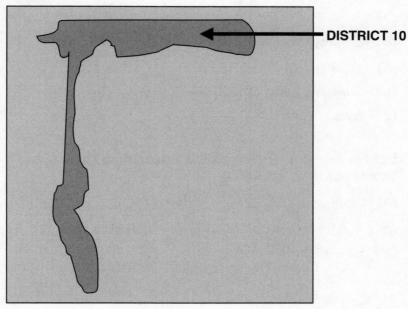

DISTRICT 10

4. District 10 is one electoral region existing in square-shaped State Y, shown on the map above. District 10 was most likely formed through

    (A) gerrymandering   (D) balkanization

    (B) maladaptation   (E) supranationalism

    (C) devolution

5. Which of the following states is NOT a permanent member of the United Nations Security Council?

    (A) China   (D) France

    (B) Russia   (E) Germany

    (C) United States

6. Which of the following is a forward capital?

    (A) Paris, France

    (B) Bombay (Mumbai), India

    (C) Rome, Italy

    (D) Putrajaya, Malaysia

    (E) Sydney, Australia

7. Sikhs in India, Muslim Palestinians in Israel, and Kurds in the former Iraq are all considered

    (A) multinational states   (D) frontiers

    (B) stateless nations   (E) landlocked states

    (C) nation-states

8. According to world-systems analysis, which of the following countries would be best classified as being in the global economic periphery?

    (A) England   (D) China

    (B) Singapore   (E) Colombia

    (C) France

9. The current Canadian governmental organizational structure is best character-ized as

    (A) theocratic

    (B) confederate (or confederal)

    (C) federal

    (D) unitary

    (E) apartheid

10. In its application to the European Union, which state faced criticisms by some of its opponents for not being "European enough" to gain admission to the EU?

    (A) Italy   (D) England

    (B) Russia   (E) Iceland

    (C) Turkey

11. The political boundary dividing much of India from China is classified as

    (A) cultural

    (B) geometric

    (C) physical (or natural)

    (D) relict

    (E) superimposed

12. The United States and its allies entered the Vietnam conflict in part to prevent Communists from gaining control of the Eurasian periphery, because that control would have led to domination of the world, according to some geopolitical thinkers of the time. This justification is most closely associated with which of the following geographic concepts?

    (A) Rimland theory

    (B) New world order

    (C) World-systems analysis

    (D) Neocolonialism

    (E) North–south gap

13. Egypt and Ethiopia have developed a tense relationship over control of water from the Nile River. This conflict is best classified as which type of boundary dispute?

    (A) Definitional

    (B) Allocational

    (C) Operational

    (D) Locational

    (E) Demarcation

14. Italy fought against Austria to annex Italian-speaking regions controlled by Austria. This is an example of

    (A) Balkanization

    (B) an exclusive economic zone

    (C) devolution

    (D) irredentism

    (E) colonialism

15. All the following were included in the UN Convention on the Law of the Seas EXCEPT:

   (A) Coastal states can claim control of waters up to 12 nautical miles from their shorelines.

   (B) Coastal states can claim up to 200 nautical miles from their shorelines in exclusive economic zones.

   (C) Coastal states sharing waters with other states that are less than 200 nautical miles offshore will split the waters according to the median-line principle.

   (D) Ships have rights of passage through all waterways.

   (E) Straits are internationally operated and owned, not belonging to any one country.

16. The state borders drawn by the U.S. government over what used to be Native American lands are examples of

   (A) subsequent borders   (D) natural borders

   (B) superimposed borders   (E) land-grant borders

   (C) antecedent borders

17. Which of the following countries was not a member of the Warsaw Pact established during the Cold War?

   (A) Poland   (D) France

   (B) East Germany   (E) Romania

   (C) USSR

18. Which of the following is the usual order of the steps in boundary creation between countries?

   (A) Definition, delimitation, demarcation

   (B) Delimitation, definition, demarcation

   (C) Delimitation, demarcation, definition

   (D) Definition, demarcation, delimitation

   (E) Demarcation, definition, delimitation

19. Which of the following is not a centripetal force?

    (A) Religious variation   (D) Common language

    (B) National anthem   (E) Schools

    (C) Common heritage

20. The Berlin Wall today would represent a(n)

    (A) subsequent boundary   (D) natural boundary

    (B) relict boundary   (E) superimposed boundary

    (C) antecedent boundary

Free-Response Review Questions

(A) Explain the *unitary* governmental structure. Give an example of a unitary state, and explain one advantage of having a unitary structure in this example.

(B) Explain the *federal* governmental structure. Give an example of a federal state, and explain one advantage of having a federal structure in this example.

(C) Define *devolution*. Choose a state from either Europe or Asia that has recently experienced devolution, and explain the causes that led the state to devolve.

PART 7 — Pre-Exam Practice Answers

Terms Review Answers

1. Nation
2. Territoriality
3. Delimitation
4. Multinational state
5. Frontier
6. Operational boundary dispute
7. Perforated state
8. Benelux
9. Warsaw Pact
10. New world order
11. Heartland theory
12. Forward capital
13. Centripetal forces
14. Geopolitics
15. Mercantilism
16. Federal structure
17. Median-line principle
18. Subsequent boundary
19. Compact state
20. Ethnonationalism
21. Sovereignty
22. State
23. Territorial morphology
24. Imperialism
25. World-systems analysis

Multiple-Choice Answers

1. **(E)**

   Devolution is the transfer of some power from the central government to local governments, usually done to reduce ethnonationalism and/or regional separatism. (A) is a piece of a country geographically separated from the mother country and surrounded by another state. (B) is a state that exists geographically between two warring or conflicting states, (C) is a very small state like Singapore, and (D) is when legislators redesign electoral districts in a way to give a political party an advantage in an election.

2. **(C)**

   An elongated state has a long, thin shape, like Slovakia. A fragmented state (A) is splintered or geographically separated into several pieces, like Malaysia. In a compact state (B), no point on the state's boundary is significantly further from the geographic center than any other point. A prorupt, or protruded, state (D) has a piece of land jutting off of a core region, like Thailand. A perforated state (E) has a hole punched in it by another state, like South Africa.

3. **(B)**

   An enclave is a region in which a particular group is concentrated in one area and surrounded by people who are not members of that group. Because Region B is ruled by State X's government, the same as Region A, it is not considered an exclave of any other state (A). (C) is a force that helps bind a country together, such as a charismatic leader, a flag, or national anthem. (D) is a region that dominates a state economically or politically, and nothing in the questions suggests that Region B does so. (E) is the area 200 nautical miles off the coast that a state can claim as its exclusive economic zone.

4. **(A)**

   Gerrymandering is the design by legislators of electoral districts to create advantages for a particular party. In linking people registered with a particular party together in one district, gerrymandering often results in very strange-shaped regions. (B) is the adoption of a trait by a population that is impractical for the population. (C) is the transfer of some political power from a central government to regional units; (D) is the breakup of a unified state into various independent subunits; and (E) is an alliance of three or more states for mutual benefit.

5. **(E)**

   The UN Security Council has 15 member states, five of which are permanent, veto-empowered states: China, Russia, United States, France, and

England. Germany was not allowed permanency because of its actions during World War II.

6. **(D)**

A forward capital is a city to which a government moves its capital to achieve a national objective. Malaysia is constructing Putrajaya to replace Kuala Lumpur as its political capital. Putrajaya is being planned from all conceivable aspects to create a city that represents urban innovation.

7. **(B)**

A stateless nation is a unified cultural group without a state to call its own, as in each of the mentioned cases, in which the named group wants its own countries. (A) are states each containing more than one nation; (C) are states each containing only one nation and with political boundaries that match cultural boundaries; (D) are regions that are officially unassigned and unoccupied territories with thinly defined boundaries and undeveloped territoriality; and (E) are countries without coastal access to bodies of water.

8. **(E)**

According to world-systems analysis, the world's states exist in one of three categories: core, periphery, and semiperiphery. A peripheral country is controlled by and serves the countries in the core. Colombia is not in an economic driver's seat, the core; it is not in a state of upward, near-core existence, the semiperiphery; but it is controlled by the core and, as a former colony, serves in a dependent relationship with the core. The other choices are, arguable, in the core or fringes of the semiperiphery near the core.

9. **(C)**

The Canadian government is organized as a constitutional monarchy with a parliamentary democracy that is also a federation of 10 provinces. This means that the central parliament shares power with 10 empowered provincial governments. (A) is a government run by religious leaders; (B) is a structure of a weak central government trumped by more powerful regional governmental units, like provinces; (D) is a structure with a strong central government and weak or nonexistent regional governments; and (E) was the racially segregating governmental structure in South Africa.

10. **(C)**

Turkey, a country that straddles both Europe and Asia, has a large Muslim population and affiliations with the Middle East that have prompted criticism that the country does not share enough of the EU's political-cultural similarities (if they even exist) to be a member-state. For example, Turkey's conflict with Cyprus has been viewed as a human rights issue jeopardizing Turkey's necessary commitment to EU principles.

11. **(C)**

The Himalayan Mountains play a prominent role in creating India's northern border from China. Because this boundary is based on a natural feature, a mountain chain, it is (C). (A) are political boundaries based on cultural aspects, such as language and religion; (B) are geometric straight-line boundaries not based on natural features; (D) are boundaries no longer active in dividing space; and (E) are boundaries applied by outside forces like the United Nations.

12. **(A)**

Spykman's rimland theory is based in the idea that control of the Eurasian periphery would lead to domination of the Eurasian landmass and eventual world domination. Therefore, according to this theory, if lands like Vietnam fell, the rest of the world would have fallen to the Communists in a domino effect. (B) came into existence after the fall of the Soviet Union in the 1990s, after the Vietnam War. (C) argues that states exist in a capitalistic system. (D) argues that the poverty in most newly independent states is linked to the exploitative economic malnourishment engineered by the former colonizing powers. (E) relates to the geographic divide in wealth between countries in the Northern and Southern hemispheres.

13. **(B)**

An allocational dispute centers on fights over resources, such as water, and boundaries. (A) is a dispute over the language in a boundary's creation; (C) is a conflict over how a boundary should function; (D) is a conflict over the location of a boundary; and (E) is a phase in boundary formation involving the marking of a boundary on the territory.

14. **(D)**

Irredentism is an effort by a government to take over (or reclaim) a place or people it believes is naturally part of its state but exists outside its borders. (A) is the breakup or splintering of a unified state into several distinct pieces. (B) is a region of the sea extending 200 nautical miles from a country's coast, unless it overlaps with another's state's zone of control. (C) is the transfer of power from a central authority to local units. (E) is the control by a more powerful country over a place that is less developed.

15. **(E)**

Although straits are open to the passage of ships, they are owned and operated by specific states, which can lead to conflict. The other choices are all a part of stipulations reached in UNCLOS.

16. **(B)**

The borders of western states were drawn by a conquering government to the detriment of the conquered groups. (A) are boundaries drawn after substantial settlement by the people who settled the area, (C) are boundaries created before settlement occurs, (D) are features of the landscape that are used as borders, and (E) is fictitious.

17. **(D)**

The Warsaw Pact was an alliance of communist states founded for mutual protection. (A), (B), (C), and (E) were communist governments during the Cold War and originally signed the treaty. (D) is the only country of the five choices that was neither communist nor a member of the Warsaw Pact.

18. **(A)**

First, definition is the phase in which the exact location of a boundary is legally described and negotiated. Second, delimitation is the step when the boundary's definition is drawn onto a map. Third, demarcation is the marking of a boundary on the landscape with something visible, such as a fence, line, sign, or wall. Demarcation is not always reached because some countries choose not to create a physical border between themselves.

19. **(A)**

Religious differences are a major cause of instability within countries. The other choices tend to unite citizens around common values or beliefs and instill a sense of national unity.

20. **(B)**

The Berlin Wall marks the border between East and West Berlin. Although it was superimposed on the people of Berlin after the start of the Cold War and was a subsequent boundary (being created after substantial settlement), it is considered today to be a relic boundary because it no long functions as a border.

Free-Response Answers

The following is a list of suggested main points for each part of the question.

Part A

- A unitary state has a strong central government, where most governmental power is concentrated for the entire state.

- Sometimes the regional governments are weak and serve only as administrative units of the central government.

- Usually, the regional governments do not have guaranteed powers.

- The following is a list of some acceptable examples of unitary states: New Zealand, France, Zimbabwe, Namibia, Norway, Denmark, and Sweden. England is often used as an example of a unitary state, but with recent developments in Wales and Scotland, it is devolving into a decentralized unitary state.

- The most obvious advantage of having a unitary state is greater unity resulting from one national body representing the people. Often unitary states are smaller, more homogenous states; however, a multinational state may opt for a unitary organization so that no ethnonational region becomes empowered enough to break away. Although a state facing strong ethnonationalistic tension may play a dangerous game in not empowering its regions with more autonomy, minority nations are often not well represented in unitary governments because minority groups may feel even more angered and desirous of secession.

Part B

- A federal state has a government in which powers are divided equally between a central national government and regional governments, usually states or provinces.

- The division of power is guaranteed.

- Examples of federal states include the United States, Nigeria, Switzerland, and Australia.

- One advantage of a federal state is usually seen in a multinational state in which national regions are empowered by a sense of autonomy and power over their destinies, rather than dominated by a central government without adequate representation. A federal state can help bind diverse states by empowering regions with a sense of self-definition and bring government closer to the people. Of course, this can backfire when the devolved power fuels the fires of secession, as seen in the dissolution of the Soviet Union.

Part C

- Devolution is the process of transferring some power from a central government to regional or local governments.

- Devolution often occurs in unitary states with regions that desire greater autonomy and self-definition. England is a classic example of a unitary state that devolved powers to the Scottish people, who wanted their own parliament.

- Some strong examples include the USSR, Yugoslavia, and England. Students must include reasons for devolution; in each of these cases, devolution was highly related to ethnonationalism and multinationalism.

Chapter 6

Agricultural and Rural Land Use

Introduction

Like many teenagers in the United States, you may start your day by pouring cereal from a box or popping frozen waffles into the toaster or microwave. Imagine waking up and having to roam for most of the day to hunt for your food. Before the domestication of plants, humans were primarily nomadic **hunters and gatherers**, unable to settle in one place for too long before they had to move on to new food resources. Today, farms provide humans with the ability to stay in one place and build cities. In fact, fewer than 250,000 people in the world are hunters and gatherers. Instead, most people on the earth practice **agriculture**, the process of growing plants or raising of animals to produce food for sustenance or sale at the marketplace.

Despite the widespread adoption of agriculture, the farming practices used in more-developed countries are substantially different from those used in less-developed countries. Most people in Asia are farmers who can grow only enough food to feed their own families, a type of farming called **subsistence farming**. In more-developed countries like the United States, **commercial farming** predominates, with farms producing food to be sold in groceries and markets, not just to be eaten by the farmers themselves. Worldwide, commercial farming is increasing as subsistence farms are being incorporated into the global farming market.

Key Questions

- *Where did agriculture originate? How and where did it spread?*

- *What are the characteristics of the world's agriculture regions? How do these regions function?*

- *How has agricultural change affected the environment and people's quality of life?*

- *How does diet, energy use, and varying agrarian technology relate to agriculture's origination?*

- *What are different types of extensive and intensive agricultural practices? What are settlement patterns and landscapes related to each agriculture type?*

- ***What are land survey systems, environmental conditions, and cultural values linked to each agriculture type?***

- ***Why do different agricultural practices exist where they do?***

- ***What is the von Thünen model?***

- ***What is the status of food supplies throughout the world? Can humans increase the food supply and reduce starvation and malnourishment?***

PART 1 Development and Diffusion of Agriculture

Origin of Agriculture

How did humans make the leap from being hunters and gatherers to stationary farmers? Geographers generally believe that it was an evolution of knowledge that occurred over thousands of years, in various places, as humans constantly touched and handled plants while gathering their food. Geographers believe that agricultural innovation occurred in and diffused from multiple hearths, or places of origin. According to Carl Sauer, humans first learned how to grow plants through a process of simply cutting off a stem of another plant or by dividing up roots of a plant, a practice known as **vegetative planting**.

Geo Factoid

Women are widely believed to be responsible for discovering vegetative planting because of their typical sociological position as gatherers and medicinal healers.

Later, humans made the leap to **seed agriculture**, which is farming through planting seeds rather than simply planting part of the parent plant. Seed agriculture leads to higher crop yields because there are so many seeds.

Agricultural Hearths

Carl Sauer's theory of a vegetative hearth argues that vegetative farming knowledge first originated in Southeast Asia, where the climate and terrain would have supported the growth of root plants that are easily divided, such as the taro, yam, banana, and palm. From the hearth, it diffused north and east to China and to Japan, and then west toward Southwest Asia, Africa, and the Mediterranean region.

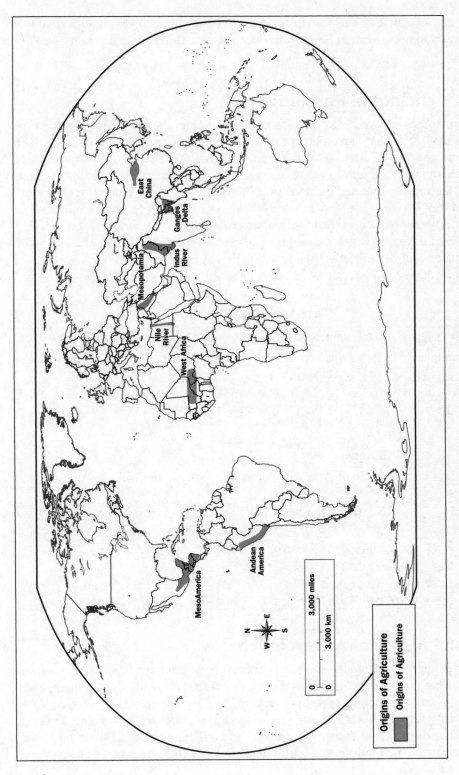

Figure 6.1. Possible cultural and agricultural hearths

Other early vegetative hearths are believed to have emerged through independent innovation in northwestern South America, near the Andes Mountains, and in West Africa.

First Agricultural Revolution

Sometimes referred to as the Neolithic Revolution, the **first agricultural revolution** saw the human development of seed agriculture and the use of animals in the farming process just 12,000 years ago. The growth of seed crops like wheat and rice, and the use of animals such as goats and sheep, replaced the nomadic hunting-and-gathering life that had existed since humanity was born. Human groups were able to stay in one place, grow their populations, and start to build communities. The ability to produce more food without roaming for it increased the carrying capacity of the earth, which charted the path toward the development of civilization. Like the advent of vegetative planting, the first agricultural revolution is believed to have occurred independently in several hearths.

Seed Agricultural Hearths

Hearth	Diffusion Route	Crop Innovation
Western India	To Southwest Asia	Wheat and barley
Southwest Asia (near Tigris and Euphrates rivers)	To Europe (first in Mediterranean regions like Greece and then north through Danube River); North Africa; and to northwestern India and Indus River area	Integrated seed agriculture with domestication of herd animals such as sheep, cattle, and goats, which helped in the farming process
Northern China	To South Asia and Southeast Asia	Millet (a small yellow grain)
Ethiopia	Remained isolated in Ethiopia	Millet (or rather an even smaller millet-like grain known as teff)
Southern Mexico	Throughout Western Hemisphere	Squash and corn
Northern Peru	Throughout Western Hemisphere	Squash, cotton, beans

Second Agricultural Revolution

After the fall of Rome around 500 CE, farming grew into a feudal village structure. During the Middle Ages most farmers worked their lands to feed themselves and their families in an **open-lot system**, one in which there was one large plot of community farmland that all villagers worked to produce a crop to eat. However, as capitalism grew, feudalism diminished and villages enclosed their farmland. This **enclosure movement** gave individual farmers their own plots of farmland, marking a major shift in agriculture. Geographers still debate where and when the second agricultural revolution began, although nearly all agree its most influential phase coincided with the Industrial Revolution in 17th- and 18th-century England and western Europe.

The growing industrial economy and the decline of feudal villages in the 1600s and 1700s caused massive urban migration, as former farmers moved into cities in England and western Europe for work. This caused a great jump in the demand for food from farms to be shipped into cities for the workers.

With this growth in demand came new innovations in farming and transportation technology that dramatically increased crop and livestock yields. New agrarian (farming) technology was invented, such as a better collar for oxen and even the use of the horse instead of the ox on the farm. New fertilizers, field drainage and irrigation systems, and storage systems were invented, all working to help increase farm outputs. Higher farm outputs also worked to encourage the population boom that accompanied the Industrial Revolution.

PART 2 — Major Agricultural Production Regions

Subsistence Agriculture

While commercial agriculture has become the dominant agricultural system in core countries, subsistence agriculture remains widely practiced in less-developed, peripheral countries. Subsistence agriculture is divided into three types: shifting cultivation, intensive subsistence agriculture, and pastoralism.

Shifting Cultivation

In **shifting cultivation**, farmers rotate the fields they cultivate to allow the soil to replenish its nutrients, rather than farming the same plot of land over and over. Shifting cultivation is different from crop rotation, in which the farmer changes the crop type, not the plot of land, to keep the soil healthy. Farming the same type of crop repeatedly on the same plot of land leaches the soil of nutrients needed for healthy crops.

Shifting cultivation is often found in the tropical zones, especially rain forest regions in Africa, the Amazon River basin in South America, and throughout Southeast Asia, because the topsoil is thin in these regions, making it necessary to change the plot of land frequently to grow healthy crops. The primary cause of such poor soil quality is the heavy tropical rains that wash away soil nutrients.

The common way that farmers in tropical regions prepare a new plot of land for farming is through **slash-and-burn agriculture**, in which the land is cleared by cutting (or slashing) the existing plants on the land and then burning the rest to create a cleared plot of new farmland, which is called **swidden**. As a subsistence agricultural form, slash-and-burn agriculture (sometimes called swidden agriculture) is not dependent on advanced technology, only on human labor and the presence of extensive acreage, because plots are frequently abandoned once the soil quality becomes poor and new land must be made swidden for a new crop. Often swidden farmers mix various seeds on the same plot of farmland, a practice known as **intertillage**. Intertillage helps grow food for a balanced diet and reduces the risk of crop failure.

The slash-and-burn method has caused environmental problems in some areas. Because of rising population pressures, farmers need to produce more food for more people on less land. Many swidden agriculturists are being forced to reduce the time the farmed land lies fallow, the period the land is not used to produce a crop. When land is repeatedly farmed and not allowed to recuperate, the soils are damaged and never fully regain their nutrients.

Because shifting cultivators use so much land in their farming process (nearly 25 percent of the earth's land) and cannot produce large amounts of food for growing populations, many shifting farmers are switching to more expedient forms of farming that allow them to remain in one place and produce more crops. Shifting cultivation is being replaced by more lucrative farming practices, like cattle ranching, logging, and production of cash crops to sell in the global marketplace. Instead of the rotating, regenerative methods of shifting cultivation, more destructive forms are being used, such as permanent clearing of the rain forests by commercial farming companies.

Intensive Subsistence Agriculture

Shifting cultivation is a form of **extensive subsistence agriculture**, using a large amount of land to cultivate food for the farmer's family to eat. Another category of agriculture is **intensive subsistence agriculture**, in which farmers cultivate small amounts of land very efficiently to produce food for their families. Remember, the intent of subsistence farming is *not* farming surpluses for sale but producing just enough food for the farming family to survive.

Whereas extensive subsistence agriculture is intended for low population densities with extensive amounts of available land, intensive subsistence agriculture is usually found in regions that are highly populated. It is widely practiced in areas where agricultural density is high, particularly China, India, and Southeast Asia. Intensive subsistence farmers make the most use of their small plots of land to feed their families, often showing ingenuity in their techniques, such as the terrace-farming "pyramids" often seen in the Southeast Asian farming landscapes.

Rice is the dominant intensive subsistence agriculture crop in areas such as South China, India, Southeast Asia, and Bangladesh, where summer rainfall is abundant. In areas with winters too cold for rice, grains like wheat, corn, and millet are grown

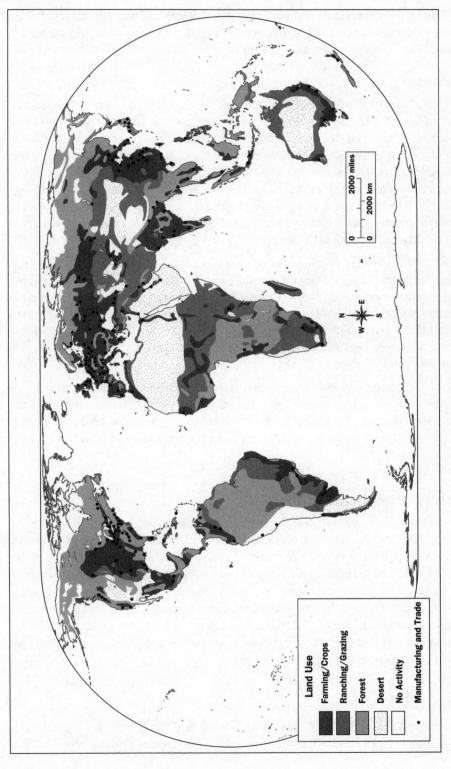

Figure 6.2. Global land use patterns

on intensive subsistence farms. Many intensive subsistence farmers practice **double cropping**, planting and harvesting a crop on a field more than once a year. An example of double cropping is growing corn in one season and wheat in another.

Pastoralism

Another form of subsistence agriculture is **pastoralism**, the breeding and herding of animals to produce food, shelter, and clothing for survival. Pastoralism is usually practiced in climates with very limited, if any, arable land, such as grasslands, deserts, and steppes. Sometimes pastoralism can be sedentary, when the pastoralists live in one place and herd their animals in nearby pastures; or it can be nomadic, when the pastoralists travel with their herds and do not settle in one place for very long. Often involving the herding of cattle, sheep, camels, or goats, pastoralism is most practiced in arid climates in North Africa, central and southern Africa, the Middle East, and Central Asia.

Contrary to popular belief, nomadic pastoralists usually do not wander aimlessly across the landscape. They most often practice **transhumance**, the movement of animal herds to cooler highland areas in the summer to warmer, lowland areas in the winter. Pastoralists usually trade animals with local farmers for food and supplies. Sometimes members of the traveling group plant some crops for use in that location before moving on. However, pastoralists depend on trading their animals for their survival.

Like other forms of subsistence agriculture, pastoralism is declining worldwide as governments work to use dry lands for other purposes, like oil drilling in the Middle East. Pastoral nomads are being confined to less and less land and encouraged to abandon their nomadic lifestyle and incorporate themselves into the global farming economy.

Mediterranean Agriculture

Mediterranean agriculture is primarily associated with the region near the Mediterranean Sea and places with climates that have hot, dry summers and mild, wet winters. California, Chile, southern South Africa, and South Australia are places where Mediterranean agriculture is found. Mediterranean farming involves wheat, barley, vine and tree crops, and grazing for sheep and goats. Olives, grapes, and figs are staple tree crops on Mediterranean farms. It can be either extensive or intensive, depending on the crop. While wheat is extensively farmed, olives are intensively farmed. Mediterranean farming can be either subsistence or commercial, depending on where it is practiced.

Commercial Farming

Commercial farming is different from subsistence farming in that commercial farmers produce crops to sell in the marketplace. Commercial farming types include mixed crop and livestock farming, ranching, dairying, and large-scale grain production. Plantation farming is a form of commercial farming, but it is practiced mostly in less-developed countries.

Mixed Crop and Livestock Farming

Mixed crop and livestock farming involves both growing crops and raising animals. Most of the crops grown on mixed farms are used to feed the farm's animals, which in turn provide manure fertilizer as well as goods for sale, such as eggs. Most of a mixed farm's income comes from sale of its animal products. Further, mixed farms reduce a farmer's complete dependence on seasonal harvests because the animal products are not as dependent on the season as the crops are.

Mixed farming exists widely throughout Europe and eastern North America, usually near large, urban areas where ample land is not available for more extensive practices. Most mixed farms practice crop rotation in which the field is subdivided into various regions, each region growing a different seed and rotating over time. Crop rotation allows the nutrients of the soil to replenish, as different seeds leach different nutrients from the soil.

Ranching

Ranching is commercial grazing, or the raising of animals on a plot of land on which they graze. It is usually extensive, requiring large amounts of land. Because meat and wool are products that are highly demanded, cattle and sheep are the most common animals on ranches. Ranching is practiced in areas where the climate is too dry to support crops, but it is declining in importance. It is most practiced in the western United States, Argentina, southern Brazil, and Uruguay. Ranching is rare in Europe, except for Spain and Portugal. Many U.S. ranches are being converted into "fattening" farms on which fixed-lot cattle are fattened before being slaughtered.

Ranching is quite common also in the tropical deciduous forest regions on the west coast of Latin America and northern Mexico. In some of these areas, such as in western Brazil, it is actually too wet to grow crops. The decline of ranching is partially caused by low grain prices and partially by a system of meat quality standards in the United States that value fat meat over lean. Latin American beef is grass fed, lean, and tough.

Dairying

Dairying is the growth of milk-based products for the marketplace. Dairy farms closest to the marketplace usually produce the most perishable fluid milk products, while those farther away produce goods like cheese and butter. It is the most economically productive type of commercial agriculture practiced near cities in northeastern United States, southeastern Canada, and northwestern Europe. Farms are usually very small and capital intensive. **Capital-intensive farms** use much machinery in the farming process, whereas **labor-intensive farms** use much human labor.

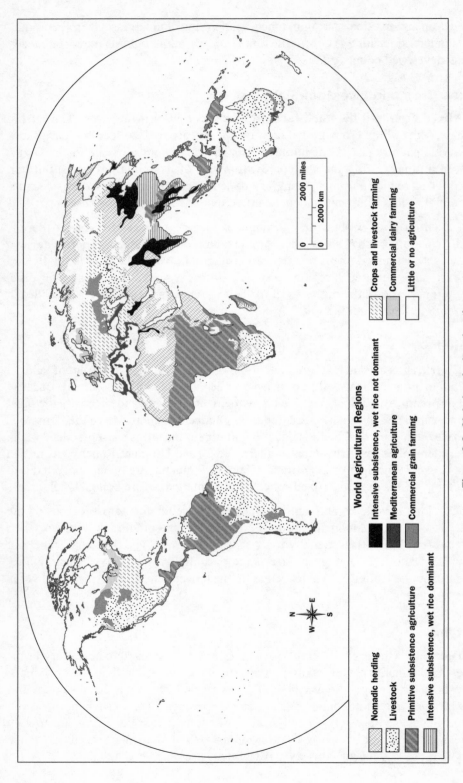

Figure 6.3. Global agricultural regions

The **milkshed** is the zone around the city's center in which milk can be produced and shipped to the marketplace without spoiling. The growth in transportation technology, such as refrigerated trucks and improved road networks, has enabled dairy farmers to locate farther from the city's center, thus increasing the area of the milkshed. In fact, improved technology and feeding systems have led to increases in the amount of milk produced per cow.

Large-Scale Grain Production

Wheat is the dominant grain on **large-scale grain farms**, where the grains are most often grown to be exported to other places for consumption. Large-scale grain production is most common in Canada, the United States, Argentina, Australia, France, England, and Ukraine (which was once considered the "breadbasket" of Russia), although the United States is the world's largest large-scale grain producer. Wheat is the world's leading export crop and is dominated by U.S. and Canadian farms, which collectively grow more than half of the world's wheat. However, many grain farms produce grain to be consumed not by humans but by the animals humans eat. Much of the land in western Europe devoted to grain farming is simply producing grain for animal feed.

Large-scale grain farms grew during the Industrial Revolution, creating large city-based populations needing wheat and other grains for consumption. Large-scale grain farms are usually highly mechanized, thus capital-intensive, operations.

Several technological innovations precipitated the growth of large-scale grain farming. The McCormick reaper, developed in the 1830s, is a machine that cuts standing grain in the field. The combine machine completes all three processes of reaping, threshing, and cleaning in one machine.

Plantation Farming

Plantation agriculture involves large-scale farming operations, known as plantations or agricultural estates, specializing in the farming of one or two high-demand crops for export, usually to more-developed regions. Plantation agriculture was introduced in tropical and subtropical zones by European colonizers who were seeking to produce crops such as coffee, tea, pineapples, palms, coconuts, rubber, tobacco, sugarcane, and cotton. Cotton was particularly important in the southern United States as an export crop produced on plantations by black Africans who were kidnapped and forced into slavery.

Today plantation agriculture is still largely reflective of global power structures. Most plantations exist in low-latitude regions of Africa, Asia, and Latin America but are owned by companies (or individuals) from more-developed countries. Most plantations exist in a location that has easy coastal access for exporting their crops to be sold in foreign markets. Though modern plantations have integrated advanced technology into their farming practices, plantation agriculture is still labor intensive, requiring the estates to hire large numbers of seasonal workers during harvest times. A form of plantation agriculture remains in the subtropical and tropical United States, where migrant workers are used for labor. Hawaii has its own plantations, but there is a strong growers' union and the products are therefore more expensive.

Rural Land Use and Settlement Patterns

Factors Affecting Decisions on Farm Locations

As usual, geographers apply the "why of where" concept to agriculture in analyzing the locations of various farming activities. Why, for example, is a dairy farm closer to the city marketplace than is a grain farm? The factors affecting farming location decisions are physical, political-cultural, and economic.

Physical Factors

Obviously, the appropriate environment for cultivating varies depending on the type of crop. However, farmers can choose to mold the environment as much as possible to fit the crops they want to harvest by adding irrigation systems, greenhouses, and other aids to farming. Usually, farmers evaluate several physical factors in making such decisions:

- **Soil:** A farmer evaluates the depth, texture, nutrient composition, and acidity of the soil in the field, because different crops require different types of soil composition. Most crops require neutral to slightly acidic soils.

- **Relief:** A farmer looks at the shape of the field, or its relief, which includes its slope and altitude. The degree to which the field is exposed to the sun, for example, is a significant factor in choosing a crop. Usually, flatter lands are best for agriculture because more sloped lands can be difficult to irrigate. Altitude also affects temperatures.

- **Climate:** The most influential physical factors affecting a farmer's crop decisions are usually temperature and rainfall, the two components of climate. Different crops require different amounts of water and temperature.

Political-Cultural Factors

The environment, though a factor, does not play a determining role in all agricultural decisions. Political and cultural factors also influence farming location decisions. For example, certain religious beliefs have affected agricultural decisions: Hinduism holds that it is wrong to kill cattle, and it is taboo in Islamic regions to eat pigs. Moreover, immigrants often carry with them their homelands' farming practices and food preferences, thereby injecting their farming styles into

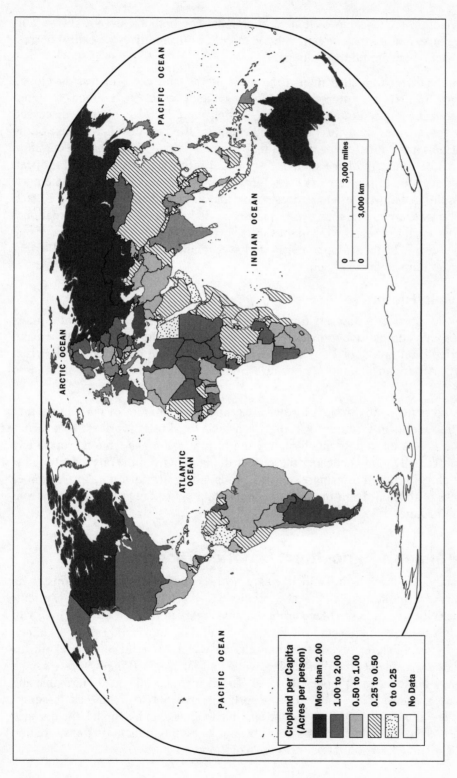

Figure 6.4. Cropland per capita

the agricultural landscapes of their destinations. Food taboos are not always religious. For example, mainstream American culture disapproves of eating horses, even though they are nutritious meat.

Political decisions also impact the agricultural landscape. In less-developed countries, farmers are often financially encouraged by the government to adopt more advanced agricultural technology. During the Green Revolution, discussed later in this chapter, many less-developed countries tried to subsidize the use of the revolution's more-efficient seed types that were more expensive than the common seeds of the time. Another example of political influence exists in the European Union's decision to pay farmers *not* to grow crops in an attempt to eliminate massive surpluses that were driving prices so low that farmers could not survive. In fact, many European countries have agricultural products that are considered national treasures, such as French wine grapes. It is very hard to remove production of one of these crops. In fact, France burns its lower-quality wines instead of allowing farmers to reduce vineyard acreage.

Economic Factors

While subsistence farmers function to feed their families, commercial farmers function in a competitive globalizing economy that has shifting levels of demand for agricultural products. For example, coffee production has dramatically risen in Latin American plantations because of the recent explosion in coffee shop crazes.

Land rent, or the price a farmer must pay for each acre of land, is another economic factor in farming location. Crops sell for different prices, so a farm's location is related to how much money the farmer can make from a crop to pay the rent. Usually, rent is cheaper the farther the land is from the city's center, thus influencing farmers requiring extensive lands (for grain farming, for example) to locate farther out from the city's center to take advantage of the cheaper rent per unit of land.

Von Thünen's Agricultural Location Theory

Johann Heinrich von Thünen was a 19th-century German economist who formulated a model explaining and predicting where and why various agricultural activities would take place around a city's marketplace. In other words, **von Thünen's model** explains and predicts agricultural land use patterns. Von Thünen began by establishing several assumptions on which to build his model. In his model, there is one central marketplace where all farmers sell their products in an attempt to make the most money they can. The farmland is all equally farmable and productive, and only one mode of transportation is available. With these assumptions, von Thünen allowed for only one variable to change in his model: the distance a farm was located from the city's market was a determining factor in transportation costs. The model's resulting patterns are as follows:

- The central marketplace is surrounded by agricultural activity zones that are in concentric rings, each ring representing a different type of agricultural land use.

- Moving outward from the city's central marketplace, the farming activities changed from intensive to more extensive.

Von Thünen's land use patterns can be explained through land rent and transportation costs. Land closest to the city's marketplace is more expensive per unit than is land father away from the city's center. Therefore, a grain farmer, who needs lots of land for his or her extensive farming operation, is going to purchase a farm farther from the city's marketplace because land is less expensive farther out. However, a milk producer is likely to buy land closer to the city's center because he or she does not need the extensive land a grain farmer needs to produce the same profit. Additionally, milk spoils quickly, so the dairy farm must be closer to the marketplace so the farmer can quickly transport milk the to the marketplace for sale before it spoils. Grazing is often farthest outside the city's marketplace in the ring with the lowest land rent because grazing requires so much land and makes the least amount of money per unit of land.

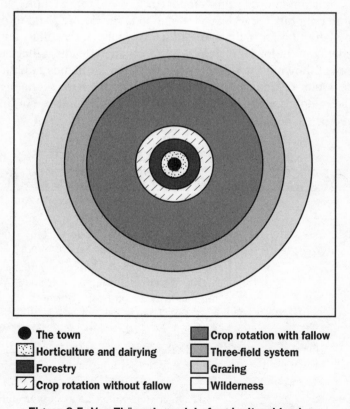

Figure 6.5. Von Thünen's model of agricultural land use

Usefulness of the von Thünen Model

Von Thünen's model is useful in comparing real situations to his theoretical farming situation—one that is restricted to only one variable, transportation costs. In the real world, agricultural land use patterns depend on more than one variable. Von Thünen knew his work was based on his theoretical assumptions, so he introduced some variations, such as the existence of a river running through the city and more than one market. Also, he played with the assumption of all soil quality being equal in productivity and introduced the idea of different areas of land having higher-quality soil than others. Overall, the model further illuminates the influence of distance as a factor in human location decisions. Farming decisions, like so many other spatial patterns, relate to distance. Geographers analyze farming land uses in particular areas and compare them to von Thünen's hypothetical situation as a way of explaining what they see and predicting future land use patterns.

Settlement Patterns in Villages

The definition of the term *village*, including its size, may vary according to the culture using it. However, historically the shape of a village's spatial layout has related to its function and its environment. In Europe, for example, villages were often clustered on a hillside to leave the flatlands for farming and to offer people protection by being on an incline. Additionally, many early villages were walled to keep invaders out. In lowland areas with rivers and streams, villages were often linear in shape, following the water source, with the farmlands radiating from the linear village. Other villages in Europe, Asia, and Africa were round in shape, with a space in the middle for the cattle. Many villages were built according to a grid plan, with geometric boundaries.

Housing Building Materials

Material	Regions Commonly Found
Wood	Eurasia, U.S. Pacific Coast, North America, Australia, Brazil and Chile
Stone	Europe, Egypt, India, western China, Yucatan, Mexico, South-Central Africa, Middle East
Grass and brush	Low-latitude regions: African savanna, East African highlands, upland South Africa, South American highlands, Amazon Basin; northern Australia
Poles and sticks (wattle)	Africa, Southeast Asia, West Africa, Amazon Basin in South America
Sun-dried brick (more traditional; note that brick is often used where wood is not as available)	Middle East, Middle and South America, northern China, African savanna, and North Africa
Oven-baked brick	Modern, contemporary areas in more-developed countries

PART 4 · Modern Commercial Agriculture

Third Agricultural Revolution

Beginning in the late 1800s, the **third agricultural revolution** began in North America and saw the globalization of industrialized agriculture and new technologies that increased the food supply. Whereas the first agricultural revolution ushered in the growth of stationary plant and animal domestication and the second agricultural revolution saw new farming and storage capabilities increase food supplies to meet and facilitate a growing and industrializing population, the third agricultural revolution distributed mechanized farming technology and chemical fertilizers on a global level. Importantly, during the third agricultural revolution, farming and food processing were completed at different sites.

Industrialization of the Farming Process

With the advent of the third agricultural revolution, it became more common for commercial farmers to harvest their crops and ship them off to food-processing sites to be packaged for marketing and distribution. Like a factory system in which different parts of the production process are completed by different departments before the finished product hits the market for sale, food production became increasingly "industrialized" with the start of the third agricultural revolution. In the 1700s, the local milk farmer produced, processed, bottled, and shipped the milk to the marketplace for sale. By the 1900s, the milk production process had evolved as part of the third agricultural revolution into an industrialized, agricultural process.

Purity Dairies in Nashville, Tennessee, provides a strong example of this evolution in agriculture. Today this large agricultural corporation subcontracts with local farms to buy unprocessed milk that is shipped to the Purity Dairies factory in Nashville, near the market. At the city-based factory, the milk is processed, packaged, and put on trucks for distribution within the milkshed. The milk farm itself is only one component in this multilayered agricultural process.

Agribusiness System

The commercialization and industrialization of the food production process has led to the development of a modern farming concept called **agribusiness**, the system of food production involving everything from the development of seeds to the marketing and sale of food products at the market. Agribusiness is the combination of the various pieces of the food production industry, including the farms, processing plants, packagers, fertilizer laboratories, distributors, and advertising agencies. Although the percentage of farmers in the U.S. workforce has markedly declined, the number of workers involved in some way in agribusiness shows that

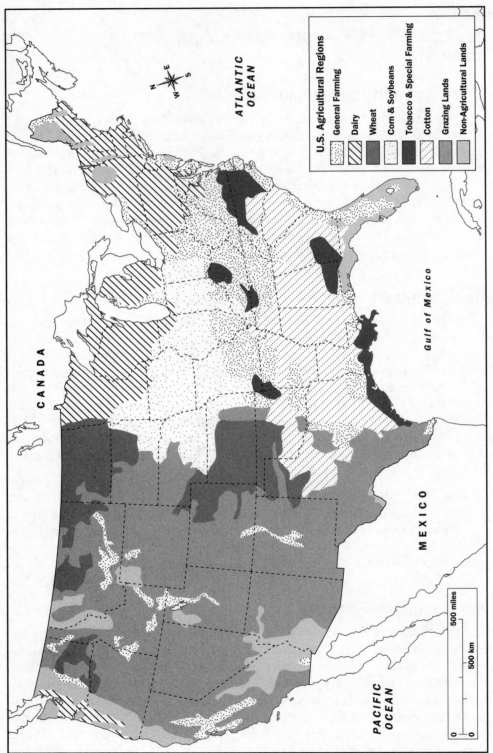

Figure 6.6. U.S. agricultural regions

food production is still an integral part of the U.S. and global economy. Even the graphic designer drawing the images for a child's lunchbox is part of the increasingly complex agribusiness system.

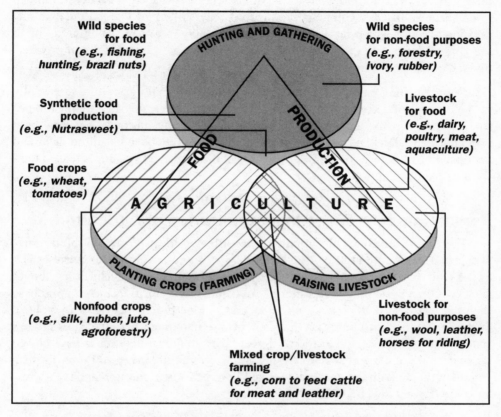

Figure 6.7. The relationship between food production and agriculture

Globalization of the Farming Process

The colonial and imperial campaigns of the 18th and 19th centuries built a system between the core and peripheral regions in the world. European colonizers took over lands in peripheral regions like Africa, South America, and Asia. The Europeans used these colonies to supply their people with raw goods. By the late 1800s and 1900s, the economies of the colonized countries were entrenched in a master-dependent relationship with the colonizers. Even after gaining political independence, former colonies essentially continued to survive by providing crops for export to more-developed countries that were once their imperial masters. This neocolonial, or postcolonial, dependent relationship has fueled the globalization of the farming process.

Food sold in grocery stores throughout more-developed countries is often grown in peripheral less-developed regions of the world that ship food to factories for processing and to markets in the more-developed world. Even flowers in your local grocery are often flown in from commercial gardens, called **truck farms**, in tropical zones. Just as a computer production process often involves an international division of labor—with production in Asia, assembly in Europe, and marketing in the United States—the farming process has become a "food production process" divided on an international level into an "agribusiness system."

Truck farming can also refer to intensive commercial agriculture, especially in the context of a core country. Share-based organic farming is a major type of truck farming in the United States and Europe. Organic farms often grow both vegetables and chickens, with the chickens used to produce eggs and to clear and fertilize plots. Pigs are sometimes raised to eat plants that are for some reason unfit for human consumption.

Human Impacts of the Industrialization of Agriculture

The industrialization of agriculture has affected local farmers in both more- and less-developed countries. Local farmers in more-developed countries, such as the United States, have been forced to integrate into the agribusiness system to survive. Often agriculture corporations subcontract with local farmers to purchase their harvests and then process, package, and sell the produce at the marketplace; or the corporation will purchase the local farm to integrate it into the corporation's food production process. Most local flower farms in the United States have closed down because of the globalization of industrial agriculture; the local flower farmers cannot compete with the corporate-owned flower farms in foreign lands that grow and ship flowers to U.S. groceries.

In 1920, about one in three U.S. citizens lived on farms. By 1978, only one in 28 U.S. citizens lived on a farm (Knox and Marsten).

Many farmers in less-developed countries have been forced to sell their lands to foreign corporations to survive. Foreign corporations often come into these poorer countries and purchase land to grow cash crops for export, such as coffee and rubber. A problem arises from this when the farms become totally export oriented and do not produce food for consumption in their local regions. While corporations from richer countries often own the large farms in poorer countries, they do provide local people with income sources. Yet much of the profits harvested on these corporate farms are channeled directly back to their corporations' already-wealthier countries. Often, these profits are not reinvested in infrastructural growth in these poorer countries in which the export-driven farms are located. Additionally, the communities associated with subsistence farming are changed because the farming process becomes profit driven and commercialized.

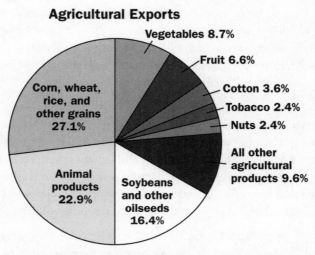

Agricultural Exports

Figure 6.8. U.S. agricultural exports

Green Revolution

An outgrowth of the third agricultural revolution, an effort known as the **Green Revolution**, began in the 1940s and developed new strains of hybrid seeds and fertilizers that dramatically increased the crop output possible on every farm. The Green Revolution began with agricultural experiments that were funded by U.S. charities to find ways of improving Mexico's wheat grain production capabilities to reduce hunger in that region. Scientists soon found new hybrid strains of wheat, maize, and rice that were higher yielding, meaning they were seeds capable of producing more food at a faster pace. Scientists also developed new fertilizers and pesticides to support the higher-yielding Green Revolution seeds because the new seeds required nitrogen-enriching fertilizers and increased protection from diseases and pest infestations. Green Revolution scientist Norman Borlaug won a Nobel Peace Prize in the 1970s for his work to increase world peace through spreading hunger-reducing technology to poorer regions of the world.

The "miracle" of the Green Revolution was in its global diffusion of higher-yielding varieties of wheat, rice, and maize crops. Globally, grain production increased by 45 percent between 1945 and 1990. Asia was able to increase its rice production by 66 percent by 1985, and India was able to supply its own wheat and rice by the 1980s. Hunger and famine were reduced, but not eliminated, through the diffusion of Green Revolution technology. Farmers were simply able to grow more food per unit area of farmland at a faster pace.

The diffusion of Green Revolution technologies has its downside, too. The technologies have reduced the amount of human labor needed on the farm in some areas. But the higher-yielding crop strains are often more prone to viruses and pest infestations, leading to higher levels of crop failure in some areas. Many of the higher-yielding Green Revolution crops, such as rice and wheat, are not farmable in dryer African regions, where millet and sorghum are grown. Additionally, research in more African-appropriate crops has not kept pace. Less than 5 percent of African farmers use Green Revolution seeds.

Some analysts argue that the Green Revolution has increased economic inequality in peripheral countries. Local farmers in peripheral countries often have a difficult time purchasing the more-expensive Green Revolution seeds and technologies, often driving them out of the market and causing them economic ruin. Mechanized farming also requires expensive fuels to power farm machines which also increases pollution and fossil fuel consumption. In some of these countries, governments have subsidized, or helped pay for, the use of Green Revolution technology.

Environmentally, Green Revolution pesticides have arguably caused pollution and soil contamination problems because they drain through the ecosystems in which they are used. Workers frequently exposed to these chemicals have suffered health problems from poisoning. Furthermore, some argue Green Revolution crops often require more watering, causing water resources to be strained. Interestingly, Green Revolution seeds are being adopted so widely that the genetic diversity in seeds is rapidly reducing, with local strains being phased out. This genetic uniformity places the food supply at an increased vulnerability to diseases and pest infestations similar to the problem faced with the overuse of antibiotics to which bacteria are adapting and becoming resistant.

Biotechnology

Agricultural **biotechnology** is using living organisms to produce or change plant or animal products. **Genetic modification** is a form of biotechnology that uses scientific manipulation of crop and animal products to improve agricultural productivity and products. Reorganizing plant and animal DNA as well as tissue culturing are two examples of genetic modification processes in agricultural biotechnology. Recent innovations in biotechnology have led to plant and animal cloning as well as "superplants" that grow at much faster rates, even in nutrient-poor soils, and already have pesticides and fertilizers integrated into their DNA. Scientists have created some crops that are drought resistant and others that are not susceptible to plant diseases. Genetically modified animals are manipulated and cloned to produce larger, better agricultural outputs, such as the "superchicken," which is beefed up

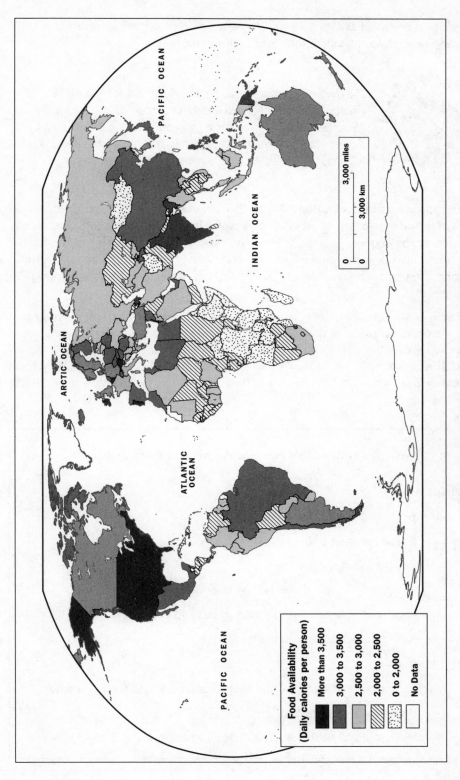

Figure 6.9. Global patterns in food availability

to produce more meat at a faster rate. This extension of scientific innovation to all crops and animal products is known as the biorevolution.

The United States produces nearly 63 percent of the world's genetically modified crops. Nearly 33 percent of U.S. corn and 55 percent of U.S. cotton come from genetically modified crops. Among other innovations, biotechnological research is designing bananas containing vaccines against the hepatitis disease.

Supporters of biotechnology argue that in addition to increasing food output, it also reduces costs of farming and can help the environment. Genetically modified crops require less of the expensive fertilizers, thereby reducing the environmental pollution caused by the chemicals. Innovations in agricultural biotechnology are seen by many to be the human innovation to growing population pressures.

There is also criticism of agricultural biotechnology. Cloned plants are often more susceptible to crop diseases and reduce genetic diversity, as discussed earlier. Cloned plants, therefore, require more chemical pesticides and herbicides. Similar to criticism of the Green Revolution discussed earlier, many local farmers suffer because they cannot afford to use newly-invented agricultural biotechnology.

Genetically Modified Foods: Benefits and Controversies

Benefits

- **Crops**
  - Enhanced taste and quality
  - Reduced maturation time
  - Increased nutrients, yields, and stress tolerance
  - Improved resistance to disease, pests, and herbicides
  - New products and growing techniques
- **Animals**
  - Increased resistance, productivity, hardiness, and feed efficiency
  - Better yields of meat, eggs, and milk
  - Improved animal health and diagnostic methods

- **Environment**
  - — "Friendly" bioherbicides and bioinsecticides
  - — Conservation of soil, water, and energy
  - — Bioprocessing for forestry products
  - — Better natural waste management
  - — More efficient processing
- **Society**
  - — Increased food security for growing populations

Controversies
- **Safety**
  - — Potential human health impact: allergens, transfer of antibiotic resistance markers, unknown effects
  - — Potential environmental impact: unintended transfer of transgenes through cross pollination, unknown effects on other organisms (e.g., soil microbes), and loss of flora and fauna biodiversity
- **Access and Intellectual Property**
  - — Domination of world food production by a few companies
  - — Increasing dependence on industrialized nations by developing countries
  - — Biopiracy—foreign exploitation of natural resources
- **Ethics**
  - — Violation of intrinsic values of natural organisms
  - — Tampering with nature by mixing genes among species
  - — Objections to consuming animal genes in plants and vice versa
  - — Stress for animal
- **Labeling**
  - — Not mandatory in some countries (e.g., United States)
  - — Mixing genetically modified crops with non-genetically modified crops confounds labeling attempts
- **Society**
  - — New advances may be skewed to interests of rich countries

(Source: U.S. Department of Energy)

Hunger and the Food Supply

The causes of world hunger exist largely in the distribution of food supplies and people's ability to access food supplies, not in humans' ability to grow food. Although biotechnological research in agriculture promises innovations in humans' ability to further master environmental constraints, it is the social and economic structure inherent in inequality that causes food security issues, undernutrition, and famine.

Undernutrition is the lack of sufficient calories or nutrients, whereas **famine** is mass starvation resulting from prolonged undernutrition in a region during a certain period. In some cultures, women have higher rates of undernourishment than do men because of practices such as men eating first, leaving only scraps for the women to eat. Often a civil war, severe drought, or some other "trigger" starts a period of famine. While food is stockpiling and rotting in some more-developed countries, food shortages and periods of famine are occurring in others areas. Most, but not all, people in more-developed countries have food security, or the ability to access food so that they do not become undernourished.

Nearly 25,000 people in the world die each day because of undernutrition.

The innovative agricultural methods being produced in the biorevolution must be integrated into the agricultural economies of less-developed countries in such a way that people in those countries can afford them and use them to grow more food. Thus, the solution to ending world hunger is believed to exist not just in growing enough food but also in distributing it and empowering people with the *ability* to obtain their needed food and produce **sustainable yields**, or rates of crop production that can be maintained over time.

According to the prominent geographer Ester Boserup, food production methods are derived from human needs. Boserup believed that subsistence farmers want the most leisure time they can have, so they farm in ways that will allow them to feed their families and maximize free time as well. They will change their approach to farming if the population increases and more food is needed. Boserup considered the food supply to be dependent on human approaches. This contrasts with Thomas Malthus's theory of human overpopulation outpacing growth of the food supply. Most evidence shows Boserup's theory is true in a subsistence economy but not in a technologically advanced industrialized society.

Desertification and Soil Erosion

Chemical pollution and loss of biological diversity are not the only harmful consequences of contemporary farming. Because of population pressures, farmers in many regions are trying to grow food at faster rates, often not allowing their soils enough time to recuperate from the last harvest before starting another. Such a practice leads to the negative consequence of **soil erosion**, the loss of the nutrient-rich top layer in soil. Some geographers estimate that nearly 7 percent of the world's rich topsoil is being destroyed each decade.

It takes the earth 100 to 500 years to naturally regenerate half an inch of nutrient topsoil. Soil erosion destroys 55 billion tons of topsoil each year.

Another negative consequence related to human overuse of the earth's land is **desertification,** the loss of habitable land to the expansion of deserts. Though desertification can result from both human and natural causes, humans have contributed to the expansion of the Sahara Desert (and others) because of their overly intense use of the land. The loss of forested areas, or deforestation, is caused by humans chopping down wooded areas at rates so fast that the areas cannot regenerate. Some estimates predict that the rain forest centered on the equator will be completely destroyed in less than a century. To try to save precious land resources, governments and organizations have organized **debt-for-nature swaps**, which forgive international debts owed by developing countries in exchange for these countries protecting valuable, natural land resources from human destruction.

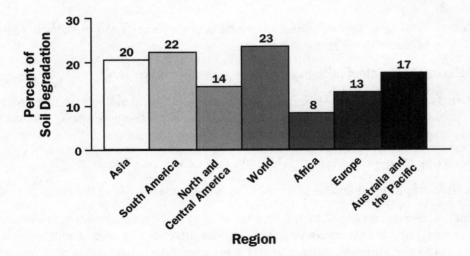

Figure 6.10. Percentage of soil degradation by world region

PART 5	**Chapter Review**

Models Review

Von Thünen Model

Developed by German geographer Johann Heinrich von Thünen, this model explains and predicts agricultural land use patterns in a theoretical state by varying transportation cost. Given the model's assumptions, the pattern that emerges predicts more-intensive rural land uses closer to the marketplace, and more-extensive rural land uses farther from the city's marketplace. These rural land use zones are divided in the model into concentric rings.

Terms Review

Agribusiness—System of food production involving everything from the development of seeds to the marketing and sale of food products at the market.

Agriculture—Growing plants or raising animals to produce food for sustenance or sale at the marketplace.

Biotechnology—Using living organisms to produce or change plant or animal products.

Capital-intensive farm—Farm that makes heavy use of machinery in the farming process.

Commercial farming—Growing food to be sold in groceries and markets, not just to be eaten by the farmers themselves.

Dairying—Growth of milk-based products for the marketplace.

Debt-for-nature swaps—Efforts to preserve natural farmland by forgiving international debts owed by developing countries in exchange for those countries protecting natural land resources from human destruction.

Desertification—Loss of habitable land to the expansion of deserts.

Double cropping—Planting and harvesting a crop on a field more than once a year.

Enclosure movement—As feudalism faded away and capitalism grew, this movement divided the common farm—one the villagers all farmed together—into individual farming plots. Many farmers who did not get private plots moved to the growing cities.

Ester Boserup—Geographer who developed the theory that subsistence farmers want the most leisure time they can have, so they farm in ways that will allow them both to feed their families and to maximize free time. Boserup's theory also posited that farmers will change their approach to farming if the population increases and more food is needed, thus making the food supply dependent on human innovation, rather than humans dependent on the food supply.

Extensive subsistence agriculture—Using a large amount of land to farm food for the farmer's family to eat.

Famine—Mass starvation resulting from prolonged undernutrition in a region during a certain period.

First agricultural revolution—Period marked by the development of seed agriculture and the use of animals in the farming process just 12,000 years ago; also called the Neolithic Revolution.

Genetic modification—Form of biotechnology that uses scientific, genetic manipulation of crop and animal products to improve agricultural productivity and products.

Green Revolution—As an outgrowth of the third agricultural revolution, this effort began in the 1940s and developed new strains of hybrid seeds and fertilizers that dramatically increased the crop output possible from each farm.

Hunters and gatherers—Nomadic people who do not remain stationary but follow herds of wild animals and forage for plants for survival.

Intensive subsistence agriculture—Cultivating a small amount of land very efficiently to produce food for the farmer's family.

Intertillage—Practice of mixing many types of seeds on the same plot of land.

Labor-intensive farm—Farm that uses much human labor.

Land rent—Price a farmer must pay for each acre of land.

Large-scale grain farm—Extensive commercial grain farm where the grain typically is grown to be exported to other places for consumption.

Mediterranean agriculture—Type of farming involving wheat, barley, vine, and tree crops and grazing for sheep and goats; primarily associated with the region near the Mediterranean Sea and places with climates that have hot, dry summers and mild, wet winters.

Milkshed—Zone around the city's center in which milk can be produced and shipped to the marketplace without spoiling.

Mixed crop and livestock farming—Category of agriculture in which farmers both grow crops and raise animals.

Open-lot system—System of agricultural land distribution in which all villagers worked on one large plot of community farmland to produce a crop to eat.

Pastoralism—Breeding and herding of animals to produce food, shelter, and clothing for survival.

Plantation agriculture—Farming that involves large-scale operations, known as plantations or agricultural estates, specializing in the farming of one or two high-demand crops for export, usually to more-developed regions.

Ranching—Raising animals on a plot of land on which they feed or graze.

Seed agriculture—Developed later than vegetative planting, this type of farming involves planting seeds rather than simply planting part of the parent plant.

Shifting cultivation—Form of extensive subsistence agriculture in which farmers rotate the fields they cultivate to allow the soil to replenish its nutrients, rather than farming the same plot of land over and over.

Slash-and-burn agriculture—Common way that subsistence farmers prepare a new plot of land for farming; system in which the land is cleared by cutting (or slashing) the existing plants on the land and then burning the rest to create a cleared plot of new farmland.

Soil erosion—Loss of the nutrient-rich top layer in soil.

Subsistence farming—Growing only enough food to feed the farmer's own families.

Sustainable yield—Rate of crop production that can be maintained over time.

Swidden—Plot of land prepared by subsistence farmers using the slash-and-burn method.

Third agricultural revolution—Period in which agriculture became globalized and industrialized, and new technologies increased the food supply.

Transhumance—Movement of animal herds to cooler highland areas in the summer to warmer lowland areas in the winter.

Truck farm—Commercial flower farm or garden.

Undernutrition—Case of not getting enough calories or nutrients.

Vegetative planting—Process of cultivating by simply cutting off a stem of another plant or by dividing roots of a plant; developed before seed agriculture.

PART 6 Some Suggested Web Resources for Further Exploration

United States Department of Agriculture: http://www.usda.gov/

This site provides federal government statistics and processes related to U.S. farming, including an interesting nutritional evaluation called "My Pyramid."

European Union's Agriculture Commission: http://ec.europa.eu/agriculture/info.htm

This is the official site of the EU's branch in charge of agricultural affairs.

United Nations Food and Agriculture Organization (FAO): http://www.fao.org/

This organization is dedicated to ending world hunger. Its mission statement declares, "Serving both developed and developing countries, FAO acts as a neutral forum where all nations meet as equals to negotiate agreements and debate policy. FAO is also a source of knowledge and information."

World Resources Institute (WRI): http://www.wri.org/

Motivated by its mission "to move human society to live in ways that protect Earth's environment and its capacity to provide for the needs and aspirations of current and future generations," the WRI provides useful statistics and projections related to climate change, resource consumption and abuse, farming practices, and more.

Food First: http://www.foodfirst.org/

A nonprofit organization, Food First works to eliminate the injustices that cause hunger. Its website provides information on the Green Revolution, biotechnology, and genetically modified foods, among other topics. It looks at undernutrition and hunger related to the current distribution of resources and food supplies.

PART 7 Pre-Exam Practice

Terms Review Quiz

Use the Terms Review list or your own memory to determine the extent of your knowledge of key terms and concepts. Remember, the AP exam does not include this kind of exercise, but it is included here as a review tool.

1. _____ Planting and harvesting a crop on a field more than once a year.

2. _____ Common way that subsistence farmers prepare a new plot of land for farming; system in which the land is cleared by cutting the existing plants on the land and then burning the rest to create a cleared plot of new farmland.

3. _____ Cultivating a small amount land very efficiently to produce food for the farmer's family.

4. _____ Type of farming involving wheat, barley, vine, and tree crops and grazing for sheep and goats; primarily associated with climates that have hot, dry summers and mild, wet winters.

5. _____ Growth of milk-based products for the marketplace.

6. _____ Farming that involves large-scale agricultural estates, specializing in farming one or two high-demand crops for export, usually to more-developed regions.

7. _____ System of food production involving everything from the development of seeds to the marketing and sale of food products at the market.

8. _____ As an outgrowth of the third agricultural revolution, this effort began in the 1940s and developed new strains of hybrid seeds and fertilizers that dramatically increased the crop output possible from each farm.

9. _____ Case of not getting enough calories or nutrients.

10. _____ Category of agriculture in which farmers both grow crops and raise animals.

11. _____ As feudalism faded away and capitalism grew, this movement divided the common farm—one that the villagers all farmed together—into individual farming plots.

12. _____ Developed later than vegetative planting, this type of farming involves planting seeds rather than simply planting part of the parent plant.

13. _____ Growing plants or raising animals to produce food for sustenance or sale at the marketplace.

14. _____ Period marked by the development of seed agriculture and the use of animals in the farming process just 12,000 years ago; also called the Neolithic Revolution.

15. _____ Process of cultivating by simply cutting off a stem of another plant or by dividing roots of a plant; developed before seed agriculture.

16. _____ Form of extensive subsistence agriculture in which farmers rotate the fields they cultivate to allow the soil to replenish its nutrients, rather than farming the same plot of land over and over.

17. _____ Nomadic people who do not remain stationary but follow herds of wild animals and forage plants for survival.

18. _____ Using a large amount of land to farm food for the farmer's family to eat.

19. _____ Growing food to be sold in groceries and markets, not just to be eaten by the farmers themselves.

20. _____ Zone around the city's center in which milk can be produced and shipped to the marketplace without spoiling.

21. _____ Farm that makes heavy use of machinery in the farming process.

22. _____ Raising animals on a plot of land on which they feed or graze.

23. _____ Movement of animal herds to cooler highland areas in the summer to warmer lowland areas in the winter.

24. _____ Period in which agriculture became globalized and industrialized, and new technologies increased the food supply.

25. _____ Efforts to preserve natural farmland by forgiving international debts owed by developing countries in exchange for those countries protecting valuable, natural land resources from human destruction.

Multiple-Choice Review Questions

1. Which of the following agricultural practices is most likely to be found in the Tibetan plateau?

    (A) Slash and burn   (D) Pastoralism

    (B) Mediterranean   (E) Plantation

    (C) Truck

2. According to the von Thünen model of rural land use, which of the following agricultural products would most likely be produced farthest from its London marketplace?

    (A) Fruits and vegetables   (D) Wool and hides

    (B) Feed grains   (E) Wheat and flour

    (C) Butter, cheese, and eggs

3. All of the following are associated with the second agricultural revolution EXCEPT

    (A) the Industrial Revolution

    (B) improved food storage capacity

    (C) the invention of barbed wire

    (D) the enclosure movement

    (E) recombinant DNA splicing

4. All of the following are modern states existing in land postulated to be agriculture hearths EXCEPT

    (A) Ethiopia   (D) China

    (B) Iraq   (E) India

    (C) England

5. Which of the following regions produces the least amount of wheat?

    (A) Ukraine   (D) France

    (B) United States   (E) Greece

    (C) Canada

6. The house shown in this picture is most likely located in which of the following regions?

    (A) Southern Africa   (D) Central Africa

    (B) Northeastern Europe   (E) South Asia

    (C) Southeast Asia

7. Beef consumption is at the lowest level in which of the following regions?

    (A) Italy   (D) China

    (B) United States   (E) India

    (C) Romania

8. Which of the following statements would least support an argument criticizing the Green Revolution?

    (A) Many of its initial hybrid crops could not grow in African regions.

    (B) It is making developing countries more dependent on Western technology than before.

(C)   The original intent of the Green Revolution was to increase the profits of agricultural corporations seeking to expand their markets.

(D)   Green Revolution seeds are often more expensive for local farmers in less-developed regions.

(E)   The global diffusion of its crops has threatened the genetic diversity in local agricultural landscapes.

9.   Which of the following is an accurate statement regarding agriculture and the United States economy?

(A)   Agriculture is no longer an important piece of the U.S. economy.

(B)   The number of farms in the United States has decreased in the last 50 years.

(C)   United States food exports have declined steadily since World War II.

(D)   Farming is now an outsourced process in the United States, where nearly all foodstuffs are imported from foreign farms.

(E)   Wheat production in the United States has remained stagnant since the start of the 20th century.

10.   The seasonal movement from highlands to lowland pastures is known as

(A)   slash-and-burn agriculture

(B)   Mediterranean agriculture

(C)   transhumance

(D)   mixed crop and livestock farming

(E)   crop rotation

11.   Which of the following export-oriented cash crops is often grown in formerly European colonial regions?

(A)   Wheat   (D)   Corn

(B)   Rubber   (E)   Millet

(C)   Sorghum

12. All the following are assumptions in the classical von Thünen rural land use model EXCEPT:

    (A) Rural land is equally productive, regardless of its proximity to the central city.

    (B) More-extensive land uses will develop farther from the city than intensive farming practices.

    (C) There is only one marketplace.

    (D) Transportation costs are unrelated to distance.

    (E) The land was flat throughout the rural plane.

13. Geographer Ester Boserup would most likely agree with which of the following statements?

    (A) Population growth will outpace the growth of the food supply.

    (B) Population growth is unrelated to the food supply.

    (C) The food supply is adapted by farmers to meet the changing population.

    (D) Farmers cannot affect the level of the food supply.

    (E) Subsistence farmers exist in isolation rather than in community.

14. Which of the following statements accurately applies to agribusiness?

    I. Agribusiness is associated with the vertical and horizontal integration of the processes involved in the agricultural process.

    II. Agribusiness involves the increasingly global division of the agricultural production process.

    III. Individual farmers do not play a role in agribusiness, only corporate conglomerates.

    IV. Agribusiness is contributing to agricultural industrialization.

    (A) I and II

    (B) I, III, and IV

    (C) II, III, and IV

    (D) I, II, and IV

    (E) I, II, III, and IV

15. A farmer in China is statistically most likely to be a(n)

    (A) extensive subsistence farmer

    (B) nomadic herder

    (C) intensive subsistence farmer

    (D) shifting cultivator

    (E) hunter and gatherer

16. The earliest form of agriculture was

    (A) seed planting   (D) pastoralism

    (B) vegetative planting   (E) the Green Revolution

    (C) agribusiness

17. The use of large amounts of land to grow food to feed only the farmer's family is

    (A) intensive subsistence agriculture

    (B) intensive commercial agriculture

    (C) extensive subsistence agriculture

    (D) extensive commercial agriculture

    (E) ranching

18. The term *swidden* refers to a plot of land formed by what type of agriculture?

    (A) Transhumance   (D) Double cropping

    (B) Truck farming   (E) Slash and burn

    (C) Open-lot system

19. The loss of the nutrient-rich top layer in soil is called

    (A) soil erosion   (D) undernutrition

    (B) swidden   (E) shifting cultivation

    (C) transhumance

20. Biotechnology, or the process of using living organisms to produce or change plant or animal products, is an integral part of which agricultural revolution?

    (A) First agricultural revolution

    (B) Second agricultural revolution

    (C) Third agricultural revolution

    (D) Open-lot system

    (E) Plantation agriculture

Free-Response Review Questions

1. Agriculture has been evolving since its inception some 12,000 years ago.

    (A) Explain the major trends in innovation that characterize the third agricultural revolution.

    (B) Define *agribusiness* and relate it to the third agricultural revolution.

    (C) Explain one positive effect of agribusiness on the individual farmer in the periphery.

    (D) Explain one negative effect of agribusiness on the individual farmer in the periphery.

PART 8

Pre-Exam Practice Answers

Terms Review Answers

1. Double cropping
2. Slash-and-burn agriculture
3. Intensive subsistence agriculture
4. Mediterranean agriculture
5. Dairying
6. Plantation agriculture
7. Agribusiness
8. Green Revolution
9. Undernutrition
10. Mixed crop and livestock farming
11. Enclosure movement
12. Seed agriculture
13. Agriculture
14. First agricultural revolution
15. Vegetative planting
16. Shifting cultivation
17. Hunters and gatherers
18. Extensive subsistence agriculture
19. Commercial farming
20. Milkshed
21. Capital-intensive farm
22. Ranching
23. Transhumance
24. Third agricultural revolution
25. Debt-for-nature swaps

Multiple-Choice Answers

1.   **(D)**

Because of the dryer landscape of the plateau, farming is limited to pastoral activities such as nomadic movements of herders with their animals. (A) is found more in tropical and subtropical zones; (B) obviously, in climates commensurate with the Mediterranean zone; (C) in well-watered tropical zones; and (E) in less-developed regions with climates conducive to cash crop harvests targeted for export.

2.   **(D)**

In von Thünen's model, all land is equally productive. Thus, farming activities requiring the most extensive land use without expensive transportation costs locates farthest from the city's center. Dairying, for example, uses the land intensively and requires expensive trucking to prevent the milk from spoiling, so dairy farms locate close to the city's center. Ranching to produce wool and hides, however, requires extensive amounts of land because the livestock must graze and move about, but it has fewer transportation costs associated with it than a practice such as dairying.

3.   **(E)**

Recombinant DNA splicing is part of the biorevolution during the third agricultural revolution. The other choices were all a part of the wave known as the second agricultural revolution, even (D), which was the closing in of public crops into private properties. This movement caused many people without land to move into the cities to find opportunity in the industrial sector; the enclosure of formerly public crops also led to increased efficiency, related to private property and direct responsibility.

4.   **(C)**

While the other choices are countries located on lands believed to be sites of ancient agriculture hearths, (C) is not believed to be a place where farming first evolved. Rather, farming practices likely originated in southern Europe and diffused northward toward modern-day England.

5.   **(E)**

Greece's Mediterranean climate allows for wheat production but also for farming olives, figs, and other Mediterranean crops that can be highly profitable for the region's farmers, who often do not have extensive lands. Wheat production is dominated particularly by the United States, Canada, and France.

6. **(B)**

    The picture is of a house in Lithuania, a northeastern European state. Notice the wood and stone materials, both of which are common in European homes. Wood, in the form of paneling, is not common in African regions, particularly because of the heat and need for ventilation, not insulation. Thus, the combination of wood and stone indicate a place needing insulation from a cold winter, like Lithuania.

7. **(E)**

    India's cultural taboo against eating beef is related to a Hindu belief that a divine power is vested in the cow. Hence, beef consumption is lowest in India than in the other states listed.

8. **(C)**

    The original intent of the Green Revolution was humanitarian because it was funded by a charitable organization in the United States. Original researchers were sent to Mexico to try to help find a solution to boost Mexican harvests for the benefit of the Mexican people. What developed from their work was a set of technologies that diffused to other less-developed countries as means to boost global food supplies, intentionally in poorer regions. The other arguments are common criticisms of the Green Revolution.

9. **(B)**

    As farming has become increasingly industrialized and corporate, the family farmer in the United States has become incorporated into larger farming aggregates. Thus, the number of family farmers has drastically declined as farms have been merged into corporate-owned operations within the industrialized agribusiness system that now constitutes the U.S. farming landscape. (A) is false because agriculture is still an integral part of the U.S. economy, employing in some facet more than 30 percent of U.S. workers. (C) is false because exports have increased since World War II. (D) is false as many consumed foods are of U.S. origin, especially wheat, meat, and dairy-based products. (E) is false because wheat production dramatically increased with the advent of Green Revolution hybrid seeds and improved farming technologies continually being implemented with the modern biorevolution.

10. **(C)**

    Transhumance is the movement of seasonal nomads and their respective herds from highland to lowland pastures. (A) is subsistence farming that clears land by first slashing the vegetation and then burning it to prepare the soil for planting. (B) is farming wheat, figs, olives, and other crops in Mediterranean zones. (D) is farming that has both animals and crops on the same, stationary farm. (E) is a farming technique that divides the farm into zones and plants varying seeds in each zone to prevent leeching the soil of its nutrients.

11. **(B)**

Rubber was a cash crop focused on by colonizers to aid the colonizers' industrializing populations. It is still grown in former colonies like India, but it has also expanded to other countries such as China. The other choices were not cash-crop exports in former European colonies.

12. **(D)**

At the heart of von Thünen's conclusions is the variation of transportation costs associated with changing distances from the central marketplace. All other factors are held constant in the model, which results in concentric rings according to transportation costs. The remaining choices accurately state assumptions in the model.

13. **(C)**

Boserup looked at subsistence farmers as having direct power over the food supply and responding to population changes by increasing or decreasing their farming efforts to meet food demands. In contrast, Malthus did not empower farmers with the ability to meet food demands made by what he saw was geometrically increasing population rates.

14. **(D)**

The only statement that does not apply is III, because individual farms do play a role in the process. Many individual farms supply foodstuffs to agribusiness corporations, such as an individual beef farm supplying a meat-packing and distributing company with its raw meat. Perhaps (I) was difficult to understand: integration is the combination of pieces into one unit, so agricultural integration involves the coming together of different pieces of the farming process into one corporate-driven system.

15. **(C)**

While it is industrializing, China is still largely a subsistence agricultural economy. Most of its farmers exist on small plots of farmland that they farm intensively, often employing ingenious tactics like pyramids and terraces.

16. **(B)**

Vegetative planting, the process of simply cutting off a stem of another plant or dividing up roots of a plant, developed before seed agriculture (A). (C) is the modern economic system surrounding agriculture, (D) is the raising of animals by moving from place to place, and (E) is the use of scientifically created fertilizers and pesticides to increase crop yields.

17. **(C)**

Subsistence agriculture is the growing of food to feed just your own family. Extensive agriculture uses large amounts of land, as opposed to intensive agriculture, which tries to maximize yields from small amounts of land. (A) is using smaller plots of land; (B) and (D) are commercial, meaning they raise crops for sale, not just private use; and (E) is the raising of animals for sale.

18. **(E)**

Swidden is another name of a field prepared by cutting down existing vegetation and then burning it to enrich the soil; the process is also known as slash-and-burn agriculture. (A) is the movement of animal herds to cooler highland areas in the summer to warmer, lowland areas in the winter. (B) are commercial flower farms and gardens; (C) is a system of agriculture where the land is distributed in one large plot of community farmland that all villagers work; and (D) is growing two crops on the same plot of land in a year.

19. **(A)**

Soil erosion is the process of losing the nutrient-rich topsoil needed to raise crops. (B) is a field produced by slash-and-burn agriculture; (C) is the movement of animal herds to cooler highland areas in the summer and to warmer, lowland areas in the winter; (D) is the condition of having too few calories and nutrients in your diet; and (E) is the practice of rotating fields to allow the soil to replenish its nutrients.

20. **(C)**

Biotechnology is an aspect of the third agricultural revolution that relies on scientific means to improve crop yields. (A) started humans on the path to growing their own food instead of collecting it; (B) used industrial advances to improve agricultural output; (D) is a system of agriculture in which the land is distributed in one large plot of community farmland that all villagers work; and (E) are large-scale farming operations specializing in the farming of one or two high-demand crops for export.

Free-Response Answers

The following is a list of some suggested main points for each part of the question.

Part A

- Beginning in the late 1800s, the third agricultural revolution began in North America and saw the globalization of industrialized agriculture and new technologies that increased the food supply.

- Whereas the first agricultural revolution ushered in the growth of stationary plant and animal domestication, the second agricultural revolution saw new farming and storage capabilities increase food supplies to meet and facilitate a growing, industrializing population. The third agricultural revolution distributed mechanized farming technology and chemical fertilizers on a global level.

- During the third agricultural revolution, farming and food processing were completed at different sites in an increasingly "industrialized," mechanical, more corporate-like structure.

Part B

- Agribusiness is the system of food production involving everything from the development of seeds to the marketing and sale of food products at the market.

- Agribusiness is the combination of all the elements of the food production industry, including farms, processing plants, packagers, fertilizer laboratories, distributors, and advertising agencies.

- Agribusiness, an outgrowth of the third agricultural revolution, is the child of agricultural industrialization and commercialization, processes fueled by the globalization of farming technology and mechanization. In other words, the third agricultural revolution saw the growth and development of new farming technologies and transportation systems that have precipitated the commercialization and industrialization of agribusiness.

Part C

- Possible positive effects of agribusiness on individual farmers in the periphery are diffusion of new farming technology to the area (which is also a double-edged sword that can cause farmers harm if the new technology is too expensive for them and makes them unable to compete), growth and development of the local economy, and possible ties to a global marketplace for their farming products.

Part D

- Possible negative effects of agribusiness on individual farmers in the periphery are being pushed out of the marketplace by large corporate farms that can produce more food with more expensive technology and land; loss of subsistence agricultural community; loss of land to multinational corporations in agribusiness and political dealings; water shortages because of intense irrigation needs of the new, large, corporate farms built in the peripheral countries.

Chapter 7

Industrialization and Economic Development

Introduction

Economic geographers study the locations and reasons for economic patterns in the world's human landscape. They analyze the patterns in economic wealth, poverty, growth, and decline. Inherent in this analysis is the genesis of industrialization, which revolutionized economic interaction and moved human resource consumption to a new level. The human and environmental consequences to industrialization and industrialization's impact on varying development levels are carefully analyzed by geographers, partly through the lens of models and theories attempting to explain and predict economic activities. In their quest to understand the "why of where," geographers search for both explanations and solutions to current economic inequalities.

Geo Factoid

Almost half of the people in the world live on the equivalent of less than $2 a day, and about 20 percent live on less than $1 a day. Meanwhile, people in the 20 richest countries on average earn 37 times more than people in the 20 poorest countries.

Key Questions

- *What is industrialization? What is development?*

- *How do natural resources, culture, politics, and history influence the spatial character of economic activity?*

- *What are the key sectors in the economy?*

- *How do places acquire comparative advantages? Where do they exist?*

- *How do key economic models help explain the world's division between core and peripheral economic regions?*

- *What is economic globalization?*

- *How do space–time compression and the international division of labor affect market orientation and the production process?*

- *What are key patterns in economic growth and decline in North America?*

- *What are the modern patterns of economic inequality, and how do they relate to global economic interdependence?*

- *What are the environmental consequences of industrialization and globalization?*

- *What are the socioeconomic and political ramifications of deindustrialization? How is deindustrialization related to the disaggregation of the production process?*

PART 1 · Key Concepts and the Growth and Diffusion of Industrialization

Economic Classifications

The system of production, consumption, and distribution is called the **economy**. The economy can be divided into different parts to understand its whole. At its most basic core is its **primary sector**, the part of the economy in which activities revolve around getting raw materials from the earth. Farming, fishing, and raw mining are examples of primary economic activities.

Secondary economic activities deal with processing the raw materials acquired through primary activities into finished products of greater value, such as taking raw corn and processing it into baby food. Factories and manufacturing fall into the secondary economic activity category, taking raw materials and transforming them into finished products.

Tertiary economic activities focus on moving, selling, and trading the products made in primary and secondary activities. Tertiary economic activities also involve professional and financial services, such as banks, carpet cleaning businesses, and fast-food restaurants.

A fourth category of economic activity, termed **quaternary economic activity,** involves information creation and transfer. Quaternary economic activities assemble, distribute, and process information; they also manage other business

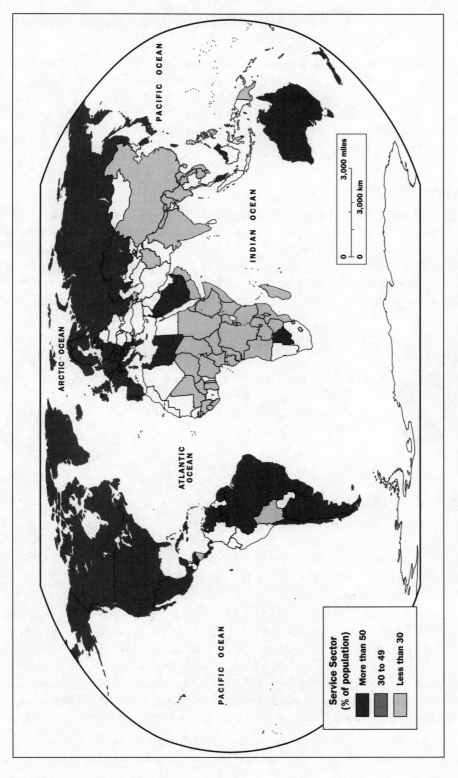

Figure 7.1. Percentage of workers in the service sector throughout the world

operations. University research and investment analysis are examples of quaternary economic activities.

Within the quaternary sector exists a subclassification known as **quinary economic activities**, which involve the highest level of decision making, like that of a legislature or a presidential cabinet. High-level government-targeted research is also included in the quinary subclassification. Finally, it is important to note that some consider both quaternary and quinary activities to be subsets of the tertiary economic sector.

Industrialization

Industrialization is the growth of manufacturing activity in the economy or a region and usually occurs alongside a decrease in the number of primary economic activities within a country. Even before the Industrial Revolution, manufacturing, a secondary economic activity, transpired. From bread making to clothes making, industrial activity was located nearest the urban cores and close to the raw materials needed in the production process. However, these manufacturing-like activities were small and localized, like preindustrial communities in less-developed regions today.

The amount of world trade since 1950 has increased 20-fold, from $320 billion to $6.8 trillion. This increase in the trade of manufactured goods is three times larger than the increase in the rate of the production of those goods.

The Industrial Revolution

The **Industrial Revolution** began in England in the 1760s, when the industrial geography of England changed significantly and later diffused to other parts of western Europe. In that period of rapid socioeconomic change, machines replaced human labor and new sources of inanimate energy were tapped. Coal began as the leading energy source, fueling England's textile-focused industrial explosion.

What most defined England's Industrial Revolution was the rise of assembly-line manufacturing. Although assembly lines existed first on a small scale in homes where people made goods before the revolution, the 1760s saw the growth of large mechanized factories. Because early factories were powered by coal sources, they tended to clump around the coalfields. North-central England's coalfields fostered major industrial cities such as Manchester and Liverpool. The emergence of many factories led to the development of a clear industrial landscape and working-class housing areas.

Along with this industrial growth, England's transportation infrastructure improved to allow for shipping supplies into urban factories. Further, farming

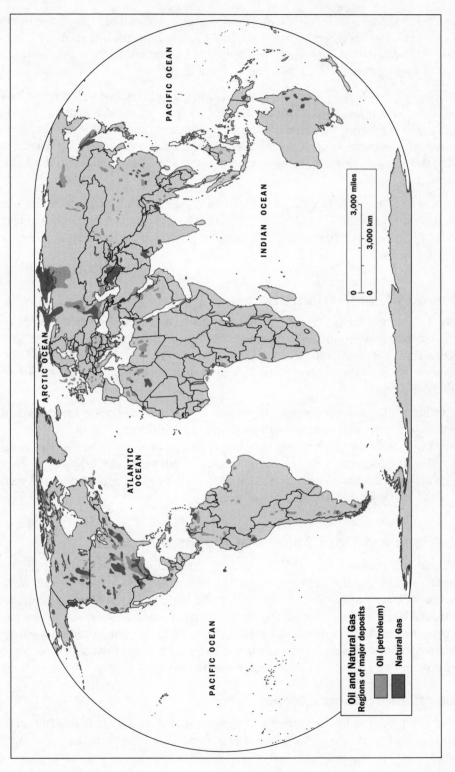

Figure 7.2. Oil and natural gas deposits

became more mechanized with the infusion of greater technology into the agricultural process. One result of industrialization was the **commodification** of labor, with factory owners looking at their human labor as commodities (objects for trade) with price tags per hour, rather than seeing them as people.

While original factory-like labor was conducted in households, the growth of factories first occurred around water sources, such as rivers and lakes. As coal-powered manufacturing increased, factories could move away from water sources that formerly supplied energy through steam and water-mill methods. Factories could locate in coalfields and occupy larger areas of space, eventually building out, rather than up.

By the 1960s, oil replaced coal as the dominant source of industrial energy in the world. Although the United States, Russia, and Venezuela had been the chief sources of oil, the surge in oil demand allowed for the Middle East to take over the market for oil in the 1960s.

Diffusion of Industrialization

By 1825, the technology of the industrialization in England had spread to North America and countries in western Europe like Belgium, Germany, and France. Again, industrialization thrived in places with rich coal deposits, like Ohio and Pennsylvania in the United States, Ukraine in Russia, and the Ruhr region in Germany.

By the 1920s, the production process in the U.S. automobile factories had broken down into differentiated components, with different groups of people performing different tasks to complete the product, a process known as the **Ford production (or Fordist) method**. Fordist factories built out rather than up, meaning that they were built on only one story so that the product could be transported throughout the assembly line without problems.

Weber's Least Cost Theory of Industrial Location

Where will factories locate? What factors affect industrial location? Predicting where factories will grow was the focus of German economist Alfred Weber's work in the early 20th century. Just as von Thünen studied the locations of agricultural activities, **Alfred Weber** studied the locations of industrial activities by setting up a hypothetical state with several assumptions. Weber's model predicted where industries would locate based on the places that would be the lowest cost to them. Appropriately, his model was called **least cost theory.**

Assumptions in Weber's Model

Weber's model is based on the assumptions that the cost of transportation is determined by the weight of the goods being shipped and the distance to the market; the heavier the good and/or the farther the distance, the more expensive it is to ship. He assumed that industries are competitive and aim to minimize their costs and maximize their profits. He also assumed that markets are in fixed locations. Labor, he assumed, exists only in certain places and is not mobile. Like von Thünen, he also assumed that the physical geography (land quality) and political-cultural landscape are uniform across the model's space. In other words, he assumed a uniform landscape with equal transportation paths and routes throughout the space (no mountains, lakes, or rivers would get in the way). With these assumptions, the location of industry is driven by four factors: transportation, labor, agglomeration, and deglomeration.

Transportation and Distance

Industries wanting to locate where transportation costs are minimized must consider two issues: the distance to the market and the weight of the goods. Distance is a premier factor in the location of industries on several levels besides shipping. For instance, the distances from the factory to its sources of energy and raw materials are also important. Factories established in the early part of the Industrial Revolution had to locate close to their energy sources, but the invention of electricity and other innovations in energy production and transportation enabled modern factories to locate far from energy sources without incurring high costs.

Early factories also had to consider their proximity to the raw materials they needed. A factory had **spatially variable costs**—costs that varied (or changed) depending on the space in which it was located. For example, a factory using heavy or perishable raw materials in its production process might be built as close as possible to its source of raw materials to minimize the cost of transporting the materials into the factory. **Weight-losing processes** are manufacturing processes that create a product lighter than the raw materials that went into making it. Paper production is an example of a weight-losing production process: many paper mills are located near forests, the source of the heavy wood the factory converts into lighter paper products to be shipped long distances. When weight-losing industries locate near the raw resource supply, they are said to have a **material orientation.**

Weight-gaining processes take raw materials and create a heavier final product. Beverage bottling is a weight-gaining industry. Early factories involved in weight-gaining processes were built near the marketplace because the product was heavier to transport in its final form. When weight-gaining industries locate near the place where the heavier product will be sold, that industry is said to have a **market orientation.**

Some industries maintain the same cost of transportation and production regardless of where they choose to locate. These industries have **spatially fixed costs**—costs that remain the same no matter where they choose to locate. These industries often produce lightweight products of extremely high value, like computer chips. Geographers often refer to these types of industries as **footloose**

industries, because they are not bound by locational constraints and can choose to locate wherever they want. Footloose computer chip industries often locate near advanced university research areas.

Labor Costs

Labor cost is another key factor in least cost theory. Can the factory owner hire the workforce needed for the factory? Included in labor considerations is the availability of industrial capital, which consists of machinery and the money to purchase the tools and workers the factory needs. Sometimes an industry will move to a place to access lower labor costs, even though transportation costs might increase as a result. In the long run, these factories will save more because of the cheaper labor. Such a decision is called the **substitution principle**.

Agglomeration

Weber also focused on the advantages and savings made when industries clump together for mutual advantage, a process called **agglomeration**. Factories that are in the same area can share costs associated with resources such as electrical lines, roads, pollution control, and so forth. In other words, agglomeration has positive effects (usually manifested in lower costs and prices) for both the clustered industries and the consumers of their products, a phenomenon known as an **agglomeration economy**.

An example of agglomeration is the **high-tech corridor**—a place where technology and computer industries agglomerate—established in California's Silicon Valley. Many technology-related companies located in this **technopole**, or region of high-tech agglomeration, to benefit from shared resources, like a highly-trained workforce, similar ancillary activities or support businesses, like computer repair shops and electrical wiring services. As a consequence of this agglomeration, other areas suffered an out-migration of talented computer engineers and other skilled workers who migrated to Silicon Valley. This negative consequence of agglomeration, when other regions suffer a drain of resources and talent, is called the **backwash effect**.

Related to agglomeration is the theory of **locational interdependence**, which states that industries choose locations based on where their competitors are located. Industries want to maximize their dominance of the market, so they are influenced by their competition. A common sight near a highway exit is an agglomeration of gas stations. The theory of locational interdependence would assert that these gas stations know that one gas station cannot serve all the cars needing gas, so clustering around the exit allows them a slice of the market share.

Deglomeration

When an agglomerated region becomes too clustered, too crowded, agglomeration can begin to negatively affect the industries in the form of excessive pollution, traffic congestion, lack of resources and labor, and so forth. These industries might then choose to move for more space in a process called **deglomeration**, or the "unclumping" of factories because of the negative effects and higher costs associated with industrial overcrowding.

Criticisms of Weber's Model

Weber's theory does not identify the fact that markets and labor are often mobile, and that the labor force varies in age, skill sets, gender, language, and other traits. Some transportation costs, too, are not directly proportional to distance as his model assumes.

 Contemporary Patterns and Impacts of Industrialization and Development

PART 2

Development

Why are some countries continually so rich and others so poor? The diffusion of economic growth and the increasingly interconnected world has led geographers to see differences in levels of development in the countries of the world. **Development** is the process of improving the material condition of people through the growth and diffusion of technology and knowledge. Human development is continuous and unending in its drive to improve the human condition. Every place, regardless of size, exists at some level of development. Geographers have grouped countries into identifiable categories, more developed and less developed, based on where they are clumped on the spectrum of development.

More-Developed Versus Less-Developed Countries

More-developed countries are on the wealthier side of the development spectrum, while **less-developed countries** are those on the economically poorer side of the spectrum. Both sides have related challenges, with more-developed countries facing issues such as maintaining economic growth and less-developed countries trying to improve their economic condition. Yet it is difficult to qualify and rank countries according to their level of development. Development is not simply a metric of the amount of money a country has. Rather, economic, social, and demographic factors enter into the measurement.

UN Human Development Index

The United Nations uses a formula to generate the **Human Development Index (HDI),** a measure of development that can be used to compare the various

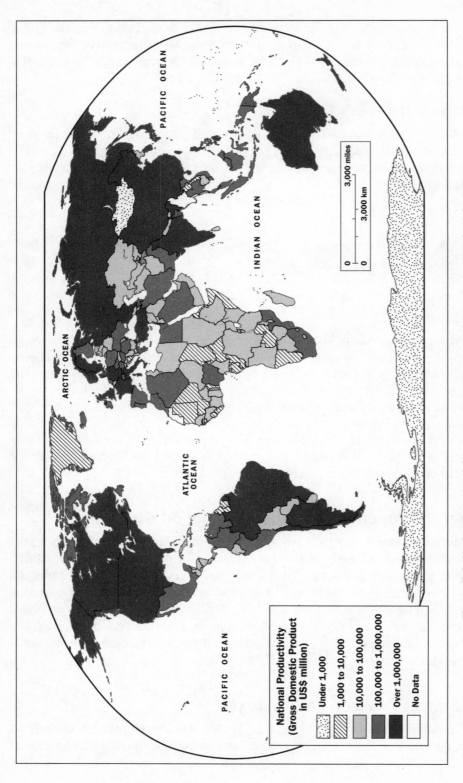

Figure 7.3. National productivity as measured by gross domestic product in U.S. dollars

development levels of regions and countries. According to the UN, the Human Development Index is based on the idea that development is a process of expanding choice. It is an equation that factors into its measurements three areas: life expectancy, average educational levels, and standard of living.

The economic component of HDI is the country's **gross domestic product (GDP)**, the value of total outputs of goods and services produced in a country, usually over one year. GDP per capita is simply the GDP divided by population. In more-developed countries, the GDP per capital is greater than $20,000, and in less-developed countries it is less than $1,000. In the United States, the GDP per capita is nearly $35,000, or $10 to $15 per hour, while in less-developed countries it is 50 cents per hour. (Gross national product includes all goods and services owned and produced by a country overseas.)

Importantly, GDP data are used in calculating **purchasing power parity (PPP)**, a measurement tool for calculating the exchange rates required for each currency to buy an equal amount of goods. In other words, PPP might demonstrate how many colas $1 can buy in Lithuania compared with in the United States. PPP is used to make "apple-to-apple" data comparisons. For example, although the GDP per capita in sub-Saharan African countries is at or below $750, an evaluation of PPP for that income level shows that the buying power in those countries is closer to $4,000 in the United States. PPP puts number comparisons into perspective.

One drawback to using GDP as a factor in evaluating human development is that it is an average that does not reflect the inequality that may exist among people in a country. For example, a country may have a high GDP that is concentrated in one small, elite class of people, while large numbers may be very poor. In fact, in the United States, the richest 10 percent of its citizens holds 15 times more money than the poorest 10 percent of Americans, thus illustrating a large gap between the rich and poor. In less-developed countries, however, the gap is often even more severe. In Guatemala, for example, the richest 10 percent of the population has 75 times more money than the poorest 10 percent.

In addition to GDP per capita, the other three factors used in the UN's HDI equation are life expectancy at birth, educational level attained, and degree of literacy in the region or country. The highest score a country could get on the HDI is 1.000, whereas the lowest is 0.000. In 2006, the lowest country on the list was Niger, with a score of 0.311. The highest country on the list was Norway, with a score of 0.965. The United States ranked eighth among the 177 listed countries.

Informal Sector

Another drawback in using GDP is that many countries do not know and/or do not report data from their **informal sector**, a network of business transactions that are not reported and, therefore, not included in the country's GDP and official economic projections. For example, when parents pay a high school student to baby-sit their children, that transaction is typically "under the table," or not reported to the government. Other examples of workers performing informal-sector economic activities include street vendors selling goods to pedestrians, undocumented aliens working as domestics, prostitutes, and drug traffickers. In many less-developed countries, the informal sector is a prominent portion of overall economic activity, making GDP of limited use in measuring development levels.

The informal sector exists for several reasons. First, the goods produced in the informal sector may be meeting a need that the formal sector has ignored. Second, the goods produced in the informal sector may be in high demand because they are inexpensive. However, because their products are inexpensive, the owners of informal-sector operations, whether they are lunch carts or backroom purse shops, do not make enough money to buy permanent stores and transition into the formal sector. Another part of the informal sector involves illegal immigrants who risk being deported if they and their employers report their earnings to the government.

Other Indicators of Development

Given the problems with solely relying on GDP per capita, geographers sometimes use other measures to analyze economic development, such as access to raw materials, amount of consumer goods, and even the number of TVs and radios per person. Importantly, geographers are beginning to include analyses of women's rights and level of equality as other factors in measuring development levels.

Another interesting indicator of development is the **Big Mac Index**, which compares prices of a Big Mac throughout the world. For example, a Big Mac costs roughly $1.78 in Thailand, where the gross national income per person was $8,440 in 2005. In contrast, the cost of a Big Mac is $3.22 in the United States, where the average income per person is about $42,000. Thus, while Americans earn nearly five times as much as Thais, the U.S. Big Mac costs only two times as much as the Thai version, making it a comparatively expensive meal in Thailand. The Big Mac Index is also used to evaluate exchange rates.

The Development Gap

Geographers are also concerned with the **development gap**, the widening difference between development levels in more- and less-developed countries. Simply put, more-developed countries are improving in their development levels faster than are less-developed countries, and the difference in development levels between the two is widening. In the last decade, the GDP tripled in more-developed countries but only doubled in less-developed countries. The rate of natural population increase fell by nearly 85 percent in more-developed countries but by only 5 percent in less-developed countries.

The world's countries even fall into a regional division based on development, with more-developed countries located primarily in the Northern Hemisphere and less-developed countries primarily located in the Southern Hemisphere. This division is known as the **north–south gap**. Charitable foundations like the Willy Brandt Foundation have called for countries in the north to increase their donations and commitment to less-developed countries in the south to help reduce the widening development gap.

Structuralist Reasons for the Development Gap

How and why do some countries become less developed while others are more developed? Why are many less-developed countries entrenched in their low economic status? Geographers are divided into two camps on this issue. One group of geographers subscribes to **structuralist theories**, which argue that less-developed countries are locked into a vicious cycle of entrenched underdevelopment by the global economic system that supports an unequal structure.

Dependency theory exemplifies this structuralist perspective, arguing that the political and economic relations among countries limit the ability of less-developed countries to modernize and develop. Structuralists see the world's countries as existing in a system, wherein one country's actions directly impact the development paths of other countries in the system. Countries are, therefore, interdependent, not independent.

Immanuel Wallerstein's world-systems analysis (discussed in detail in Chapter 5) is an example of a dependency perspective. Remember, world-systems analysis divides the world into three groups: core, periphery, and semiperiphery. Wallerstein did not assert that all countries can become part of the core, or reach a developed state. Rather, his theory is based on the notion that the core depends on the existence of a periphery. If there is a core, there is a periphery, because the core gains its power through the exploitation of the peripheral and semiperipheral countries. However, the list of countries in the core can change over time, as core countries become peripheral and vice versa.

Dependency theorists point to Europe's colonial occupation of Africa as a reason for continued African poverty. They argue that European colonialism locked African nations into a dependent relationship to their European occupiers. Dependency theory sees little hope for less-developed countries because the dominance of more-developed countries is highly linked to the continued economic and political inferiority of less-developed countries. Dependency theory is criticized for not allowing for cultural and contextual geographic differences.

Liberal Theories of Development: The Rostow Modernization Model

Liberal development theories contrast with structuralist theories and claim that development is a process through which all countries can move. Walt Rostow's **modernization model**, often called the ladder of development, is one such model that assumes all countries follow a similar path of development toward becoming modernized.

Developed in the 1950s, Rostow's modernization model is similar to the demographic transition model in predicting that countries move through stages of structural change to attain development. Rostow's model comprises five stages of development. More-developed countries exist in stages 4 and 5, whereas less-developed countries are in stages 1 through 3. According to the Rostow model, once a country starts investing money in capital—building factories, for instance—its development path is ignited. The following is a description of each stage in Rostow's modernization model.

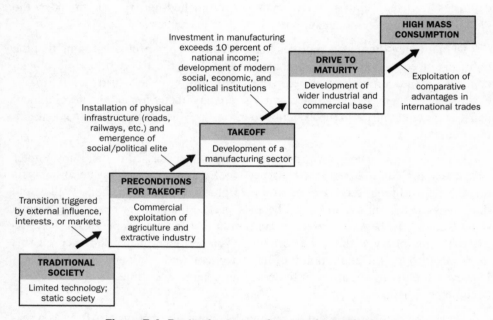

Figure 7.4. Rostow's stages of economic development

- **Stage 1: traditional society.** Economic activity at this stage focuses on subsistence, and the outcome of the activity is consumed primarily by those producing the products. For example, families practicing subsistence farming ate the crops they grew, rather than trading them at markets. Rostow believed that in this first stage, a large amount of national wealth is allocated to tasks that are not economically productive, such as building a military or constructing religious temples.

- **Stage 2: preconditions to takeoff.** As a region begins to develop, a small group of people initiates innovative economic activities that pave the way to economic development. Those few influential people begin to invest in new technologies and infrastructure, such as better water systems and modes of transportation, which sets the stage for economic takeoff. Meanwhile, the region develops surpluses for trading, and productivity increases.

- **Stage 3: takeoff.** The small number of new industries in which the elite invested during stage 2 begin to show rapid economic growth. Industrialization increases as workers shift from agricultural activities into manufacturing jobs created by the takeoff industries. However, the other sectors of the country's economy remain dominated by traditional predevelopment activities like agriculture.

- **Stage 4: drive to maturity.** At this stage the region shows the diffusion of advanced technology beyond just the few initial industries. Other industries experience rapid growth, workers become more skilled and specialized, and the economy begins to diversify and grow in many directions.

- **Stage 5: high mass consumption.** The economy shifts from the dominance of secondary manufacturing jobs to the dominance of service-sector tertiary jobs. High incomes characterize much of the workforce, and masses of people become consumers of produced goods.

Criticisms of Rostow's Model

Some geographers question the applicability of the Rostow modernization model to all countries. After all, the model is based on western European and Anglo-American development patterns and does not account for roadblocks to development, such as the postcolonial dependency on former colonizer that many countries experience while struggling to develop their economies. Another criticism of the model is that it considers each country an independent agent, rather than one piece of an interlocking system of countries.

Reducing the Development Gap: The Self-Sufficiency Approach

To reduce the development gap between rich and poor countries, less-developed countries must build their economies more rapidly. However, geographers debate how to achieve this growth. A method popular in the 1900s is developing **self-sufficiency**, the ability to provide for its own people, independent from foreign economies.

An African woman faces a 1 in 16 chance of dying in childbirth in her lifetime. For a woman in the industrialized world, the chance is 1 in 2,800.

According to the self-sufficiency approach, a country should spread its investments and development equally across all sectors of its economy and regions. Rural areas must develop along with urban areas, and poverty must be reduced across the entire country. The self-sufficiency approach favors a closed economic state, in which imports are limited and heavily taxed so that local businesses can flourish without having to compete with foreign companies.

In the 20th century, China, India, eastern Europe, and Africa were using this self-sufficiency approach to improve development in their regions. However, drawbacks became evident when corruption and inefficiency limited development. In India, for example, the government paid failing businesses to stay open and continue their work. Some economists argue that if the Indian government had allowed those failing businesses to face foreign competition, they would have been forced to improve their products and compete.

Reducing the Development Gap: International Trade

Another approach to improving the economic underdevelopment of less-developed countries is through encouraging **international trade**. This approach pushes a country to identify its unique set of strengths in the world and to channel investment toward building on those strengths. To compete internationally, this approach argues, a country must find out what it can offer the world and capitalize on that good or service.

Eventually, the country will develop a comparative advantage over the rest of the world in producing that good or providing that service. A country has a **comparative advantage** when it is better at producing a particular good or offering some service than another country. The place with a comparative advantage can fill the market's need for a good or service at a lower production cost than other places can. For example, Japan invested much money and power into developing a comparative advantage in high-technology products. Japan could produce computer chips and such much more efficiently than other places could, thereby giving Japan a comparative advantage in high-technology goods. Japan could then specialize in exporting high-tech products to other countries, which could then trade with Japan for the products Japan needed to survive.

Globalization

Spatial interaction has existed throughout human history, at large and small scales: tribe to tribe, village to village, empire to empire. Along with improved communication and transportation technologies, spatial interaction has increased in speed and distance, leading to a continued trend toward space–time compression.

Globalization is the term used to describe this increasing sense of interconnectedness and spatial interaction among governments, cultures, and economies. Originally, *globalization* was used in reference to the spread of economic activities from a home country to other parts of the world, but its reach has profoundly influenced cultural and political realms.

For example, the globalization of brand-name coffee shops is essentially the spread of an economic activity (the coffee shop), but it is also the diffusion of a piece of American culture. The spread of MTV to other parts of the world is also inherently economic, in the diffusion of music sales and videos, but it is also very much a cultural force. Globalization of Western culture is resented in some places that wish to maintain the "purity" of their cultures without the perceived invasion, or cultural imperialism, of Western forces. Hence, the global diffusion of products and their related values by companies such as Disney, MTV, and McDonald's has given way to phrases such as the "Disneyification," "MTVization," and "McDonaldization" of the world.

Multinational Corporations

Multinational corporations (MNCs), sometimes called transnational corporations, are the primary agents of globalization. MNCs are businesses with headquarters in one country and production facilities in one or more other countries. They are usually **conglomerate corporations**, meaning that one massive corporation owns and operates a collection of smaller companies that provide it with specific services in its production process. For example, a conglomerate corporation might own a bottling company and a food-coloring company. An MNC can also include companies that own completely unrelated businesses, such as one owning not only film studios but also television networks and many other smaller companies.

Usually, MNCs locate their headquarters in core countries and build production facilities in peripheral countries. **Outsourcing** is the practice of an MNC to relocate a piece (or all) of its manufacturing operations to factories in other countries. For example, a company headquartered in the United States, outsources its shoe production process to workers in Malaysia and other less-developed countries. MNCs outsource to take advantage of lower labor costs, lower tax rates, and cheaper land prices in countries outside the United States. Remember the substitution principle: that companies might choose to take on higher transportation costs of moving their industrial location farther from their market because they will end up saving money in the long run by hiring less expensive labor.

New Industrial Countries and the Asian Tigers

MNC headquarters tend to exist in the United States, Canada, Germany, the United Kingdom, France, and Japan. However, several states have climbed the economic ladder and have established an industrialized economy based on manufacturing and global trade, countries geographers refer to as **new industrial countries (NICs)**.

Four East Asian countries experienced rapid economic growth by riding the technology boom in the late 20th century and becoming NICs. Taiwan, South Korea, Hong Kong, and Singapore, collectively known as the **Asian Tigers**, are NICs that followed the growth pattern of post–World War II Japan by developing a global reach for high-tech products. Together with China and Japan, the four Asian Tigers make up the core of the Asian economic engine, known as the **Pacific Rim economic region**.

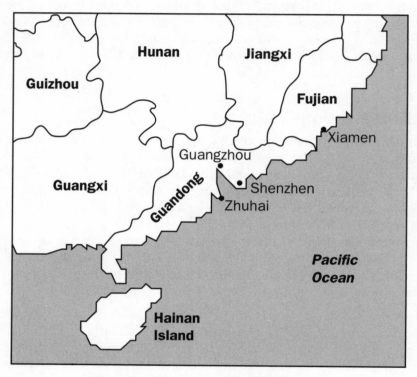

Figure 7.5. Chinese special economic zones

Foreign Direct Investment

As a tactic to improve their economic development, many less-developed countries actively solicit foreign corporations' investment in their countries, referred to as **foreign direct investment**. Often countries wanting to attract MNCs establish **special economic zones**—regions offering special tax breaks, eased environmental restrictions, and other incentives to attract foreign business and investment. China's communist government has designated special economic zones within its territory to allow foreign companies to have free-trade rights and to outsource. Another related term, **export-processing zones,** refers to regions that offer tax breaks and loosened labor restrictions in less-developed countries to attract export-driven production processes, such as factories producing goods for foreign markets. Often,

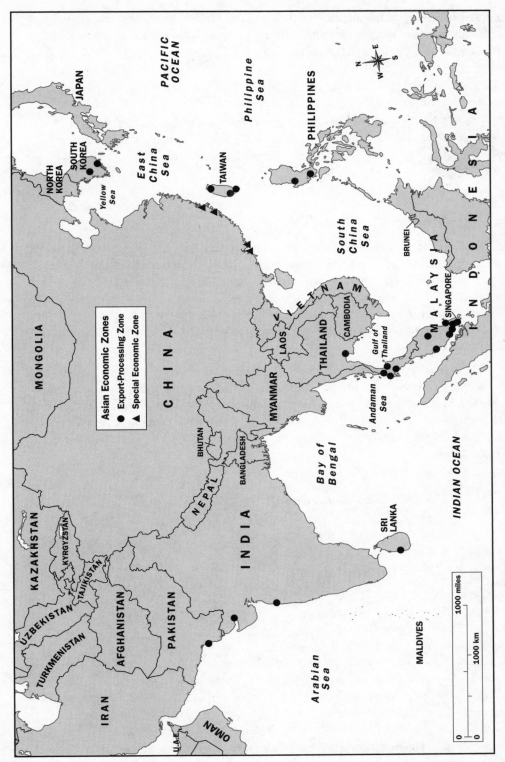

Figure 7.6. Asian export-processing zones

export-processing zones are referred to as **free-trade zones**, because duties and tariffs are waived by governments wanting to encourage MNCs to invest in their countries.

In 1982, the global total of foreign direct investment flows was nearly $57 billion. By the year 2000, that number had grown to nearly $1.3 trillion — almost 20 times larger than in 1982!

Maquiladoras

Mexico established **maquiladora zones**, which are special economic zones on its northern border with the United States. MNCs can outsource labor to these maquiladoras, taking advantage of labor costs in Mexico that are far below those required for U.S. workers to manufacture the same products. Additionally, the Mexican government gave tax breaks to U.S. MNCs that located in maquiladora zones, and the products made in maquiladoras could be shipped to U.S. markets tariff free.

The Mexican government created the maquiladora program to create jobs for Mexican farmers no longer able to make a living off the land. Now nearly 500,000 Mexicans work in the maquiladoras, and the areas where the factories are located are besieged by overpopulation and pollution problems. As part of the North American Free Trade Agreement, the maquiladora program is supposed to be phased out.

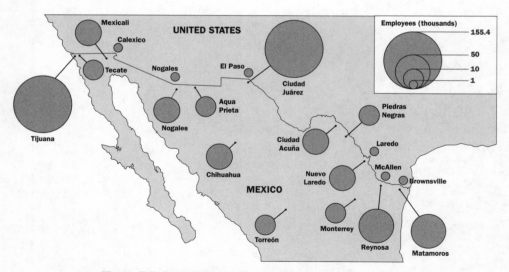

Figure 7.7. Maquiladora zones on the Mexico-U.S. border

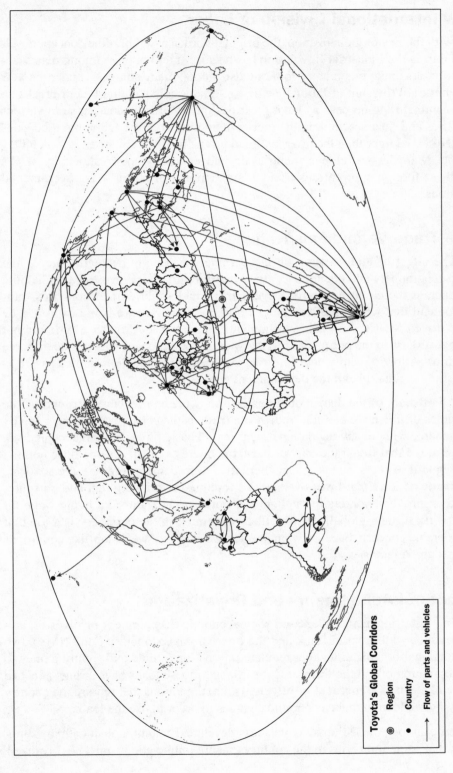

Figure 7.8. An example of an international division of labor: Toyota's global assembly process

Toyota's Global Corridors
- ◎ Region
- ● Country
- → Flow of parts and vehicles

New International Division of Labor

With the rise of globalization, the original Fordist assembly-line concept developed during the Industrial Revolution has been split up not only among many factory workers under one factory roof but also among many countries under the **new international division of labor**. The new international division of labor breaks up the manufacturing process by having various pieces of a product made in various countries and then assembling the pieces in another country. Often the total sales of MNCs are larger than the gross national products of the countries in which they operate. Many less-developed countries depend so heavily on investment by MNCs that these foreign corporations wield a large amount of power over governmental decisions.

Free Trade Versus Fair Trade

The effect of globalization on the periphery is a hotly debated topic. While some geographers and economists argue that foreign direct investment is helping to generate increased economic development in less-developed countries, others contend that workers and resources in those countries are being exploited by profit-driven MNCs. According to human rights advocates, many MNCs are not paying workers in the periphery a living wage, enough to survive on in their home countries. Allowing capitalism to direct such spatial interaction, critics assert, is deepening inequality and the development gap.

An offshoot of the debate on globalization is the controversy surrounding the principles of free trade and fair trade. **Free trade** is the concept of allowing MNCs to outsource without any regulation except for the basic forces of market capitalism. Critics argue that free trade only protects the interests of MNCs and does nothing to safeguard workers' rights. As an alternative to free trade, some people advocate **fair trade** policies that favor oversight of foreign direct investment and outsourcing to ensure that workers throughout the world are guaranteed a living wage for their work. In fact, globalization's effect on women in the periphery is a topic of considerable concern, because women often work in the sweatshop-like conditions of outsourced factories.

Structural Adjustments and Privatization

The fight to generate increased socioeconomic development involves organizations such as the World Bank and the International Monetary Fund (IMF), two supranational organizations that regulate international trade and supply money to developing regions in the form of loans. Many of these loans have strings attached to them known as **structural adjustments**, or stipulations that require the country receiving the loan to make economic changes in order to use the loan.

For example, the IMF may issue a less-developed country a loan with the stipulation that some industries in the country that are public goods must be privatized, or sold off to private companies for profit. In many African countries, this involves selling off publicly operated goods, such as water systems, to private companies that begin charging people for the products that were free when owned and operated by the government.

Privatization, the selling of publicly operated industries to market-driven corporations, is one proposed solution to increasing economic efficiency in less-developed countries. However, privatization can cause social hardship for many families that once depended on the government-owned and operated resources being sold off to profit-driven corporations. Further, the movement of foreign companies into local economies threatens the survival of local businesses driven out of the market by the larger MNCs. Advocates of structural adjustments champion the idea that the long-term economic benefits to countries will outweigh the immediate and often difficult side effects of making the economic changes.

Nongovernmental Organizations

To assist in boosting economic development and human rights throughout the world's peripheral regions, nonprofit organizations like *Doctors Without Borders* and *Save the Children* enter the scene. Thousands of **nongovernmental organizations (NGOs)** represent a myriad of causes, including women's rights, health care, the eradication of poverty, and animal rights. NGOs often supply resources and money to local businesses and causes advancing economic and human development. NGOs have also been instrumental in helping combat HIV/AIDS and hunger.

Globalization and the Environment

With the diffusion of industrialization and increased economic interaction, geographers wonder if the increased rate of production and development can be maintained. Fossil fuels and natural resources, including land, are being depleted. With the increase of affordable, efficient transportation methods, humans can travel to places once considered too distant. Consequently, landscapes in exotic and "vacationable" areas are being transformed to meet tourists' desires, often at the expense of local communities and environments. One response to the negative environmental and cultural effects of increasing tourism is to create environmentally friendly tourist operations. **Ecotourism** comprises tourist operations that aim to do as little harm to the environment as possible. For example, instead of tearing down a forest to build a theme park, an ecotourist business might build a tourist attraction around hiking through the forest and celebrating its ecological diversity.

Costa Rica has turned a huge percentage of its land into protected areas that can be used for ecotourism. Many of the activities center on doing something inside the protected area, such as a "jungle swing," where tourists hike into the rain forest and then climb a small tower. At the top of the tower is a guidewire that runs slightly downhill to a tree. Tourists are hooked to the guidewire by a harness and

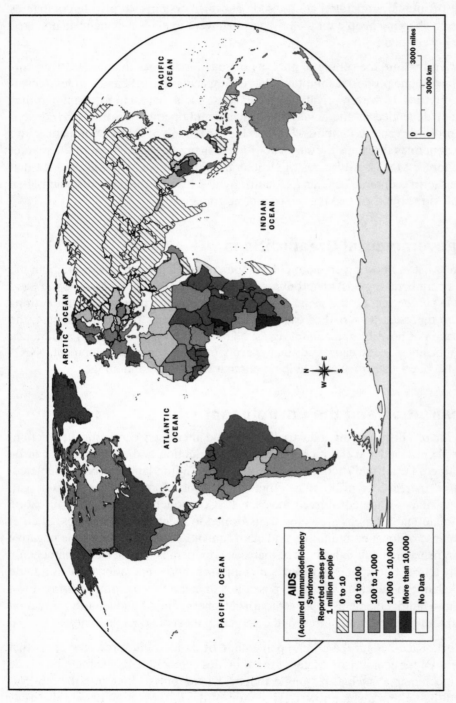

Figure 7.9. Reported AIDS cases per 1 million people

then slide from tree to tree over the top of the lower canopy. At one point tourists are about 100 feet above the ground sliding among the trees. The only "damage" to the ecosystem is caused by the wires attached to the trees and the landing platforms they install. As such, Costa Rica is a strong example of the ecotourism movement on a national scale.

The question still remains: Will our rate of resource consumption eventually rob the earth of the natural resources required to keep pace with human development? To protect future generations, many geographers argue that humans must embrace **sustainable development**, a rate of growth and resource-consumption that can be maintained from one generation to another. At its meeting in 1992, the UN Commission on Sustainable Development called for conservation and careful use of resources. The commission focused on caring for the soil, avoiding overfishing the oceans and rivers, preserving the forests, protecting species from extinction, and reducing air pollution. Recycling and alternative sources of fuel were championed at the meeting.

Geographers are also concerned with the rising average global temperature, caused in part by the **greenhouse effect**. When industrial outputs such as carbon dioxide, methane, chlorofluorocarbons, and water vapor combine in the atmosphere, they create a spongelike vapor that transforms radiation into heat, causing the earth's temperature to rise. The greenhouse effect is much like what happens when you park your car with the windows closed on a hot day and return to find it so hot inside that you can barely sit in the seat. Related to the greenhouse effect and depletion of the ozone layer, **global warming theory** argues that the earth's rise in temperature is causing negative consequences, such as premature melting of the polar ice caps, which could cause sea levels to rise and an interruption of oceanic patterns. The merits and impacts of global warming are hotly debated by geographers and other scientists.

Average temperatures in the Arctic have risen at almost twice the rate as temperatures in the rest of the world over the past few decades. Moreover, the warmest global average temperatures on record have occurred within the past 15 years, with the warmest two years being 1998 and 2005.

Industrialization and its diffusion throughout the world are directly linked to these global changes, for industrialization has caused human resource consumption and pollution emissions to dramatically increase. Industrializing humans are abandoning subsistence livelihoods and moving toward consumption-oriented lifestyles in a race toward more "development." Some scholars see irony in the fact that staying up to speed in the global race toward more *development* requires countries to increase their levels of environmental *destruction*.

PART 3	**Chapter Review**

Models Review

Least Cost Theory

This is Alfred Weber's theory of industrial location, explaining and predicting where industries will locate based on cost analysis of transportation, labor, and agglomeration factors. Weber assumes an industry will choose its location based on the desire to minimize production costs and thus maximize profits. Drawbacks to the model include its assumption of an immobile and equal labor force.

Locational Interdependence

Hotellings theory of locational interdependence asserts that an industry's locational choices are heavily influenced by the location of their chief competitors and related industries. In other words, industries do not make isolated decisions on locations without considering where other, related industries exist.

Rostow's Modernization Model

Developed in the 1950s, this model exemplifies the liberal development ideology, as opposed to structuralist theory. Under the model, all countries develop in a five-stage process. The development cycle is initiated by investment in a takeoff industry that allows the country to grow a comparative advantage, which sparks greater economic gain that eventually diffuses throughout the country's economy. Drawbacks to this model include its not identifying cultural and historic differences in development trajectories because it is based on North American and western European development histories.

Terms Review

Agglomeration—Clumping together of industries for mutual advantage.

Agglomeration economy—Positive effects of agglomeration for clustered industries and for the consumers of their products, often in the form of lower costs to the industries and consumers.

Alfred Weber—Twentieth-century German geographer who created the least cost theory to predict the locational decisions made by industrial operations.

Asian Tigers—Group of new industrial countries comprising Taiwan, South Korea, Hong Kong, and Singapore.

Backwash effect—Occurs when other regions suffer a drain of resources and talent due to agglomeration in another region.

Big Mac Index—Tool for calculating purchasing power parity that compares prices of a Big Mac throughout the world.

Commodification—Giving a price tag or value to something that was not previously perceived as having a money-related value.

Comparative advantage—Ability of a country (or place) to produce a good or offer a service better than another country can.

Conglomerate corporation—Massive corporation operating a collection of smaller companies that provide it with specific services in its production process.

Deglomeration—Unclumping of industries because of the negative effects and higher costs associated with overcrowding.

Dependency theory—Theory that exemplifies the structuralist perspective, arguing that the political and economic relations among countries limit the ability of less-developed countries to modernize and develop.

Development—Process of improving the material condition of people through the growth and diffusion of technology and knowledge.

Development gap—Widening difference between development levels in more-developed and less-developed countries.

Economy—System of production, consumption, and distribution.

Ecotourism—Type of tourist attraction built around an environmentally friendly activity that aims to preserve the earth and its resources.

Export-processing zone—Region of a less-developed country that offer tax breaks and loosened labor restrictions to attract export-driven production processes, such as factories producing goods for foreign markets; sometimes called free-trade zone.

Fair trade—Policies that favor oversight of foreign direct investment and outsourcing to ensure that workers throughout the world are guaranteed a living wage for their work, enough to survive in their home countries.

Footloose industry—Industry not bound by locational constraints and able to choose to locate wherever it wants.

Ford production (Fordist) method—Manufacturing process broken down into differentiated components, with different groups of people performing different tasks to complete the product.

Foreign direct investment—Investment by a multinational corporation in a foreign country's economy.

Free trade—Concept of allowing multinational corporations to outsource without any regulation except for the basic forces of market capitalism.

Globalization—Originally, this buzz term referred to the spread of economic activities from a home country to other parts of the world, but its reach has profoundly influenced cultural and political realms.

Global warming theory—Argues that the earth's surface temperature is gradually rising because of the greenhouse effect, which is responsible for changing global climate patterns.

Greenhouse effect—Rise in the average temperature on the earth as a result of the buildup of chlorofluorocarbons, methane, and other polluting outputs of industrialization.

Gross domestic product (GDP)—Value of total outputs of goods and services produced in a country, usually over one year.

High-tech corridor (technopole)—Place where technology and computer industries agglomerate.

Human Development Index (HDI)—Measurement developed by the United Nations to rank development levels of countries.

Industrialization—Growth of manufacturing activity in an economy or a region; usually occurs alongside a decrease in the number of primary economic activities within a country.

Industrial Revolution—Social and economic change that began in England in the 1760s when the industrial geography of England changed significantly and later diffused to other parts of western Europe. In this period of rapid socioeconomic change, machines replaced human labor and new sources of inanimate energy were tapped. Coal was the leading energy source, fueling the industrial revolution in England's textile-focused industrial explosion.

Informal sector—Network of business transactions that are not reported and therefore not included in the country's GDP and official economic projections.

International trade approach—Method of improving a country's development that pushes the country to identify its unique set of strengths in the world and to channel investment toward building on these strengths. To compete internationally, this approach argues, a country must find out what it can offer the world and capitalize on that good or service.

Less-developed country—Country on the economically poorer side of the development spectrum.

Liberal development theories—Theories that claim development is a process through which all countries can move.

Locational interdependence—Theory that industries choose locations based on where their competitors are located.

Maquiladora zone—Special economic zone on Mexico's northern border with the United States.

Market orientation—Result of locating weight-gaining industries near the marketplace for the heavier product.

Material orientation—Result of locating weight-losing industries near the supply of raw resources.

More-developed country—Country on the wealthier side of the development spectrum.

Multinational corporation (MNC)—As one of the primary agents of globalization, this business has headquarters in one country and production facilities in one or more other countries; sometimes called a transnational corporation.

New industrial country (NIC)—Country that has recently established an industrialized economy based on manufacturing and global trade.

New international division of labor—Division of the manufacturing process across several countries, wherein different pieces of the product are made in different countries, and then the pieces are assembled in yet another country.

Nongovernmental organization (NGO)—Organization not run by a government but by a charity or private organization that supplies resources and money to local businesses and causes advancing economic and human development.

North–south gap—Pattern of development levels in which most most-developed countries exist in the Northern Hemisphere whereas most less-developed countries exist in the Southern Hemisphere.

Outsourcing—An MNC relocating a piece (or all) of its manufacturing operations to factories in other countries.

Pacific Rim economic region—Together with China and Japan, the four Asian Tigers make up the core of the Asian economic engine.

Primary economic activities—Economic activities that revolve around getting raw materials from the earth.

Privatization—Selling of publicly operated industries to market-driven corporations.

Purchasing power parity (PPP)—Measurement tool of calculating exchange rates so that each currency buys an equal amount of goods as every other currency.

Quaternary economic activities—Include assembling, distributing, and processing information, and managing other business operations.

Quinary economic activities—Subset of quaternary activities that involves the highest-level of decision making, such as that of a legislature or a presidential cabinet.

Secondary economic activities—Economic activities related to processing raw materials (acquired through primary activities) into a finished product of greater value.

Self-sufficiency approach—Approach to improving economic development by building a country's independence from foreign economies and fostering its ability to provide for its own people.

Spatially fixed costs—Costs that remain the same no matter where a business chooses to locate.

Spatially variable costs—Costs that vary (or change) depending on the location of an industrial activity.

Special economic zone—Region offering special tax breaks, eased environmental restrictions, and other incentives to attract foreign business and investment.

Structural adjustments—Stipulations that require the country receiving an international loan to make economic changes in order to use the loan.

Structuralist theories—Argue that less-developed countries are locked into a vicious cycle of entrenched underdevelopment by the global economic system that supports an unequal structure.

Substitution principle—Asserts that an industry will choose to move to access lower labor costs despite higher transportation costs.

Sustainable development—Balance between the pace of human development and the environment that supports that development. A level of development that does not destroy the earth's ability to regenerate its resource supply for future generations of inhabitants of the earth.

Tertiary economic activities—Economic activities that move, sell, and trade the products made in primary and secondary activities.

Weight-gaining process—Process that takes raw materials and creates a heavier final product.

Weight-losing processes—Manufacturing process that takes raw materials and converts them into a product that is lighter than the raw materials that went into making the finished product.

PART 4 — Some Suggested Web Resources for Further Exploration

World Bank: http://www.theworldbank.org/

The official site of the World Bank includes valuable data resources, graphs, charts, and discussions related to development levels and economic trends throughout the world.

International Monetary Fund: http://www.imf.org/

This site, like the World Bank's, contains many valuable data resources on economic trends and efforts throughout the world. Particularly interesting is the section on debts owed by various countries.

U.S. Agency for International Development: http://www.usaid.gov/

This is the primary arm of the U.S. government responsible for extending financial assistance to foreign countries. Check out this site to learn more about the countries receiving money from the U.S. government.

European Union Commission on Humanitarian Aid: http://ec.europa.eu/echo/index_en.htm

This is the EU's primary arm for extending financial aid to foreign countries needing humanitarian assistance.

Doctors Without Borders: http://www.doctorswithoutborders.org/

One of the world's largest nongovernmental organizations, Doctors Without Borders has a mission of providing medical care to some of the world's most desperately poor people. The organization provides health care to people who are victims of armed conflict, epidemic diseases, and disasters and those excluded from health care.

Globalization 101: http://www.globalization101.org/

This site contains a look at the key issues related to globalization, sponsored by the Carnegie Foundation for International Peace. The site is very valuable for students and includes lessons for teachers.

PART 5   Pre-Exam Practice

Terms Review Quiz

Use the Terms Review list or your own memory to determine the extent of your knowledge of key terms and concepts. Remember, the AP exam does not include this kind of exercise, but it is included here as a review tool.

1. _____   Economic activities related to processing raw materials (acquired through primary activities) into a finished product of greater value.

2. _____   Giving a price tag or value to something that was not previously perceived as having a money-related value.

3. _____   Manufacturing process that takes raw materials and converts them into a product that is lighter than the raw materials that went into making the finished product.

4. _____   Occurs when other regions suffer a drain of resources and talent due to agglomeration in another region.

5. _____   Asserts that an industry will choose to move to access lower labor costs despite higher transportation costs.

6. _____   Costs that vary (or change) depending on the location of an industrial activity.

7. _____   Clumping together of industries for mutual advantage.

8. _____   Process of improving the material condition of people through the growth and diffusion of technology and knowledge.

9. _____ Value of total outputs of goods and services produced in a country, usually over one year.

10. _____ Network of business transactions that are not reported and therefore not included in the country's GDP and official economic projections.

11. _____ Industry not bound by locational constraints and able to choose to locate wherever it wants.

12. _____ Pattern of development levels in which most most-developed countries exist in the Northern Hemisphere whereas most less-developed countries exist in the Southern Hemisphere.

13. _____ As one of the primary agents of globalization, this type of business has headquarters in one country and production facilities in one or more other countries.

14. _____ Include assembling, distributing, and processing information, and managing other business operations.

15. _____ Process that takes raw materials and creates a heavier final product.

16. _____ Twentieth-century German geographer who created the least cost theory to predict the locational decisions made by industrial operations.

17. _____ Growth of manufacturing activity in an economy or a region; usually occurs alongside a decrease in the number of primary economic activities within a country.

18. _____ Place where technology and computer industries agglomerate.

19. _____ Widening difference between development levels in more-developed and less-developed countries.

20. _____ Theory that exemplifies the structuralist perspective, arguing that the political and economic relations among countries limit the ability of less-developed countries to modernize and develop.

21. _____ Ability of a country (or place) to produce a good or offer a service better than another country can.

22. _____ Massive corporation operating a collection of smaller companies that provide it with specific services in its production process.

23. _____ Region offering special tax breaks, eased environmental restrictions, and other incentives to attract foreign business and investment.

24. _____ Organization not run by a government but by a charity or private organization that supplies resources and money to local businesses and causes advancing economic and human development.

25. _____ Division of the manufacturing process across several countries, wherein different pieces of the product are made in different countries, and then the pieces are assembled in yet another country.

Multiple-Choice Review Questions

1. Which of the following best captures a structuralist interpretation of the development gap?

   (A) Less-developed countries fall behind more-developed countries in levels of wealth and development because people in less-developed countries do not work efficiently.

   (B) Less-developed countries are in stages 2 and 3 of Rostow's model.

   (C) More-developed countries have reached higher development levels because of coal deposits beneath their soils.

   (D) Less-developed countries remain poor because they are continually exploited by more-developed countries seeking resources and labor.

   (E) Less-developed countries will develop in the same pattern as more-developed countries have, but it will take time and self-improvement.

2. A factory process transforming raw corn into processed baby food falls into which economic category?

   (A) Primary   (D) Quaternary

   (B) Secondary   (E) Quinary

   (C) Tertiary

3. Fashion Incorporated, a company headquartered in New York, has contracted with a clothing factory in Thailand to make its sweaters. Fashion Incorporated has determined the value of the workers in the factory to be $1.50 per hour of work. This scenario exemplifies which of the following geographic concepts?

   (A) Privatization   (D) Structural adjustments

   (B) Commodification   (E) Deglomeration

   (C) Fair trade

4. All the following are areas of early industrialization EXCEPT

    (A) England   (D) Ohio region

    (B) Ukraine   (E) Madrid

    (C) the Ruhr region

5. Which of the following is most likely a footloose industry?

    (A) Automobile production   (D) Bottled-water production

    (B) Computer chip production (E) Paper production

    (C) Steel production

6. All the following are used in the human development index equation EXCEPT

    (A) average income per person (D) literacy rate

    (B) average life expectancy   (E) infant mortality rate

    (C) women's level of equality

7. All the following were Asian Tigers EXCEPT

    (A) South Korea   (D) Singapore

    (B) Taiwan   (E) Hong Kong

    (C) Japan

8. Murthy Industries owns a factory located in northern Mexico, on the border with the United States. Given this information, which of the following terms most likely applies to the factory that Murthy Industries owns?

    I.   Maquiladora

    II.   New industrial country

    III. Special economic zone

    IV.   Export-processing zone

    (A) I   (D) I, III, and IV

    (B) I, II, and IV   (E) I, II, III, and IV

    (C) II and III

9. Shanghai, China, is industrializing and growing at exponential rates. The urban migration stream into Shanghai is one of the largest in Chinese (and urban) history. As a consequence of this pattern, many smaller surrounding villages and cities are losing talented workers and resources that are being channeled into Shanghai's rapid growth. This situation best illustrates

    (A) backwash effects   (D) footloose industries

    (B) Fordism   (E) ubiquitous industries

    (C) foreign direct investment

10. Which country has been a high-volume destination for global firms from the United States outsourcing their tertiary-sector jobs?

    (A) Mexico   (D) Indonesia

    (B) China   (E) Malaysia

    (C) India

11. Which of the following geographic theories would be used to explain the concept of neocolonialism and postcolonial dependency?

    (A) world-systems analysis

    (B) Rostow's modernization model

    (C) concentric zone model

    (D) locational interdependence

    (E) demographic transition theory

12. Maquiladora areas in Mexico and free-trade regions in China are examples of

    (A) growth poles   (D) special economic zones

    (B) trade blocs   (E) high-tech corridors

    (C) exclusive economic zones

13. Which of the following people performs activities most likely to be classified as part of the informal sector of the economy?

    (A) Broadway-musical dancer

    (B) Janitor at a public high school

    (C) Street hot-dog vendor

    (D)   Doctor

    (E)   Newspaper journalist

14.   The IMF agreed to give Kenya a $2 million loan on the condition that the government would sell an electrical company in its northern region to a private corporation. This situation demonstrates which of the following concepts?

    (A)   Commodification   (D)   Arbitrage

    (B)   Cumulative causation   (E)   Structural adjustments

    (C)   Fair trade

15.   Which of the following currently claims the highest percentage of workers in the United States?

    (A)   Primary   (D)   Quaternary

    (B)   Secondary   (E)   Quinary

    (C)   Tertiary

16.   In Weber's least cost theory, what are the two major factors he assumed controlled cost of transportation?

    (A)   Value of the good being transported and distance to market

    (B)   Size of the market and price of the good

    (C)   Durability of the good and size of the market

    (D)   Distance to market and terrain

    (E)   Weight of the good and distance to market

17.   A company that produces a weight-gaining product decides to locate a factory near its market. This is an example of

    (A)   material orientation   (D)   locational interdependence

    (B)   market orientation   (E)   deglomeration

    (C)   footloose orientation

18. The value of a country's total output of goods and services in that country during a year is called its

    (A) foreign direct investment   (D) inflation rate

    (B) purchasing power parity   (E) gross domestic product

    (C) human development index

19. Allowing MNCs to outsource without any regulation except for the basic forces of market capitalism is known as

    (A) free trade   (D) market orientation

    (B) foreign direct investment   (E) a primary economic activity

    (C) the informal sector

20. As a country first industrializes, a decrease in jobs usually occurs in which sector?

    (A) primary   (D) quaternary

    (B) secondary   (E) quinary

    (C) tertiary

Free-Response Review Questions

Globalization has been praised and criticized by geographers and economists.

(A) Define the concept of *multinational corporation (MNC)* and relate it to the new international division of labor. Give an example to illustrate this relationship.

(B) Define *outsourcing*, and explain its effect on economic conditions both in the core and the periphery with reference to two of the following regions:

   • North America

   • Latin America

   • East Asia

   • Western Europe

Terms Review Answers

1. Secondary economic activities
2. Commodification
3. Weight-losing process
4. Backwash effect
5. Substitution principle
6. Spatially variable costs
7. Agglomeration
8. Development
9. Gross domestic product (GDP)
10. Informal sector
11. Footloose industries
12. North–south gap
13. Multinational corporation (MNC)
14. Quaternary economic activities
15. Weight-gaining process
16. Alfred Weber
17. Industrialization
18. High-tech corridor (technopole)
19. Development gap
20. Dependency theory
21. Comparative advantage
22. Conglomerate corporation
23. Special economic zone
24. Nongovernmental organization
25. New international division of labor

Multiple-Choice Answers

1. **(D)**

   The structuralist perspective argues that the structure of the world's economy inherently keeps less-developed countries poor at the benefit of more-developed countries. (A) places the blame on the citizens of a less-developed country, which does not hit at the structure of the global economic system. (B) represents Rostow's modernization model, which is the antithesis of the structuralist perspective in that it assumes that all countries can move through the same development pattern and does not account for the economic system of interlocking, interrelated economies. (C) might be related to the structuralist perspective in a weak way in that it hints at resource inequalities, but its relationship to the structuralist perspective is more removed than the clearer relationship of (D). (E) is representative of liberal theories similar to Rostow's modernization model and does not account for cultural and contextual differences within the global economic system.

2. **(B)**

   Secondary economic activities take raw materials gathered in the primary sector and transform them into marketable products.

3. **(B)**

   Commodification is placing a price tag or priced value on something never thought to have a price or value, like a person. (A) is selling a publicly owned business to a private corporation for profit, (C) is moderating free-market capitalism to protect workers' interests, (D) are required changes that a country must agree to make in its economy to receive a loan for which it has applied, and (E) is when companies move out of an agglomerated region because the costs of agglomeration outweigh its benefits.

4. **(E)**

   All the other answer choices were early dominant centers of industrialization.

5. **(B)**

   Computer chip production is not usually tied to any one location and can move around the globe, free of locational restraints, because the resources that go into the final product are not related to one particular place. The other answer choices depend on resources tied to a location, preventing these production processes from moving freely about the world.

6. **(C)**

Though some geographers argue that analyses of women's rights and levels of equality should be included in the HDI equation, those issues are not officially included in the equation.

7. **(C)**

Japan industrialized before the rise of the Asian Tigers, which followed Japan's pattern of industrial and economic development by developing a comparative advantage in a high-tech industrial activity.

8. **(D)**

Located in northern Mexico, this plant is likely in a maquiladora zone, or Mexican factory zone constructed to attract U.S. factories. This zone is also a special economic zone and an export-processing zone because it gives U.S. factories incentives to move there and produce their goods targeted for export. However, Mexico is not an NIC because its economy has not transitioned toward industrialization and dominance.

9. **(A)**

Backwash effects are the negative consequences of agglomeration and growth that pull talented workers and resources from the surrounding regions. (B) is the model of industrial production that breaks down the production process into an assembly line of differentiated operations. (C) is when a company invests or spends money in a foreign country to build a factory or employ its workers. (D) are industries that are not tied down to one particular place but can move freely throughout the world to find the ideal location, and (E) are industries that cannot be separated from their market because their sole purpose is to provide immediate goods to their market (like a dairy farm).

10. **(C)**

India's service-related sector is soaring so high that many U.S. industries are relocating (outsourcing) their service-related jobs to India. Mexico, Indonesia, China, and Malaysia are other places where U.S. global firms are outsourcing secondary-sector jobs, such as factory labor.

11. **(A)**

Neocolonialism and postcolonial dependency describe the continued economic and sociopolitical dependence experienced by countries that were once colonies but are now intricately dependent on their former colonial masters. World-systems analysis divides the world into a core, semiperiphery, and periphery, and it describes core growth as related to an exploitation of the periphery, which supports this exploitative concept of postcolonial relations. (B) assumes that all countries can develop in an equal way and makes no mention of structural impediments to develop as seen in neocolonial explanations of inequality. (C) is a model of urban land use; (D) explains industrial location as related to competition; and (E) explains population change, which could be related to neocolonialism but is not as explanatory of it as is world-systems analysis.

12. **(D)**

Special economic zones offer trade incentives and free trade to companies that locate their industries within the boundaries of the zones. Maquiladora zones in northern Mexico offer U.S. industries special incentives and trade options for locating their factories there, as do free-trade zones in communist-controlled China. (A) are regions experiencing extraordinarily fast industrial growth centered on one particular start-up industry, (C) are areas in the ocean or territorial waters that are exclusively controlled by one country, and (E) are growth poles centered on a high-tech industry.

13. **(C)**

The informal sector of the economy comprises jobs and activities undetected and unreported to the government, the "under the table" operations, such as a hot-dog vendor who takes cash and does not report it to the government. The other jobs are more likely to be reported because they are linked to a greater organizational structure that will pay taxes and health care for their employees.

14. **(E)**

Structural adjustments are changes a country must make in its economy to gain access to the loans it needs; (A) is putting a price on something that has not had a price or been viewed as needing a price before. (B) is the exponential, "snowball" growth that a region experiences once it becomes successful, such as when one city draws all the investment, while the others suffer. (C) is trade that is regulated to ensure that workers' rights are protected, and (D) is when a company produces a product at a very low price and then sells it for many more times its production cost.

15. **(C)**

With the Industrial Revolution in the 20th century, the U.S. economy shifted toward the secondary sector, but the United States is currently transitioning away from the secondary sector in a massive deindustrialization trend that has boosted the service-oriented tertiary sector into dominance.

16. **(E)**

Weber assumed the weight of the good and the distance were the two most important factors in the cost of transportation. All the other answer choices were not considered in Weber's model.

17. **(B)**

A company that locates a factory near its market is trying to reduce the cost of shipping the heavier end product as opposed to the lightweight raw materials. (A) occurs when a company locates near its source of raw materials to reduce the cost of shipping heavy raw materials used to produce a lighter final product. (C) describes a company that is not tied to any location by the cost of shipping. (D) is when industries choose their location based on where their competitors are located. (E) is the "unclumping" of industries because of the negative effects and higher costs associated with overcrowding.

18. **(E)**

A country's gross domestic product (GDP) shows the total of all of the goods and services counted within a country's domestic borders over the course of a year. Usually, the (GDP) is a helpful measure of the country's overall economic strength. (A) is money invested by firms in countries outside of their home country's borders; (B) is a metric often used to compare standards of living among countries; (C) is an equation developed by the United Nations to compare development among countries; (D) is a measure of the devaluation of money and currency.

19. **(A)**

Free trade is the idea that governments should not inhibit companies but should allow market forces to determine how businesses operate. (B) is the investment by an MNC in a foreign country's economy, (C) is a network of business transactions that are not reported and therefore not included in the country's GDP and official economic projections, (D) occurs when weight-gaining industries locate near the place where the "heavier" product will be sold, and (E) are economic activities that revolve around getting raw materials from the earth.

20. **(A)**

As industrialization spreads through a country, it usually leads to a decrease in primary-sector jobs because machines make it possible for fewer people to harvest raw materials from the earth while at the same time creating jobs that process the increased amount of materials gathered. (B) Industrialization is a secondary-sector activity, producing goods from raw materials. (C), (D), and (E) are economic sectors that can follow the growth of industrialization.

Free-Response Answers

The following is a list of suggested main points for each part of the question.

Part A

- A multinational corporation is a company, often a conglomerate corporation, which has headquarters in one country and owns production sites in other countries.

- MNCs are the commanding heights behind the new international division of labor, in which production processes are broken down not only under the roof of one factory but also among countries and across borders. A computer's parts may be made in several different countries before it is finally assembled into its marketable product.

- An example of a multinational corporation is Nike, which has its headquarters in the United States but has production sites and factories in other countries.

Part B

- Outsourcing occurs when a multinational corporation sends part of its production process to a site in another country, such as when a modem company outsources its customer service call center to a city in Indian.

- Outsourcing has affected both the core and the periphery in different ways.

- Often the headquarters of MNCs exist in the core countries in North America and western Europe, while their labor-intensive production sites exist in peripheral less-developed countries in East Asia and Latin America.

- The profits reaped are often shipped back to the countries in the core rather than being reinvested in the peripheral production regions.

- The peripheral countries are left with higher pollution levels.

- The core countries' workforces must adapt to the outsourcing of secondary economic activities. They must train for service-sector and high-tech jobs.

- Workers in peripheral regions are often paid much lower wages than what the MNCs would have to pay workers in their headquarter countries (hence, a potential reason the MNCs outsource).

- Workers in the periphery rarely get to buy the goods they are manufacturing, because the goods are produced for export to the countries in which the

MNCs are headquartered. Further, these products are often too expensive for purchase in the less-developed countries.

- Maquiladoras are U.S.-owned factories in northern Mexico. U.S. companies are given incentives, such as lower taxes and lower labor costs, to move their factories into northern Mexico.

- Northern Mexico benefits from the job opportunities provided, though it suffers from the industrial agglomeration—pollution and overcrowding.

- One possible response would discuss the Asian Tigers and the economic growth of China through industrialization and special economic zones.

- Women often suffer the most in less-developed countries because they must work in the often poorly regulated factories that exploit their labor.

Chapter 8

Cities and Urban Land Use

Introduction

While riding atop the tallest Ferris wheel in the world, a resident of London looked down at the sprawling mass of the city whose history spans millennia. The rider wondered how and why London grew and developed in the brilliant way that it did. As the wheel rotated down and the rider's bird's-eye view of the dazzling cityscape, or city landscape, refocused earthward, the Londoner once again became an urban dweller, walking through the "mighty heart" of the urban settlement, almost like an ant in its hill.

Permanent settlements like London developed after human groups learned to practice agriculture. Such permanent places evolved from clans and villages, eventually, into larger urban city structures that reflect layers and generations of **urbanization**, the growth and diffusion of city landscapes and urban lifestyles. Heavy

(Photo by: M. Paananen)

Figure 8.1. The London Eye, the tallest Ferris wheel in the world

urbanization in more-developed countries is typical, but even in less-developed countries, the number of urban dwellers has grown massively in recent years. Many city governments in less-developed regions are struggling to manage the explosive urbanization. In fact, about 10 million people die each year because of hazardous conditions caused by overcrowding and inadequate infrastructural support in areas experiencing explosive urbanization.

Geographers analyze where urbanization developed and why these places became hearths of urban civilization, or **urban hearth areas**. Geographers analyze the path of urbanization's diffusion from these hearths and the related gaps in urban development among different countries, some of which are nearly 100 percent urban, while others are still largely rural. In addition to analyzing the patterns of urbanization, geographers look into internal spatial relationships in cities. For example, geographers ask why there are socioeconomic ghettos and how a city's transportation system affects its spatial development. Further, geographers compare cities. How does Mumbai, India, compare in organization and development to Moscow, Russia?

Key Questions

- *What is the definition of city, and how do cities across the world vary?*

- *Where are cities located and why do they exist where they do?*

- *What are the paths through which urbanization diffused?*

- *What are the political, economic, and cultural functions of cities?*

(Photo by: Morguefile)

Figure 8.2. A view of the British Parliament from the London Eye

- *What are the differences in the ways cities have grown and developed?*

- *Why are there differences in levels of urbanization throughout the world?*

- *How do urban places interact spatially through communication and transportation?*

- *How do theories like Christaller's central place theory and the rank-size rule help explain and predict settlement geography?*

- *What is urban hierarchy? How and why have cities' rankings changed over time?*

- *What do patterns in urban land use look like, and how do they compare to rural land use patterns?*

- *Where and why do patterns in ethnic and racial segregation exist in urban places?*

- *What types of inner-city transportation systems exist? How do those systems affect city development and spatial organization?*

- *What types of agricultural traditions exist in various urban cultures?*

- *How do comparative models of internal city structure—like the concentric zone, sector, and multiple-nuclei models—explain and predict city growth and development?*

- *How do urban places differ across the world? For example, how do Middle Eastern cities differ from western European cities in layout and design?*

- *What are modern trends in urban development, such as edge cities and gentrification?*

- *What will cities look like in the future?*

PART 1 — Defining Urbanism

Urban Population Size

At least 3 billion people, nearly half of the world's population, live in areas considered urban. But what makes a place urban rather than rural? What is the definition of *urbanism*? The answer is that the definition depends on time and culture. The size of a stationary population is part of the equation but varies according to historical context and location. Ancient cities had populations ranging from 2,000 to 20,000. However, Mesopotamia's Ur, one of humanity's most ancient, massive urban civilizations, was home to 200,000 city dwellers, and that pales in comparison to its modern-day neighbor, Baghdad, with a population of nearly 7 million. The size of a city also varies geographically. In Portugal, any population of more than 10,000 people makes up a city; in Ethiopia, a city is at least 2,000 people; and in Norway, a population of only 200 is considered a city. Thus, a city usually is qualified by a population considered large for its time and place.

As of 2005, China, India, and the United States had the largest numbers of urban dwellers in the world.

However, "cityness" is not simply measured by the number of people in a given place. For example, the congregation of people at the Super Bowl may be as large as the populations of some cities, but no one would consider that gathering of football fans a city. The presence of a government and some form of boundaries, though often difficult to determine, is part of the definition of cityness. A city's boundaries often become unclear as the city sprawls and merges with other growing urban places. For example, Cool Springs is a growing urban area near Nashville, Tennessee. Many urban dwellers in Cool Springs consider themselves Nashville citizens, while others call themselves residents of Franklin, another nearby city. Yet Cool Springs is intricately linked to the Greater Nashville economy and culture.

Metropolitan Statistical Areas

Because it is often difficult to determine city boundaries, the U.S. Census Bureau uses the term **metropolitan statistical area (MSA)** to describe a geographic unit of area that includes a central city and all its immediately interacting counties, with commuters and people directly connected to the central city. An MSA is an urbanized region with a minimum of 50,000 people in it. Often the boundaries of MSAs overlap. For example, the cities in what is called the Triangle in North Carolina—Raleigh, Durham, and Chapel Hill—started out as individual cities or towns and have grown into one another, becoming so interrelated that they are now seen as one MSA. Such a massive urban "blob" of overlapping, integrated metropolitan areas, whose distinctive boundaries are increasingly becoming difficult to find, was named a **megalopolis** by the geographer Jean Gottmann, who originally applied the term to the metropolitan areas of Washington, D.C., and Boston.

The U.S. Census Bureau also uses a unit called a **micropolitan statistical area**, an area of the surrounding counties integrated into a central city with a population of 10,000 to 50,000. Many formerly rural areas have been reclassified as micropolitan statistical areas.

With 35 million residents in 2005, the metropolitan area of Tokyo was by far the most populous urban agglomeration in the world.

Economic Diversity

The economy of a place is another layer in classifying it as rural or urban. Economically, cities often have more diversity in economic activities, from dog walking and hair styling to surgery and broadcast journalism. For example, Japan defines a city as a place with at least 50,000 inhabitants, 60 percent or more of whom are engaged in trade, manufacturing, or other nonagricultural activities.

Once ancient humans domesticated animals and began to grow crops, they could produce surpluses of food, leading to permanent settlement and eventually economic diversification, with people performing various jobs rather than just farming. Money developed, records were written, laws were codified, and services were provided. Surrounding farmlands grew to support cities. Traditionally, larger cities have shown a high degree of economic diversity.

Cultural Diversity

A cultural layer also plays a role in defining a place's degree of urbanity, or cityness. A tourist in Paris can visit the Paris Opera House, tour the Louvre Museum and see the Mona Lisa, and eat delicious Indian food. Cultural diversity, complexity, and vibrancy also contribute to a geographer's classification of a place as a city.

A Definition?

Thus, our search for a clear definition of what makes a city has led us to more of a process of comparison than a sentence or two. Geographers use factors such as the size of the population in a given historical and geographic context, economic diversity, governmental organization, delineated boundaries, and cultural complexity to analyze the degree to which a place is considered urban.

PART 2	**Origin and Evolution of Cities**

Hearths of Urbanization

Where did cities and urbanism, or urban life, begin? The earliest cities were born around 3500 BCE and were spawned from agricultural villages. Earliest hearths of urbanism existed in Mesopotamia, between the Tigris and Euphrates rivers in former Iraq; the Indus River region in modern Pakistan; the Nile Valley in modern Egypt; the Huang He River valley in modern China; and in Mexico and Peru. Several qualities are common among places that were urban hearths: a dependable water supply, a long growing season, domesticated plants and animals, plenty of building materials, and a system of writing and records.

In addition to cities that evolved from agricultural villages, some cities grew as established marketplaces, where traders came together to buy and sell goods from across the region. Many such points of exchange grew near waterways and long-distance overland trade routes. Urbanism spread westward throughout the Mediterranean region because of Phoenician, Greek, and Roman traders, and it spread eastward through overland and caravan trade routes through Persia and Pakistan to India, China, and then Japan. Even at this early stage, specialization began to occur, as certain cities began to focus economic development on the goods over which they had a comparative advantage. Specialization would evolve into a global economic network of specialized cities, each defined largely by its dominant economic specialty, such as Hollywood's specialization in movie making.

Greeks and Romans erected cities as centers of political and administrative control over their conquered regions. Such cities often were built in a planned gridlike pattern. Other cities grew as centers of religious ceremony, such as urban places in China that were determined to be holy sites and designed in geometric shapes to reflect related religious beliefs.

Preindustrial Cities

City landscapes varied significantly across the world before industrialization. However, **preindustrial cities** did share some traits across time and space. Many rural settlements surrounding urban spaces provided agricultural products and foodstuffs to the urban dwellers, who in turn provided various economic functions. Cities have always provided economic functions from their surrounding rural lands. Preindustrial cities served as trade centers and gateways to foreign lands and markets. After the fall of the Roman Empire by 600 BCE, European preindustrial cities experienced a decline in development. Exploration and trade associated with the growth of mercantilism led to a surge in urban growth. Mercantilism is the system in which European governments controlled economic activity and aimed to gain as many new colonies as possible to increase their nations' wealth and supplies. The European drive to grab foreign land and resources fueled the construction and creation of cities in the conquered colonies. Many **colonial cities** contained European imprints, such as wide boulevards and prominent structures evoking classical architecture. Importantly, colonial cities were constructed with the aim of exporting raw resources from the colonial city back to the "mother country." (The colonial city is discussed in more detail in the section on the Latin American city model.)

By the beginning of the 1500s, most cities were located in an arch of trade centers that extended from London to Tokyo, a line of cities known as the **urban banana** because of its crescent or banana-like shape. Thus, the focus of urbanization existed in powerful cities, like London, Paris, Constantinople, Venice, Cairo, Nanking, Hanchow, and Osaka. The urban banana of dominant cities resulted from both site and situation factors. Site factors are the physical and cultural characteristics of a place that help us learn something about the city, factors like arable land, street layout, and building materials. Situation factors relate to how a city fits into the larger urban network, such as proximity to major trade routes and other urban places.

Internally, preindustrial cities often had a diverse mix of economic functions in any given space, rather than the specific zoning that came with industrialization. This meant that shops, markets, homes, and government offices were typically found jumbled together in urban space. However, economic segregation often existed, with the wealthier elite living closer to the city center. Also, in feudal European cities, guilds led to the clumping of certain functions in particular areas of the towns, which suggests the existence of a crude form of zoning, or functional differentiation. Again, though, cultural differences affected internal, urban spatial organization.

Industrialization and City Structure

In 1800, only 5 percent of the world's population lived in cities; by 1950, 16 percent lived in cities; by 2000, nearly 50 percent of the world's population lived in cities. What caused this explosion in urbanization? Largely, the diffusion of industrialization is responsible for urbanizing the world's people, albeit at unequal levels. More than 75 percent of the world's population living in more-developed countries is considered urban. However, only about 40 percent of the world's population living in less-developed countries is considered urban. Specifically, Africa and Asia are the least urbanized continents on the earth, while North America is the most urbanized continent, with nearly 80 percent of its people living in urban places. In 2001, only 35 percent of the African population was considered urban.

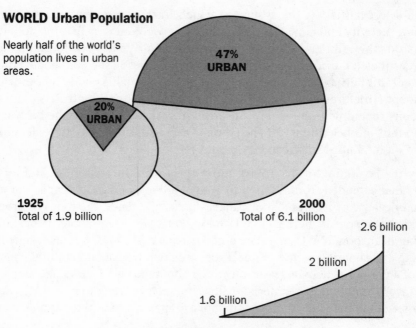

Figure 8.3. Urban growth on a global scale

The European Industrial Revolution and its related imperialism triggered this diffusion of city growth. Urbanization grew in a snowball process, as the growth of factories and urban jobs provided attractive opportunities to rural people struggling to make a living farming. Thus, the Industrial Revolution, which started in England and then diffused to other parts of the world, created a steady rural-urban migration pattern. Supporting this pattern was the demographic transition linked to the second agricultural revolution, which led to an increasing population size to supply more people to work in the cities and fuel industrialization.

England's population was 24 percent urban in 1800 and 99 percent by 1999.

Population growth and rural-urban migration led to massively growing urban spaces that were, in many ways, overwhelmed with the influx of urban in-migrants. Manchester, England, grew from having less than 80,000 residents in 1750 to nearly 500,000 urban dwellers just a century later. As industrialization and urbanization spread to North America after it developed in western Europe, the U.S. city of

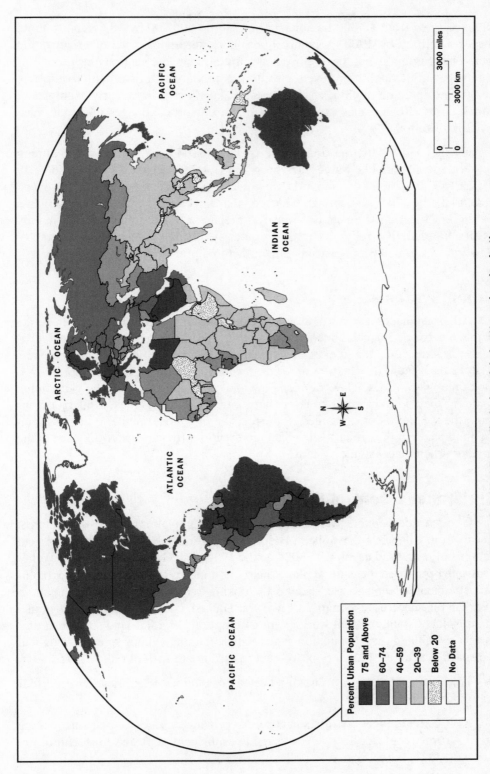

Figure 8.4. World map displaying global patterns in urbanization

Chicago grew from 30,000 inhabitants in 1750, to 500,000 by 1830, and to more than 1.5 million by 1900. Accompanying those surprising rates of urbanization were challenging social, economic, and cultural changes, such as the growth of slums, hazardous pollution levels, deadly fires, the growth of urban prostitution, and the exploitation of children. Manchester and Chicago were early examples of **shock cities**, urban places experiencing infrastructural challenges related to massive urbanization.

By the mid-1700s, the dominance of land-based trade cities was declining as sea-trade centers like Saint Petersburg and Bombay began to grow rapidly. By the early 1900s, most of the world's greatest cities were American or European industrial cities, like Manchester, Chicago, and Barcelona. The **industrial city** had a different function from its preindustrial precursor. Rather than serving mainly as an administrative, religious, trade, or gateway city, the industrial city's primary function was to make and distribute manufactured products.

Urban Systems

All urban places are part of an interlocking **urban system** of cities that operate within a network of spatial interaction. In other words, urban places are *interdependent*, not independent, and exist in a spider web of interacting parts. Geographers analyze the spatial distribution of cities, trying to determine why the spider web looks the way it does. They wonder how and why cities grow in the geographic locations they do. Why are there fewer large cities than small cities? Do larger cities drain the smaller cities of needed resources, keeping those smaller cities lower on the food chain of the urban system? Do larger cities provide needed services to the smaller urban places in the system?

Christaller's Central Place Model

German geographers were very interested in explaining land use patterns. Recall from Chapter 6 that Johann Heinrich von Thünen studied the geographical patterns of *rural* land use in the 1800s. In the 1930s, the German geographer Walter Christaller proposed the **central place theory** as a means of studying the geographical patterns of *urban* land use, specifically looking to explain and predict the pattern of urban places across the map. Just like von Thünen, Christaller created his model in an isolated state, or ideal world, with assumptions of a flat land surface, a uniformly distributed rural population, equal transportation methods spread throughout the space, and an evolutionary movement toward the growth of cities.

To explain the pattern of urban places across the world, Christaller used four main ideas in his model:

1. **Central places** are urban centers that provide services to their surrounding rural people, collectively referred to as the central place's **hinterland**.

2. The **threshold** is the *minimum* number of people needed to fuel a particular function's existence in a central place. The more unique and special an economic function, the higher its threshold. For example, the threshold of a doughnut shop is lower than the threshold of a neurosurgical center for several reasons. First, a doughnut shop's services are used by a higher percentage of people than a neurosurgery center. Therefore, the doughnut shops can exist in a smaller population to fulfill its customer base. A brain surgery center, on the other hand, serves a smaller percentage of people; therefore, it requires a larger population to fulfill its customer base. Second, the doughnut shop has a lower maintenance cost than a state-of-the-art neurological center. Third, the workforce needed in the neurological center of a hospital requires a higher degree of specialized training compared with the workers in a doughnut shop.

3. The **range of a good or service** is the maximum distance a person is willing to travel to obtain that good or service. The range of a doughnut shop is much smaller than the range of a neurological brain surgery center because a person is willing to travel much farther for lifesaving brain surgery than for a chocolate doughnut.

4. **Spatial competition** implies that central places compete with each other for customers.

With these ideas, Christaller's model illustrated how and why economic functions drive the locational pattern of cities across geographic space. Central places contain economic functions with high thresholds and high ranges that require large

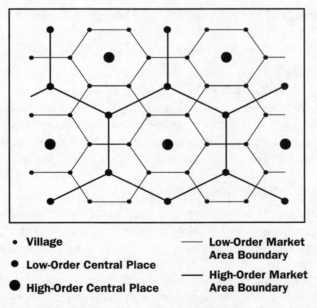

- • Village   —— Low-Order Market Area Boundary
- ● Low-Order Central Place
- ⬤ High-Order Central Place   — High-Order Market Area Boundary

Figure 8.5. Hexagonal market areas predicted by Christaller's central place theory

populations to serve groups of smaller central places existing around them. Even the smallest central places, with low-threshold, low-range functions (like the doughnut shop or a gas station) serve a surrounding population, usually a rural settlement. Whereas von Thünen's model resulted in concentric rings of rural land use, Christaller's model predicted a hexagonal pattern of urban central places. In this pattern, smaller central places will be located closer together, because consumers will not be willing to travel as far for lower central place functions, like doughnut shops and gas stations. However, larger central places will be located farther away from each other because consumers are more willing to travel a longer distance to obtain higher central place functions, like brain surgery.

Urban Hierarchy

Essentially, the central place theory predicts that if a population is evenly distributed, there will be a hierarchy of evenly spread central places to serve that population. Such an **urban hierarchy** is a system of cities consisting of various levels, with only a few cities at the highest level and increasingly more settlements on each lower level. The position of a city within the hierarchy is determined by the types of central place functions it provides. The higher the position on the hierarchy, the higher the population being served by the central place, and the more variety of central place functions performed in the city. It is the volume of choices in an urban center that makes it more dominant in the urban hierarchy than a smaller town.

In other words, central places at the top of an urban hierarchy provide functions with the highest ranges and highest thresholds, whereas cities at the lower levels of the urban hierarchy provide lower-range, lower-threshold functions. Providing the highest-range, highest-threshold functions that could not be supported in smaller urban places, Chicago sits at the very top of the urban hierarchy. Actually, some geographers argue that Chicago is a second-level city now, behind Los Angeles and New York.

In the hierarchy, few urban central places are at the top of the hierarchy, while many urban central places are at the bottom. This is logical if you think about it. Few large cities provide functions like those of Broadway and Wall Street in New York City, and many smaller cities provide gas stations and fast-food restaurants. Cities like Chicago sit atop the urban hierarchy in the United States, whereas urban places like Miami and Saint Louis occupy the next level of the urban hierarchy.

Applying the Central Place Theory

The central place theory provides one piece in the jigsaw of understanding and predicting geographic patterns of urban places. Theoretical models like the central place theory can add analytical power to understanding patterns, such as urban growth. Since the 1970s, U.S. urban places in the South and the West have been growing much faster than cities in the old manufacturing areas of the Northeast and Midwest. Many people attribute this pattern to the larger numbers of people, like retirees, moving to those areas for warmer weather and more fun and relaxation. However, the central place theory offers another piece of the explanation.

Over the last 30 years, populations in the U.S. South and West have increased and become wealthier overall. Several factors have contributed to this trend, including increased immigration into the regions from Latin America; construction of military bases and space stations by the U.S. government, and the official ending of legal segregation. With more people and wealth, more services were needed. Several cities stepped up to fill this need. Cities like Phoenix, Atlanta, and Dallas moved up on the urban hierarchy as they grew to offer more central place functions to the newly growing populations. While cities like Atlanta have been important for the past 100 years, their levels of importance on the national level have increased.

As with any hierarchy, as these cities moved up the ladder, other cities moved to fill their places. Cities like Tampa, San Antonio, and Charlotte moved up to fill the new spots. Consequently, some older, manufacturing cities in the Northeast and Midwest began to suffer. Remember, the central place theory assumes that people needing a particular service (from buying a doughnut to getting brain surgery) will travel to the *closest* available option to obtain that service. For example, if a southerner needed to access central place functions, such as neurosurgery, he or she no longer needed to travel to Chicago. Instead, he could go to a major surgery center in Atlanta.

Rank-Size Rule and Centrality

With the existence of an urban hierarchy, there is a pattern in city size distribution across geographic space. In other words, there is a relationship to a city's population size and its place on the urban hierarchy within its urban system. Statistically, this is predicted by the **rank-size rule**, which states that the nth largest city's population size in a region is $1/n$ the size of the region's largest city's population. For example, the fourth largest city in a region is predicted to be one-fourth the size of the region's largest city's population size.

While the urban hierarchy in the United States urban system roughly conforms to the rank-size rule prediction, some urban systems have disproportionately large cities, known as *primate cities*, as mentioned in Chapter 5. Cities with such **primacy**, like Buenos Aires, London, Paris, and Rio de Janeiro, are often much larger than the second-largest city in the country's urban hierarchy. Buenos Aires, Argentina, is nearly 10 times the size of its second-largest city, Rosario, and thus would have a high degree of *primacy*. Additionally, when a city dominates economic, political, and cultural functions more than expected based on its population size, the city demonstrates a high degree of centrality, or the possession of central place functions. For example, Managua, Nicaragua, demonstrates urban centrality because its population accounts for only about 30 percent of Nicaragua's total population, but the city controls nearly 40 percent of the country's economy.

World Cities

Within the network of interacting cities comprising the world's urban system are **world cities**, powerful cities that control a disproportionately high level of the world's economic, political, and cultural activities. World cities, sometimes called global cities, have a high degree of centrality in the global urban system. The group of world cities has shifted with the changing nature of the global urban system. In the 1600s, London, Lisbon, and Amsterdam were world cities in the mercantile economy of that century, and by the 1700s, Rome and Paris had become world cities. In the rising industrialization of the nineteenth century, Berlin, Chicago, New York, and Saint Petersburg became world cities.

Today's world cities are less concerned with serving as administrative centers of power over imperialism and trade. Instead, modern world cities are centers of global financial decisions, flows of information, and multinational (or transnational) corporations driving the global economic and political landscape. Another term related to being a world city is *panregional influence*. New York City is a world city with **panregional influence**, meaning its range extends beyond North America into the other two centers of economic control, Europe/Africa/Middle East and Asia/Oceania. Home to powerful media outlets, financial institutions, global corporate headquarters, and political organizations like the United Nations, New York City is a world city because it influences a larger percentage of world affairs than its share of the world's population would suggest. In other words, New York City is a world city because its global influence is larger than its share of the earth's population. Also, a city can be considered a world city when it dominates a distinct area of global affairs. For instance, Amsterdam is a global financial center, and Milan exerts powerful influence over fashion and design.

Megacities

Though not considered world cities, **megacities** have a high degree of centrality and primacy, thereby exerting high levels of influence and power in their countries' economies. All megacities are large, having more than 10 million inhabitants. Beijing, Cairo, Mexico City, and Jakarta are examples of megacities that serve to connect the earth's world cities with the smaller central places in their countries' urban hierarchies. Thus, Jakarta's businesses and political units connect with New York City's services and bring them to Indonesia's people through spatial interactions in the form of trade, transportation, communication, and even migration.

Modern Trends in Urbanization

In 1950, only 30 percent of the world was urbanized and 83 urban places had a population of 1 million or more people. By 2000, the number of urban places with 1 million or more people had risen to nearly 400. Estimates project that by 2010 nearly 500 such cities will be spread across the earth.

There is an important distinction between level and rate of urbanization. **Rate of urbanization** is the speed at which the population is becoming urban, while **level of urbanization** is the percentage of people already considered urban. For example,

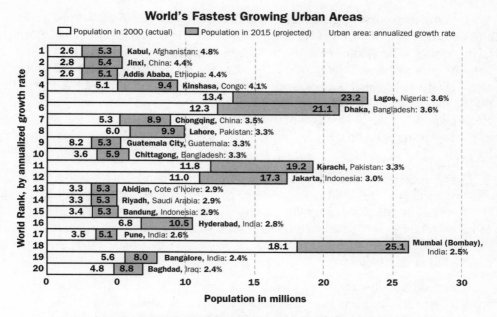

World's Fastest Growing Urban Areas

☐ Population in 2000 (actual) ▨ Population in 2015 (projected) Urban area: annualized growth rate

World Rank, by annualized growth rate

1. 2.6 | 5.3 Kabul, Afghanistan: **4.8%**
2. 2.8 | 5.4 Jinxi, China: **4.4%**
3. 2.6 | 5.1 Addis Ababa, Ethiopia: **4.4%**
4. 5.1 | 9.4 Kinshasa, Congo: **4.1%**
5. 13.4 | 23.2 Lagos, Nigeria: **3.6%**
6. 12.3 | 21.1 Dhaka, Bangladesh: **3.6%**
7. 5.3 | 8.9 Chongqing, China: **3.5%**
8. 6.0 | 9.9 Lahore, Pakistan: **3.3%**
9. 8.2 | 5.3 Guatemala City, Guatemala: **3.3%**
10. 3.6 | 5.9 Chittagong, Bangladesh: **3.3%**
11. 11.8 | 19.2 Karachi, Pakistan: **3.3%**
12. 11.0 | 17.3 Jakarta, Indonesia: **3.0%**
13. 3.3 | 5.3 Abidjan, Cote d'Ivoire: **2.9%**
14. 3.3 | 5.3 Riyadh, Saudi Arabia: **2.9%**
15. 3.4 | 5.3 Bandung, Indonesia: **2.9%**
16. 6.8 | 10.5 Hyderabad, India: **2.8%**
17. 3.5 | 5.1 Pune, India: **2.6%**
18. 18.1 | 25.1 Mumbai (Bombay), India: **2.5%**
19. 5.6 | 8.0 Bangalore, India: **2.4%**
20. 4.8 | 8.8 Baghdad, Iraq: **2.4%**

Population in millions (0, 0, 10, 15, 20, 25, 30)

Figure 8.6. The fastest-growing urban areas in the world

the level of urbanization in the United States is nearly 75 percent, meaning that nearly 75 percent of the U.S. population lives in urban places. However, the rate of urbanization in the United States is much lower than the rate of urbanization in China, for example, which is experiencing a rapid rate of urbanization despite its lower level of urbanization, which is nearly 30 percent.

After the communist takeover of China in 1949, Chairman Mao Zedong committed China to agricultural development, not urbanization, and restricted his people's movements into cities. After Mao's death in 1976, his successor, Deng Xiaoping, charted a course of urbanization for China, a course that has led to the doubling of its urban population from 1981 to 2001. Among the less-developed, peripheral countries experiencing high rates of urbanization are Nigeria, Pakistan, Indonesia, and Egypt, where the megacity of Cairo is the focus of urban growth.

An important trend in modern urbanization is its diffusion to less-developed parts of the world and its uneven spread. Overall, the highest rates of urbanization are occurring in places with the lowest levels of urbanization, in less-developed, peripheral countries. In 1950, nearly 60 percent of urbanized places were in *more*-developed countries. By 1980, 19 of the largest 30 metropolitan areas in the world were in the *less*-developed world, indicating a clear surge in the growth of urban cities in less-developed countries. Although rates of urbanization in core countries are relatively low, their levels of urbanization are already high. The populations of most core countries are already above 75 percent urban. In semiperipheral countries, rates of urbanization are also high.

Cities in more-developed countries are fading from the list of the world's largest cities. According to the United Nations, between 1980 and 2000, Lagos, Dhaka, and Cairo, among others, joined the list of 30 largest cities in the world. By 2010, the Nigerian city of Lagos is projected to become the third-largest city on the globe, after Tokyo and Mumbai. European cities like Milan and London will have dropped off the list of the 30 largest cities. By 2010, New York City, Osaka, and Paris will have fallen down the ladder as well. Some projections speculate that nearly all 30 of the largest metropolitan places in the world will be in less-developed countries by 2010.

As we have seen, urbanization in less-developed countries is often focused on one or two major cities with a high degree of primacy and centrality, rather than being spread evenly throughout the country's landscape. Such intensely high rates of urbanization in less-developed countries are straining the infrastructures of the growing cities. Their growth has happened so quickly that these cities are often referred to as shock cities.

Large migration streams of young adults moving from rural areas to urban areas in pursuit of job opportunities challenge already-strained urban places. These young rural-urban migrants are often depressed to find filthy living conditions and demeaning working conditions. Unable to find housing, many new migrants build **squatter settlements (or *barriadas*)**—makeshift, unsafe housing constructed from any scraps they can find on land they neither rent nor own. The 1996 United Nations Conference on Human Settlements estimated that 600 million people were living in unsafe and life-threatening conditions in cities. Further, as much as 33 percent of the world's urban households live in absolute poverty.

Nearly 60 percent of households in Lagos, Nigeria, and Nairobi, Kenya, are not connected to running water.

Models of Urban Systems

As you walk through London, the sense of place you see and feel is quite different from the sense of place you perceive as you walk through Moscow, Russia, or even Nashville, Tennessee. Cities vary greatly in aspects such as their architecture, layout, density, social organization, depending on the political factors, cultural context, and how they have evolved over time.

Although two cities may have similar sizes, economic functions, and standards of living, like Chicago and New York, they can vary in their spatial layout and

Key Finding from the 2001 United Nations Conference on Human Settlements

"A country's global success rests on local shoulders. For the good of all citizens, city and state must become political partners rather than competitors. If accommodation requires new political arrangements, institutional structures or constitutional amendments, it is never too early or too late to begin making changes. . . . Gathering of evidence by putting in place proper information systems and diagnostic tools is a practical first step. Good information will provide the common platform for dialogue among stakeholders—an essential part of the process—as they approach a vision for the future and set priorities for conservation and change. *The main goal is to make the structures of governance more responsive to individuals, households and communities so that both national and local authorities can better serve civil society, each through separate but complementary instruments.*"

unique sense of place. Even as cities become more interconnected with globalization and even as people travel and communicate more frequently among the world's urban places, cities still show the imprints of the generations of people and economic functions that have influenced their growth. Just as the rings within old trees reflect layers of growth, city landscapes reflect the periods of their greatest development. Even the relatively young cities of the United States (compared with ancient cities like Rome) vary significantly depending on their historical eras of growth, their "growth spurt" phases, if you will.

Borchert Model of Urban Evolution

In the 1960s, **Samuel Borchert** studied U.S. cities and linked historical changes to urban evolution. **Borchert's model of urban evolution** defined four categories of cities based on the transportation technology that dominated during the era when the city hit its initial growth spurt and found a comparative advantage in the economy.

In stage 1 of this model are cities that first grew during the "sail wagon" era of 1790–1830 mostly near ports and waterways for transportation. In stage 2, "iron horse" cities were born and grew around the rivers and canals, during the early industrial years of 1830–1870, when the railroad and steamboats were rapidly spreading. By stage 3, the "steel rail" epoch of 1870–1920, the Industrial Revolution was at full steam in the United States. Powered by the steel industry, industrial cities blossomed, particularly around the Great Lakes. Stage 4 cities were born around 1920 and were intricately linked to car and air travel, leading to a maze of road networks and the rapid spread of suburbs. Stage 4 saw the growth of new, more-influential cities in the South.

For example, Pittsburgh began as Fort Duquesne and was on the landscape by 1760. Pittsburgh hit its peak in stages 2 and 3, and then its level of influence began decreasing. The reason a city becomes more or less prominent is related to its comparative advantage. In 1720, Pittsburgh had less of a comparative advantage because no one could reach it by ocean. By 1900, Pittsburgh had developed into a powerhouse because of its central location (situation) and the fact that it had railroads and canals feeding it all the raw materials needed to fuel its industrial revolution.

Such a comparative advantage, though, can weaken as other cities hit their growth spurts and begin to develop dominant comparative advantages. For example, Flint, Michigan, hit its growth spurt and developed a comparative advantage grounded in the Industrial Revolution but lost its dominance as the U.S. economy shifted away from an industrial, factory-based economy toward a more service-based economy.

Cultural and Regional Urban Diversity

Differences among cities often result from their cultural and national contexts. Monuments, temples, and pyramids dominate ancient Chinese and Mexican cityscapes to show the dominance of their governments and religious philosophies, as well as to provide settings for important functions. In contrast, medieval Islamic cities were organized with tiny, winding, dead-end streets into which mosques and government buildings were woven and not prominently displayed. Medieval Muslims believed their buildings should blend into the urban landscape, usually to ensure privacy and protection from outsiders. Visiting Europeans often described such Islamic cities as "mysterious," showing how different the Europeans' outlook on urban structure was from the Muslim view.

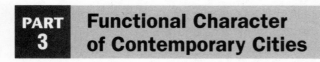

PART 3 **Functional Character of Contemporary Cities**

Basic Versus Nonbasic Jobs

What do cities do, and what types of products do they make to bring in the goods their people need to survive? First, we need to distinguish between basic and nonbasic employment sectors of a city's economy. The **basic employment sector** brings money into an urban place and gives the city its primary function (think *basic brings in* money). For example, Flint, Michigan, was dominated by its

Figure 8.7. Two different urban architectural styles in Shanghai, China, reflecting different influences on the city's urban culture and landscape

Figure 8.8. Islamic architecture often puts windows and openings above human reach and covers windows to increase the privacy of the inhabitants

basic employment sector of automobile manufacturing. The cars made in Flint's basic employment sector were exported to other places, which in turn sent money into Flint's economy for the cars. Chapel Hill, North Carolina, is a small city with a basic employment sector dominated by the existence of the University of North Carolina, a basic employment function that exports information and knowledge in exchange for bringing money into Chapel Hill.

The **nonbasic employment sector** in a city comprises jobs that shift money within the city, not outside the city as basic jobs do. Teachers, janitors, fire departments, dry cleaners, street cleaners, and air-conditioner repair companies are all examples of nonbasic employment. In other words, the nonbasic sector is largely responsible for maintaining a city's infrastructure.

Usually, the larger the city, the higher the percentage of nonbasic jobs, because these larger cities often have more infrastructural needs, from window washers, dry cleaners, and parking attendants, to expert subway technicians and financial consultants. In a smaller city, gas stations and restaurants may be part of its basic employment sector because residents from nearby rural regions may come into the small town to purchase those services, thereby bringing money into the town from outside.

Since most cities have the same types of nonbasic jobs, it is the basic employment sector that defines a city and gives it more of its unique sense of place and presence in the economy. Steel-mill towns, warehouse port facilities, oil refineries, country music towns, movie industry hotspots—all are examples of elements of the basic employment sector that heavily influence a city's sense of identity. Nashville is defined by its country music industry, an integral part of its basic employment sector.

Multiplier Effect

Cities often try to build their economies around the basic employment sector, which brings in money from the outside. For example, a car factory will bring money in because the cars are produced and sold to people outside the city. In fact, the addition of one basic job tends to give rise to more jobs, including non-basic jobs. This pattern is called the **multiplier effect**. For example, the addition of production line jobs in an automobile factory, which are basic jobs producing a good for export and interaction with other places, creates the need for new janitors, air-conditioning repair people, electricians, and building inspectors, among others—nonbasic jobs. Likewise, adding a movie production company requires nonbasic jobs like carpenters, hair stylists, and costume makers to keep it operating. Thus, the addition of a basic job multiplies the number of jobs within a community. Adding a nonbasic job does not have the same multiplying effect.

Agglomeration

Sometimes a successful industry that generates a multiplier effect becomes a leader in its field throughout the world. When a business achieves such a recognized status as an industry leader, it is called a growth pole, and it often acts as a magnet, attracting other industries and businesses near it to take advantage of its "shine" and innovation. When these businesses locate near the growth pole, it leads to agglomeration. As discussed in Chapter 7, agglomeration is the clumping of industries to take advantage of each other's resources.

For example, the University of North Carolina at Chapel Hill has had success in health research that has led to its becoming a growth pole, attracting other research industries to the area. The resulting agglomeration of research industries has led to a powerful economic multiplier effect, with the number of new jobs skyrocketing and generating new wealth. However, traffic buildup and overcrowding have occurred in the region as a result of the growing Research Triangle Park. Another negative result of agglomeration is the backwash effect; recall from Chapter 7 that this is caused when the growth poles and related agglomeration draw talent and economic growth out of the surrounding regions and do not allow for equal development and the even spread of development throughout the landscape.

Changing Employment Mix of Contemporary Cities

North America's basic employment sectors were once dominated by manufacturing and industrial activities. However, the nature of America's basic employment sector is moving away from industrial jobs and toward professional and financial services. Instead of being dominated by factory-based production processes, modern **postindustrial city** economies are focused more on display and consumption. Old factories are being converted into shopping malls; former waterfront industrial ports are being turned into parks for recreation; old warehouses are turning into art galleries. Postindustrial architecture is often characterized by **postmodernism**, a style that emphasizes diversity and free form rather than the uniformity and symmetry that characterize the classical Greco-Roman roots of Renaissance- and Enlightenment-era architecture.

While the Industrial Revolution changed cities into smog-laden centers of manufacturing and distribution, the modern economy is moving cities back to the Greco-Roman concept of a city, one in which the resources needed by vibrant economic diversity and lifestyles come from centers of production outside the city. Most of the factory-produced goods that Americans buy are now made in foreign countries and shipped into the United States. In exchange, U.S. cities provide services to the foreign production regions, like financial and entertainment services.

Thus, the old industrial cores of the United States, like Chicago and Manhattan, are becoming **deindustrialized**, with their factory-based economies transitioning to economies dominated by the service sector. Such cities have experienced "boom and bust" cycles, in which their service sectors boomed while their manufacturing sectors busted. Some Sunbelt cities, like Austin, Texas, never had any manufacturing base, so their service sectors have boomed without any commensurate bust. Critics of the changing functional nature of U.S. cities worry that if cities become heavily dependent on foreign producers, Americans could be left out economically because they cannot make their own products. Also, factory jobs often offered more security to workers than the increasingly dominant retail and fast-food-type service-sector jobs dominating urban economies. Moreover, factory work required few computer skills and little education. In modern-city economies, people without training and education are left out of the mix, leading to higher rates of crime and unemployment. There are simply fewer factory jobs that provide adequate incomes. Educators are having to analyze and adjust to this prominent economic shift to train students to fill the more highly skilled jobs now in demand.

 PART 4 **Built Environment and Social Space**

Comparative Models of Urban Systems

To understand why cities are spatially organized in various ways, geographers have developed models that explain and predict the internal structures of cities. Most focus on patterns of internal growth within U.S. cities, but some of the following models can be extended to explain and predict foreign cities. Each model described here possesses a **central business district (CBD)**, or original core of its economy, like the nucleus of a cell. However, the degree of influence and geographic location of the CBD varies throughout the models.

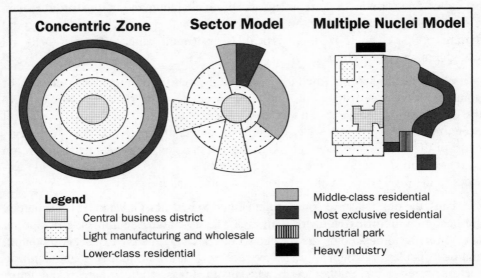

Figure 8.9. Three urban land use models

Concentric Zone Model

Developed in the 1920s, the **concentric zone model** was the first model to explain and predict urban growth. Based on urban growth in Chicago, the concentric zone model is the original foundation on which the other models of urban growth were built. The model suggests that a city's land use can be viewed from above as a series of concentric rings, like the rings of a tree trunk that has been cut. As the city grows and expands, new rings are added and older rings change their function and character. For example, a ring of land use that was once where houses were built might become more of a business sector. Old houses may be transformed into offices. The model assumes a process called **invasion and succession (or succession migration)**, in which new arrivals to cities tend to move first into the inner rings, near the CBD. Eventually, people and economic activities in the center are pushed out into farther rings. Invasion and succession is essentially a series of migration waves, with one group moving in and establishing itself.

For example, let's consider the arrival of European immigrants to a hypothetical U.S. city. As German immigrants start to move in (or invade), the English immigrants already living in the city become aggravated and choose to leave, thus making more room for more Germans. This creates a German-dominated center and an English-dominated outer ring. When Italian immigrants decide to move in, they cannot afford to live in the English areas, so they head for the German center. The arrival of new immigrants causes aggravation in the German-dominated core, prompting the Germans to "push out" toward the next ring where the English had settled, thus pushing the English settlers further out. In this example, each new group is looked down on by all the others as the "new guys" who are "ruining" things.

Because of this constant invasion and succession pattern, often a ring known as the **zone in transition** forms just outside the CBD. This ring never becomes developed because investors know it will constantly be caught in the shifting urban pattern. Sometimes this zone of transition is called skid row.

One of the most important components of the concentric zone model is the CBD, known as "downtown" in the United States. In the concentric zone model, the CBD is the land use ring nearest the point of maximum accessibility and visibility in the city, a point known as the **peak land value intersection**. The highest real estate prices and competition for land are found in this model's CBD. Land values decrease moving in all directions away from the CBD, so that the farther out a ring of urban land use, the less expensive the land. This pattern is known as a **bid-rent curve**, which predicts that land prices and population density decline as distances from the central business district increase. A ritzy real estate firm would want to buy a sleek headquarters in the heart of the CBD to show importance in the community and to have access to the downtown's powerful people and businesses. However, a factory would probably not choose to locate in the CBD. Rather, a factory would most likely move away from the CBD, where it can purchase more land for less money to build its horizontal factory.

The concentric zone model shows a pattern in which the architecture and function of buildings match in each concentric ring of urban land use. In other words, the architecture of the houses in a concentric ring occupied by suburban families matches its function to provide families with houses. A suburban-style house is not a likely sight in the heart of Chicago's CBD.

Sector Model

The concentric zone model assumes that a city offers equal access to the CBD in all directions radiating from it. However, in the 1930s, geographers discovered a twist on the concentric zone pattern, known as the **sector model**. The sector model grew out of geographers' observations that there were urban land use zones of growth based on transportation routes and linear features like roads, canals, railroads, and major boulevards, not just concentric zones around the CBD. However, both the concentric zone and sector models feature a strong CBD. The sector model explains that similar land uses and socioeconomic groups clumped in geometric sectors radiating outward from the CBD along particular transportation routes. Therefore, in urban patterns conforming to the sector model, many factories and industrial activities follow rail lines, lower socioeconomic housing follows lines of public transportation, and sectors that service visitors are located along major highways. By the late 1940s, the assumptions of both the concentric zone and sector models no longer applied to urban growth patterns. Therefore, a new model was born: the multiple-nuclei model.

Multiple-Nuclei Model

Unlike previous models that focused on a strong CBD, the **multiple-nuclei model** suggests that growth occurred independently around several major focal points, like airports, universities, highway interchanges, and ports. These focal points may be distant from the "original" CBD and only loosely connected to it, suggesting a reduced dominance of the CBD in urban growth. The multiple-nuclei model recognizes that land use zones often pop up at once, in chunks. Industrial parks, shopping centers, and housing zones are built in one giant sweep of construction and are only very loosely connected to the original heart of the city. In the 1950s, suburban neighborhoods were created overnight.

The model does not suggest that the CBD is necessarily unimportant, but it does show that new areas of intense urban growth (the nuclei) can grow simultaneously around key nodes of access or industry. In the 1950s, geographers saw the growth of **exurbs** (extra-urban areas) or rings of wealthier rural communities that grew just outside of the suburbs and were hotbeds of continued urban growth and development. Early inhabitants of exurbs commuted over parkway systems and commuter rails.

Urban Realms Model

As the automobile became increasingly prevalent in the 1970s, the **urban realms model** was developed to explain suburban regions that were functionally tied to mixed-use suburban downtowns with relative independence from the CBD. This model grew from the increasing independence developed by the nuclei within the multiple-nuclei growth pattern. Beyond simply being focal points of urban growth, these nuclei had evolved into independently functioning "urban realms." The urban realms model recognized that many people's daily lives and activities occurred within a fixed activity space within a portion, or urban realm, of a larger metro region. In these urban realms, one could find suburban downtowns, filled with all the amenities needed for living, including businesses, eateries, medical care, and so forth.

Importantly, many North American city and suburb dwellers want to escape from the bustling pace of modern urban life. Beginning in the 1970s, larger numbers of middle- and later-aged (older) citizens were leaving cities and suburbs and moving to more rural areas and small towns outside the city's busy way of life in a pattern called **counterurbanization**. Plus, with the advent of the Internet and telecommunications technology, people no longer had to commute physically; they could work from home and send everything electronically, a trend called **telecommuting**.

A Comment on All the Models

Importantly, the classic models can be combined to understand a particular city's urban growth pattern. A CBD may be encircled by rings and sectors with a variety of nuclei and realms existing farther from the CBD along a beltway, for example.

Latin American Cities and the Three Models

The classic models can be applied to illustrate urban growth patterns in various cultural settings, such as those in Latin America, especially in formerly Spanish colonial regions. During the medieval period, cities in Europe were laid out in unplanned jumbles of open spaces and intertwined streets, but the 1400s saw a rebirth in Greco-Roman architecture and urban design. Europeans then diffused those classical structures throughout their colonies. In fact, Spain passed a law in 1573 ordering that all its colonial cities would be built according to Greco-Roman designs, with prominent, rectangular plazas dominated by a cathedral and major governmental buildings. These plazas resembled the sectors featured in the sector model.

As with the CBD, a ring of commercial and residential areas formed close to the plaza. The CBD was more important in the focus of Latin American cities because suburbanization was not nearly as strong in Latin America. Instead of rings of wealthy residential areas outside the CBD, as in the suburban rings of North American cities, the zones of the Latin American city model typically decrease in wealth moving away from the CBD. Squatter settlements and abject poverty often mark the rings outside of the centers of Latin American cities. Moreover, Latin Americans traditionally live downtown, giving the inner cities more of a residential nature than is typical of North American cities. Because of the intensity of use, a Latin American city usually has no zone of transition. Further, because Latin Americans people tend to stay in the inner cities (and cannot get loans to move), they tend to upgrade their existing homes, rather than moving out to different neighborhoods as residents of North American cities usually do.

Like other less-developed regions, many Latin American cities have struggled to meet the demands of rapid urbanization. For example, Latin American urban governments are finding it difficult to provide infrastructural support to the growing urban populations. The massive numbers of rural-urban migrants often find shelter by building makeshift homes in the **periferico**, or zone of peripheral squatter settlements. However, industrial parks and government housing projects are starting to pop up in Latin American cities, like nuclei in North American cities, although these urban focal points are less common in Latin American cities because of the limited amount of capital available for development and investment in such projects by developers.

Transportation and Urban Infrastructure

How does transportation infrastructure affect the development of land use and building types? Consider a colonial city built for walking and horse-riding citizens, before motorized transport. The general store, market shops, government offices, bank, and doctor's office were usually located on one block, because people would come to town for their general needs and not be able to transport themselves long distances to obtain each service.

As modes of transportation became more efficient and speedier, the organization and use of urban space changed. Land use and building types could be more specialized and more widespread. As people increasingly used public transportation lines, various districts of urban land use developed along those lines of urban growth, which radiated out from the downtown in a **star-shaped pattern**. Department stores, urban housing zones, and office parks grew around the lines of transportation, which provided the threshold population needed for business to continue. Paris, London, New York City, and Chicago were among the first cities to develop subways and elevated trains to transport massive amounts of people and products into and out of the urban core.

By the 1920s and 1930s, the use of the car had exploded on the scene. City streets were widened and a few parkways were constructed, but the pattern of a strong CBD and zones of straight-line urban growth radiating from it continued until after the 1950s, when the U.S. government enacted the National Defense Highways Act, which ordered the construction of highways to facilitate the movement of military equipment, such as nuclear missiles, during the cold war. Although urban growth continued in the star-shaped pattern established with earlier transportation modes, by the 1970s and 1980s, a new urban form was born with the construction of beltways, or highways that encircled urban areas. With the growth of these outer-belt freeways, people could quickly access areas around the CBD, which led to the growth of regional offices, industrial parks, and shopping centers in new nuclei within the metropolitan complex. Often these new nuclei of urban growth were located in places of urban accessibility, such as on highway exits.

Urban Sprawl

Joel Garreau referred to the self-sufficient urban villages that developed within a greater metropolitan complex, often at highway exits, as **edge cities**. The result of this explosive growth empowered by the growth of highways and beltways is referred to as **urban sprawl**, the diffusion of urban land use and lifestyle into formerly nonurban, often agricultural lands. The pattern of urban sprawl has raised continued problems related to uneven development and changing land use patterns.

Political Organization and Urban Sprawl

The political organization of urban areas largely contributes to the sprawling nature of U.S. cities. Suburbs often fight for independence from the metropolitan government so that their inhabitants can have their own mini-governments and tax bases. A central city surrounded, even strangled, by independently governed suburbs is left with a limited tax base.

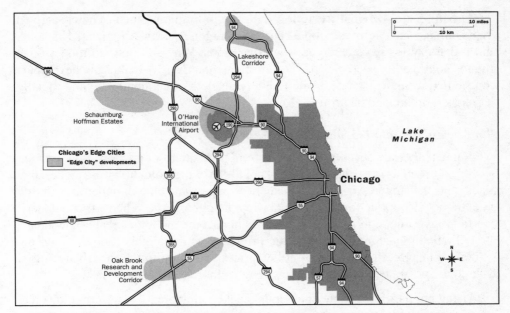

Figure 8.10. Edge cities linked to Chicago

If the inner city is predominantly occupied by a lower socioeconomic (poorer) tax base, then the amount of taxes the inner city can collect for its schools and infrastructure is limited. Saint Louis, Missouri, had nearly 1 million residents in 1950, but by 2000 the city proper had only 300,000 residents, because most people had fled to the independently governed suburbs surrounding the city. Many suburbs have legislated their exclusivity, passing **restrictive covenants**, or laws prohibiting low-income housing. The wealthy town of Franklin, Tennessee, has recently passed a law requiring all homeowners to pay a hefty fee to have all their power lines put underground because "it looks better." Obviously, this would be financially impossible for anyone with a low income.

Ghettoization and Uneven Development

Because of political influences, transportation infrastructures, and location preferences, urban sprawl has led to uneven development and **ghettoization**, the growth of areas of concentrated poverty. **Uneven development** refers to urban development that is not spread equally among a city's areas, leaving some areas richly developed and others continually poor and decrepit. Uneven development is often caused by **cumulative causation**, when money flows to areas of greatest profit, places where development has already been focused, rather than to places of greatest need. Agglomeration is another process related to cumulative causation. Opulent skyscrapers and multimillion-dollar malls often exist only minutes from some of the poorest, most underdeveloped regions. Racially and ethnically uniform neighborhoods continued to exist even after the 1960s Civil Rights Act prohibited legal racial segregation.

Urban ghettos originally comprised mostly immigrants, such as newly arrived Irish, Italian, and German people, but even larger African American, Hispanic, and Asian ghettos have emerged since the 1950s. Why and how do modern-day ghettos continue to exist? Several surreptitious practices by real estate developers contributed to the existence of modern-day clusters of economically and racially segregated urban land use zones.

Blockbusting, Redlining, and Racial Steering

Some real estate developers profited from this pattern of ghettoization, preying on racism to sell as many houses as they could. They used **blockbusting** tactics, like placing advertising in African American newspapers and church bulletins, offering an extremely low price for a house in a white neighborhood. When African American families came to look at the advertised house, the malicious real estate agents incited racially charged turmoil in the primarily white neighborhood, urging the white families to sell their homes at low prices and move to the suburban fringes, where they would be "safe" from "invading" minority groups.

Using another form of the malicious blockbusting practice, unscrupulous real estate agents vandalized houses in a neighborhood to induce panic and urge people to move out. Then the same real estate agents would profit from the turnover and clear the land to build large, urban housing structures, which often degenerated into tenements. Blockbusting is now illegal.

Some less-obvious tactics influenced the continued existence of urban ghettos and segregated urban land use patterns. Real estate agents, either intentionally or unintentionally, steered people to certain neighborhoods and not others based on their race, a practice known as **racial steering**, which is now illegal. Further, banks would **redline** minority districts, refusing to give loans to people moving to minority-dominated areas on the grounds that the statistical improbability of successful development in these zones meant the loans would not be repaid. Though redlining is now illegal, the practice contributed to a vicious cycle wherein developers and minority families wanting to develop and improve ghettoized regions could never get money to do so, which only contributed to the continually impoverished character of those zones.

Several real estate trends today contribute to the continued uneven pattern of development in many urban places. The development of gated communities is often based on an underlying fear of crime and, sometimes, racial integration. These types of developments are often constructed with strict regulations and covenants, binding their residents to specific house colors, sizes, and rules, even as to the size of the dogs they can have.

Gentrification

Gentrification is a process wherein older, urban zones are "rediscovered and renovated" by people who move back to the inner city from their suburban fringes.

Gentrification is a trend that is bringing money into urban areas thought to be underdeveloped and poor. Have you driven through your city's inner area and seen a trendy new loft-apartment complex built in an old, abandoned factory warehouse? If so, that is gentrification. Many people see gentrification as a great solution to recharging a city's inner core that was suffering because of **suburbanization**, the growth of suburb neighborhoods and commuter families, and the continued flight of wealthier classes out of the inner city.

However, critics of gentrification see it as only increasing uneven development. They think gentrification is pushing lower-income families from their homes to make way for glitzy, trendy buildings that only the rich can afford. New businesses do come to the region to cater to the rich "gentrifiers," but the people who were living in the neighborhood in the first place cannot afford to patronize the new businesses or buy into the gentrified housing complexes. In this sense, critics claim, gentrification does not help reduce poverty and uneven development but actually pushes the urban poor from their neighborhoods and divides the urban landscape into ghettos and highly priced gentrified districts.

(Photo by: J. Dabu)

Figure 8.11. A block that has been renewed, or gentrified, by investors

Strategies to Curb the Negative Effects of Urban Sprawl

Urban sprawl is one of the greatest challenges facing North American cities. In larger metropolitan cities, you often find suburbs, shopping malls, and industrial parks only miles from the original CBD. However, it is rare to find effective mass transit systems in North American cities. Often this is a result of the high cost of installing subways and other mass transit systems that were not built into the urban infrastructure as the city grew. Some strategists suggest building railways for commuters, more bike paths, government-organized carpools, and special bus lanes. In fact, in Nashville, a new train system is being developed for commuters coming from edge cities into the downtown area.

European cities like London have worked to limit urban development to a particular area. London installed a **green belt** to contain its urban core, forcing all urban development to occur within that boundary and not sprawl. North American cities have a difficult time setting such boundaries because they can attract investors who want to develop these lands and grow the city at the expense of rural lands. Also, city governments profit from new taxes in suburbs. Portland, Oregon, has effectively instituted a boundary to contain urban sprawl. There developers must focus on the land within the established boundary, forcing revitalization of the inner city, not outward growth. Portland also built an effective mass transit system.

Another approach to lessening the negative effects of urban sprawl exists in **street morphology**, or the organization of street patterns. Many newer suburbs are built around cul-de-sacs and loop streets, rather than the traditional grid design of inner cities. Developers tend to favor cul-de-sacs and looping streets to provide privacy for their neighborhoods, reducing traffic and noise throughout the neighborhood by allowing only one or two entrances and exits into and out of the neighborhood.

However, such a street morphology channels all traffic in the same direction toward the major highways. Drivers have no way to escape the traffic, often leading

(Photo by: Derek Jensen)

Figure 8.12. Urban sprawl and its effect on landscape distinctiveness

to backups at the few entrances and exits to the development. Pedestrians cannot walk and cars cannot escape traffic jams by going around the block.

Related to urban morphology are zoning laws. In many shock cities, governments have not effectively created boundaries to channel growth and development into organized sectors, or zones. For example, in some cities experiencing high rates of urbanization, makeshift low-income housing may exist next to large polluting factories. Such lack of zoning contributes to infrastructural decay and problems in functional land use.

Recent Trends in Neo-Urbanism

Recent innovations in neo-urbanism, or the new urban landscape, include **planned communities**, which are neighborhoods with master-planned housing designs, recreational facilities, security systems, and other features that stress uniformity and common identity in the landscape. One planned community in Memphis includes a small grocery store and ice-cream shop, pedestrian-friendly walkways, a Starbucks, and a golf cart for each family in the neighborhood.

Health experts are encouraging North American developers to build pedestrian walkways to help reduce cardiovascular disease, which is increasing in the United States, partly because of Americans' total reliance on automobile travel rather than walking. The Memphis planned community also includes a picnic area and community gathering spot for everyone in the neighborhood to use. In fact, many recent urban designs include **festival settings**, or large recreational areas for communities, such as waterfront parks along the rivers in Nashville, Tennessee, and Louisville, Kentucky. Another feature of the new urban landscape is **office parks,** zones of urban land exclusively set aside for corporate offices and often include incentives to businesses for locating offices in them.

The popular name for neo-urbanism is the livable city movement. Portland, Oregon was an innovator in the movement and is one of the best examples of it. Other well-known examples are Chattanooga, Tennessee; Asheville, North Carolina; and Fort Collins, Colorado. Fort Collins calls itself a "wellness city" and requires a certain percentage of the businesses to focus on wellness. Chiropractors, massage therapists, bike shops, gyms, and other businesses that help people finding "wellness" without using drugs are highly encouraged by the city's planners.

PART 5   Chapter Review

Models Review

Borchert's Model of Urban Evolution

Borchert created this model in the 1960s to predict and explain the growth of cities in four phases of transportation history: stage 1, the "sail wagon" era of 1790–1830; stage 2, the "iron horse" era of 1830–1870; stage 3, the "steel rail" epoch of 1870–1920; and stage 4, the current era of car and air travel that began after 1920.

Central Place Theory

Developed in the 1930s by Walter Christaller, this model explains and predicts patterns of urban places across the map. In his model, Christaller analyzed the hexagonal, hierarchical pattern of cities, villages, towns, and hamlets arranged according to their varying degrees of centrality, determined by the central place functions existing in urban places and the hinterlands they serve.

Concentric Zone Model

This model was devised in the 1920s to predict and explain the growth patterns of North American urban spaces. Its main principle is that cities can be viewed from above as a series of concentric rings; as the city grows and expands, new rings are added and old ones change character. Key elements of the model are the central business district and the peak land value intersection.

Sector Model

This model predicts and explains North American urban growth patterns in the 1930s in a pattern in which similar land uses and socioeconomic groups clustered in linear sectors radiating outward from a central business district, usually along transportation corridors.

Multiple-Nuclei Model

Developed in the 1950s, this model explains the changing growth pattern of urban spaces based on the assumption that growth occurred independently around several major foci (or nodes), many of which are far away from the central business district and only marginally connected to it.

Urban Realms Model

This model was developed in the 1970s to explain and predict changing urban growth patterns as the automobile became increasingly prevalent and large suburban "realms" emerged. The suburban regions were functionally tied to a mixed-use sub-urban downtown, or mini-CBD, with relative independence from the original CBD.

Terms Review

Basic employment sector—Group of economic functions that bring money into an urban place and represent the city's primary functions.

Bid-rent curve—Graph showing the predicted decline in cost of land and population density as you move away from the central business district in the concentric zone model.

Blockbusting—Tactic (now illegal) that contributed to ghettoization; used by real estate agents to get people to move out of their homes because of fear of racial integration.

Central business district (CBD)—Original core of a city's economy, like the nucleus of a cell.

Central place—Urban center that provides services to people living in the surrounding rural areas.

Colonial city—City whose primary identity is as a colony of an invading or conquering imperial power, often showing forced cultural imprints of the colonizer.

Counterurbanization—Increase in rural populations resulting from the out-migration of city residents from their city and suburban homes in search of the peace and tranquility of nonurban lifestyles.

Cumulative causation—Contributing factor to uneven development; occurs when money flows to areas of greatest profit, places where development has already been focused, rather than to places of greatest need.

Deindustrialized—Refers to an industrial city whose factory-based economy has transitioned to an economy dominated by the service sector.

Edge city—Self-sufficient urban area within a greater metropolitan complex; often develops on highway exits.

Exurb—Area of growth outside the central city and surrounding suburbs; its growth is fueled by people exiting the city and suburbs in search of the peace and tranquility of more-rural lifestyles.

Festival setting—Area within an urban place built for community gatherings, such as a park or waterfront.

Gentrification—Process in which older urban zones are rediscovered and renovated by people who move back into the inner city from their suburban fringes;

resulting influx of new money raises prices and pushes out lower-income residents.

Ghettoization—Growth of areas of concentrated poverty in urban places.

Green belt—Boundary encircling an urban place and limiting the sprawl of the city, forcing inward development and reinvestment in a city's core.

Hinterland—Area serviced by a central place.

Industrial city—City that grew during the Industrial Revolution. Rather than serving mainly as an administrative, religious, trade, or gateway city, the industrial city's primary function was to make and distribute manufactured products.

Invasion and succession (or succession immigration)—Pattern of inflow of new migrants to the central business district in the concentric zone model and then the related pushing of existing inhabitants outward to rings outside the center, thereby causing changing land use patterns.

Level of urbanization—Percentage of people considered urban.

Megacity—City that has a high degree of centrality and primacy; although not a world city, it exerts high levels of influence and power in the country's economy. All of megacities have populations over 10 million inhabitants.

Megalopolis—Massive, urban "blob" of overlapping, integrating metropolitan areas whose distinctive boundaries are increasingly becoming difficult to find.

Metropolitan statistical area (MSA)—U.S. Census Bureau geographic unit of area including a central city and all its immediately interacting counties populated by commuters and people directly connected to the central city. An MSA is an urbanized region with a minimum of 50,000 residents.

Micropolitan statistical area—U.S. Census Bureau geographic unit comprising a central city and the surrounding counties integrated into it, and having a population of 10,000 to 50,000.

Multiplier effect—Increased economic success and energy created by the addition of new basic-sector jobs.

Nonbasic employment sector—Group of economic functions in a city that shift money within the city, not outside the city as in the basic employment sector.

Office park—Zone of urban land exclusively set aside for corporate offices. Often office park developers offer incentives to businesses to locate there.

Panregional influence—Influence that extends beyond the city's own region into the other centers of economic control.

Peak land value intersection—Point of land with maximum accessibility and visibility in the city, usually the center of the CBD in the concentric zone model.

Periferico—Most peripheral zone of a Latin American city marked by squatter settlements and abject poverty.

Planned community—Master-planned neighborhood with preformulated architectural designs, built-in community gathering spots, and restrictive covenants.

Postindustrial city—City whose economy and urban organization are conforming to the dominance of service-sector, nonindustrial economic functions.

Postmodernism—Postindustrial school of architecture and urban design that frowns on symmetry and balance and looks more toward diversity and individuality in expression.

Preindustrial city—City existing before the Industrial Revolution that served as a trade center and gateway to foreign lands and markets. Often the rural settlements surrounding the urban space provided agricultural products and foodstuffs to the urban dwellers, who in turn provided different economic functions.

Primacy—Degree to which a primate city dominates economic, political, and cultural functions in a country. The degree of primacy is calculated using the formula P_1/P_2, where P_1 is the population size of the primate city and P_2 is the second-largest city in the country.

Racial steering—Tactic (now illegal) contributing to ghettoization; real estate agents would show people neighborhoods and houses according to their race.

Range of a good or service—Maximum distance a person is willing to travel to obtain a good or service.

Rank-size rule—In a region, the nth-largest city's population is $1/n$ the population of the region's largest city.

Rate of urbanization—Speed that the population is becoming urban.

Redlining—Practice (now-illegal) of banks and lending agencies refusing to give loans to people moving to minority-dominated districts because the banks/agencies feared the loans would not be repaid based on the statistical improbability of successful development in the districts.

Restrictive covenants—Special laws passed by communities usually to exert control over the way their neighborhood will look and grow, such as laws restricting how people can use their space.

Shock city—Urban place experiencing infrastructural challenges related to massive and rapid urbanization.

Spatial competition—Assumption in the central place theory that implies that central places compete with each other for customers.

Squatter settlement (or *barriada*)—Makeshift, unsafe housing constructed from any scraps people can find on land they neither rent nor own.

Star-shaped city pattern—Early shape of city growth before automobile dominance in which lines of public transportation radiated from the central business district (or downtown) in a star pattern. The star-shaped pattern of growth maintained the dominance of the CBD.

Street morphology—Layout or pattern of streets.

Suburbanization—Growth of lower-density housing, industry, and commercial zones outside the central business district.

Telecommuting—Modern form of commuting that involves only the commuting of information, not the worker, through use of the telephone and Internet technology, allowing people to send information and communication over long distances. (For example, this book was written Tennessee, sent to California for editing, and then transmitted to New Jersey for publication, all via e-mail.)

Threshold—*Minimum* number of people needed to fuel a particular function's existence in a central place.

Uneven development—Urban development that is not spread equally among a city's areas, leaving some areas richly developed and others continually poor and decrepit.

Urban banana—Arch of the dominant overland, trade-based cities stretching from London to Tokyo in the 1500s before the rise of sea-based trade and exploration.

Urban hearth area—Area where an urban lifestyle and civilization started and from which they diffused.

Urban hierarchy—System of cities consisting of various levels, with few cities at the top level and increasingly more settlements on each lower level. The position of a city within the hierarchy is determined by the diversity and level of central place functions it provides.

Urbanization—Growth and diffusion of city landscapes and urban lifestyle.

Urban sprawl—Diffusion of urban land use and lifestyle into formerly nonurban, often agricultural lands; has raised continued problems related to uneven development and changing land use patterns.

Urban system—Network of urban places; part of an interlocking web of interacting cities.

World city—Powerful city that controls a disproportionately high level of the world's economic, political, and cultural activities. Sometimes called a global city, it has a high degree of centrality in the global urban system.

Zone in transition—Ring of land usually just around the central business district that is constantly in flux and run down because of successive waves of immigration that never allow it to develop a permanent population base and attract development.

PART 6   Some Suggested Web Resources for Further Exploration

Urban Institute: http://www.urban.org/

The Urban Institute researches public policy issues on issues related to urban lifestyle and sprawl, producing reports on issues such as schools in impoverished neighborhoods, environmental problems in urban areas, zoning issues, and more.

Best Practices: http://www.bestpractices.org/

Coordinated by the UN Habitat, this searchable database contains thousands of proven solutions from nearly 150 countries to the common social, economic, and environmental problems of an urbanizing world.

UN Human Settlements Programme: http://www.unhabitat.org/

UN Habitat is the United Nations agency for human settlements. It is mandated by the UN General Assembly to promote socially and environmentally sustainable towns and cities with the goal of providing adequate shelter for all. The website has articles, researched data, and stories related to the UN's work in promoting shelter for the world's people.

Earth Observatory: http://earthobservatory.nasa.gov/

The Earth Observatory page is run by the National Aeronautics and Space Administration (NASA) and provides interesting images related to NASA's research on urbanization and its relationship to global warming and other environmental issues.

UN Department of Economic and Social Affairs (DESA): http://www. un.org/esa/desa/

According to its website, the mission of the DESA is as follows: "Under the overall authority of the General Assembly, DESA coordinates the economic and social work of the United Nations and the UN family of organizations. As the central forum for discussing international economic and social issues and for formulating policy recommendations, the Council plays a key role in fostering international cooperation for development. It also consults with nongovernmental organizations (NGOs), thereby maintaining a vital link between the United Nations and civil society."

Earth Institute: http://www.earthinstitute.columbia.edu/

Issues addressed on this website, run by Columbia University, include challenges facing the planet and its inhabitants, with particular focus on sustainable development and the needs of the world's poor. As its mission states, "The Earth Institute is motivated by the belief that science and technological tools already exist, and could be expanded, to greatly improve conditions for the world's poor while preserving the natural systems that support life on Earth."

Pre-Exam Practice

Terms Review Quiz

Use the Terms Review list or your own memory to determine the extent of your knowledge of key terms and concepts. Remember, the AP exam does not include this kind of exercise, but it is included here as a review tool.

1. _____ Makeshift, unsafe housing constructed from any scraps people can find on land they neither rent nor own.

2. _____ System of cities consisting of various levels, with few cities at the top level and increasingly more settlements on each lower level.

3. _____ Growth of lower-density housing, industry, and commercial zones outside the central business district.

4. _____ Graph showing the predicted decline in cost of land and population density as you move away from the central business district in the concentric zone model.

5. _____ Growth of areas of concentrated poverty in urban places.

6. _____ Ring of land usually just around the central business district that is constantly in flux and rundown because of successive waves of immigration that never allow it to develop a permanent population base and attract development.

7. _____ Degree to which a primate city dominates economic, political, and cultural functions in a country.

8. _____ Tactic (now illegal) contributing to ghettoization; real estate agents would show people neighborhoods and houses according to their race.

9. _____ Self-sufficient urban area within a greater metropolitan complex; often develops on highway exits.

10. _____ Contributing factor to uneven development; occurs when money flows to areas of greatest profit, places where development has already been focused, rather than to places of greatest need.

11. _____ Powerful city that controls a disproportionately high level of the world's economic, political, and cultural activities. Sometimes called a global city, it has a high degree of centrality in the global urban system.

12. _____ Urban development that is not spread equally among a city's areas, leaving some areas richly developed and others continually poor and decrepit.

13. _____ *Minimum* number of people needed to fuel a particular function's existence in a central place.

14. _____ Growth and diffusion of city landscapes and urban lifestyle.

15. _____ Urban place experiencing infrastructural challenges related to massive and rapid urbanization.

16. _____ Original core of a city's economy, like the nucleus of a cell.

17. _____ Layout or pattern of streets.

18. _____ Assumption in the central place theory that implies that central places compete with each other for customers.

19. _____ City that has a high degree of centrality and primacy; although not a world city, it exerts high levels of influence and power in the country's economy.

20. _____ Maximum distance a person is willing to travel to obtain that good or service.

21. _____ Massive, urban "blob" of overlapping, integrating metropolitan areas whose distinctive boundaries are increasingly becoming difficult to find.

22. _____ Most peripheral zone of a Latin American city marked by squatter settlements and abject poverty.

23. _____ U.S. Census Bureau geographic unit comprising a central city and the surrounding counties integrated into it, and having a population of 10,000 to 50,000.

24. _____ Arch of the dominant overland, trade-based cities stretching from London to Tokyo in the 1500s before the rise of sea-based trade and exploration.

25. _____ Area serviced by a central place.

Multiple-Choice Review Questions

1. Chicago's relative location near other major city networks gave the urban place a comparative advantage for successful economic growth. This statement best describes Chicago's

   (A) threshold

   (B) site

   (C) situation

   (D) density

   (E) functional zonation

2. Tony and Jacob are brothers who decided to move into an old warehouse in downtown New York City and fix it up into a slick loft apartment complex. Tony and Jacob's actions are most closely classified as

   (A) suburbanization

   (B) urban morphology

   (C) social stratification

   (D) gentrification

   (E) redlining

3. All the following are processes that have contributed to ghettoization in North American cities EXCEPT

   (A) blockbusting

   (B) redlining

   (C) racial steering

   (D) green belts

   (E) suburbanization

4. Tokyo is many times larger than the second-ranked city in Japan, thus making Tokyo a(n)

   (A) periferico

   (B) central business district

   (C) hinterland

   (D) squatter settlement

   (E) primate city

5. All of the following are common preconditions found in areas that became urban hearths EXCEPT

    (A) access to water sources

    (B) access to building materials

    (C) arable land

    (D) a long growing season

    (E) social stratification

6. Which of the following processes most influences the existence of a zone of transition in concentric urban growth patterns?

    (A) Exurbanization   (D) Decentralization

    (B) Successive immigration   (E) Zoning

    (C) Agglomeration

7. The Latin American city typically differs from the North American city in which of the following ways?

    (A) The Latin American city often has higher densities in peripheral zones and less population density in the central business district.

    (B) The central business district is more dominant in its influence over its related urban land in the North American city than in the Latin American city.

    (C) The Latin American city typically does not show as strong a trend toward suburbanization as does the North American city.

    (D) The North American city shows more influence of the sector model growth patterns than does the Latin American city.

    (E) The urban realms model is more strongly explanatory and predictive of Latin American urban growth than it is of North American urban growth.

8. Which of the following is the smallest scale of geographic inquiry by the U.S. Census Bureau?

    (A) Metropolitan statistical area

    (B) Micropolitan statistical area

    (C) Metropolitan area

    (D) Census tract

    (E) County

9. Which of the following central place functions is most likely to have the highest range of goods and highest threshold population?

    (A) Used car lot   (D) Steakhouse

    (B) High school   (E) Furniture store

    (C) Hand-surgery center

10. Which of the following is a strong example of postmodern urban landscape?

    (A) Cairo, Egypt   (D) Washington, D.C.

    (B) Brasilia, Brazil   (E) Rome, Italy

    (C) London, England

11. According to the rank-size rule, if the largest city in Country X has 100,000 inhabitants, how many people will live in Country X's fourth-largest city?

    (A) 80,000   (D) 25,000

    (B) 75,000   (E) 10,000

    (C) 50,000

12. The concept of exurbanization is illustrated in which of the following scenarios?

    I. Thirty-three-year-old Marqueze and his wife move from Chicago to San Fransico to take advantage of a new job opportunity.

    II. Twenty-five-year-old Tina decides to move to the heart of New York City to enjoy the cultural vibrancy and diversity during her youth.

III.   Fifty-year-olds Margaret and Tom pack up and move to a rural, country-style home outside Louisville, Kentucky, to escape the fast pace of city life.

IV.   Nineteen-year-old Marcus decided to move from the city he grew up in to a peripheral farm, both to experience rural labor and to write poetry

(A)   I

(B)   II and III

(C)   I and II

(D)   III and IV

(E)   I, II, III, and IV

13.   Which of the following is an example of a person working in the nonbasic employment sector?

(A)   Assembly-line worker in an iPod factory

(B)   Video game software engineer

(C)   International public relations agent

(D)   University medical researcher

(E)   High school English teacher

14.   Which of the following statements correctly describes the economic employment mix that began to emerge in many U.S. cities after World War II?

(A)   U.S. cities have become increasingly dominated by industrial activities.

(B)   Workers' unions are reaching their highest level of influence in American history.

(C)   Urban jobs are becoming increasingly service oriented and required learned skills.

(D)   Most U.S. jobs are being outsourced to foreign labor supplies.

(E)   The majority of U.S. jobs are moving from being consumption related to more of a production orientation.

15.   Which of the following best illustrates the concept of a shock city?

(A)   Chicago

(B)   Paris

(C)   Madrid

(D)   Osaka

(E)   Lagos

16. Planned communities would most likely be found in what type of urban setting?

    (A) Transition zones   (D) American suburbs

    (B) CBDs   (E) Ghettos

    (C) Perifericos

17. This model is based on the assumption that growth occurred independently around several major foci, many of which were far away from the CBD and only marginally connected to it.

    (A) Sector model   (D) Urban realms model

    (B) Central place theory   (E) Model of urban evolution

    (C) Multiple-nuclei model

18. Which of the following rivers was NOT a cultural hearth of urbanism?

    (A) Tigris   (D) Rhine

    (B) Euphrates   (E) Nile

    (C) Huang He

19. The star-shaped city pattern resulted from the dominance of which transportation system?

    (A) Beltways surrounding cities

    (B) Lines of public transportation extending from the CBD

    (C) Pedestrian walkways within the CBD

    (D) Interstate highways linking cities

    (E) Roads leading to airports that link cities

20. The area serviced by a central place is called a

    (A) hinterland   (D) threshold

    (B) sphere of influence   (E) redline

    (C) range

Free-Response Review Questions

Urban sprawl has contributed to inner-city decay in many North American urban places.

(A)   Define *urban sprawl*.

(B)   Explain how urban sprawl has contributed to inner-city decay in some North American urban places.

(C)   Choose two of the following categories of solutions to uneven development, and for each, explain one related approach to reducing uneven development:

- Political

- Urban morphology

- Cultural

- Legal

PART 8 Pre-Exam Practice Answers

Terms Review Answers

1. Squatter settlement (or *barriada*)
2. Urban hierarchy
3. Suburbanization
4. Bid-rent curve
5. Ghettoization
6. Zone in transition
7. Primacy
8. Racial steering
9. Edge city
10. Cumulative causation
11. World city
12. Uneven development
13. Threshold
14. Urbanization
15. Shock city
16. Central business district (CBD)
17. Street morphology
18. Spatial competition
19. Megacity
20. Range of goods
21. Megalopolis
22. Periferico
23. Micropolitan statistical area
24. Urban banana
25. Hinterland

Multiple-Choice Answers

1. **(C)**

   Situation is equivalent to *relative location*, whereas *site* (B) refers to a city's internal features, such as resources and natural landscape. (A) is the number of people needed to support the existence of a central place function; (D) is the number of a certain phenomenon in a given space; and (E) refers to the division of urban space into many areas of use, or zones.

2. **(D)**

   Gentrification is the buildup or renovation of decaying or neglected urban space, usually in an inner city or a formerly industrial region. (A) is the growth of less-dense housing rings for middle and upper-class families within commuting distance to a city's CBD. (B) is the study of urban landscapes and how they evolved into their current forms. (C) is the division of an egalitarian society into various economic and social classes. (E) is the malicious practice of banks not granting loans to people living in certain areas of a city.

3. **(D)**

   Green belts are boundaries that contain a city's development and refocus development and investment energy back into a city's core, rather than allowing the city to sprawl and lose its focus. They help prevent uneven development and ghettoization trends. (A), (B), and (C) are all malicious real estate practices that lead to increased segregation and create ghettos. (E) also contributes to the creation of urban ghettos; suburbs drain the inner city of needed capital and development energy, leaving the core to decay because its predominantly low-income residents are stuck without a tax base for schools and infrastructure.

4. **(E)**

   A primate city is much larger than the next-largest city in the country and is usually overwhelmingly representative of national culture and identity. (A) is a region typically found on the outskirts of a Latin American city and marked by squaller and poverty. (B) is a region in a city that contains the peak land value intersection, the point of highest accessibility and visibility as well as the traditional origin of the city's growth. (C) is the region served by a central place. (D) is a region of a city containing makeshift homes.

5. **(E)**

   All the choices represent preconditions (or traits of urban hearths) except social stratification, which often followed city development. Urban growth led to the division of society along social and economic levels, or social stratification.

6. **(B)**

The constant influx of new arrivals to the city in the concentric zone model brings a new group into the city's center rings, pushing those already living in the inner rings to move outward to rings farther out, forcing a change in function in many rings. Residential rings become commercial rings, and so on. Because of this constant shifting process, there usually exists a ring near the CBD that never develops but is a zone of transition and constant uprooting; often, this is referred to as skid row, and developers avoid investing in it. (A) is the movement of city dwellers out to rural areas beyond the suburbs; (C) is the clumping of industries to take advantage of being together; and (D) is the spread of economic and urban features away from their center around the CBD into becoming more diversely spread throughout an urban space. Though (E) may have been tempting, zoning is the restrictions on land use that can be placed on urban space to segregate office parks from housing areas, for example.

7. **(C)**

Latin American cities tend to grow up, not out, because city inhabitants typically do not have capital and discretionary income to buy new houses; rather, they renovate their current homes. Also, most Latin American cities do not have the development energy and capital that North American cities have. Also, transportation, electricity, and water infrastructural grids tend to focus on the inner city in Latin America, rather than being available for urban sprawl. (A) is reversed, because Latin American cities are denser in the center than in peripheral zones. (B) is reversed, because the CBD is more dominant in Latin American cities and becoming less dominant in North American cities with suburbanization and urban sprawl. (D) is not necessarily true, because many Latin American cities show urban growth that is a mix of the classic models, as in North America. (E) is totally false, because urban realms are more applicable to North American cities than Latin American urban areas.

There is also an interesting cultural trend at work in many Latin American cities: the rich *want* to live in city centers. In contrast, the middle and upper socioeconomic classes in the United States, want to live in the suburbs (though this is changing in many cities). That means that the middle class in Mexico are trying to get *into* the city so they can show they are moving up the economic/social ladder, the middle class in many U.S. cities is trying to get *out* of the inner city for the same reason. Because all the money is in the center of most Latin America cities, that's where the best infrastructure is often found; the opposite is true in the United States.

8. **(D)**

(A)   includes a region of at least 50,000 within a greater metropolitan area (C), while a micropolitan area includes from 10,000 to 50,000 inhabitants of a region within a greater metropolitan area. A census tract is like a neighborhood, whereas a county often includes many census tracts.

9. **(C)**

A central place function with a high range and high threshold must be one that is going to require a very specialized set of customers and workers and is therefore going to attract people to travel far for its specialized services; a hand-surgery center's specialty will attract doctors who specialize and patients who need this specialty and are willing to travel far and wide for it.

10. **(B)**

A postmodern landscape is one that emphasizes diversity of thought and landscape without the obsession with symmetry and form that is found in classical architecture. Brasilia was designed with an emphasis on diversity in form rather than on the balance and emphasis on reason found in Renaissance and Enlightenment forms.

11. **(D)**

The rank-size rule asserts that the fourth-largest city will be one-fourth the size of the largest city.

12. **(D)**

Exurbanization occurs when city dwellers leave their urban homes and urban pace of life in search of more-rural lifestyles outside the central city and beyond the suburbs. Each of these scenarios (III and IV) describes a person in search of a less-urban, more-rural lifestyle.

13. **(E)**

Nonbasic jobs cause a shift of money within the urban place's economy, whereas basic jobs create an exchange of money between the urban place and another place (exports and imports). All choices except (E) are involved in creating a product that will bring money into the city's economy from outside of it. (E) provides a service to the residents and does not bring money in from the outside.

14. **(C)**

The current shift in the employment mix of North American cities is a movement away from unskilled, factory work toward service-oriented employment that often requires some knowledge of technology.

15. **(E)**

A shock city is an urban place usually in a less-developed region that is experiencing rapid rates of urbanization and in-migration. Such growth is straining to a shock city's ill-prepared infrastructure, which cannot provide housing and services, as well as jobs, to the rapidly growing population.

16. **(D)**

Planned communities are master-planned neighborhoods with preformulated architectural designs and often with community gathering spots and restrictive covenants. (A) are the areas outside the CBD that are constantly in flux and run down because of the invasion and succession pattern that never allows it to develop a permanent population base and attract development. (B) are the original cores of cities' economies; (C) are the peripheral zones of squatter settlements and abject poverty on the outskirts of many Latin American cities; and (E) are areas of concentrated poverty in urban places.

17. **(C)**

(A)   predicts urban growth in a pattern in which similar land uses and socioeconomic groups are clustered in linear sectors radiating outward from a central business district, usually along transportation corridors. (B) theorizes that cities can be viewed from above as a series of concentric rings. (D) attempted to explain and predict changing urban growth patterns as the automobile became increasingly prevalent. (E) is Borchert's model explaining the growth of cities in four phases of transportation history.

18. **(D)**

Urbanism did not originally spawn from the Rhine river valley in Germany, whereas hearths existed in the other choices.

19. **(B)**

Star-shaped city growth resulted from public transportation systems (mainly streetcars) that extended out from the CBD. Growth took place along these corridors that offered easy access into the city and back out before automobiles became common.

20. **(A)**

The hinterland is the area serviced by a central city. (C) is the distance a person is willing to travel for a certain good or service. (D) is the number of people needed to make a good or service profitable and sustainable. (E) is a practice of not loaning money to individuals or businesses in certain areas. (B) is not a geographic term.

Free-Response Answers

The following is a list of suggested main points for each part of the question.

Part A

- Urban sprawl is the spread of the urban landscape into areas that were formerly nonurban or rural.

- The term *urban sprawl* often includes a negative connotation, implying the unplanned and reckless invasion of rural lands by urban developers and fast-paced, crowded lifestyles.

Part B

- Urban sprawl has contributed to the decay of inner-city zones for several reasons:

- Suburbanization has caused an out-migration of the middle and upper socioeconomic classes from residing in the inner-city zones. This has caused the tax base to be dramatically reduced, causing schools and infrastructure to have less money.

- Sprawl and suburbanization have "strangled" the inner city from being able to grow outward because many of the newer communities, or nuclei, have seceded and become politically independent from the metropolitan government.

- Poor zoning laws in some areas have allowed housing complexes and industrial zones to be juxtaposed, causing polluted living environments.

- Because of sprawl, the focus of development and renovation is often directed away from the inner-city areas, particularly the fringes between the newer suburban zones and the original CBD—the zone of transition, or skid row.

Part C

- Political—discussion of incorporation and fusing of metropolitan governments with country governments to create one, unified system of support services and tax base; increasing support for mass transit options within the city.

- Urban morphology—discussion of increasing grid-patterned streets and reducing cul-de-sac and one-entrance properties that channel traffic into only a few outlets.

- Cultural—possible discussion of gentrification, though gentrification is not seen by some geographers as a cultural method of controlling sprawl. Other cultural methods might entail our changing beliefs that led to the end of racial segregation in real estate practices or the movement to building smaller homes with smaller environmental footprints and better energy usage.

- Legal—discussion of green belts and zoning laws to restrict out-migration and urban sprawl.

BIBLIOGRAPHY

AP Human Geography

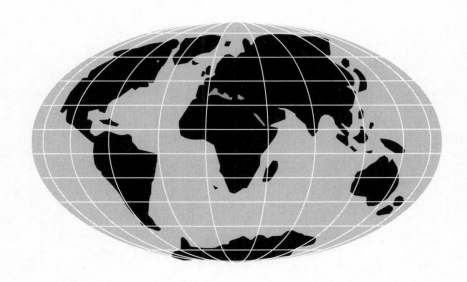

Bibliography

De Blij, Harm J., and Alexander B. Murphy. *Human Geography: Culture, Society, and Space*. 7th ed. New York: Wiley, 2003.

De Blij, Harm J., and Peter O. Muller. *Concepts and Regions in Geography*. New York: Wiley, 2003.

Diamond, Jared. *Guns, Germs, and Steel: The Fates of Human Societies*. New York: Norton, 1999.

Fuller, Charles. *Conquering Human Geography: A Manual for Successful Completion of AP Human Geography*. New York: Wiley, 2007.

Gabrys-Alexson, Randy. *Advanced Placement Student Companion*. New York: Wiley, 2003.

Jordan-Bychkov, Terry G., and Mona Domosh. *The Human Mosaic: A Thematic Introduction to Cultural Geography*. 9th ed. New York: W. H. Freeman, 2003.

Knox, Paul L., and Sallie A. Marston. *Places and Regions in Global Context: Human Geography*. 3rd ed. Upper Saddle River, NJ: Prentice Hall, 2004.

Kuby, Michael, John Harner, and Patricia Gober. *Human Geography in Action*. 3rd ed. Hoboken, NJ: Wiley, 2004.

Norton, William. *Human Geography*. 4th ed. New York: Oxford University Press, 2002.

Nunley, Robert E., George W. Ulbrick, and Bernard O. Williams. *Study Guide to the Cultural Landscape*. 7th ed. Upper Saddle River, NJ: Prentice Hall, 2003.

The Nystrom Desk Atlas. Chicago: Nystrom Herff Jones Education Division, 2004.

Pitzl, Gerald R. *Encyclopedia of Human Geography*. Westport, CN: Greenwood, 2004.

Rubenstein, James M. *The Cultural Landscape: An Introduction to Human Geography*. 8th ed. Upper Saddle River, NJ: Pearson/Prentice Hall, 2005.

Sowell, Thomas. *Conquests and Cultures: An International History*. New York: Basic Books, 1998.

Tuan, Yi-Fu. *Space and Place: The Perspective of Experience*. Minneapolis: University of Minnesota Press, 1977.

PRACTICE EXAMS

AP Human Geography

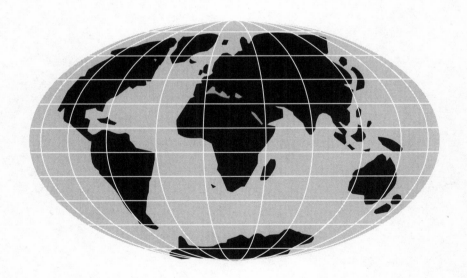

PRACTICE EXAM 1

**This exam is also on CD-ROM in our
special interactive AP Human Geography TestWare®**

AP Human Geography

Section I

TIME: 60 minutes
75 multiple-choice questions

(Answer sheets appear in the back of this book.)

Directions: Each of the following questions is followed by five suggested answers or completions. Select the best answer choice.

---

1. All the following have been considered new industrial countries EXCEPT

   (A) Hong Kong   (D) China

   (B) South Korea   (E) Indonesia

   (C) Brazil

2. Which of the following is an example of a quinary-sector economic activity?

   (A) Working at a cash register at McDonald's

   (B) Serving as a researcher for human genetic cloning

   (C) Serving on the U.S. president's cabinet

   (D) Converting crude oil into gasoline

   (E) Plowing land in preparation for planting a crop

3. London has become a world city in part because of its proximity to ports and other places that foster development. This reason for London's historic growth relates to the city's

    (A) site   (D) situation

    (B) sovereignty   (E) distance decay

    (C) redlining

4. Which of the following is a valid difference between the urban patterns of the United States and those of Latin America?

    (A) Unlike U.S. cities, Latin American cities have ghettos.

    (B) U.S cities follow a sector pattern, whereas Latin American cities follow concentric zones.

    (C) Gentrification is more present in Latin American cities.

    (D) Latin American cities have more-defined industrial sectors.

    (E) Unlike U.S. cities, Latin American cities show patterns of wealthy residents emanating from the city's central business district.

5. The number of people under the age of 15 plus the number of people above the age of 64 divided by the number of the people aged 15 through 64 is defined as

    (A) carrying capacity   (D) age-sex pyramid

    (B) primary economic sector (E) infrastructure

    (C) dependency ratio

6. Governments such as those once controlled by the Taliban in Afghanistan and the Ayatollah Khomeini in Iran are classified as

    (A) landlocked   (D) theocratic

    (B) parliamentary   (E) microstates

    (C) federal

7. All the following were original members of the European Community, the predecessor to the European Union, EXCEPT

    (A) France

    (B) Belgium

    (C) United Kingdom

    (D) Italy

    (E) The Netherlands

8. In 1492, Christopher Columbus's voyage took nearly 40 days to cross the Atlantic Ocean, a trip that would take a modern ship less than one week. This difference best reflects the geographic concept of

    (A) distance decay

    (B) uneven development

    (C) stimulus diffusion

    (D) space-time compression

    (E) distribution

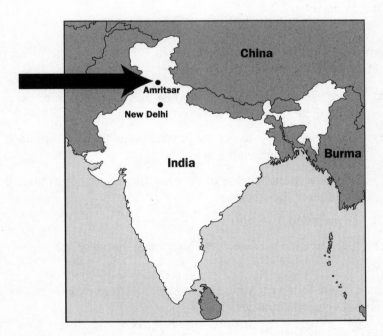

9. The arrow on the map above points to a city in India containing the largest number of shrines from which of the following religions?

    (A) Sikhism

    (B) Shintoism

    (C) Buddhism

    (D) Christianity

    (E) Hinduism

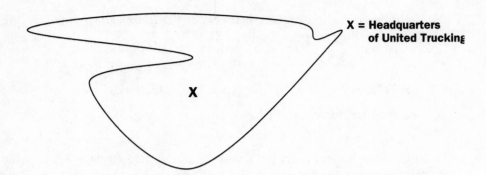

10. The region outlined above contains delivery destinations served by United Trucking. Which of the following classifications best fits this region?

    (A) Functional   (D) Mental

    (B) Formal   (E) Perceptual

    (C) Vernacular

11. Compared with the world pattern of crude birth rates, the world pattern of crude death rates shows

    (A) more variation because of the vast inequalities in minimal health care throughout the world

    (B) less variation because of the general availability of minimal health care facilities throughout the world

    (C) equal variation because of the offsetting effect of birth and death rates throughout the world

    (D) no variation

    (E) high variation because of the high infant mortality in some world regions

12. Which of the following would be most attracted to export-processing zones in less-developed countries?

    (A) Transnational corporations assembling products that are bulk reducing or not weight gaining

    (B) Multinational firms wanting to build world headquarters

    (C) Quaternary-sector workers wanting to find jobs

    (D) Technopoles

    (E) International lending agencies

13. The second agricultural revolution developed at the same time as

   (A) growing urban markets were demanding increased food production

   (B) improved genetic modification of food allowed for increased harvests
        in developing countries

   (C) humans were forming communes and practicing open-field farming

   (D) vast shortages in laborers existed because of communicable diseases

   (E) large streams of migrants moved from core to peripheral countries

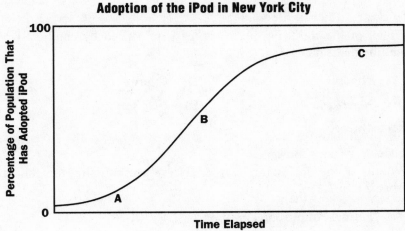

14. Which of the following most likely explains the diffusion pattern of the iPod
     depicted in the graph above?

   (A) In the innovation stage, at point A, only a small number of iPod pur-
        chases were made, but by point B the number of adopters had grown
        exponentially as the early buyers spread the word of the iPod.

   (B) The highest exponential growth rate was achieved by point C, where
        the fastest adoption of the iPod occurred.

   (C) The highest adoption rate occurred at point A because, as a new inven-
        tion, the iPod aroused excitement.

   (D) Point C represents the late-adopter stage, when adoption of the iPod
        reached all people in the population.

   (E) The pattern represents relocation diffusion.

15. All the following are true of truck farming EXCEPT:

    (A) Among the most common truck crops are tomatoes, strawberries, and lettuce.

    (B) Most often it is characterized by the use of mechanized farming tools.

    (C) Labor costs are often relatively high on these large-scale farming operations.

    (D) It is the predominant agricultural practice found in the southeastern United States.

    (E) Truck farmers' harvests are usually intended for distant markets.

16. Which of the following places is least influenced by conflicts related to multilingualism?

    (A) Nigeria   (D) Cyprus

    (B) Venezuela   (E) Belgium

    (C) Quebec

17. Which of the following was the first prerequisite for the start of urbanization?

    (A) Formal political organization

    (B) Agricultural surplus

    (C) Monarchial control

    (D) Privatization of land ownership

    (E) Development of currency

18. Which of the following regions is most threatened by desertification?

    (A) South America   (D) Africa

    (B) Australia   (E) Asia

    (C) Europe

19. Which of the following significantly weakened the strength of Mackinder's geopolitical heartland theory?

    (A) Ascendance of the United States' international influence after World War II

    (B) Existence of a pivot area

    (C) Growth of Soviet power in eastern Europe

    (D) Influence of Eurasia in world affairs

    (E) Rise of Nazi Germany

20. Which of the following factors had the greatest effect in proving the demographic theorist Thomas Malthus incorrect?

    (A) Decreased land supply after the Industrial Revolution

    (B) Improved fertilizers and crop strains

    (C) Increased contraceptive technology in the Western Hemisphere

    (D) The decline of the Roman Catholic Church's influence on politics in Britain

    (E) Improved trade routes enabling improved food transport and cross-national trade

21. Country X can produce televisions at 50 percent of the cost that Country Y can produce televisions. Country Y can produce pencils at 70 percent of the cost that Country X can produce pencils. Therefore, Country X chooses to produce televisions and trade them with Country Y for pencils. This scenario best reflects which concept?

    (A) Substitution principle

    (B) Topocide

    (C) Foreign direct investment

    (D) Footloose industry

    (E) Comparative advantage

22. A banking company wanted to open a new branch in the New York City area. In order to study the region, the bank used a map to analyze potential locations. The map the bank's leadership used in its decision-making process showed a layer of regional data displaying per capita income; another layer displaying the frequency of bank deposits made; and another layer showing the average value of the deposited amount. With this map, the banking company was able to choose the optimum location for its new branch. All of the following are tools that the bank (or its geographic team) most likely used to create and display this layered map of geographic data EXCEPT

(A) GPS

(B) GIS

(C) remote sensing

(D) desalination

(E) satellite imagery

(Photo by: M. Savage)

23. A pilgrim to the religious site depicted in the photograph above would most likely be a(n)

(A) Taoist

(B) Buddhist

(C) Eastern Orthodox Christian

(D) Muslim

(E) Hindu

24. In the 1980s the demographic trend in China was best characterized by a(n)

(A)   rapidly rising crude birth rate

(B)   falling life expectancy

(C)   decreasing general fertility rate

(D)   increased total fertility rate

(E)   surge in refugees emigrating from China

25. The United Nations Human Development Index is based on the assumption that a country's development

(A)   is directly related to its position in the core or periphery

(B)   is a function of social, demographic, and economic factors

(C)   can improve if countries liberalize trade policies

(D)   is indicated most accurately by its gross domestic product

(E)   is a reflection of its population count

26. The photograph above shows a farm most likely located in which of the following regions?

(A)   Sub-Saharan Africa   (D)   North Africa

(B)   Southwest Asia   (E)   Southeast Asia

(C)   Eastern Europe

27. All the following resulted from the British enclosure movement in the 1850s EXCEPT

    (A) agricultural efficiency increased

    (B) urban migration increased

    (C) feudal village life was disrupted

    (D) the number of farm owners rose dramatically

    (E) communal fields were consolidated

28. In 1998 an estimated 350,000 asylum seekers were from Croatia. What were their primary destinations in that year?

    (A) Kosovo and Albania

    (B) Germany and France

    (C) Yugoslavia and Bosnia-Herzegovina

    (D) Austria and Hungary

    (E) Macedonia and Romania

29. On which of the following map projections is direction true everywhere on the map?

    (A) Mollweide   (D) Robinson

    (B) Mercator   (E) Miller cylindrical

    (C) Peter

30. Which among the following has the highest-threshold, highest-range central place function?

    (A) Doughnut shop   (D) Neurosurgery complex

    (B) Post office   (E) Department store

    (C) Movie theatre

31. "Women are inherently better preservationists of Earth because women have traditionally been nurturers and men have been destroyers." This argument exemplifies

    (A) economic determinism

    (B) the Gender Empowerment Measure

    (C) ecofeminism

    (D) the convergence hypothesis

    (E) ethnogenesis

32. You would most expect to find a linguistic refuge area in a(n)

    (A) relatively flat country   (D) river bank

    (B) mountainous area   (E) marketplace

    (C) international airport

33. By 2015 life expectancy in several African countries, such as Namibia, is expected to decline by more than 10 years. What is the principal factor causing this demographic projection?

    (A) Cyclical poverty   (D) Infrastructural decay

    (B) Crop shortage   (E) HIV/AIDS

    (C) Ecoterrorism

34. Both Ulaanbaatar in Mongolia and Lagos in Nigeria are examples of

    (A) primate cities   (D) edge cities

    (B) world cities   (E) postindustrial cities

    (C) exclaves

35. A coffee shop and an ice-cream shop are often found on the same block, in close proximity. This is an example of

    (A) deglomeration   (D) purchasing-power parity

    (B) agglomeration   (E) an urban heat island

    (C) an export-processing zone

36. The size of an urban place's *hinterland* is an indication of its

(A) government structure   (D) degree of centrality

(B) religious diversity   (E) urban design

(C) social distance

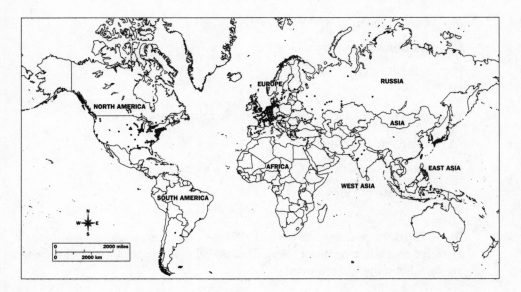

37. Which of the following is the most accurate title for the map above?

(A) Map of World Democratic Voters

(B) Map of Nuclear Power Reactors

(C) Map of Dravidian Languages Spoken

(D) Map of Avian Flu Outbreaks

(E) Map of HIV-1 Infections

38. The informal sector in a developing country exists for all the following reasons EXCEPT:

(A) Tertiary economies in the formal sector are not developed well enough to absorb all the economies of the informal sector.

(B) The demand for informal-sector goods and services keeps prices low.

(C)   Informal-sector workers and businesses cannot afford permanent business sites.

(D)   The government benefits from taxing informal-sector workers and their small businesses.

(E)   The quality of products and the quality of work in the informal sector are low.

39.   Two unrelated people are trying to decide whether to travel to Houston, Texas, from their homes in Germany for a special vacation package offered on television. One German decides Houston is too far away, while the other decides to purchase the vacation package. This scenario best demonstrates the effects of

(A)   brain drain   (D)   doubling time

(B)   concentration   (E)   expansion diffusion

(C)   cognitive distance

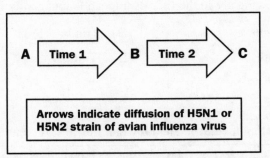

Population at place A = 1.5 million chickens
Population at place B = 6 million chickens
Population at place C = 15 million chickens

40.   The trend above best demonstrates which pattern of diffusion of the H5N1 or H5N2 strain of the avian influenza virus?

(A)   Hierarchical diffusion   (D)   Uneven development

(B)   Stimulus diffusion   (E)   Reverse hierarchical diffusion

(C)   Maladaptive diffusion

41. Which of the following is best classified as a centrifugal force?

    (A) National flag

    (B) State-owned news station

    (C) National research laboratories

    (D) Ethnic discrimination

    (E) Common language

42. By 2006 the states of northern Nigeria came under the governance of

    (A) the Sharia law   (D) secularists

    (B) the African Union   (E) Ibo speakers

    (C) Christian theocrats

43. All the following are in the Indo-European language family EXCEPT

    (A) Portuguese   (D) Hindi

    (B) Bengali   (E) Turkish

    (C) German

Population Increases and Growth Rates in Five-Year Periods

	1980–1985	1985–1990	1990–1995	1995–2000	2000–2005	2005–2010	2010–2015	2015–2020
Net population added per year (in millions)	80	87	83	79	76	76	75	72
Annual population growth rate (%)	1.8	1.8	1.6	1.4	1.2	1.2	1.1	1.0

44. The table on the previous page best illustrates which demographic trend?

(A) Hidden momentum

(D) Doubling time

(B) North–south gap

(E) Zero population growth

(C) Counterurbanization

China Population Density

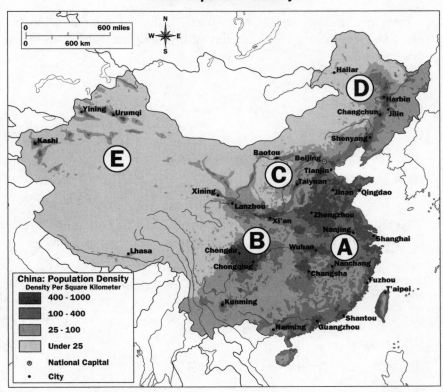

45. Based on the population density map of China above, in which region is extensive subsistence agriculture most heavily practiced?

(A) Region A

(D) Region D

(B) Region B

(E) Region E

(C) Region C

46. In 1990 Iraq invaded Kuwait, in part over an oil resource that Iraq and Kuwait both claimed fell within their national boundaries. This type of boundary dispute is classified as

    (A) locational   (D) operational

    (B) definitional   (E) subsequent

    (C) allocational

47. A computer production process involves creating the computer chip in Indonesia and assembling the motherboard in Malaysia. This is, most closely, evidence of

    (A) maquiladora districts

    (B) the post-Fordist production process

    (C) an infrastructure

    (D) the new international division of labor

    (E) a cottage industry

48. Which of the following asserts that ethnic minorities often live in the geographically peripheral regions excluded from the core of a country's power?

    (A) Demographic transition model

    (B) Cleavage model

    (C) Von Thünen's model

    (D) Central place theory

    (E) Locational interdependence model

49. In von Thünen's theory, the key variable in an agricultural location decision is

    (A) labor cost

    (B) value of agglomeration benefits

    (C) climate type

    (D) cost of irrigation

    (E) transportation cost

50. Currently, the world's *third*-largest religion, in terms of number of adherents, is

    (A) Sikhism

    (D) Christianity

    (B) Hinduism

    (E) Judaism

    (C) Islam

Female Literacy Rates, 2007

	Region A	Region B	Region C
Females Literate in Region (%)	53	73	88

51. Which of the following accurately lists in order the regions in the above table corresponding to A, B, C, respectively?

    (A) Asia, Latin America and the Caribbean, sub-Saharan Africa

    (B) Latin America and the Caribbean, Asia, sub-Saharan Africa

    (C) Asia, sub-Saharan Africa, Latin America and the Caribbean

    (D) sub-Saharan Africa, Asia, Latin America and the Caribbean

    (E) sub-Saharan Africa, Latin America and the Caribbean, Asia

52. Which of the following cities best represents a forward capital?

    (A) Paris, France

    (D) Canberra, Australia

    (B) Algiers, Algeria

    (E) Warsaw, Poland

    (C) Putrajaya, Malaysia

53. Which of the following best describes shifting cultivation?

    (A) Primarily a subsistence practice, it involves a farmer using a plot and then abandoning it for return at a later time.

    (B) Usually a commercial agriculture endeavor, it involves rotating one crop type on a plot for another in a sequential pattern.

    (C) It is the movement of pastoral nomads from one food source to another.

    (D) Only used in wetlands, it is the use of pyramid-style farms for rice farming.

    (E) It involves the intensive, commercial integration of crops and livestock into a farming system.

54. Which of the four stages in the demographic transition model are considered "homeostatic" stages, when the forces of demographic change are in equilibrium?

    (A) Stages 1 and 3   (D) Stage 4

    (B) Stages 2 and 3   (E) Stages 1, 2, 3, and 4

    (C) Stages 1 and 4

55. An essential difference between the standard language of a people and an official language is that the standard language is

    (A) the chosen, generally accepted variant of a language, while the official language is the legally declared language of a country to be used in all government interactions

    (B) usually spoken by outsiders, while the official language is what is on all official documents

    (C) the form spoken by commoners, while the official language is the "king's form" of the language, taught in the grammar books

    (D) used widely throughout society, while the official language is only used for government documents

    (E) unchanging, while the official language changes with changes in governments

56. Which of the following most accurately matches the country to its territorial shape?

    (A) Russia: fragmented   (D) Philippines: elongated

    (B) Poland: compact   (E) Chile: protruded

    (C) Singapore: perforated

57. Where would you most likely find the greatest concentration of feedlots in America?

    (A) Chicago   (D) South Dakota

    (B) California   (E) Kentucky

    (C) Florida

58. The seasonal migration of animal livestock from lowland pastures to mountainous regions is termed

    (A) intensive subsistence agriculture

    (B) mixed crop and livestock farming

    (C) double cropping

    (D) transhumance

    (E) swidden agriculture

59. Which of the following strategies was identified by the 2004 United Nations International Conference on Population and Development as the most powerful approach for reducing the global population growth rate?

    (A) Increasing the amount of exports to less-developed countries

    (B) Retracting anticontraception laws throughout conservative countries

    (C) Reducing hunger throughout the world

    (D) Empowering the socioeconomic status of women in less-developed countries

    (E) Enforcing demographic growth rate targets in specific countries through coalition building

60. Which of the following is a true statement about popular culture?

    (A) Technology is reducing the scale of territory covered by popular culture.

    (B) The scale of territory covered by folk culture is often much larger than that of popular culture.

    (C) The heart of popular culture customs is often found in less-developed regions.

    (D) Folk culture is often the result of cultural isolation, while popular culture often results from cultural diffusion.

    (E) Popular culture customs remain the same for long periods of time.

61. In Rostow's economic development model, the stage in which workers become more skilled and modern technology spreads to industries beyond the innovating "takeoff" industry is called the

    (A) traditional society

    (B) preconditions for takeoff

    (C) takeoff

    (D) drive to maturity

    (E) age of high mass consumption

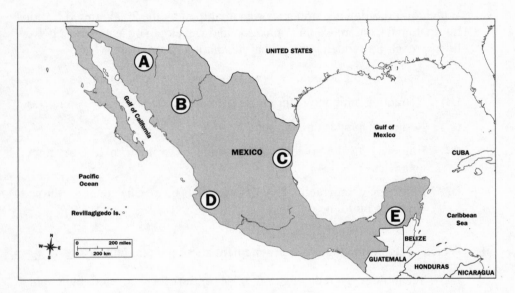

62. On the map of Mexico above, a maquiladora is most likely found at which point?

    (A) Point A   (D) Point D

    (B) Point B   (E) Point E

    (C) Point C

63. The migration of a Hildegarde von Pabst to Dayton, Ohio, from Berlin, Germany, because of a cousin living in Dayton is most closely an example of

    (A) forced migration   (D) periodic movement

    (B) chain migration   (E) a refugee

    (C) internal migration

64. The actual number of live births per 1,000 women in the fecund range refers to

    (A) total fertility rate   (D) infant mortality rate

    (B) fecundity   (E) general fertility rate

    (C) crude birth rate

65. Which of the following correctly sequences Sino-Tibetan languages from largest to smallest in terms of the number of native speakers?

    (A) Mandarin, Cantonese, Wu, Hakka (Kejia), Min

    (B) Cantonese, Wu, Mandarin, Min, Hakka (Kejia)

    (C) Hakka (Kejia), Mandarin, Wu, Cantonese, Min

    (D) Mandarin, Wu, Cantonese, Min, Hakka (Kejia)

    (E) Mandarin, Min, Cantonese, Hakka (Kejia), Wu

66. Which of the following is NOT a usual characteristic of an edge city?

    (A) Accessibility   (D) Suburban sense of place

    (B) Tenement housing   (E) Office park

    (C) Varied urban functions

67. The relationship among power structures, the environment, and economic inequalities is termed

    (A) ecoterrorism   (D) gerrymandering

    (B) political ecology   (E) balkanization

    (C) cultural diffusion

68. The focus of the Green Revolution was

    (A) improving crop yields in commercial agribusiness corporations

    (B) reducing starvation in less-developed countries

    (C) inventing new forms of food to add variety to the human diet

    (D) saving undeveloped land from urban sprawl

    (E) encouraging the use of fertilizers less damaging to the environment

69. All the following are factors motivating the conflict surrounding Quebec, Canada, EXCEPT

    (A) language   (D) economic inequality

    (B) sovereignty   (E) colonial roots

    (C) religion

70. Which of the following countries produces the most woven cotton fabric?

    (A) Italy   (D) Egypt

    (B) India   (E) United States

    (C) China

71. The picture above shows an abandoned factory warehouse that was remodeled into a loft apartment complex near the central business district of a major U.S. city. This is an example of

    (A) an edge city   (D) blockbusting

    (B) commodification   (E) gentrification

    (C) counterurbanization

72. A primary differentiation between a state and a nation is that a state is a

    (A) political abstract, whereas a nation is a human group

    (B) mutable concept, whereas a nation is permanent

    (C) fixed geographic item, whereas a nation is not linked to a territory

    (D) product of history, whereas a nation is a product of people

    (E) controversial issue, whereas a nation is more peaceful

73. Structural adjustment programs often encourage all the following EXCEPT

    (A) selling off public resources to private corporations

    (B) higher taxation rates

    (C) closing of export-processing zones

    (D) reducing government expenditures

    (E) charging citizens more for government services

74. Which of the following would have the steepest bid-rent curve?

    (A) Textile factory

    (B) Family desiring a plot of land for a suburban home

    (C) Urban real estate brokerage firm

    (D) Pig farmer

    (E) Trash dump

75. When a barge stops in Louisville, unloads its cargo, and transfers it onto a train to be transported to Ohio, Louisville is referred to as a(n)

    (A) trading bloc

    (B) export-processing zone

    (C) shatter belt

    (D) break of bulk

    (E) special economic zone

Section II

TIME: 75 minutes

3 free-response questions

> **Instructions:** You have 75 minutes to answer all three free-response questions in this section. Take a few minutes to outline your answers. Illustrate your essay with substantive examples when appropriate. It is not enough to answer a question by merely listing facts. You should present a cogent argument based on your critical analysis of the question posed and your understanding of geography.

1. Through the years, geographers have developed various perspectives on cultural ecology.

    (A) Define *cultural ecology*.

    (B) Contrast environmental determinism and possibilism.

    (C) Compare and contrast the spatial distribution of the cities of Chongqing and San Francisco, as shown in the maps below.

    (D) How would the theory of possibilism explain the human constructions shown in the map of San Francisco?

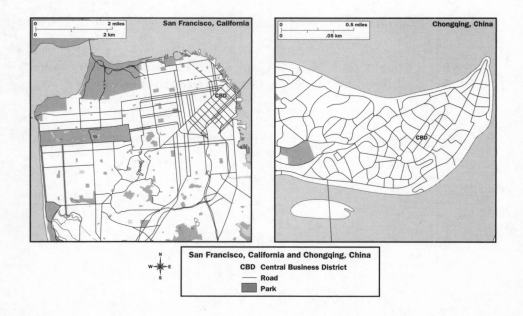

2. (A) Define *demographic dependency ratio*.

    (B) Look at the population pyramids below. Describe and explain the demographic trends in fertility and longevity depicted in China from 1950 through 2050 and relate those trends to China's dependency ratio.

    (C) With reference to the demographic trends you identified in part B, forecast any social and/or economic problems facing China related to its dependency ratio.

China's Age Distribution

Population Structures by Age and Sex
Millions

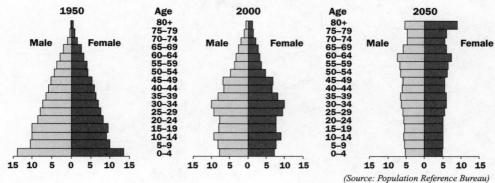

(Source: Population Reference Bureau)

3. Urbanization is affecting nearly all parts of the world.

    (A) Define *urbanization*.

    (B) Describe and explain the current trends in levels and rates of urbanization in two of the following regions:

    • North America

    • Southeast Asia

    • Latin America

    (C) Explain counterurbanization. Explain the demographic trends linked to current patterns in counterurbanization in the United States.

PRACTICE EXAM 1

AP Human Geography

Answer Key

Section I

1.	(E)	20.	(B)	39.	(C)	58.	(D)
2.	(C)	21.	(E)	40.	(E)	59.	(D)
3.	(D)	22.	(D)	41.	(D)	60.	(D)
4.	(E)	23.	(E)	42.	(A)	61.	(D)
5.	(C)	24.	(C)	43.	(E)	62.	(A)
6.	(D)	25.	(B)	44.	(A)	63.	(B)
7.	(C)	26.	(C)	45.	(E)	64.	(E)
8.	(D)	27.	(D)	46.	(C)	65.	(D)
9.	(A)	28.	(C)	47.	(D)	66.	(B)
10.	(A)	29.	(B)	48.	(B)	67.	(B)
11.	(B)	30.	(D)	49.	(E)	68.	(B)
12.	(A)	31.	(C)	50.	(B)	69.	(C)
13.	(A)	32.	(B)	51.	(D)	70.	(C)
14.	(A)	33.	(E)	52.	(C)	71.	(E)
15.	(C)	34.	(A)	53.	(A)	72.	(A)
16.	(B)	35.	(B)	54.	(C)	73.	(C)
17.	(B)	36.	(D)	55.	(A)	74.	(C)
18.	(B)	37.	(B)	56.	(B)	75.	(D)
19.	(A)	38.	(D)	57.	(D)		

Section I Diagnostic Instrument

> **Instructions:** Use these charts to see where your "weaknesses" exist in the curriculum.

Geography: Its Nature and Perspectives

Item #	3	8	10	22	29	39
Correct/Incorrect						

Population

Item #	5	11	14	20	24	33	40	44	51	54	59	63	64
Correct/Incorrect													

Cultural Patterns and Processes

Item #	9	16	23	32	43	50	55	60	65	69
Correct/Incorrect										

Political Organization of Space

Item #	6	19	28	37	41	42	46	48	52	56	67	72
Correct/Incorrect												

Agricultural and Rural Land Use

Item #	2	13	15	18	26	45	49	53	57	58	68
Correct/Incorrect											

Industrialization and Economic Development

Item #	1	7	12	21	25	35	47	61	62	70	73	75
Correct/Incorrect												

Cities and Urban Land Use

Item #	4	17	27	30	31	34	36	38	66	71	74
Correct/Incorrect											

PRACTICE EXAM 1

AP Human Geography

Detailed Explanations of Answers

Section I

1. **(E)**

   A new industrial country has a strong manufacturing base that enables it to maintain a competitive presence in the global economy rather than remaining a neocolonial country dependent on its former colonial masters. Indonesia is primarily attracting foreign direct investment from transnational corporations, which is a form of neocolonialism. (A) and (B) are part of the Asian Tigers, a group of Asian countries that developed a strong technology manufacturing base that propelled them into a competitive and relatively independent global economic position rather than remaining economically dependent on their former colonial masters.

2. **(C)**

   Serving on the president's cabinet is a quinary-sector economic activity because it involves decisions at the highest level of the government and economy. (A) is a tertiary-sector economic activity because it is service related. (B) is a quaternary-sector economic activity because it involves higher education; jobs in the quaternary sector can also be in financing, technological services, governmental operations, and the media. (D) is an example of a secondary-sector economic activity, which involve converting or processing raw materials (in this case, crude oil) that have been extracted from the earth (which is a primary economic activity) into a product (in this case, gas) to be sold at the marketplace. (E) is an example of a primary-sector economic activity because it involves extracting natural resources.

3. **(D)**

   Situation describes a place's location relative to other places, whereas (A) is the physical character of a place. (B) describes a place's ability to control its own territory and internal affairs, (C) is a discriminatory practice used by banks and lending agencies, and (E) is the decreasing impact a phenomenon has on something as the distance from its origin increases.

4.   **(E)**

In Latin American (and western European) cities, the wealthy cluster nearer the central business districts and push outward from the focal point of the city, whereas in the United States the wealthy often live in suburbs outside the central cities. (A) is incorrect because many U.S. cities have ghettos. (B) is incorrect because many Latin American cities also show sector and concentric patterns. (C) is incorrect because U.S. cities show an equal (if not greater) influence of gentrifiers compared with Latin American cities. (D) is incorrect because U.S. cities have industrial sectors that are as defined as those found in Latin American cities.

5.   **(C)**

The dependency ratio is a measure of the economically dependent members of the population—people considered either too old or too young to work. (A) is the maximum population that could be supported by a region's resources. (B) is the sector of the economy engaged in direct extraction of natural resources from the earth, such as farmers. (D) is a tool demographers use to illustrate trends in population by gender and age group. (E) is the "backbone of a society," including schools, health care institutions, and transportation systems.

6.   **(D)**

Governments ruled by religious authorities are termed theocracies. The Afghani Taliban and the Ayatollah in Iran were religious authorities, both Muslim, who governed their countries. (A) describes countries without coasts on open seas. (B) describes countries with a representative body comprised of officials elected at the national level. (C) describes governments wherein the country is divided into districts, each with a sense of protected sovereignty (like the states in the United States) and a national government that represents those subunits. (E) are states that are so small in their territory that they are usually only a dot on the map, such as Singapore.

7.   **(C)**

The six original countries in the 1958 European Community, which was renamed the European Union (EU), were Belgium, France, West Germany, Italy, Luxembourg, and the Netherlands. By 1973 Ireland, Denmark, and the United Kingdom joined. The EU has effectively improved the economy of western Europe and has made it highly competitive in the world market.

8.   **(D)**

Space-time compression is defined as the decreasing effect of distance on the speed of human travel across space, in movement of people and communications. (A) is the decreasing impact a phenomenon has on something as the distance from its origin increases. (B) refers to the negative impact of globalization in causing a growing divide between countries in the periphery and those in the core. (C) is diffusion of an innovation that takes a newer form in the new place to match cultural customs. (E) is a measurement of the way a feature is arranged in space.

9. **(A)**

Amritsar, India, is the city wherein the Sikh's holiest religious site, the Golden Temple, is found. (B) is practiced mainly in Japan and involves the worship of natural elements like rivers, rocks, and mountains. The rest of India is primarily Hindu (E), although minority pockets of Buddhists (C), Christians (D), and Muslims as well as other religious minorities are present.

10. **(A)**

A functional region consists of a node and the places linked to that central point through some sort of movement. In this case the region is created by the movement of United Trucking's services to customers in the places within the boundaries shown in the diagram. (B) describes a place with a uniform trait, such as language, present throughout the area. (C), (D), and (E) describe regions like the Bible Belt or the South in the United States—regions with boundaries marked by people's ideas rather than overtly measurable characteristics.

11. **(B)**

While the crude birth rate reflects varying human decisions related to cultural expectations and requirements, the crude death rate reflects the spread of basic health care throughout the world. Because minimal health care has diffused even to places with very high birth rates, death rates do not display the particularly vast discrepancies among countries that birth rates do, thus invalidating (A), (C), (D), and (E). Further, (C) is illogical in that birth rates do not always offset death rates.

12. **(A)**

Transnational corporations (TNCs, also called multinational corporations) are firms that have different parts of their production processes in different countries. Export-processing zones (EPZs) are special zones, often in less-developed countries, where industrial parks and export-oriented production occurs. Often countries establishing EPZs will grant those regions special tax exemptions to lure foreign direct investment. Typically a TNC contracts with factories to use their low-cost, low-skilled labor to make lightweight products for export to distant markets. (B) is incorrect because a TNC usually establishes its world headquarters in a world city, not in an EPZ. (C) is incorrect because quaternary-sector workers are involved in high-level information processing and decision making, not in industrial assembly; their work is usually found in world cities. (D) is incorrect because technopoles are regions in which technological research and innovation is abundant, for example, Silicon Valley in California. (E) would most be attracted to places with high amounts of capital, such as world cities and global investment capitals.

13. **(A)**

The second agricultural revolution, which occurred at the end of the 19th century, saw improved farming and storage practices that allowed for increased farming efficiency and output to feed the growing urban populations forming to fuel the Industrial Revolution's hunger for city-based workers. (B) refers to the advent of the third agricultural revolution in the 20th century, whereas (C) refers to preindustrial farming practices that colored much of medieval (feudal) times. (D) describes the opposite of what was happening at the time, because improved sanitation and inoculations helped prolong human life and improve health. (E) is also untrue because migrants moved into core countries for industrial work.

14. **(A)**

The graph depicts a typical spatial diffusion S curve. In the innovation stage (point A) the phenomenon (the iPod) is invented and first used by the innovating class of users, usually a small group. Once the innovation hits the greater community and becomes popular, it enters the majority-adopter stage (point B) with the fastest rate of adoption, as indicated by the slope of the graph. Once the innovation saturates the marketplace, or adopter class, the adoption rate (slope of the curve) lowers and the diffusion pattern reaches the late-adopter stage, when the innovation is adopted by the laggards or latecomers. (B) is incorrect because the highest growth rate occurs in the majority-adopter stage, not the late-adopter stage. (C) is not correct because in the innovator stage, the adoption rate is low, not high. (D) wrongly claims that the iPod had reached the whole population, but the y-axis of the graph indicates a saturation below 100 percent. (E) is incorrect because it is not possible to determine whether the diffusion represented in the graph was relocation or contagious diffusion.

15. **(C)**

Truck farming refers to commercial farming of fruits and vegetables intended for sale in places where such harvests are not possible (E). The market is now dominated by large agribusiness farms that grow tomatoes, strawberries, and lettuce (A), among other fruits and vegetable crops. These often corporate-owned and operated farms employ the use of machinery to irrigate and process the crops (B). Southeastern U.S. states like Florida dominate truck farming (D), along with California and Texas. (C) is false because migrant workers often supply less-expensive labor on large-scale truck farms.

16. **(B)**

Nigeria (A) has hundreds of local languages, which is one of the centrifugal forces challenging its unity. A major factor influencing the conflict over control of Quebec (C) is the division between French- and English-speaking Canadians, because Quebec is where most French-speaking Canadians are clustered. The political conflict in Cyprus (D) is highly related to the division between Greek speakers and Turkish speakers on the small island. Belgium (E) is highly divided along linguistic lines because the Flemings, the French-speaking Belgians, and the Walloons, the Dutch-speaking Belgians, are in conflict over control of Belgium. By contrast, Venezuela (B) is considered by many to be as near to monolingual as a country can get in today's society. Spanish is spoken by a high percentage of Venezuela's population.

17. **(B)**

The development of food surpluses, or more food than farmers need, allowed a population of nonfarmers to exist. Those nonfarmers could specialize in the fields and conduct the services needed for the development of cities, which were fed by the farmers. After the development of agricultural surpluses, people could perform nonfarming jobs, including those related to politics, and formal political organizations could develop (A). (C) and (D) existed before urbanization. (E) was primarily an outgrowth of the social stratification that occurred as trade grew between farmers and nonfarmers.

18. **(B)**

Desertification is the spread of desert-like conditions into more arable regions as a result of human overuse and, perhaps, environmental shifts. According to de Blij and Murphy's research, South America (A) is at a 20 percent risk; Europe (C), 9 percent; Africa (D), 57 percent; and Asia (E), 37 percent; by contrast, Australia (B) is at an 83 percent risk.

19. **(A)**

The growth of the United States' influence after World War II beyond that of the Soviet Union most significantly challenged Mackinder's theory that dominance of Eurasia would yield world domination for a superpower, because the United States existed outside the Eurasian "world island" that Mackinder defined. (B) was the area of focus of Mackinder's theory, the area of eastern Europe and much of Russia that was considered prime real estate for world domination and that the Soviets dominated after World War II. (D) was the heart of Mackinder's heartland theory. (E) is related to Mackinder's theory because Hitler supposedly subscribed to it. (C) was largely predicted by Mackinder's theory.

20. **(B)**

Thomas Malthus lived in England during the late 18th century, when cities were growing explosively as a result of the Industrial Revolution. As urban migration hit a new high mark, Malthus was convinced that the food supply would only grow arithmetically and would not match the exponential growth of the human population "explosion." What Malthus could not see was the Green Revolution on the horizon, when the development of new farming technologies, such as improved fertilizer and crop hybrids, allowed the food supply to grow faster and provide more nourishment for the exponentially growing population. Although (E) may seem reasonable, it was improved farming technologies, not trade routes, that directly proved Malthus's ideas false. If anything, reduced land supply (A) would have supported Malthus's alarmist theory. (C) and (D) are not directly related to Malthus's theory of food production being outpaced by population growth.

21. **(E)**

Comparative advantage is the idea that a region (or country) will produce goods it can make at a lower cost than other regions can and will trade them for goods that other regions can make more efficiently than it can. In this case Country X is better at making televisions, whereas Country Y specializes in pencil production. The two countries will find greatest economic efficiency if each one produces what it has a comparative advantage in producing, and then they trade with each other. (A) relates to industrial location theory—for example, when a company chooses to outsource its factory work and substitute higher transportation costs in exchange for the lower labor costs it will have. (B) is the planned destruction of a place to make way for an industrial center. (C) is the investment of foreign companies in countries outside their headquarters, such as when an American company builds a factory in Indonesia. (D) is a type of industry that does not have high transportation costs and is therefore free to locate wherever it wants; an example is a computer chip manufacturing plant whose final product is extremely lightweight.

22. **(D)**

Desalination (D) refers to the technology used to convert salt-water into potable, drinking water. GPS (A) refers to the global positioning system that activates satellites to pinpoint locations and gather geographic data. GIS (B) refers to geographic information systems that collect, store, and analyze geographic data in the form of layered map displays. Remote Sensing (C) is the process of collecting geographic information from remote locations, most often through satellite collection systems. Satellite imagery (E) is often used to create layers in maps.

23. **(E)**

The temple in the image, with its many statues of gods and goddesses, is most likely a Hindu temple. Another defining feature of a Hindu temple is its peaceful integration into the landscape. Hindu temples are built to house shrines of deities rather than for worship. (A) Taoist temples are usually filled with bright colors, especially red, with broad, curving rooftops and sculptures of traditional deities like the dragon and the carp. (B) Buddhists often decorate their temple complexes with pagoda towers, which are usually tall, with many tiers and slanted roofs. (C) Typically, Eastern Orthodox Christian churches are ornate, with domes and pointed arches. (D) Muslims construct mosques that usually include a central worship building with four towers used to call worshippers to prayer.

24. **(C)**

Whereas the Communist leader Mao Zedong implemented an aggressively pronatalist campaign to raise the birth rate in China, his successor, Deng Xiaoping, realized that high birth rates could destroy China's infrastructure. Thus he imposed a strict one-child policy, which rapidly reduced the Chinese birth rate. As a result, the number of children born per 1,000 women (the general fertility rate) decreased rather than increased (A). Life expectancy (B) was not directly affected. The total fertility rate was forcibly reduced to one child per family in many areas, making (D) invalid. (E) is not a documented claim.

25. **(B)**

The United Nations (UN) measures countries' development with its Human Development Index (HDI), ranking countries up to 1.0, or 100 percent. The equation for the index includes social, demographic, and economic factors, such as literacy rate and amount of education, life expectancy, and gross domestic product. (A) relates to core periphery models. (C) is one side of the economic globalization debate. (D) captures too narrowly the meaning of HDI, because the intent of the UN equation was to broaden analysis of development beyond gross domestic product. (E) is not a factor in the HDI equation because the size of a population is not the sole determinant of the level of human development.

26. **(C)**

The photograph shows large-scale, extensive grain farming, most likely mechanized. This is highly common in places like North America and eastern Europe, especially Ukraine (called the breadbasket of Russia). (A) is dominated by primitive subsistence agricultural and livestock production. (B) and (D) are known for their desert-like terrains and nomadic herding agriculture. (E) is dominated by intensive, primitive subsistence agriculture.

27. **(D)**

The enclosure movement closed in the public field system and consolidated individual strips of land that jutted off feudal villages, forming one large farmstead owned by one or a few farm owners (E). This effectively reduced the number of individual farm owners, making (D) false. Efficiency rose because one owner could push best practice and reduce the chaos that characterized land organization before the enclosure movement (A). People who were pushed off their lands moved into the cities, where they could find work in the growing industrial complexes (B). Thus the number of feudal village communities fell because people lost their lands to the enclosure movement (C).

28. **(C)**

By 1998 the Croats living in Croatia had successfully found independence from their Serb occupiers governing from Belgrade, Serbia. Remember, Croats are a unique nationality, Serbs are a unique nationality, and the Muslims throughout the region are considered a nationality as well. However, following the Croatian victory, many of the ethnic Serbs living in Croatia did not want to be governed by the Croats, who had formed a new government. Therefore, nearly 400,000 ethnic Serbs fled Croatia for their "homeland" of Yugoslavia and Bosnia. Soon thereafter Yugoslavia devolved even further into Serbia-Montenegro, and the dictator Slobodan Milosevic was removed from power by his own people.

29. **(B)**

The Mercator projection, while drastically distorting the dimensions of higher-latitude land masses, accurately displays direction everywhere on the map, making it particularly useful to navigators on sea vessels. (A) is considered an equal-area projection, which accurately depicts the relative sizes of land masses while distorting the other properties of maps: shape, direction, and distance. (C) is also an equal-area map. (D) is considered an average projection in that it distorts all four properties so as not to drastically distort one. While (E) avoids the relative-size distortions of the Mercator projection, direction is only accurate along the equator.

30. **(D)**

In Christaller's central place theory, a high-threshold function requires a large population to make the economic endeavor work; a high-range function draws people from far away to purchase the good or use the service. (D) requires a large population, because a small percentage of people need brain surgery, so it has a high threshold; it has a high range because people would probably travel far for life-saving brain surgery. (A) and (B) are low range and low threshold, whereas (C) and (E) are a bit higher but not as high as (D).

31. **(C)**

Ecofeminism expresses the idea in the quote and is a new facet of study in cultural ecology. (A) is the notion that human behavior and development is dictated by economic factors and causes. (B) is a measurement tool available to geographers to compare the abilities of men and women to excel in economic and political leadership and work. (D) argues that cultures are becoming more similar as regional disparity is being reduced through improved transportation and communication. (E) is the process of all cultures originating somewhere, somehow.

32. **(B)**

A linguistic refuge area is a place that is relatively free from forces of language diffusion and convergence. Mountainous regions such as the Alps, the Himalayas, and the Caucasus Mountains often divide groups geographically and allow for isolation and refuge from invading forces trying to assimilate a people to a particular culture or language. Mountains often provide this geographical separation, preventing language convergence that requires constant contact with other languages or forced change. A marketplace (E), like an international airport

(C), is a place where contact with other languages is likely to occur in trade and thus would not allow for linguistic refuge or shelter from convergence. (A) provides little geographic protection for the forces of diffusion and convergence. (D) is also unlikely to include a linguistic refuge area because riverbanks are often invasion points and centers of cultural contact.

33. **(E)**

Life expectancy in African countries such as Namibia and South Africa is being critically reduced by HIV/AIDS, in some cases by as much as 10 years. While (A) has a cumulative effect that keeps life expectancy low, it is not immediately reducing life expectancy as HIV/AIDS is, although some people argue that cyclical poverty is related to HIV/AIDS in Africa. (Remember, the AP test requires you to select the *best* answer, and cyclical poverty is not as exact as HIV/AIDS.) (C) is the term for the violent terrorist actions taken by environmental activists against organizations linked to ecologically destructive practices.

34. **(A)**

A primate city is a large urban center that is disproportionately representative of its national economic, political, and social power. Often a primate city is found in a developing country where former colonizers set up their colonial headquarters. Both Ulaanbaatar and Lagos are much larger than the next largest cities in their countries and are disproportionately powerful. (B) are economically powerful global "headquarters" cities that generally have populations greater than 10 million people. (C) are portions of a country's territory separated from its main body by the territory of another country. (D) are clusters of new urban settings with varied functions that often exist off highway exits and beltways surrounding central business districts of older downtown regions. (E) are cities in which the dominant economic activities are no longer secondary but have transitioned toward tertiary, quaternary, and quinary sectors. Ulaanbaatar and Lagos are both still in their industrializing phases.

35. **(B)**

Agglomeration is best exemplified in the modern shopping mall, wherein stores are clumped to take advantage of like-minded shoppers who may walk out of one store and be attracted to another. Coffee shops and ice cream shops tend to clump on blocks with the marketing strategy that customers may leave the coffee shop and want ice cream, or may decide against ice cream for coffee or mochas, or vice versa. (A) is the "unclumping" or spreading out of formerly clustered industries that occurs when staying together becomes too expensive or cramped. (C) is a region set up to lure factories, such as maquiladoras. (D) is an equation used to compare the value of a good in two countries; for example, the Big Mac index compares the price of a Big Mac in two places. (E) is the phenomenon of the temperature being somewhat higher in an urban area as a result of industrialization and increased human population density.

36. **(D)**

An urban place's hinterland is defined as the surrounding area serviced by the functions in an urban center; the larger the urban place, the larger is its hinterland (usually). Thus, as you move "up" a country's urban hierarchy, the economic reach (or hinterland) of each urban place increases in size. (A), (B), and (E) might be tempting answers, but (D) is a much more concrete, logical relationship to the hinterland concept. (C) has no relationship to the concept.

37. **(B)**

This map was created by the International Nuclear Safety Center in 2005 to show the clustered spread of nuclear power throughout the world. Notice that nuclear power is positively correlated with GDP. (A) is incorrect because there are dots in China and not enough throughout India. (C) is incorrect because Dravidian is more widely spoken in India than is indicated on the map, and Dravidian is uncommon in western Europe and the United States. (D) is incorrect because western Europe and the United States had proportionately fewer outbreaks than in China. (E) is incorrect because HIV should be more represented on the map in Africa and less in the United States and western Europe, proportionately, than indicated.

38. **(D)**

The informal sector consists of workers who do not report their incomes or jobs to the government. The government cannot tax informal-sector workers because it does not know officially of their work activities, and the informal sector is not included in GDP calculations.

39. **(C)**

Cognitive distance shapes the effects of friction of distance because a person's perception of distance impacts their travel decision. (A) is massive emigration of educated elites, (B) is a measurement of a phenomenon's spread over space, (D) is the time needed for a population to double in size, and (E) is the spread of a phenomenon from one place to another with the continued addition of adopters along the way.

40. **(E)**

Hierarchical diffusion is the spread of something from large or powerful places to areas that are smaller or less powerful. Reverse hierarchical diffusion is the inverse of that; it is the spread of something from smaller (or less-powerful) places to larger (or more powerful) places. The map shows its spread from A to B to C, each with a larger population of chickens than the other, thus moving from smaller to larger populations. (B) is the diffusion of the basic idea or principle but the failure for the entire concept to spread (e.g., the spread of the idea of a hamburger to India, where it was adopted as a vegetarian burger). (C) is the spread and adoption of a culture trait that does not seem to be appropriate for the adopting population, such as ranch-house architecture in snowy climate regions. (D) is unrelated but describes the gap in development in places, often between more-developed countries and less-developed countries.

41. **(D)**

Centrifugal forces are those that either pull people away from the city's center or pull a state (e.g., a country) toward falling apart and dividing into separate states. (D) can cause people who are being oppressed to become so frustrated that they will try to secede or at least revolt against discrimination by others. (A), (B), (C), and (E) are all centripetal forces, which help bind a state together or pull people toward a city's center. A national flag usually inspires loyalty and unification around a national identity, as does a state-owned news station, which can spin news in favor of the state's power. A national research laboratory could be seen as a centripetal force because of its findings of new health initiatives, but it would not be a centrifugal force in usual scenarios. A common language also binds people together into more of a cohesive whole.

42. **(A)**

Linguistically and religiously divided, Nigeria is nearly split along a north-south axis, with its northern states conforming to Islamic Sharia law and its southern states aligning along Christian lines, thus making (C) and (D) incorrect. Hausa is the dominant language in the north, while Yoruba and Ibo dominate the southern region, making (E) incorrect. (B) is a political, supranational organization similar to the European Union in its aim of uniting African countries in working toward progress.

43. **(E)**

Languages in the Indo-European family are spoken by more of the world's people than any other family, though Chinese, in the Sino-Tibetan family, has the largest number of speakers of any single language. (A), (B), (C), and (D) are all Indo-European languages. Turkish is in the Altaic family, which dominates the Anatolian Plateau region.

44. **(A)**

According to the table, the growth rate declines steadily beginning in 2000. However, between 2015 and 2020, 72 million people will be added to the global population annually. This is a trend called hidden momentum, which is the continuous growth in population despite a growth rate decrease. This occurs because the size of the generation of women having babies is very large as a result of the high fertility rates in the preceding generations. Their mothers and grandmothers had lots of babies. (B) is the divide in development levels that roughly corresponds to the equator, where most of the world's global south population lives in poverty. (C) is the pattern of human migration away from cities into villages and towns. (D) is the amount of time it would take for a population to double in size. (E) is the point at which the natural growth rate equals zero, which is not when no babies are born but is the point when, generally, the birth rate equals the death rate.

45. **(E)**

Extensive agriculture involves farming practices requiring large plots of land, such as wheat farming or animal herding. Intensive agriculture is farming a small plot of land more heavily, as in rice farming. As you move eastward into China's capital interior, intensive subsistence farming increases, and more people live near water-rich, arable lands close to Beijing and Shanghai (regions A, B, and C). Nomadic herding, the movement of animals to find food sources, is an example of extensive subsistence agriculture, most likely to occur in Region E.

46. **(C)**

Allocational boundary disputes involve the distribution of a precious commodity or resource, such as oil. (A) are disputes over the location of a boundary, whereas (B) are arguments over the language in the boundary's definition—for example, the exact height of a boundary's expanse. (D) are fights over the nature of a boundary—for example, how a boundary will be enforced. (E) is a type of border, not a type of border dispute.

47. **(D)**

The new international division of labor is a production process involving outsourcing of some parts of an assembly line to other countries. When one part of a computer is made in one country and another in a different country and final assembly takes place in yet another country, the labor has been divided among three countries. This process is facilitated by improved transportation links and time-space compression, or the reduction of the friction of distance. (A) are production or factory districts in Mexico on the U.S. border where American factories are built to take advantage of Mexico's low-cost labor, usually provided by women. (B) is the new factory production process that contrasts with the original assembly-line process developed by Henry Ford, in which a worker performed one piece of the assembly line process all day. In the post-Fordist assembly line, workers are trained to complete several tasks as a group to increase efficiency. (C) is the "backbone" of a country or region composed of various operations that enable a place to function; examples include the water system, roads, and the electrical grid. (E) refers to manufacturing of goods in homes rather than in factories; this was found in England and the United States before the Industrial Revolution and is often found in less-developed countries that have not yet industrialized.

48. **(B)**

The cleavage model was developed as an explanatory factor in electoral patterns. These patterns often show the power core being dominated by a particular nation (or cultural group) and in tension with minority groups, which are often marginalized politically and geographically. (A) explains and predicts the changes in population patterns in countries, (C) explains and predicts patterns of agricultural land use, and (D) explains and predicts the patterns of city development and their relationship to urban hierarchy. (E) was developed by Harold Hotelling to study the placement of industries in relationship to each other and their markets.

49. **(E)**

The key variable in von Thünen's theory is distance to the marketplace from the harvest site as measured by the transportation cost. He concluded that zones of similar agricultural land use will develop around a central marketplace in relation to the intensity of the farming being done and the cost of transporting the harvest to the market.

50. **(B)**

With nearly 1.5 billion adherents, Christianity is the world's largest, followed by Islam, with 1.2 billion, and then Hinduism, with 757 million. Sikhism, with nearly 22 million believers, is larger than Judaism, with 17 million.

51. **(D)**

Nearly all men and women can read in more-developed countries. Literacy rates for females vary significantly in less-developed regions. In general, more men than women are literate, a pattern true throughout history. However, this gap is lessening in many places throughout the world, though literacy rates continue to be especially divergent between males and females in Arab states, where only 50 percent of females are literate but nearly 75 percent of men are literate. This question requires general knowledge of demographic trends, very accessible through the Population Reference Bureau (www.prb.org). Of the three regions, sub-Saharan Africa has historically had lower literacy rates in general, particularly among women, largely because of that region's earlier stage in the demographic transition. This would eliminate (A), (B), and (C), leaving the correct answer choice dependent on the rates of Latin America and the Caribbean and Asia.

52. **(C)**

A country creates a forward capital when it moves its capital city to a new site to achieve some national aim, such as moving the power base to a more central location. The Malaysian government is currently moving its headquarters from the colonial capital city of Kuala Lumpur to the forward capital of Putrajaya, a move intended to demonstrate the country's economic modernity.

53. **(A)**

Shifting cultivation is primarily associated with subsistence farming, although it is also used by commercial farming systems. It is essentially farming a plot of land and then shifting to another plot to allow the fertility of the soil in the farmed plot to regenerate. (B) is incorrect because shifting cultivation is primarily a subsistence practice. Further, the rotation of crop types in a pattern on the same piece of land is known as crop rotation, not shifting cultivation. (C) describes pastoral nomadism; (D) is intensive subsistence terrace farming often found in China; and (E) describes mixed farming, a technique often found in Europe and North America.

54. **(C)**

Stage 1 is characterized by high crude birth and death rates, leading to equilibrium and nearly a natural rate of increase of nearly zero, which is equilibrium. Stage 2 is when the crude death rate begins to fall as a result of technological improvements in health care, causing the rate of natural increase to rise from its zero position in stage 1. Once a country reaches stage 3 in its demographic transition, the crude birth rate falls toward the death rate, and they finally meet again in stage 4, when the "forces of change," birth rate and death rate, are again equal, or at equilibrium.

55. **(A)**

An official language is the designated language of a government for all government purposes, such as legislation and all records. The standard language is the generally accepted dialect in a language that has various forms. For example, the standard language in the United States is American English, whereas in England, it is British Received Pronunciation. (B) is untrue because the standard language is what is generally spoken by the "insiders" of a population and can be used as a culturally divisive moment when newcomers try to integrate into a region and speak a different dialect. (C) is incorrect because it simply describes what is generally known as the standard language. (D) is untrue because the official language of a country can be (and often is) the standard form of the language. Standard languages can change, with invasion or governmental change, making (E) false.

56. **(B)**

In a compact-shaped country the distance from the center of the country to any of its extremities (or points on its boundaries) is about equal. Russia (A) is more of an elongated shape, Singapore (C) is a compact shape, the Philippines (D) is fragmented, and Chile (E) is elongated.

57. **(D)**

The greatest concentration of cattle feedlots, where cattle are fattened in a mechanized, factory-like process, exists in a corridor from South Dakota to Texas. Feedlots are also found in large numbers in Washington, Utah, Idaho, and Arizona. Some feedlots can hold more than 1 million head of cattle.

58. **(D)**

Transhumance is the practice of pastoral nomads when they circulate with their herds from lowland pastures to mountainous regions in a learned pattern that is often passed down through generations of family members. (A) involves farming one small plot of land to yield high output per acre. (B) is the integration of livestock and crops on one plot of land. (C) is an intensive farming practice using one plot of land to produce two harvests each year. (E) involves clearing unfarmed land by first cutting and then burning the present vegetation, allowing the cleared land to rest for a period, and then planting crops.

59. **(D)**

The 2004 UN conference related increasing women's rights to lowering birth rates, because women can enter the workforce and find opportunities outside the home. Additionally, increased women's rights lead to better health care for women because women can push for reforms in health care and research that focus on their needs. One of the effects of better maternal health care is a lower infant mortality rate. When babies live longer, parents do not have to have more babies to fill their family needs. (E) may seem like a reasonable answer, but enforcing target goals in specific countries was an approach taken by earlier conferences that did not emphasize enough the significance of the structural change necessary to change birth rates, which are an expression of cultural decisions.

60. **(D)**

Folk and popular culture are the two primary divisions of material culture, which comprises the aspects of culture that can be seen or are tangible. Nonmaterial culture, on the other hand, comprises the intangible aspects of a culture, such as beliefs. Folk culture represents homogeneity, or sameness, and is usually practiced by those who live in isolated regions, free from the influence of popular culture's diffusion. Popular culture diffuses over wide areas of diverse peoples, while folk culture defines a much smaller group of more-homogenous people, thereby making (B) incorrect. The Internet and television have increased the speed and expanse of popular culture's diffusion, because new ideas can reach farther places faster, thus making (A) incorrect. Popular culture is often spread from the most-developed regions of the world—regions with the capital resources to induce the diffusion— thus (C) is incorrect. Because of the rapid diffusion of popular culture, the actual customs rapidly change from place to place, as new ideas quickly come and adapt to the new people's needs, thus making (E) incorrect.

61. **(D)**

In the drive to maturity stage of Rostow's model of economic growth, the innovation and growth that benefited the society's takeoff industry spread to other areas of the economy, enabling workers to specialize and grow more skilled. During (A) a large number of people in the society are farmers. (B) involves the identification of and initial investment in the infrastructure needed for an industry to take off. (C) is the stage in which the selected industry grows and prospers. By (E) the economy has developed to the extent that consumer goods, such as cars and radios, are produced for consumption by a wealthier workforce.

62. **(A)**

Maquiladoras are U.S.-owned factories built at any point along the U.S.– Mexico border, such as point A. These factories are built because the maquiladora regions offer companies low-cost labor and other tax breaks. The North American Free Trade Agreement (NAFTA) is highly related to the growth of maquiladoras. The maquiladora regions are also considered export-processing zones.

63. **(B)**

Chain migration is when migrants move to a location because of information from friends or relatives who have made the same migration previously. (A) is when people are pushed from their home regions against their will (e.g., to escape ethnic cleansing) and become refugees (E). (C) is the migration of people within their country or region, and (D) is the movement of people in similar patterns over time, such as traveling from a boarding school to home for the summer holiday.

64. **(E)**

This is the definition of the general fertility rate. (A) is the number of children each woman is expected to bear. (B) is the ability of a woman to conceive. (C) is the number of children born per 1,000 people (not just women) in a given year. (D) is the number of deaths among infants under one year of age per 1,000 live births in a given year.

65. **(D)**

Mandarin, with nearly 875 million speakers, is the largest language from the Sinitic branch of the Sino-Tibetan family, followed by Wu (77 million), Cantonese (71 million), Min (55 million), and then Hakka, also known as Kejia (33 million).

66. **(B)**

An edge city is an urban complex that typically grows off a highway or beltway surrounding an inner city (A). Edge cities often have their own malls, health care facilities, entertainment complexes, and other necessities and conveniences (C). Often manufacturing jobs and facilities exist in edge cities, built in suburban settings (D). A cluster of office buildings on the side of a highway or beltway often forms the heart (or nucleus) of an edge city, and suburban housing and family restaurants grow around the office zone. Tenements, or slums, are not found in most edge cities but are more typical of the original inner-city regions.

67. **(B)**

Political ecology is the arm of geography that analyzes political structures and their relationship to natural resources and habitats. (A) refers to terrorist actions taken by groups frustrated with their perception of corporate abuses of natural habitats, (C) is the spread of a cultural trait across space, (D) is redefining electoral districts to give certain parties an advantage, and (E) is the fracturing of a cohesive state into splinters.

68. **(B)**

The 20th century's Green Revolution was aimed at reducing hunger in less-developed countries by giving farmers in those regions greater access to the fertilizers and seeds they needed to increase their crop yields and improve their farming practices. It did not focus on commercial agriculture or improving profits for agribusiness corporations, as (A) suggests; and it did not focus on improving the human diet (C) or land preservation (D). Although (E) may imply the use of fertilizers that aid in increasing crop yields, (B) is more related to the focus of the Green Revolution.

69. **(C)**

Religion is not a motivating factor in the conflict within Quebec. French-speaking inhabitants of Canada are known as Francophones and English-speaking inhabitants are Anglophones. Quebec was first settled by the French in the 1600s and then taken by the British in the 1700s, making (E) a factor in the conflict. The Francophones desire more control over Quebec's economic and political affairs, which have been traditionally dominated by the Anglophone minority, making (B) another factor. Quebec has traditionally been Canada's poorest province, and this inequality has created tensions that straddle cultural and economic lines, making (D) a factor. Language (A) is a preeminent factor in the dispute, with Francophones seeing their French language as a defining factor in their national identity. They have even created a commission to transfer toponyms from English names into French names.

70. **(C)**

China is the leading producer of woven cotton fabric, a labor-intensive part of the clothing and textile production process. India is second in line, followed by the United States.

71. **(E)**

Gentrification is the upgrading and remodeling of rundown buildings in low-income neighborhoods in inner-city regions. (A) is a suburban complex that has developed on the edge of an inner city, usually off a highway exit. (B) is the process of transforming something not priced into something traded as a product—for example, putting a price on a human working in a factory. (C) is the process of moving away from inner cities toward a more rural, suburban life. (D) is the illegal practice by real estate brokers of stirring up racially grounded fear in residents that leads to segregation and prompts some residents to sell their homes.

72. **(A)**

A state is essentially a country, which is a political term for a sovereign, bounded territory that has a government. A nation, on the other hand, is a group of people with a shared culture and history. A state can change its borders, and a nation can realign its identity, thus making (B) incorrect. (C) is incorrect in its assertion that a nation is not linked to a territory, because nationhood often is tied powerfully to a piece of land; and (D) is incorrect because a state and a nation are both products of history and people. (E) is flawed in its oversimplified suggestion that a nation cannot be controversial; the explosive conflict between the Serbs and Croats in the former Yugoslavia is just one example of a nation steeped in controversy.

73. **(C)**

Structural adjustment programs encourage countries to develop economies that can participate in the globalizing economic landscape through international trade. To achieve such growth, the structural adjustments often end popular, but economically inefficient, practices. This involves all the steps listed except for (C), because a structural adjustment program often leads to the creation of zones to lure foreign direct investment, which can generate growth in a country. However, the program can be quite painful in the short run because people may lose jobs and services that were cut in favor of the "more efficient" economic solutions advocated by proponents of the structural adjustment program.

74. **(C)**

The highest land value in a city is usually found at the point called the peak land value intersection (PLVI), which is near the city's central business district, or city center. The bid-rent curve shows how much a firm or person is willing to pay for land. The stronger the desire to be near the PLVI, the steeper the curve. (C) is a business that needs visibility and accessibility to downtown areas. (A), (B), (D), and (E) require larger plots of land with lower returns on their investments, so it would be illogical, not to mention costly, for them to buy the more expensive land closest to the PLVI. By contrast the real estate firm could afford the property and can expand by building up rather than out.

75. **(D)**

A break-of-bulk is a place where cargo (or people) change from one type of transportation to another, such as from barge to train. (A) is a group of countries that create an open trading relationship through reduced tariffs and improved transportation among their borders. (B) is a region in a less-developed country where foreign direct investment is courted through tax breaks and other incentives to companies. (C) is an unstable zone between two regions of conflicting political or cultural values. (E) is a region in a communist country (such as China) where special capitalistic trade is allowed.

Section II

Sample Response and Scoring Rubric for FRQ 1

Sample Response

A.   Cultural ecology is the study of the relationship between a human cultural group and its natural environment. It is closely related to human–environment interactions.

B.   Environmental determinism is a doctrine holding that human activities are controlled by the environment. Possibilism is a school of thought created in response to environmental determinism. One fundamental belief of possibilism is that humans, not the physical environment, are the primary active force. Another belief is that any environment offers a culture numerous possible ways to develop.

C.   Both cities developed along elongated, hilly sites flanked on one side by water. Both are connected by bridges leading to adjacent land across the water. Both use tunnels for arterial roads. There are differences in street patterns. In Chongqing the streets are laid out to accommodate the rugged terrain. San Francisco, however, shows relatively little deviation from a gridiron pattern. Also, San Francisco covers a much larger land area.

D.   San Francisco seems to have adapted the environment to fit its gridiron pattern. Possibilists would point to the innovative technologies in the bridges and tunnels that both cities built to adapt to environmental constraints. Also, possibilists would point to San Francisco's parks and the construction of streets through them as human adaptation, molding the environment to fit its needs. Further, the city parks in San Francisco are on the coast, rather than inland.

Scoring Rubric for FRQ 1

PART A: 1 point

1 point for any of the following:

- Cultural ecology is related to the study of human–environment interactions.

- It is the study of a human group's interaction with its environment.

- It is the study of the cultural landscape.

PART B: 2 points

1 point for any of the following:

- Environmental determinism sees the environment as directing human action, predetermining the course humans will take.

- Possibilism sees the environment as providing a set of broad constraints that limit the possibilities of human choice.

PART C: 2 points

1 point for accurate similarity; 1 point for accurate difference:

- Both cities developed along elongated, hilly sites nearly surrounded by water, both are connected by bridges leading to adjacent land across the water, and both use tunnels for arterial roads.

- The cities have different street patterns. In Chongqing the streets are laid out to accommodate rugged terrain, whereas San Francisco shows relatively little movement away from the gridiron pattern; also, San Francisco covers a much larger land area compared with Chongqing.

PART D: 2 points

1 point for each of the following:

- Possibilists would point to the innovative technology in bridges and tunnels used by the cultures to adapt to environmental constraints.

- Possibilists would point to San Francisco's parks and the construction of streets through them as indications of human adaptation, molding the environment to fit human needs.

OVERALL SCORE FOR FRQ 1   _____/ 7 points

Sample Response and Scoring Rubric for FRQ 2

Sample Response

A.   The group of people in a country composed of active workers, usually aged 15 through 64, is considered nondependent. The people who are older or younger than the working group form the group considered dependent. The dependency ratio shows the relationship between the dependents and the workers (who take care of the dependents).

B.   These population pyramids illustrate China's shrinking working-age, nondependent population and its growing elderly population. A sharp decline in China's fertility rate was seen starting in the 1980s with the imposition of the antinatalist one-child policy. That policy successfully reduced the number of babies each woman was having, which is the country's total fertility rate. The improvements in medical and industrial technology are increasing the life expectancy of Chinese citizens, or their longevity. This is causing China to have a higher dependency ratio, because a large number of elderly nonworkers are dependent on a shrinking number of people in the working cohort (the nondependents).

C.   Because of its high dependency ratio, China is facing the problem of having too few working-age people to support its growing elderly population. As the number of older people rises, health care costs will rise rapidly and the number of working-age people able to support these rising costs will decrease. Therefore, many older people may not receive the care that they need because they cannot pay for it; they are also more likely to become homeless. Moreover, many jobs may be unfilled because the domestic workforce is not large enough to replace the positions once occupied by the retiring population. This could lead to an economic downturn.

Scoring Rubric for FRQ 2

PART A: 1 point

1 point for the following:

- The dependency ratio is the number of people considered dependent (under age 15 and above age 64) divided by the number of people in the workforce (nondependents).

PART B: 5 points

1 point for each correct description of demographic trend, 1 point for each correct explanation of demographic trend, and 1 point for correct relation of demographic trends to dependency ratio:

- Decreasing working-age, nondependent population

- Rising elderly dependent population

- Decreasing fertility linked to one-child policy

- Increasing longevity linked to improved medical technology and industrialization

- Increasing dependency ratio in China as number of dependents is rising and number of people in the workforce (aged 15 through 64) is decreasing

PART C /4 points

1 point for each correct identification of social and/or economic problem related to China's dependency ratio:

- Higher number of dependents means higher health care costs

- Lower number of workers means fewer people to support rising health care costs

- Potential homelessness and insufficient care provided for elderly people

- Economic downturn because jobs not filled after older workers retire

OVERALL SCORE FOR FRQ 2   _____/ 10 points

Sample Response and Scoring Rubric for FRQ 3

Sample Response

A.   Urbanization is generally equivalent to city building. It is the spread and growth of cities, or the transformation of rural space into urban space. Urbanization includes political, social, and cultural shifts. It is the evolution of a location into a city structure with an urban population that has migrated, usually, from rural areas to supply labor and inhabitants.

B.   "Rate of urbanization" refers to how fast urbanization is growing, while "level of urbanization" refers to the amount of the population that is already considered urban. Although urbanization is increasing globally, certain areas are experiencing faster rates of urbanization because more of their space is becoming urban. Southeast Asia is experiencing rapid rates of urbanization, with many countries industrializing and converting formerly rural places into urban spaces. Southeast Asia's level of urbanization, or the percentage of its people considered urban, is lower than North America's level of urbanization. Simply explained, North America experienced an earlier industrial revolution, therefore it has already developed a higher level of urbanization than Southeast Asia. Since most North Americans are urban already, its rate of urbanization is lower—urbanization has nearly reached 100 percent.

C.   Counterurbanization is the return of city-dwellers (or urban people) to more-rural places because of the pull factors present in more-rural landscapes, including a slower pace of life, less traffic, less pollution, and less noise, among others. It is most likely to be found in more-developed countries among retired individuals, usually older than 55 and in the middle- to upper-income ranges.

Scoring Rubric for FRQ 3

PART A: 2 points

1 point for each of the following observations (2 points maximum):

- Urbanization is the spread and growth of cities.
- It is the growth of city-based populations.
- It includes social, political, and cultural impacts as populations transform into city-based ways of living.

PART B: 4 points

1 point for each of the following correct descriptions and explanations (4 points maximum):

- North America: low rate of urbanization and high level of urbanization; already reached industrial revolution, so population is already largely urban
- Southeast Asia: high rate of urbanization and low level of urbanization (ongoing city building); currently experiencing industrialization and growth of cities, massive urban migration patterns in many countries (although not all; Singapore, for instance, is 100 percent urban)
- Latin America: low level of urbanization and high rate of urbanization; similar to Southeast Asia, with high rates of rural-to-urban migration, causing higher rates of urbanization and increasing levels of urbanization

PART C: 3 points

1 point for each of the following (3 points maximum):

- Counterurbanization is the process of a population becoming less centralized and generally moving from urban spaces into more-rural spaces.
- The factors that influence counterurbanization are higher costs of living in cities, less traffic and congestion in outlying areas, and the availability of improved transportation and communication technology (allowing commuting and working from home in more-remote areas).
- Demographically, most people in U.S. counterurbanization trends are retired (older than 55) and in the middle- to upper-income ranges, allowing them the freedom to be spatially mobile and the ability to move into the "countryside" for a more peaceful retirement than the traffic and congestion in the cities would allow.
- Younger people, in their 20s and 30s, often enjoy the bustle and diversity of the cities. Unmarried people also are statistically more likely to live in urban spaces.

OVERALL SCORE FOR FRQ 3 _____ / 9 points

PRACTICE EXAM 2

This exam is also on CD-ROM in our
special interactive AP Human Geography TestWare®

AP Human Geography

Section I

TIME: 60 minutes
75 multiple-choice questions

(Answer sheets appear in the back of this book.)

Directions: Each of the following questions is followed by five suggested answers or completions. Select the best answer choice.

1.   The diagram below most clearly illustrates the geographic process of

(A)   deglomeration

(B)   accessibility

(C)   scale

(D)   placelessness

(E)   agglomeration

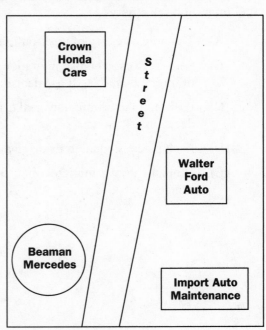

2. According to the rank-size rule, a country's fourth-largest city is what fraction of the country's largest settlement?

    (A) 1/2   (D) 1/12

    (B) 1/4   (E) 1/16

    (C) 1/8

3. Which of the following countries has a government organized in a federal structure?

    (A) United Kingdom   (D) France

    (B) China   (E) Czech Republic

    (C) India

4. Which of the following religions did not originate with a founder or innovating prophet?

    (A) Buddhism   (D) Taoism

    (B) Hinduism   (E) Confucianism

    (C) Islam

5. Which of the following assumptions underlies push-pull reasoning in human migration selectivity?

    (A) The only category of push-pull factors is economic.

    (B) Some factors in human migration decisions are beyond the total control of migrants making those decisions.

    (C) Push-pull factors are universal truths that apply to all human migration decisions.

    (D) Each place is equal in its original favorability to humans.

    (E) Humans always migrate when forced to live in unfavorable circumstances.

Word Usage for Term Meaning "Soda"

Line indicates boundary between two terms' dominance

6.   The diagram above most closely demonstrates the geographic concept of

(A) language groups   (D) the isogloss

(B) ideograms   (E) language pollution

(C) pidgin language

7.   All the following are often preconditions for the construction of a federal government EXCEPT

(A) compact shape

(B) multiculturalism

(C) wide expanse of territory

(D) multicore region (or lack of core)

(E) regionalism

8. In sub-Saharan Africa,

    (A) caloric intake has reached nearly adequate levels because genetically modified food crops are being shipped from foreign markets

    (B) malnutrition has most affected children in urban areas

    (C) the impact of the Green Revolution has been the highest, though still insufficient to mitigate malnutrition

    (D) agribusiness investments have improved local agricultural economies

    (E) food production has declined since 1980 and continues to drop

9. Which of the following accurately lists regions in order of decreasing levels on the Human Development Index ?

    (A) Anglo-America, western Europe, eastern Europe, Southeast Asia, Middle East

    (B) Anglo-America, western Europe, eastern Europe, Middle East, Southeast Asia

    (C) Anglo-America, western Europe, Middle East, eastern Europe, Southeast Asia

    (D) Western Europe, Anglo-America, eastern Europe, Southeast Asia, Middle East

    (E) Western Europe, Anglo-America, eastern Europe, Middle East, Southeast Asia

10. Bank USA refused to approve loans to people living in a particular neighborhood of Nashville, Tennessee. This is an example of

    (A) blockbusting   (D) ghettoization

    (B) redlining   (E) racial steering

    (C) gerrymandering

11. Approximately how many independent states exist on the earth's surface?

    (A) 2,500   (D) 500

    (B) 1,800   (E) 200

    (C) 1,000

12. A pilgrim wishing to visit the hearth of Islam would most likely visit which modern-day country?

    (A) Iran   (D) Saudi Arabia

    (B) Syria   (E) Lebanon

    (C) Israel

13. After the 1991 Gulf War, the Kurdish people residing in and near Iraq are best classified as a

    (A) nation-state   (D) perforated state

    (B) multinational state   (E) supranational organization

    (C) stateless nation

14. Which of the following is not one of the key assumptions in von Thünen's agricultural location model of an isolated state?

    (A) The isolated state involves flat, uninterrupted land without barriers to farming or transportation.

    (B) Farmers transport their harvests by accessing the most direct routes.

    (C) Farmers wish to maximize their profits by minimizing their transportation costs.

    (D) It costs more to transport produce longer distances.

    (E) Different soil types and qualities exist throughout the isolated state.

Percentage of *Specific* Ethnic Groupings in Former Yugoslavian Regions

	% Serb	% Croat	% Muslim	% Slovene	% Albanian
Serbia	85				
Croatia		75	12		
Slovenia				91	
Bosnia-Herzegovina	32	18	40		
Montenegro			13		6
Macedonia					20
Kosovo	13				77

15. Based on the table above, in the Yugoslavian civil wars, which region was most intensely the focus of Serb irredentism?

    (A) Serbia   (D) Macedonia

    (B) Bosnia-Herzegovina (E) Slovenia

    (C) Croatia

16. Which of the following countries is predominantly Shiite Muslim?

    (A) Saudi Arabia   (D) Iran

    (B) Indonesia   (E) Philippines

    (C) Pakistan

17. Which of the following states has only one core region?

    (A) United States   (D) Malaysia

    (B) Japan   (E) India

    (C) Nigeria

18. When Dutch traders and Japanese traders meet, they often use English to conduct their business transactions. This use of English is an example of a(n)

    (A) pidgin language   (D) lingua franca

    (B) creole language   (E) monolingualism

    (C) official language

19. On the map of Azerbaijan above, point Z most closely represents which concept?

    (A) Assimilation   (D) Multiculturalism

    (B) Exclave   (E) Multiplier effect

    (C) Ghetto

20. Human geography is best defined as the study of

(A) where and why human activities are located as they are

(B) where and why natural forces exist

(C) populations and birth rates

(D) human civilizations and their changes

(E) governments and their impacts on the earth's surface

Demographic Data: Ireland

Year	Total Fertility Rate	Dependency Ratio (dependents:workers)
1970	3.9	10:14
1995	1.9	10:18
2006	1.6	10:22

21. Based on the trend demonstrated by data in the table above, which of the following statements can be inferred about Ireland?

I.   When children born in the 1960s entered the workforce in Ireland, fewer children were in the generation behind them.

II.   Fewer Irish women were able to enter the workforce in the mid-1990s.

III. Laws restricting contraception were lessened in Ireland in the 1970s.

IV.   By 2006 Ireland was experiencing an economic downturn.

(A) I   (D) III

(B) I and III   (E) I , II, III, and IV

(C) I, II, and IV

22. Niamey, the capital of Niger, is located at 13 degrees 31 minutes north latitude and 2 degrees 7 minutes east longitude. This is Niamey's

    (A) relative location   (D) node

    (B) region   (E) site

    (C) absolute location

Berlin Wall, circa 2005   *(Photo by: Davax)*

23. Which of the following boundary classifications fits that shown in the picture above?

    (A) Natural-political   (D) Relic

    (B) Subsequent   (E) Antecedent

    (C) Superimposed

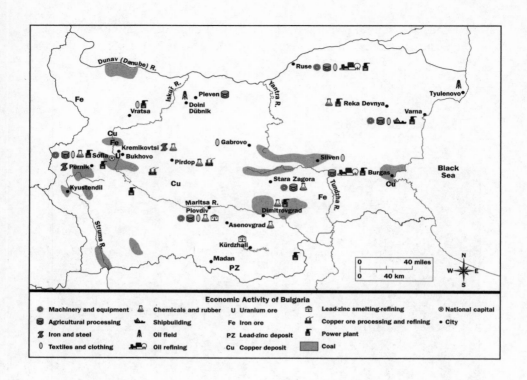

24. Based on the map of Bulgaria's economic activity above, which of the following regions contains the most agglomeration of secondary economic activities?

   (A) Reka Devnya   (D) Sofia

   (B) Dimitrovgrad   (E) Stara Zagora

   (C) Vratsa

25. The image above shows an example of a(n)

(A) pinyin   (D) shatter belt

(B) isoline   (E) isolated language

(C) ideogram

26. Which of the following states is most similar to the concept of a geopolitical nation-state?

(A) Canada   (D) Belgium

(B) Russia   (E) Japan

(C) United Kingdom

27. The Middle East has been called the "crossroads of the world." Which fact would best support this statement?

(A) Most of the world's oil reserves are there.

(B) The Strait of Hormuz is an important waterway.

(C) Parts of three continents intersect there.

(D) Water bodies surround most of the region.

(E) It is characterized by regional, tribal conflict over land.

28. The Gravity Model predicts

(A) population density

(B) agricultural land use patterns

(C) urban land use patterns

(D) birth rates and death rates

(E) spatial interaction between places

29. Which of the following statements accurately applies to theories of development?

    (A) While liberal models assume that every country can develop along the same projection for growth, structuralist models assume that countries are withheld from growth by constraints built into the global economy.

    (B) Liberal models include the core-periphery models, while structuralist models include Rostow's economic development model.

    (C) Structuralist models reject the theory of neocolonialism.

    (D) Structuralist models assume that economic inequalities between countries are a result of inefficient structure in local or countrywide government policies.

    (E) Liberal models argue that less-developed countries cannot grow economically because the core countries unfairly suppress the less-developed countries' opportunities for economic growth.

30. Which of the following regions has the lowest percentage of urban dwellers?

    (A) Eastern Europe   (D) Southeast Asia

    (B) Middle East   (E) Western Europe

    (C) Latin America

31. Which of the following is true of U.S. agriculture?

    (A) Most U.S. farms are owned by agribusiness corporations.

    (B) Nearly 20 percent of the U.S. workforce is involved in agribusiness.

    (C) The amount of U.S. land devoted to agriculture has decreased.

    (D) The number of U.S. farms has increased since 1900.

    (E) The largest farms, nearly 4 percent of total U.S. farms, account for only 10 percent of U.S. agricultural output.

32. According to world-systems analysis, the world's states

    (A) strengthen when involved in supranational organization

    (B) are divided into a heartland and rimland

    (C) compete for Eurasian dominance

    (D) exist in a mobile structure of economic advancement

    (E) must be seen in the context of a global capitalist economy

(Photo by W. McLean)

33. The photograph above was taken in which of the following cities?

    (A) Mecca, Saudi Arabia   (D) São Paulo, Brazil

    (B) Jerusalem, Israel   (E) Tehran, Iran

    (C) Kuala Lumpur, Malaysia

34. Which of the following correctly sequences the evolution process of boundaries, starting with the first stage and ending with the last?

    (A) Definition, delimitation, demarcation

    (B) Definition, demarcation, delimitation

    (C) Demarcation, definition, delimitation

    (D) Delimitation, demarcation, definition

    (E) Demarcation, delimitation, definition

35. Which of the following statements best describes the growth pole concept?

    (A) Growth poles first cause deindustrialization.

    (B) The growth pole concept only operates at the national or supranational geographic scale.

    (C) The development of growth poles leads to deglomeration.

    (D) Growth pole development is often led by one particularly commanding industry or firm.

    (E) Once a region becomes a megalopolis, growth poles disappear in influence.

36. Which of the following is most likely NOT a significant factor causing the growth of favelas, barrios, and *barriadas* in Latin America?

    (A) Natural disasters   (D) Population increases

    (B) Strained infrastructure (E) Housing shortages

    (C) Urban migration

37. All the following are regions where ranching is practiced widely EXCEPT

    (A) Central Europe   (D) Southeast South America

    (B) Southern Africa   (E) Central Asia

    (C) Australia

38. Which of the following best defines the cultural landscape approach in geography?

    (A) Each region has a uniquely built environment that is constructed by social processes and their impacts on the surrounding natural features.

    (B) Geography is a result of human processes that shape the earth's features.

    (C) Humans are driven by their environments and consequently shape their surroundings.

    (D) Environmental perception drives industrial development.

    (E) Physical geography is less significant than human constructions in shaping the landscape.

COUNTRY
1. Japan
2. Italy
3. Germany
4. Greece
5. Sweden

39. The table above lists the countries with the

    A. highest natural growth rates

    B. shortest doubling times

    C. lowest percentages of dependents

    D. grayest populations

    E. largest populations of guest workers

40. Which of the following statements most closely aligns with the theory of environmental determinism?

    (A) The physical environment interacts with human groups in shaping the cultural landscape.

    (B) Humans create a series of reactions to the physical environment in which they live and choose from a set of possibilities the best course of action to suit their circumstance.

    (C) The physical environment directly causes human actions to take the forms they do.

    (D) The physical environment may affect human choices, but human groups ultimately can shape the physical environment to fit their needs.

    (E) Resources drive the creation of a set of tensions between the regions of the world rich in food and those most needing it.

41. The spread of baseball to China is most closely an example of which process?

    (A) Agglomeration

    (B) Cultural convergence

    (C) Centripetal forces

    (D) Balkanization

    (E) Conurbation

42. In which place labeled on the map above do the largest number of people live as irredenta of Albania?

    (A) Montenegro   (D) Podgorica

    (B) Kosovo   (E) Belgrade

    (C) Vojvodina

43. Which of the following examples best illustrates the impact of toponyms in contributing to human conflict?

    (A) Washington, D.C.   (D) Tokyo, Japan

    (B) São Paulo, Brazil (E) Berlin, Germany

    (C) Mumbai, India

44. Which of the following most closely qualifies as a buffer state?

    (A) China   (D) Venezuela

    (B) Mongolia   (E) Macedonia

    (C) France

45. In which of the following regions would the sawah pictured above most likely NOT exist?

    (A) Indonesia   (D) Malaysia

    (B) Northern India   (E) Vietnam

    (C) Southeastern China

46. Which of the following processes is most likely to be bulk reducing?

    (A) Automobile manufacturing

    (B) Copper refining

    (C) Computer production

    (D) Clothing manufacturing

    (E) Soda bottling

47. Ukraine, the Czech Republic, Slovenia, and the Republic of Korea share which worldwide demographic trend?

    (A) High crude birth rate

    (B) Low doubling time

    (C) High natural rate of increase

    (D) Low total fertility rate

    (E) Low dependency ratio

Figure 1

Figure 2

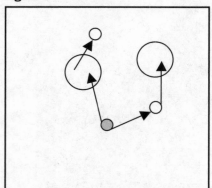
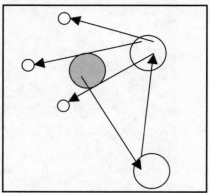

Legend
• **Shading indicates node of infection**
• **The larger the circle, the larger the community infected**
• **Arrows indicate spatial diffusion path**

48. Which of the following accurately describes the infection patterns depicted in each figure above?

    (A) Figure 1 demonstrates the pattern of hierarchical diffusion, and Figure 2 shows contagious diffusion.

    (B) Figure 1 primarily demonstrates a contagious diffusion pattern, and Figure 2 shows hierarchical diffusion.

    (C) Figures 1 and 2 primarily demonstrate contagious diffusion patterns.

    (D) Figures 1 and 2 primarily demonstrate hierarchical diffusion patterns.

    (E) Neither Figure 1 nor Figure 2 demonstrates contagious diffusion patterns.

49. Which of the following demographic tools is used more as a predictive measurement of fertility in a society?

    (A) Total fertility rate   (D) Infant mortality rate

    (B) Crude birth rate   (E) Literacy rate

    (C) General fertility rate

50. Which of the following is NOT an independent state on the current world map?

    (A) Burma (Myanmar)   (D) Albania

    (B) Yugoslavia   (E) Hungary

    (C) East Timor

51. Subsistence agriculture

    (A) does not include the herding of animals

    (B) is aimed at producing surplus crops for sale in the market

    (C) is becoming increasingly dominant in the world

    (D) is characterized by production of food for consumption by the farmers and their families

    (E) is most practiced in South America

52. Which of the following first focused world attention on global climate change, facilitating discussions by leading world countries to reduce greenhouse gas emissions?

    (A) UNCLOS   (D) Benelux

    (B) Kyoto Protocol   (E) Comintern

    (C) NAFTA

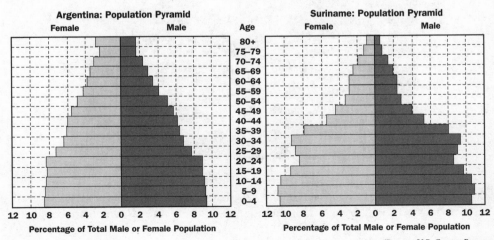

(Source: U.S. Census Bureau, International Data Base)

53. Which of the following accurately contrasts the demographic trends of Suriname and Argentina, based on the 2004 age-sex pyramids shown on the previous page?

   (A) Argentina is most likely in stage 1 of demographic transition, while Suriname is likely in stage 3.

   (B) Argentina has a higher percentage of women in the fecund range than does Suriname.

   (C) Life expectancy in Suriname is higher than Argentina.

   (D) Since the 1990s birth rates have changed more in Suriname than in Argentina.

   (E) Women have a lower life expectancy in Argentina than in Suriname.

54. In addition to India, which country is home to the largest number of Hindus?

   (A) Pakistan

   (B) Senegal

   (C) Sri Lanka

   (D) China

   (E) Nepal

55. The picture above was taken on the Paseo de la Reforma, a prominent boulevard in Mexico City, Mexico. This picture most closely reflects which concept?

   (A) Agglomeration of industries

   (B) Lasting colonial imprints

(C)   Communist ideology

(D)   Impact of greenhouse gas emissions

(E)   Creation of a forward capital

56.   The Kentucky Governor's Scholars Program, which offers scholarships covering full room and board to talented high school seniors if they choose to go to in-state universities, was established primarily to prevent

(A)   brain drain   (D)   immigration

(B)   guest workers   (E)   intervening opportunity

(C)   intraregional migration

57.   Diffusion on a microscale often occurs most intensely around the initial adopter, or innovator. This is referred to as

(A)   susceptibility   (D)   independent invention

(B)   maladaptive diffusion   (E)   neighborhood effect

(C)   stimulus diffusion

58.   The push in Northern Ireland to separate from its United Kingdom-based government and reintegrate with Catholic Ireland best exemplifies

(A)   devolution   (D)   structuration theory

(B)   neocolonialism   (E)   gerrymandering

(C)   centripetal forces

59.   Which of the following is true of commercial farming in more-developed countries?

(A)   Consumption of a particular food product is usually highly related to its market price.

(B)   Commercial farmers face surpluses of their harvests because of stagnant market demand.

(C)   The food supply in more-developed countries has remained relatively constant since the 1960s.

(D)   Low population growth has not affected agricultural markets.

(E)   Farmers in the United States are encouraged by the government to grow surpluses.

60. Newspapers, bakeries, and dairy plants are examples of

    (A) footloose industries

    (D) cultural convergence

    (B) ubiquitous industries

    (E) bulk-reducing industries

    (C) entrepôts

61. All the following are accurate generalizations of human migration in England in the 1880s EXCEPT:

    (A) Streams of migration often produce counterstreams, which are usually small.

    (B) Migrants moving long distances usually travel to one of the great centers of commerce and industry.

    (C) Most migrants travel only small distances.

    (D) Migration is a step-by-step journey.

    (E) Large towns grow more by natural increase than by migration.

62. A major change over the last 30 years in the list of the world's 20 largest (most-populated) cities is that

    (A) no South American city appears on the list

    (B) New York City has fallen off the list

    (C) the dominant presence on the list of Western industrial cities has reduced

    (D) the average annual change is nearly 30 percent

    (E) the average size of cities on the list is nearly 30 million inhabitants

63. Vegetative planting

    (A) is growing plants by dividing roots and cutting stems

    (B) involves planting seeds to cultivate a crop

    (C) is defined as the commercial farming of vegetable crops such as radishes and lettuces

    (D) most likely followed the human discovery of planting and cultivating seeds

    (E) originated in South America

Population and Agricultural Density Measurements

Country	Population Density		Agricultural Density
	Arithmetic	Physiological	
Egypt	70	3,503	1,401
The Netherlands	398	1,601	64
Canada	3	35	1

Source: Rubenstein, 2005

64. Which of the following statements is directly supported by the data in the table above?

I.   Canada has a smaller population than Egypt or the Netherlands.

II.   The Dutch use more mechanized farming tools than the Egyptians.

III. Dutch cities are more densely populated than Egyptian or Canadian cities.

IV.   Egypt has less arable land per person than the Netherlands or Canada does.

(A) I

(B) I and III

(C) I, II and IV

(D) II, III, and IV

(E) II and IV

65. Which of the following agricultural types is predominantly found in peripheral countries?

(A) Truck farming

(B) Mixed crop and livestock

(C) Mediterranean

(D) Plantation

(E) Organic

66. Feeding Kuala Lumpur's industrial growth has drained other Malaysian cities and regions of valuable workers and resources. This example best demonstrates

(A) cumulative causation

(B) territoriality

(C) the median-line principle

(D) the dependency theory

(E) counterurbanization

67. All the following are considered 21st-century world cities EXCEPT

    (A) Seoul, South Korea   (D) Kolkata, India

    (B) Istanbul, Turkey   (E) Vienna, Austria

    (C) São Paulo, Brazil

68. When Worth Industries was successful in Tokyo, Japan, it drew more jobs to the region, which in turn added more businesses and development. This case study is an example of

    (A) multiple-nuclei development

    (B) gravity model patterns

    (C) the multiplier effect

    (D) doubling time

    (E) epidemiological transition

69. The process of profits from outsourced factories flowing from the periphery back to the core is known as

    (A) machine space   (D) backwash effects

    (B) multiplier leakage   (E) terraforming

    (C) foreign direct investment

70. The surge in internal migration after 1960 of Mexican women to the border between the United States and Mexico is most influenced by which factor?

    (A) The chance of crossing the border

    (B) The construction of maquiladoras

    (C) Antinatalist policies in central Mexico

    (D) Educational opportunities

    (E) Forced migration

71. Which type of agriculture is practiced by the most people in the world?

    (A) Shifting cultivation   (D) Plantation

    (B) Pastoral nomadism   (E) Intensive subsistence

    (C) Mediterranean

72. Which of the following is the strongest example of an ecotourism industry?

    (A) Theme park with a roller coaster

    (B) Guided trail hike to view a rain forest

    (C) Beachfront resort

    (D) Oceangoing cruise ship

    (E) Go-cart track

73. A country that enacts pronatalist policies will most directly cause which of the following demographic effects?

    (A) Higher crude death rate   (D) Slower rate of natural increase

    (B) Longer life expectancy   (E) Slower doubling time

    (C) Higher total fertility rates

74. Which of the following best exemplifies exurbanization?

    (A) People in their 20s moving from farms to cities for excitement

    (B) A newly married couple moving from the rural areas to the suburbs to raise their children

    (C) A retired couple moving from their city apartment to a quiet community in a remote, rural village promising greater peace and tranquility from the city's hustle and bustle

    (D) The renovation of a warehouse into a luxurious high-rise loft apartment complex

    (E) The concentration of similar businesses around a shared resource

75. Which of the following central place functions is most likely to have the smallest range of goods and smallest threshold population?

    (A) Research university   (D) Allergy-testing clinic

    (B) Helicopter repair shop   (E) Computer store

    (C) Gas station

Section II

TIME: 75 minutes

3 free-response questions

> **Instructions:** You have 75 minutes to answer all three free-response questions in this section. Take a few minutes to outline your answers. Illustrate your essay with substantive examples when appropriate. It is not enough to answer a question by merely listing facts. You should present a cogent argument based on your critical analysis of the question posed and your understanding of geography.

1. The figure below depicts an example of U.S. intraregional migration in the 1990s.

    (A) Describe the migration pattern shown in the figure.

    (B) State at least two of Ravenstein's laws of migration and analyze the relevance of each to explaining the migration pattern depicted in the figure.

    (C) Explain the combination of factors that work to create the migration pattern demonstrated in the figure. In your response apply the demographic transition model to your explanation of the pattern demonstrated.

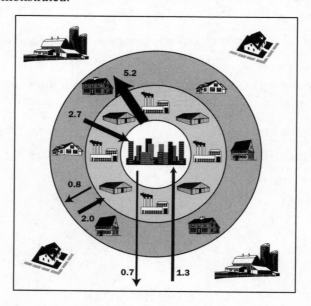

2. (A) Define *monolingualism*, and give an example of a monolingual country.

    (B) Multilingualism often reflects strong cultural pluralism and regional division.

        i. Define *multilingualism*.

        ii. Give an example of a multilingual state in either North America or Europe, and explain how linguistic diversity has contributed to regionalism in that state.

(Images Courtesy of Tennessee State Library and Archives, Nashville)

Werthan Mills Plant, circa 1950, was in an inner-city neighborhood in East Nashville, Tennessee.

The luxurious loft apartments at the former Werthan Mills Plant circa 2007.

3. (A) Define *gentrification*.

    (B) Relate gentrification to the photographs above. The modern loft apartments sell for roughly $200,000 each.

    (C) Explain one positive and one negative effect of gentrification as a proposed method of urban renewal.

PRACTICE EXAM 2

AP Human Geography

Answer Key

Section I

1.	(E)	20.	(A)	39.	(D)	58.	(A)
2.	(B)	21.	(B)	40.	(C)	59.	(B)
3.	(C)	22.	(C)	41.	(B)	60.	(B)
4.	(B)	23.	(D)	42.	(B)	61.	(E)
5.	(B)	24.	(D)	43.	(C)	62.	(C)
6.	(D)	25.	(C)	44.	(B)	63.	(A)
7.	(A)	26.	(E)	45.	(B)	64.	(E)
8.	(E)	27.	(C)	46.	(B)	65.	(D)
9.	(A)	28.	(E)	47.	(D)	66.	(A)
10.	(B)	29.	(A)	48.	(B)	67.	(E)
11.	(E)	30.	(D)	49.	(A)	68.	(C)
12.	(D)	31.	(B)	50.	(B)	69.	(B)
13.	(C)	32.	(E)	51.	(D)	70.	(B)
14.	(E)	33.	(B)	52.	(B)	71.	(E)
15.	(B)	34.	(A)	53.	(D)	72.	(B)
16.	(D)	35.	(D)	54.	(E)	73.	(C)
17.	(B)	36.	(A)	55.	(B)	74.	(C)
18.	(D)	37.	(A)	56.	(A)	75.	(C)
19.	(B)	38.	(A)	57.	(E)		

Section I Diagnostic Instrument

Instructions: Use these charts to see where your "weaknesses" exist in the curriculum.

Geography: Its Nature and Perspectives

Item #	20	22	38	40
Correct/Incorrect				

Population

Item #	5	17	21	28	39	47	49	53	56	64	70	73
Correct/Incorrect												

Cultural Patterns and Processes

Item #	4	6	12	16	18	19	25	27	33	41	42	48	54	57
Correct/Incorrect														

Political Organization of Space

Item #	3	7	11	13	15	23	26	34	44	50	58
Correct/Incorrect											

Agricultural and Rural Land Use

Item #	8	14	24	31	37	45	51	59	63	65	71
Correct/Incorrect											

Industrialization and Economic Development

Item #	9	29	32	35	46	52	60	62	66	68	69	72
Correct/Incorrect												

Cities and Urban Land Use

Item #	1	2	10	30	36	43	55	61	67	74	75
Correct/Incorrect											

PRACTICE EXAM 2

AP Human Geography

Detailed Explanations of Answers

Section I

1. **(E)**

    Agglomeration is the process of locating similarly functioning entities, such as the car dealerships, in close proximity. (A) is the inverse process in which geographic phenomena are separated. (B) refers to the general ease with which a given place can interact with other locations. (C) refers to the resolution levels in mapping and geographic research. (D) occurs when a place is indistinguishable from any other place and does not have a sense of being unique.

2. **(B)**

    According to the rank-size rule, there is a regular pattern or hierarchy in the ordering of cities according to size. A country's nth-largest city is always $1/n$ the size of the country's largest settlement. Therefore, the country's fourth-largest city is one-fourth the size of its largest city.

3. **(C)**

    A federal government structure is one in which the constituent regions in the country have protected authorities yielded to them by the central government, which shares power with them. (A), (B), (D), and (E) are unitary government structures, which are characterized by a power concentration in a central government with little or no authority yielded to provincial regions.

4. **(B)**

    Hinduism did not originate with one person or prophet who spread its teachings, whereas (A) was spread by Siddhartha Gautama; (C) is linked to Islam's prophet, Muhammad; (D) is associated with its organizer, Laozi; and (E) was founded by the philosopher Confucius.

5. **(B)**

Migration selectivity asserts that humans react to new conditions presented in their lives. As a consequence of these conditions, humans often make decisions (or are forced) to move. Push factors "push" people out of a region, or make them want to leave; examples are climate change or high taxes. Pull factors "pull" people to a particular region, or make them want to move there; examples are good schools or better job opportunities. It is important to note, however, that a person's decision to move is not entirely in that person's control. Important influences in the push-pull balance are beyond the individual's control, such as rising taxes or environmental change. (A) is incorrect because push-pull factors fall into several categories, including economic and social categories. (C) is incorrect because a push factor to one person may be a pull factor to another. For example, "being closer to Mother" may be a pull factor to one person and a push factor to another, depending on the person's relationship with Mother. (D) is incorrect because each location has a unique set of features that are valued differently by different people. (E) is incorrect because humans do not always move when forced to live in unfavorable circumstances. Sometimes people do not have the ability to move, as when living under a totalitarian regime.

6. **(D)**

Isoglosses are boundaries within which a particular word is used. North of the isogloss in the diagram, *Pop* is dominantly used, while south of it *Coke* dominates usage. (B) are symbols in a language that connote the idea being communicated rather than the sound. (C) is a simplified form of a lingua franca (or language used for trade); often pidgins are characterized by simplified vocabulary and grammatical structures. (E) is a derogatory term describing the influx of new words and phrases from other languages or regions into another; typically the word is used by people wanting to keep their language free from outside influences.

7. **(A)**

Usually states with compact shapes, ideally circular, can fit into a unitary governmental organization because regionalism is not as present as in a fragmented state, for example. The other answer choices set the stage for a federal state, or one that allows for a sense of regional semisovereignty tied to a national government of representation. For example, Australia and the United States have multicore structures (i.e., have more than one power base or region in the country), wide territories, ethnic diversity, and regionalism (i.e., competing regions).

8. **(E)**

Sub-Saharan Africa's food production has declined and is still dropping as a result of environmental damage related to overfarming and desertification, governmental corruption, disease, and the inability of local farmers to compete in the global agricultural economy. Therefore sub-Saharan Africans have the lowest caloric intake of any people on the earth, making (A) incorrect. (B) is incorrect because malnutrition most affects children in rural areas, which typically lack access to governmental aide and other food sources. (C) is incorrect because the Green Revolution has actually had a limited impact in sub-Saharan Africa compared with other world regions, such as South America. (D) is incorrect, because agribusiness investments and the globalization of agriculture have forced many local farmers out of the competition in the farming marketplace.

9. **(A)**

Following are the Human Development Index levels for the regions in the correct response: Anglo-America, 0.94; western Europe, 0.92; eastern Europe, 0.78; Southeast Asia, 0.71; Middle East, 0.66. This makes (A) the correct order.

10. **(B)**

Redlining is the illegal practice by banks and other financial institutions of refusing to lend to people and firms based on their geographic places; it had racist overtones when banks would not give African Americans loans to buy houses in certain areas, keeping those areas all white. Redlining can lead to ghettoization (D), the creation or maintenance of low-income, underprivileged neighborhoods characterized by cyclical poverty. (A) is when real estate agents create racially based fear that leads people to move out of their neighborhoods and that ultimately benefits the agents who sell the homes. (C) is the purposeful redistricting of electoral regions to benefit particular political parties. (E) is the hard-to-trace practice of real estate agents who take people of certain races to see homes in certain areas, leading to segregation patterns and racially grouped living patterns.

11. **(E)**

An independent state is a country. There are approximately 200 independent countries on the earth.

12. **(D)**

The hearth of Islam is believed to be the city of Mecca, which is on the western side of Saudi Arabia near the Red Sea. This is the point, along with the Saudi Arabian city of Medina, from which Islam diffused. Every able-bodied Muslim is called to make a pilgrimage to visit the Holy Mosque in Mecca once in a lifetime. The other choices, though they exist in the Middle East, are not the birthplace of the religion. However, (C) is a tempting choice because it is home to what Muslims believe to be the third-holiest site in Islam, the Dome of the Rock.

13. **(C)**

A stateless nation is a nation or strongly linked cultural group without a state to call its own. The Kurds form a large minority nation in Iran, Turkey, and Iraq. Although they wish to have their own state, the regime of Saddam Hussein in Iraq worked violently against it, and the Kurds face opposition to this concept from their neighboring Arab states. (A) is a country in which the borders of the dominant nation (or group) match the borders of the country, such as Iceland. (B) is a country housing several nations within its borders. (D) is a country whose land totally encompasses the land of another country. (E) is an organization involving three or more countries that are working to promote shared objectives, such as the United Nations or the European Union.

14. **(E)**

The von Thünen model makes all the listed assumptions except for (E), because von Thünen assumed that soil quality and type were similar across the isolated state. By equalizing the soil type and quality, von Thünen focused his model on analyzing farmer's choices based on cost of transportation and land nearest to the market.

15. **(B)**

Irredentism is when one group of people seeks the return of their people (or land) from a region not controlled by them. In the Yugoslavian civil wars of the 1990s, the dominating Serbs longed to keep their fellow Serbs together under one government. Since Bosnia-Herzegovina has the highest percentage (32 percent) of Serbs living outside of Serbia, the Belgrade government of the disintegrating Yugoslavian state wanted bitterly to keep Bosnia-Herzegovina from seceding and forming an independent state. Although the Serbs in Serbia (A) were experiencing irredentism, the bloodiest focus (or cause) of this desire was Bosnia-Herzegovina, where so many Serbs resided outside Serbia. Croatia (C) had a much smaller percentage of ethnic Serbs within its boundaries, as did Macedonia (D) and Slovenia (E). Consequently, their attempted secession from the crumbling Serb-controlled Yugoslavian government was much less bloody than Bosnia's attempt.

16. **(D)**

The two largest branches of Islam are Sunni and Shiite. Iran is nearly 89 percent Shiite, whereas most Islamic countries are predominantly Sunni, as in the remainder of the answer choices. Worldwide there are only about 165 million Shia compared with nearly 1 billion Sunnis.

17. **(B)**

The region of Japan that centers on Tokyo is a clear national core. This area, known as the Kanto Plain, is a highly urbanized region that is the economic and sociopolitical nucleus of the country. (A), (C), and (E) are multicore states, each with several regions that compete for dominance rather than one, clear seat of economic and sociopolitical power. (D) is a fragmented state without one clear core around which activities ambulate.

18. **(D)**

A lingua franca is a language used between two people who speak different languages. When Japanese and German traders meet and turn to English to communicate, English is being used as the lingua franca between the traders. (A) is a simplified form of a dominant language adopted by a people wanting to use that language to participate in the region dominated by that language. When that simplified form of a dominant language, a pidgin, replaces the mother tongue of those people using the pidgin, that simplified variant of the language becomes known as a creole language (B). (C) is the language selected by a government for official purposes and documents. (E) is when only one language exists in a region, which in modern countries is a rarity.

19. **(B)**

An exclave is a region of land separated from but politically controlled by its motherland. On the map, the portion of land marked Z is named Naxcivan (or Nakhichevan) and is an exclave of primarily Muslim Azerbaijan. Notice its position within Armenia, which is primarily Christian. This position has caused much conflict between the two regions, and migrants pass between the two regions. (A) is an extension of acculturation, a process in which a culture group loses some of its original traits when it comes into contact with another more dominant culture group. Assimilation is when authentic, defining traits are lost to complete integration within a new culture. A ghetto (C) is a cultural enclave, wherein people of a similar, often minority and economically or politically oppressed, culture reside or are forced to reside. (D) is the presence of many languages, races, and other culture groups within the same region. When the basic sector of the economy—that which brings money to a region from the outside (e.g., a factory)—is cultivated, the growth of the nonbasic sector doubles; that is the multiplier effect (E).

20. **(A)**

Human geography essentially attempts to answer the questions of where and why human activities occur in the patterns that they do. (B) describes physical geography, which often complements human studies. (C), (D), and (E) are components of human geography but too limited to serve as a definition.

21. **(B)**

The data displayed in the table relates to the decreasing dependency ratio in Ireland after Ireland relaxed its laws preventing contraception, which could be inferred from the table by tracing the pattern of the total fertility rate (TFR). Over the years highlighted, the TFR (the number of children born per woman) steadily declined, allowing more women to enter the workforce because they were not solely having children. By 2006 the combination of more women working and fewer children being born per woman increased the workforce and reduced the number of dependents per worker. This led to an economic surge in Ireland by the turn of the millennium, thus ruling out (C) and (E). Statement I is accurate because the number of children per woman decreased starting in the 1970s, leading to smaller generations of children in the following years.

22. **(C)**

Absolute location is defined as the exact position of a place on the global grid, using latitude and longitude. A location's address, such as 123 Main Street, Brookings, South Dakota 57007, can also be seen as a form of absolute location because only one place on the map can have that exact address. (A) is a location's place relative to other places; (B) is a general term used for a group of places sharing some sense of commonality; (D) is the hearth of a functional region, the focal point of some spreading phenomenon; and (E) comprises a place's physical characteristics.

23. **(D)**

A relic boundary is a boundary that once functioned to divide territory or people but now is only a reminder of that boundary. The remnants of the Berlin Wall are a reminder of a boundary that once divided Berlin. The Berlin Wall was a superimposed boundary when it was functioning but is a relic because it no longer functions. (A) is a boundary that follow lakes, rivers, or natural features. (B) is a boundary created and adjusted along with the cultures affected by it. (C) is a boundary forcibly placed "on top of" a culture and is not sensitive to that culture. (E) is a boundary that existed before the development of the human cultures it serves to divide.

24. **(D)**

Secondary economic activity involves the refining or processing of the earth's resources extracted in primary economic activities, such as farming. Agglomeration is the clumping or clustering of economic activities for economic advantage; the clumped businesses or industries share resources. In Sofia the machinery and equipment industry, agriculture-processing industry, textiles and clothing industry, chemicals and rubber industry, and power plant can all exchange goods and services to support each other's functions. Additionally, Sofia is Bulgaria's capital city, having the largest population and available workforce. The other choices, although they have secondary industries, do not have as much agglomeration of secondary economic activities as does Sofia.

25. **(C)**

Ideograms are written expressions in a language that communicate not a sound but an idea, so they are symbolic representations of ideas in a language. Chinese uses ideograms, such as the one displayed. (A) is the system of using roman letters to write out the phonetics of the Chinese language, instead of using ideograms. (B) is a line on a map that connects points of equal value; isolines often appear on topographic maps and weather maps. (D) is an area where many languages are spoken. (E) is a language that does not show any interaction with other languages and does not belong to a language family.

26. **(E)**

A nation-state is a country in which the boundaries of the state match the ethnographic boundaries of the people within those political borders, a place in which there is ethnic and political cohesion. Japan is most aptly termed a nation-state because it has a relatively cohesive population compared with the other nations listed. (A) exemplifies multinationalism because Canada has French-speaking and English-speaking residents. (B) has thousands of minority nations within the knit of its federation. The population of (C) includes people from prominent minority nations, such as Africans. (D) is geographically and culturally split between the Fleming and Walloon nations.

27. **(C)**

The Middle East is situated at the intersection of Europe, Asia, and Africa, which has resulted in its being both a victim of invasion and a prominent part of trade routes throughout history. Although (A), (B), (D), and (E) are true, they are too limited in scope to explain the comment linking this region to its position as a crossroads of peoples.

28. **(E)**

The Gravity Model is used by geographers to predict the spatial interaction of places, as a function of population sizes of the places in question and the distance between the places. There is no known model to predict population density (A), per se, but the demographic transition model does predict birth and death rates (D), and the von Thünen Model predicts agricultural land use patterns (B). Models such as the concentric zone model and the urban realms model (among others) predict and explain urban land use patterns (C).

29. **(A)**

Liberal models, such as Rostow's economic development model, assume that all countries can develop if they improve practices within their own economies. In contrast, structuralist models of development, such as the dependency theory and core-periphery models, argue that the structure of the international economy controls and limits the growth potential of peripheral countries. (B) has reversed the two ideas, because Rostow's is a liberal model, while core-periphery models are structuralist. (C) is not correct because structuralist models embrace the concept of neocolonialism, arguing that countries that were once colonized by core countries are now economically dependent on their former colonial masters. (D) describes liberal models, while (E) describes structuralist models.

30. **(D)**

While Southeast Asia may have large numbers of urban dwellers, it has the lowest percentage (around 40 percent) of urban dwellers, because most Southeast Asians still live in rural, subsistence farming villages. (B) is nearly 60, and (A), (C), and (E) are nearly 80 percent.

31. **(B)**

Agribusiness refers to the system of farming, processing, packaging, distribution, marketing, and sale of farm products. Agribusiness is the food production industry, which accounts for nearly 20 percent of all U.S. workers. (A) is incorrect because most U.S. farms, nearly 98 percent, are still family owned. (C) is incorrect because the amount of U.S. land devoted to farming has increased. The number of U.S. farms has decreased since 1900, making (D) incorrect. The largest farms, comprising 4 percent of the total U.S. farms, accounts for nearly 50 percent of U.S. agricultural output.

32. **(E)**

World-systems analysis asserts that the world's countries are divided into three subgroups: the core, the semiperiphery, and the periphery. The world, according to the theory, is essentially an economic system driven by capitalism and competition for resources. (A) is unrelated and a distracter, although supranational organizations can influence international structures. (B) and (C) are elements of Mackinder's heartland theory. (D) is not necessarily true because it is questionable whether states can move in a fluid manner from the peripheral zones of global power to core positions. Some geographers assert that such mobility is not something that can be achieved by individual states but is more related to global economic structures.

33. **(B)**

The photograph, taken in Jerusalem, Israel, shows the Dome of the Rock, the third-holiest site to Muslims, following Mecca and Medina in Saudi Arabia. It also shows remains of the Western Wall, which is a holy site to Jews because it is believed to be the remains of the western wall of the Temple of Solomon. The juxtaposition of these two holy sites is at the root of the Israeli-Arab conflict.

34. **(A)**

Definition, the first stage of the boundary evolution process, is when a treaty or document is written out with a description, and agreement of the boundary is spelled out. At the second stage, delimitation, the boundary is marked on a map. Finally, demarcation (which often does not occur) is when the boundary is formally marked on the land, with a line, a fence, or some other physical marker.

35. **(D)**

Growth poles are regions of extraordinarily high economic and industrial growth that are often initiated and driven around a single firm or industry leading the growth explosion, such as a new factory or research initiative. (A) is false because growth poles first cause heightened industrialization around the process causing growth. (B) is false because growth poles can be local or regional if they apply to a region, like the Ruhr region in Germany's industrial core, or a factory in a town that attracts positive growth. (C) is false because growth poles lead to agglomeration and clustering of like-minded processes around the area of magnetic growth to take advantage of the momentum and to feed the growth. (E) is not true because a megalopolis is caused by or evidence of growth poles.

36. **(A)**

Favelas, barrios, and *barriadas* are squatter settlements on the outskirts of many rapidly growing Latin American cities that are the focus of intense urban migration (C). Unfortunately, these cities cannot adequately house all the migrants (E), and the cities' support services and infrastructures, such as plumbing are strained (B). People are moving to the cities to take part in the industrialization process, coupled with population increases in part owing to improved medical care and farming practices diffusing to less-developed countries in Latin America (D).

37. **(A)**

Ranching is the raising of animals on large tracts of arid and semiarid land (extensive) on which the animals graze. It is usually practiced in more-developed countries on land where the vegetation and soil do not support crops. Mixed crop and livestock farms prevail in central Europe, whereas ranching is prevalent in the other areas listed.

38. **(A)**

The cultural landscape of a region is the imprint of human activity on the earth's surface; it is the fingerprint of human activity on the natural environment. Therefore, the cultural landscape approaches geography through the lens of both physical (natural) and social (cultural) processes. (B) is too limited in that it does not include the nature of human–environment interactions that are at the base of the cultural landscape approach. (C) describes the theory of environmental determinism, which states that people's actions are determined by the climate and natural environment in which they live. Both (D) and (E) are unrelated and not valid theories.

39. **(D)**

Except for Japan, the world's oldest countries are in Europe. These highlighted countries are experiencing "aging populations" in which the rate of natural increase is lowering and the dependency ratio is increasing. (A), (B), and (C) are the inverse of the situation in these countries, because each has a low natural growth rate and the resulting long doubling time and high dependency ratio. Although countries like Italy and Germany have high numbers of guest workers, Japan has strictly regulated the immigration of workers, thus making (E) incorrect.

40. **(C)**

Environmental determinism asserts that the physical environment directly causes human behavior, that humans are driven by their environments to take certain actions. This 19th century theory would have agreed with the idea that warmer areas create more-productive people. (A) is too vague and does not capture the theory of environmental determinism in the more exact way that (C) does. Both choices (B) and (D) more accurately reflect the theory of possibilism, a response to environmental determinism that argues that the physical environment may limit human actions by presenting a set of feasible choices that humans can work with to fit their needs. (E) is unrelated to the topic.

41. **(B)**

Cultural convergence is a result of cultural diffusion, when a trait, such as baseball, from one culture spreads into another culture and is adopted. (A) is the clumping of people and activities in one region for shared benefit, such as the grouping of factories in an industrial park to share resources. (C) are forces that unite a geographic unit, such as a national flag around which people can rally. (D) is the breakup of a country or other geographic unit into smaller (usually ethnic) units, such as what happened in the former Yugoslavia. (E) is the grouping of major metropolitan regions to form a megacomplex (sometimes called a megalopolis) of one urbanized area.

42. **(B)**

Kosovar Albanians longed desperately to be reunited with Albania, although Kosovo was an administrative unit of Serbia. This issue became a flash point in the 1990s as Yugoslavia devolved toward breaking into nation-states. (A) Montenegro is home to most ethnic Montenegrins, who also resented Belgrade's controlling presence. (C) is a region north of Belgrade with few ethnic Albanians; (D) is the largest city and the unofficial capital of Montenegro; and (E) is the capital of the Serb province and was home to the former Serb dictator Slobodan Milosevic's power base.

43. **(C)**

Toponyms are place names. Often human groups will wage war over the name of a place, because names symbolize power structures and history. Mumbai, India, is a toponym that is the result of an ongoing conflict in India over that city's name, which was recently changed from its colonially imposed name of Bombay, given by India's British occupiers. The other answer choices are places not associated with conflicts over place names.

44. **(B)**

A buffer state exists geographically between two potentially hostile or warring states. It is usually smaller and weaker. Belgium, for example, was historically a buffer state between France and Germany, and Mongolia exists as a buffer between potentially hostile Russia and China. (A) and (C) are too large and powerful to be buffers. (D) and (E) do not serve significantly to separate potentially warring neighbors.

45. **(B)**

A sawah is a flooded field in rice farming often found in all the listed regions except (B), which has too dry of a climate for wet rice farming.

46. **(B)**

A bulk- or weight-reducing process is one in which the assembly or production process creates a product that is lower in weight or volume than the original parts. All the answer choices except copper refining are weight-gaining processes, meaning that the final product weighs more than the original parts.

47. **(D)**

Ukraine, the Czech Republic, Slovenia, and the Republic of Korea are so economically depressed and their birth rates—that is, the rates of natural increase—are so low that they are classified as "graying populations." Consequently, they have very low fertility rates, extremely high doubling times, and high dependency ratios, because the younger generations are not reproducing at the levels to match the older generations, thus resulting in more dependents per worker.

48. **(B)**

Contagious diffusion is the spread of an innovation in a wave pattern. The spread pattern moves across space from the hearth or node to the next-closest place, regardless of the size or power of the receiving place. In Figure 1 the phenomenon, perhaps a disease, spreads from smaller cities to larger cities and then to a smaller city. Figure 2 diffuses from the larger cities to the smaller cities, even though the smaller cities are closer to the node than are the larger cities. The remainder of the choices incorrectly label the diffusion types.

49. **(A)**

While all the other answer choices are used to represent past behavior, the total fertility rate represents a predictive measure used to forecast how many children each woman is expected to bear. For example, the crude birth rate (B) reports how many children were born per 1,000 individuals in a society. If the total fertility rate is 3.2, demographers would predict that a woman in the fecund range would produce nearly three children during her fecund years.

50. **(B)**

Beginning in the 1990s the individual pieces of what was known as Yugoslavia began to devolve into independent countries, sometimes through what were violent, genocidal wars. By 2003 the only remaining piece renamed itself "Serbia and Montenegro," which by 2006 had even split into two distinct countries. (A), (C), (D), and (E) remain independent states as of the publication of this book.

51. **(D)**

Subsistence farmers consume what they produce. They do not produce more than what they need, or a surplus, as (B) implies. Subsistence farming often includes raising or herding animals, as in pastoral nomadism, making (A) incorrect. Subsistence agriculture has been steadily declining with the advent of new farming technologies, though it still has a large presence in less-developed countries (C). It is most practiced in Asia, particularly Southeast Asia.

52. **(B)**

The Kyoto Protocol was signed in 1997 by countries that agreed to legally binding commitments to reducing harmful greenhouse gas emissions. This was an outgrowth of the World Climate Program, initiated by the United Nations in 1979. The Kyoto Protocol was simply an overture toward a solution, because the U.S. Senate did not ratify it and President George W. Bush eliminated it from the U.S. radar. (A) established laws for delimiting shared bodies of water; (C) established free-trade relations among North American countries in 1993; (D) was an economic agreement in the 1940s by Belgium, Luxembourg, and the Netherlands that set the stage for the European Union's development; and (E) was created by the Bolsheviks in the Russian realm to spread communism throughout the world.

53. **(D)**

The base of Suriname's population pyramid is much wider than its top, indicating that Suriname is experiencing high growth rates, with more births than deaths. This puts Suriname around stage 2 of transition. Argentina's birth and death rates are more stabilized, placing it around stage 3 (with still some inequality); thus (A) is incorrect. The percentage of women in the reproducing (fecund) range is much higher in Suriname than in Argentina; as the pyramid shows, many more women in Suriname are between the ages of 15 and 40 than are older, making (B) incorrect. Life expectancy is higher in Argentina because it has more people at the top of its pyramid in the older ages than in Suriname, making (C) and (E) incorrect. Because the 1990s were as much as 14 years from the 2004 creation of the population pyramids, you need to look at the numbers for children 0–14 years old. Notice that the bars on the pyramid representing Suriname's children, male and female, 0–14 years of age are longer than the bars representing children aged 0–14 years in Argentina; thus (D) is the correct choice.

54. **(E)**

India is home to nearly 97 percent of the world's Hindu population, but the remaining percentage of Hindus live in neighboring Nepal. Pakistan and Senegal are highly Muslim; Sri Lanka is predominantly Buddhist (97 percent), and China is officially atheist.

55. **(B)**

This picture depicts the boulevard that was constructed in the late 19th century to model the Champs-Élysées in Paris. This Mexican boulevard was built by the Spanish emperor Maximilian, who came to power largely because of the support he had in France. In fact, the wide boulevard, architecture, and roundabout would make one think that this picture was taken in Paris. This shows the noticeable imprint by western European colonizers on the Latin American cultural landscape. (A) is the clumping of similar or related industries to benefit from their proximate locations. Mexico City was not a forward capital city (E) because it has been the seat of Mexican power.

56. **(A)**

Brain drain is the emigration (leaving) of well-educated members of a society for places with more opportunities suiting their needs. The Kentucky scholarship program was established to try to keep Kentucky's high-achieving high school students from migrating to universities outside the state. (B) are workers from other countries who have migrated to work temporarily in a new country. (C) is the movement within a particular region, whereas immigration (D) occurs when migrants enter a region. (E) involves an interruption in the original migration path undertaken by a migrant; essentially it is when something better comes along to prevent the migrant from completing the journey to the point he or she had planned.

57. **(E)**

The neighborhood effect occurs when diffusion is most rapid around the original innovator, or the first person affected by the diffusing element. Most simply, diffusion on a microscale most rapidly occurs through direct exposure to the diffusion phenomenon. (A) is the degree to which a person or place is likely to adopt the diffusing phenomenon. (B) occurs when a trait or phenomenon is adopted in a situation or context in which it should not fit, such as the diffusion of igloo-style homes to Florida. (C) occurs when the main idea or concept spreads but is changed to meet the adopters' needs. (D) is when two places or peoples independently invent the same (or very similar) invention or innovation.

58. **(A)**

Devolution is defined as the movement of power away from the central government in a country to its regional and local (subnational) government bodies. The movement for regional control in Northern Ireland away from U.K. control exemplifies devolution grounded in nationalism. (B) refers to the economic control that former colonial powers exert over their former political colonies. (C) are forces that unify and maintain state structures, rather than tearing down or weakening government models. (D) is the theory that individuals are a product of human structures, such as capitalism, and that humans also shape their structures. (E) is the designing of voting-district boundaries to benefit one political party over another.

59. **(B)**

Commercial farmers in more-developed countries are facing a strange irony: They are growing surpluses because farming efficiency has increased through improved farming technology, but demand for food at their markets is stagnant (and in some cases declining) because of low population growth (making C and D incorrect). In the United States, farmers receive government subsidies to encourage them not to grow surpluses, making (E) incorrect. (A) is incorrect because research shows that people will not switch from wheat products to corn products if the cost of wheat rises (within reason, of course).

60. **(B)**

Ubiquitous industries are found near their markets because of the immediacy of their products, such as a newspaper. They are not examples of (A), because footloose industries have freedom in their choice of industrial locations because they are not related to specific marketplaces and can be transported over long distances for low costs. (C) are intermediate points of trade that facilitate trade between two points or places. (D) is when a trait from one culture is adopted by another culture. (E) is an industry in which the final product weighs less than the raw materials used to create it.

61. **(E)**

Each answer choice except (E) is a generalization made by Ravenstein regarding human migration (human geographers consider Ravenstein's generalizations the only accepted rules on human migration). In the 1880s England was experiencing rapid urban migration, fueled by the Industrial Revolution (B). People were moving from the farms to the cities to find new opportunities. However, in all migration patterns, a reverse stream of people move in a return route—back to the farmlands, for example. It might not be as large as the stream into the city, but it is nevertheless present (A). Most migrants move small distances (C), not having the means or knowledge to leap great distances, and they usually move in steps (D), perhaps from town to town until they make it to their final destinations. However, large towns during the 1880s in England were growing more because of this massive urban migration into the cities than by rates of natural increase, thereby making (E) the correct choice in its inaccuracy.

62. **(C)**

The growth of populations in non-Western, peripheral countries has been the most striking change on the list, as countries such as India, South Korea, Japan, Mexico, Brazil, and China take a more prominent status on the list. In fact, cities in peripheral zones account for nearly 50 percent of cities on the list. (A) is false because Mexico City, São Paulo, Buenos Aires, and Rio de Janeiro are on the list. (B) is false because it is the second-largest city in the world as of 2007. (D) is false because annual growth averages around 15 percent. (E) is false because the average is nearly 15 million, with the largest city, Tokyo at 30 million, being far larger than the next largest, New York at nearly 17.8 million.

63. **(A)**

Vegetative planting is when agriculturalists cut the stems of plants and divide their roots to grow crops. It predated seed agriculture and likely originated in Southeast Asia, making (D) and (E) incorrect. (B) refers to seed agriculture, and (C) refers to truck farming.

64. **(E)**

The table is testing your knowledge of the definitions of arithmetic, physiological, and agricultural densities. While the arithmetic density is simply the number of people per unit of land, the physiological density measures the number of people per unit of farmland, and the agricultural density measures the number of farmers per unit of farmland. Thus, though the Dutch have the highest number of people per land, their ratio of people to farmland is less than that of Egypt's. The arithmetic density of Egypt is only 70 people per square kilometer, while its physiological density is the highest at more than 3,500, indicating that most of Egypt's peoples are clustered on farmable land; this highest physiological density indicates that Egypt has more people per unit of farmland than the others, proving that it has less farmland per person than the others (statement IV). However, the Netherlands' agricultural density is much lower than Egypt's, indicating that fewer farmers are needed on the farmlands in the Netherlands than in Egypt. This suggests that the Dutch are more mechanized in their farming than are the Egyptians, because the Dutch use machines to reduce the number of farmers to do the same job (statement II). Because the data show ratios, the actual number of people in each country is not known, so statement I cannot be accepted, thereby eliminating (A), (B), and (C). Although statement III is tempting, the table does not specifically indicate any information on urban (city) settlement, so this statement is not supported directly.

65. **(D)**

Plantation agriculture has historically been entrenched in less-developed countries' economies, with its reliance on inexpensive labor to harvest a cash crop for sale in foreign markets. (A), (B), (C), and (E) are found in both more- and less-developed countries. Mediterranean agriculture is found primarily in the region surrounding the Mediterranean Sea, which includes North Africa. Organic agriculture (E) is sometimes found in less-developed countries, when the food is produced for foreign markets where it is sold for a price higher than people living in the countries of production could afford.

66. **(A)**

Cumulative causation happens when modernization and development occur in the area of initial advantage and drain the surrounding regions of investment, labor, and resources. Growth is fed at the expense of more-equalized growth patterns. (B) is the human tendency to claim a part of space and exact control over it, much like an animal marking its territory. (C) is involved when two countries share water space that does not include the 200 miles provided for in exclusive economic zones. According to the principle, the countries must divide the water space in half at the median point. (D) claims that former colonies are still dependent on their former colonial masters, in an economic, not political, sense. (E) refers to the reverse in the trend away from urban migration. Instead, in counterurbanization trends, more people move to suburbs and rural areas to escape cities.

67. **(E)**

World cities are extraordinarily large cities with populations exceeding 10 million. Of the cities listed, only Vienna, Austria, has a population less than 10 million (in fact, its population is less than 2 million people).

68. **(C)**

The multiplier effect is highly related to cumulative causation: one successful industry or a cluster of them acts as a magnet for further development and industry, with more jobs leading to more jobs, and so on. (A) is the urban development pattern that involves many core areas. (B) is a migration theory that states that large cities attract the largest numbers of immigrants and that closer places attract each other more than more-distant places. (D) is the demographic measurement of the time it will take for a population to double in size. (E) is the transition of the causes of death within each stage of the demographic transition model.

69. **(B)**

Multiplier leakage occurs when multinational corporations invest in and build secondary industries, such as factories, in peripheral regions and send most of the profits back to their core headquarters. This contributes to uneven development. (A) is the exponential growth of space needed to feed the growing transportation space associated with cars, trucks, and planes. (C) is the investment of multinational corporations typically in peripheral regions to build factories and export operations to feed the core's needs. (D) are the negative effects of growth poles and agglomeration caused by all the energy in development and industrial growth being focused on one area, thereby draining the surrounding and supplying regions of valuable workers and resources. (E) is the negative restructuring of the earth's physical structure by industrial processes.

70. **(B)**

The Mexican government established its maquiladora program in the 1960s to allow U.S. businesses to build factories on low-cost land on the Mexican side of the U.S.-Mexico border. The program was meant to employ displaced farmers in Mexico and allow U.S. industries to outsource parts of their production processes to lower-cost areas. The labor force in the maquiladoras includes many Mexican women. Although (A) may seem reasonable, that same desire has been present since before the 1960s. (C) and (D) do not exist along the border, and there is no reason for forced migration (E), though poverty and lack of jobs are push factors.

71. **(E)**

Nearly 41 percent of the world's population comprises farmers, and most farmers grow just enough to feed their families with no surplus. In most of Asia and Africa, more than 50 percent of the people are farmers. Intensive subsistence farming involves farming a small plot of land very intensively, or to yield high output per unit area. It is labor intensive per unit area, compared with extensive agriculture, which involves using much land.

72. **(B)**

Ecotourism is ecologically responsible travel that attempts not to harm the ecosystems or well-being of the indigenous people. A trail hike in a rain forest would most likely have the least impact on the local people and environment, whereas the other choices are more invasive to the local environment. Even a cruise ship (D), because it pollutes and disrupts the oceanic ecosystem, is less ecofriendly than a rain forest hike.

73. **(C)**

Pronatalist policies encourage people to have more children, which would lead to a higher total fertility rate, or the number of children each woman is predicted to bear in her fecund years. Higher fertility rates would not likely directly affect death rates (A) or life expectancy (B), though in the long run there could be some interaction between more babies and higher death rates. More babies would lead to higher rates of natural increase and a faster doubling time, making (D) and (E) incorrect.

74. **(C)**

Exurbanization is the movement out of the city to a more quiet, peaceful, rural setting. (A) and (B) represent urban migration, (D) is gentrification, and (E) is agglomeration.

75. **(C)**

A gas station would have a small radius from which it would draw people to use its services, hence a small range. It would also require a small population to exist, hence a small threshold population. The other answer choices would require larger populations to exist, because a small percentage of people use the services rendered by the central place functions in (A), (B), (D), and (E).

Section II

Sample Response and Scoring Rubric for FRQ 1

Sample Response

A.   The figure depicts an example of U.S. intraregional migration, which is the permanent movement within a region of a country. The largest flow by far is from the central city to the suburbs, thus indicating a net out-migration from the city.

B.   British demographer Ernst Ravenstein devised several laws pertaining to internal migration within a country. (Descriptions and applications of any two of the following should be in FRQ.)

i. **Net migration amounts to a fraction of the gross migration between two places.** As seen in the figure, each of the streams has a countermigration stream, thus affecting the net migration number.

ii. **The majority of migrants move short distances.** Because of the increase of space-time compression resulting from improvements in transportation technology, modern migrants are more likely to move long distances than were migrants in Ravenstein's time. However, the migration pattern in the figure relates to Ravenstein's prediction because most migrants depicted move short distances. For example, 8 million move between the city and the suburb, a shorter distance than the approximately 1.5 million migrants moving the longer route between the city and rural areas.

iii. **Migrants who move longer distances tend to choose big-city destinations.** In this figure, the migrants moving the longest distances are moving into a "big city" destination. Technically, Ravenstein's "law" applies in this scenario. However, note that *more* migrants in the figure are moving in a counter-urbanizing trend, moving from urban areas into suburban and rural areas.

iv. **Urban residents are less migratory than inhabitants of rural areas.** The figure shows many more migrants moving from urban areas to suburban areas than it does rural residents moving into suburban and city areas. Thus, this law does not apply to the figure.

v. **Families are less likely to make international moves than young adults.** Suburbs are likely to be inhabited largely by families, while cities often attract young adults. Thus the migration pattern in the figure would seem to support Ravenstein's prediction because fewer migrants come from the suburbs than from large urban areas.

C.   People feel compelled (pushed) to emigrate from a location for political, economic, and environmental reasons. Similarly, people are induced (pulled) to immigrate to a new location because of its political, economic, or environmental attractiveness. In the figure the net out-migration from the cities is most likely related to overcrowding in the central city. In this pattern migrants from these cities are moving to the suburbs because they perceive better living conditions outside the urban areas. This pattern fits into the stage-4 prediction of the demographic transition model because major U.S. cities were in stage 4 by the 1990s. After the continued expansion and urbanization of stages 2 and 3 of the model, overcrowding in the central cities led people to seek "more room" in the American suburbs of stage 4, a typical pattern in more-developed countries.

Scoring Rubric for FRQ 1

Part A: 3 points

1 point for each of the following observations:

Note: Students should note that the movement depicted is migratory, which is permanent. Other types of movements, such as cyclic and periodic may be mentioned, but the arrows indicate migration, not cyclic or periodic movement. This is defined in the question prompt.

- Net out-migration from central city
- Largest flow from central city to suburbs
- Slightly larger migration from urban to rural areas than from rural to urban

Part B: 2 points

1 point for each law stated and analyzed.

- Accurate statement of two of Ravenstein's laws and accurate application of it to model (see each law in the sample response above)

Part C: 3 points

1 point for each of the following:

Note: Student must explain the demographic transition model mentioned to get full 3 points.

- Identification of push-pull factors:
  - Push: crowded, expensive cities
  - Pull: lifestyle and space of suburb areas
- Mention of improved transportation technology, thus allowing commuting
- Explanation of stage 4 of model

After surge of industrialization and growth of stages 2 and 3, overcrowding and expense of cities in this developed country push people to suburbs

OVERALL SCORE FOR FRQ 1 _____ / 8 points

Sample Response and Scoring Rubric for FRQ 2

Sample Response

A.   *Monolingualism* is defined as a state in which only one language is spoken. Arguably, no country in the world is truly monolingual because each has a small number of speakers of different languages. One of the closest examples of a monolingual state is Japan, which has strict immigration and naturalization policies.

B.   Multilingualism occurs in a state in which more than one language is in use. One example of a multilingual state experiencing conflict related to its linguistic diversity is Canada. French speakers in the province of Quebec desire a sense of autonomy and self-determination, separate from the English-speaking majority in Canada. Their identity as French speakers is a defining part of their nationalism, even leading to French-only laws within the province and a referendum movement to declare independence from greater Anglo-Canada.

Scoring Rubric for FRQ 2

PART A: 2 points

1 point for any of the following:

- Accurate definition of monolingualism—state wherein one language is spoken

- Possible examples include Japan in Asia; Uruguay and Venezuela in South America; Iceland, Poland, Portugal in Europe; Lesotho in Africa

PART B: 2 points

1 point for any of the following examples

1 point for correct explanation of relation between multilingualism and regionalism

- Example: Student must choose a state and specifically and accurately explain the linguistic diversity in the region and how that diversity contributes to regionalism or cultural division. Possible examples include the following

  —North America: Canada (French vs. English), United States (Spanish vs. English)

  —Europe: Greece (Greek vs. Turkish), Belgium (French vs. Dutch), Bosnia (Croatian, Serbian, Albanian), German (Turkish vs. German), France (French vs. Turkish and English), Switzerland (which has at least three major languages and one minor language)

OVERALL SCORE FOR FRQ 2   _____/ 4 points

Sample Response and Scoring Rubric for FRQ 3

Sample Response

A.   Gentrification is a process of inner-city, neighborhood urban renewal. There is also a resulting social change that occurs with this injection of money into inner-city neighborhoods and the arrival (or return) of higher social or economic groups.

B.   The old Werthan Mills Plant building has been purchased and remodeled into luxurious loft apartments in an inner-city neighborhood of east Nashville. This exemplifies the gentrification process, especially since the renovation has produced housing that is probably too expensive for the existing neighborhood dwellers.

C.   One positive effect of gentrification is that it brings renewed money and attention to decrepit, decaying infrastructures in inner cities. New middle- and upper-income citizens come to the inner-city neighborhoods being gentrified with zeal and a desire to "beautify" and commercialize the regions, generating economic development. One negative aspect of gentrification as a solution to urban renewal is its tendency to push out the people already living in the gentrified neighborhoods. Often these people have a lower socioeconomic status and cannot afford the new high-priced housing units and shops that move in. Thus gentrification can produce greater segregation, rather than unification and integration.

Scoring Rubric for FRQ 3

PART A: 1 point

1 point for the following:

- Gentrification began in the 1970s when decaying inner-city buildings in low-income neighborhoods were targeted for renovation and remodeling by developers and families in the middle and upper socioeconomic classes.

PART B: 2 points

1 point for any of the following:

- The photos show the original factory building around 1950, just as the suburbanization movement was occurring, and its remodeled, modern version.

- Gentrification occurred when a developer moved into this inner-city neighborhood and remodeled and transformed the old factory building into expensive urban-elite dwellings.

PART C: 2 points

1 point for any of the following positive factors and 1 for any of the following negative factors:

- Positives: increased economic energy in neighborhood, more aesthetically pleasing urban landscape, new businesses developed in region, efficient use of space, alternative to urban sprawl, increase in inner-city tax base

- Negatives: alienation and "pushing out" of people already living and working in region because new housing is too expensive and new businesses cater to the rich property owners moving in, political and ideological clashes between original inhabitants and influx of new "gentrifiers," increased segregation of racial and socioeconomic groups, avoiding fixing the inherent problems of cyclical poverty and suburban sprawl

OVERALL SCORE FOR FRQ 3   _____ / 5 points

Index

N

PRACTICE EXAM 1

AP Human Geography

Answer Sheet

1. (A) (B) (C) (D) (E)
2. (A) (B) (C) (D) (E)
3. (A) (B) (C) (D) (E)
4. (A) (B) (C) (D) (E)
5. (A) (B) (C) (D) (E)
6. (A) (B) (C) (D) (E)
7. (A) (B) (C) (D) (E)
8. (A) (B) (C) (D) (E)
9. (A) (B) (C) (D) (E)
10. (A) (B) (C) (D) (E)
11. (A) (B) (C) (D) (E)
12. (A) (B) (C) (D) (E)
13. (A) (B) (C) (D) (E)
14. (A) (B) (C) (D) (E)
15. (A) (B) (C) (D) (E)
16. (A) (B) (C) (D) (E)
17. (A) (B) (C) (D) (E)
18. (A) (B) (C) (D) (E)
19. (A) (B) (C) (D) (E)
20. (A) (B) (C) (D) (E)
21. (A) (B) (C) (D) (E)
22. (A) (B) (C) (D) (E)
23. (A) (B) (C) (D) (E)
24. (A) (B) (C) (D) (E)
25. (A) (B) (C) (D) (E)

26. (A) (B) (C) (D) (E)
27. (A) (B) (C) (D) (E)
28. (A) (B) (C) (D) (E)
29. (A) (B) (C) (D) (E)
30. (A) (B) (C) (D) (E)
31. (A) (B) (C) (D) (E)
32. (A) (B) (C) (D) (E)
33. (A) (B) (C) (D) (E)
34. (A) (B) (C) (D) (E)
35. (A) (B) (C) (D) (E)
36. (A) (B) (C) (D) (E)
37. (A) (B) (C) (D) (E)
38. (A) (B) (C) (D) (E)
39. (A) (B) (C) (D) (E)
40. (A) (B) (C) (D) (E)
41. (A) (B) (C) (D) (E)
42. (A) (B) (C) (D) (E)
43. (A) (B) (C) (D) (E)
44. (A) (B) (C) (D) (E)
45. (A) (B) (C) (D) (E)
46. (A) (B) (C) (D) (E)
47. (A) (B) (C) (D) (E)
48. (A) (B) (C) (D) (E)
49. (A) (B) (C) (D) (E)
50. (A) (B) (C) (D) (E)

51. (A) (B) (C) (D) (E)
52. (A) (B) (C) (D) (E)
53. (A) (B) (C) (D) (E)
54. (A) (B) (C) (D) (E)
55. (A) (B) (C) (D) (E)
56. (A) (B) (C) (D) (E)
57. (A) (B) (C) (D) (E)
58. (A) (B) (C) (D) (E)
59. (A) (B) (C) (D) (E)
60. (A) (B) (C) (D) (E)
61. (A) (B) (C) (D) (E)
62. (A) (B) (C) (D) (E)
63. (A) (B) (C) (D) (E)
64. (A) (B) (C) (D) (E)
65. (A) (B) (C) (D) (E)
66. (A) (B) (C) (D) (E)
67. (A) (B) (C) (D) (E)
68. (A) (B) (C) (D) (E)
69. (A) (B) (C) (D) (E)
70. (A) (B) (C) (D) (E)
71. (A) (B) (C) (D) (E)
72. (A) (B) (C) (D) (E)
73. (A) (B) (C) (D) (E)
74. (A) (B) (C) (D) (E)
75. (A) (B) (C) (D) (E)

PRACTICE EXAM 2

AP Human Geography

Answer Sheet

1. Ⓐ Ⓑ Ⓒ Ⓓ Ⓔ
2. Ⓐ Ⓑ Ⓒ Ⓓ Ⓔ
3. Ⓐ Ⓑ Ⓒ Ⓓ Ⓔ
4. Ⓐ Ⓑ Ⓒ Ⓓ Ⓔ
5. Ⓐ Ⓑ Ⓒ Ⓓ Ⓔ
6. Ⓐ Ⓑ Ⓒ Ⓓ Ⓔ
7. Ⓐ Ⓑ Ⓒ Ⓓ Ⓔ
8. Ⓐ Ⓑ Ⓒ Ⓓ Ⓔ
9. Ⓐ Ⓑ Ⓒ Ⓓ Ⓔ
10. Ⓐ Ⓑ Ⓒ Ⓓ Ⓔ
11. Ⓐ Ⓑ Ⓒ Ⓓ Ⓔ
12. Ⓐ Ⓑ Ⓒ Ⓓ Ⓔ
13. Ⓐ Ⓑ Ⓒ Ⓓ Ⓔ
14. Ⓐ Ⓑ Ⓒ Ⓓ Ⓔ
15. Ⓐ Ⓑ Ⓒ Ⓓ Ⓔ
16. Ⓐ Ⓑ Ⓒ Ⓓ Ⓔ
17. Ⓐ Ⓑ Ⓒ Ⓓ Ⓔ
18. Ⓐ Ⓑ Ⓒ Ⓓ Ⓔ
19. Ⓐ Ⓑ Ⓒ Ⓓ Ⓔ
20. Ⓐ Ⓑ Ⓒ Ⓓ Ⓔ
21. Ⓐ Ⓑ Ⓒ Ⓓ Ⓔ
22. Ⓐ Ⓑ Ⓒ Ⓓ Ⓔ
23. Ⓐ Ⓑ Ⓒ Ⓓ Ⓔ
24. Ⓐ Ⓑ Ⓒ Ⓓ Ⓔ
25. Ⓐ Ⓑ Ⓒ Ⓓ Ⓔ

26. Ⓐ Ⓑ Ⓒ Ⓓ Ⓔ
27. Ⓐ Ⓑ Ⓒ Ⓓ Ⓔ
28. Ⓐ Ⓑ Ⓒ Ⓓ Ⓔ
29. Ⓐ Ⓑ Ⓒ Ⓓ Ⓔ
30. Ⓐ Ⓑ Ⓒ Ⓓ Ⓔ
31. Ⓐ Ⓑ Ⓒ Ⓓ Ⓔ
32. Ⓐ Ⓑ Ⓒ Ⓓ Ⓔ
33. Ⓐ Ⓑ Ⓒ Ⓓ Ⓔ
34. Ⓐ Ⓑ Ⓒ Ⓓ Ⓔ
35. Ⓐ Ⓑ Ⓒ Ⓓ Ⓔ
36. Ⓐ Ⓑ Ⓒ Ⓓ Ⓔ
37. Ⓐ Ⓑ Ⓒ Ⓓ Ⓔ
38. Ⓐ Ⓑ Ⓒ Ⓓ Ⓔ
39. Ⓐ Ⓑ Ⓒ Ⓓ Ⓔ
40. Ⓐ Ⓑ Ⓒ Ⓓ Ⓔ
41. Ⓐ Ⓑ Ⓒ Ⓓ Ⓔ
42. Ⓐ Ⓑ Ⓒ Ⓓ Ⓔ
43. Ⓐ Ⓑ Ⓒ Ⓓ Ⓔ
44. Ⓐ Ⓑ Ⓒ Ⓓ Ⓔ
45. Ⓐ Ⓑ Ⓒ Ⓓ Ⓔ
46. Ⓐ Ⓑ Ⓒ Ⓓ Ⓔ
47. Ⓐ Ⓑ Ⓒ Ⓓ Ⓔ
48. Ⓐ Ⓑ Ⓒ Ⓓ Ⓔ
49. Ⓐ Ⓑ Ⓒ Ⓓ Ⓔ
50. Ⓐ Ⓑ Ⓒ Ⓓ Ⓔ

51. Ⓐ Ⓑ Ⓒ Ⓓ Ⓔ
52. Ⓐ Ⓑ Ⓒ Ⓓ Ⓔ
53. Ⓐ Ⓑ Ⓒ Ⓓ Ⓔ
54. Ⓐ Ⓑ Ⓒ Ⓓ Ⓔ
55. Ⓐ Ⓑ Ⓒ Ⓓ Ⓔ
56. Ⓐ Ⓑ Ⓒ Ⓓ Ⓔ
57. Ⓐ Ⓑ Ⓒ Ⓓ Ⓔ
58. Ⓐ Ⓑ Ⓒ Ⓓ Ⓔ
59. Ⓐ Ⓑ Ⓒ Ⓓ Ⓔ
60. Ⓐ Ⓑ Ⓒ Ⓓ Ⓔ
61. Ⓐ Ⓑ Ⓒ Ⓓ Ⓔ
62. Ⓐ Ⓑ Ⓒ Ⓓ Ⓔ
63. Ⓐ Ⓑ Ⓒ Ⓓ Ⓔ
64. Ⓐ Ⓑ Ⓒ Ⓓ Ⓔ
65. Ⓐ Ⓑ Ⓒ Ⓓ Ⓔ
66. Ⓐ Ⓑ Ⓒ Ⓓ Ⓔ
67. Ⓐ Ⓑ Ⓒ Ⓓ Ⓔ
68. Ⓐ Ⓑ Ⓒ Ⓓ Ⓔ
69. Ⓐ Ⓑ Ⓒ Ⓓ Ⓔ
70. Ⓐ Ⓑ Ⓒ Ⓓ Ⓔ
71. Ⓐ Ⓑ Ⓒ Ⓓ Ⓔ
72. Ⓐ Ⓑ Ⓒ Ⓓ Ⓔ
73. Ⓐ Ⓑ Ⓒ Ⓓ Ⓔ
74. Ⓐ Ⓑ Ⓒ Ⓓ Ⓔ
75. Ⓐ Ⓑ Ⓒ Ⓓ Ⓔ

INSTALLING REA's TestWare®

SYSTEM REQUIREMENTS

Pentium 75 MHz (300 MHz recommended), or a higher or compatible processor; Microsoft Windows 98 or later; 64 MB Available RAM; Internet Explorer 5.5 or higher.

INSTALLATION

1. Insert the AP Human Geography TestWare® CD-ROM into the CD-ROM drive.
2. If the installation doesn't begin automatically, from the Start Menu, choose the RUN command. When the RUN dialog box appears, type d:\setup (where D is the letter of your CD-ROM drive) at the prompt and click OK.
3. The installation process will begin. A dialog box proposing the directory "Program Files\REA\AP_HumanGeography" will appear. If the name and location are suitable, click OK. If you wish to specify a different name or location, type it in and click OK.
4. Start the AP Human Geography TestWare® application by double-clicking on the icon.

REA's AP Human Geography TestWare® is **EASY** to **LEARN AND USE**. To achieve maximum benefits, we recommend that you take a few minutes to go through the on-screen tutorial on your computer. The "screen buttons" are also explained there to familiarize you with the program.

SSD ACCOMMODATIONS FOR STUDENTS WITH DISABILITIES

Many students qualify for extra time to take the AP Human Geography exam, and our TestWare® can be adapted to accommodate your time extension. This allows you to practice under the same extended time accommodations that you will receive on the actual test day. To customize your TestWare® to suit the most common extensions, visit our Website at *www.rea.com/ssd*.

TECHNICAL SUPPORT

REA's TestWare® is backed by customer and technical support. For questions about **installation or operation of your software**, contact us at:

> **Research & Education Association**
> Phone: (732) 819-8880 (9 a.m. to 5 p.m. ET, Monday–Friday)
> Fax: (732) 819-8808
> Website: www.rea.com
> E-mail: info@rea.com

Note to Windows XP Users: In order for the TestWare® to function properly, please install and run the application under the same computer-administrator level user account. Installing the TestWare® as one user and running it as another could cause file access path conflicts.